To: Is~~~~lla

From: Elvis Pe~~~

Sep 21, 2007

Illustrated
Lives of the Saints II

This edition is dedicated to
SAINT JOSEPH
Patron of the Universal Church

ILLUSTRATED

LIVES OF THE SAINTS

II

FOR EVERY DAY OF THE YEAR

In Accord with the Norms and Principles of
the New *Roman Martyrology* (2004 Edition)

Companion Volume to
Illustrated Lives of the Saints

By
Rev. Thomas J. Donaghy

Illustrated

CATHOLIC BOOK PUBLISHING CORP.
New Jersey

NIHIL OBSTAT: Rev. Msgr. James M. Cafone, M.A., S.T.D.
    Censor Librorum
IMPRIMATUR: ✙ Most Rev. John J. Myers, J.C.D., D.D.
    Archbishop of Newark

DEDICATED TO

SISTER MARY HENRY O'CONNELL, S.H.C.J.

devoted daughter of

VENERABLE CORNELIA CONNELLY

(T-865)

PREFACE

THIS new book of short biographies of the Saints is a companion to the best-selling volume *Lives of the Saints* originally written by Father Hugo Hoever, S.O.Cist. whose latest revision appeared in 2005. Father Hoever's book includes all the Saints who appear in the official post-Vatican II liturgical calendar for the Universal Church and for the United States.

Over the years, readers have asked for the biographies of other Saints who do not form part of that calendar. Accordingly, this companion book contains a new series of saintly men and women for each day of the year—many of them newly canonized or beatified by the latest Popes. Other Saints given are taken from the 2004 Edition of the *Roman Martyrology*.

The dates assigned to the Saints are those given for them in the *Martyrology*. Most of the Saints are assigned to the date of their death, their birthday into heaven. If this fact is not known, they are given the traditional date on which their feast was celebrated. The ultimate source for the data of many of the early Saints is *Butler's Lives of Saints* (1756-1759).

A diligent attempt has been made to include in this selection of Saints a wider circle of persons— lay as well as clergy, women as well as men. In this way, a greater range of people, vocations, and virtues is offered to today's Christians for edification and imitation.

A new feature of this volume is the *Reflection* at the end of each biographical entry. This addition is intended to make it easier for readers to recall and emulate one of the outstanding characteristics of each Saint.

After the *Reflection*, there is a *Prayer* patterned after the official liturgical prayers of the Church. This feature enables readers to ask God's help in imitating the Saint who is in the final analysis an imitator of Christ, the crown of all Saints.

Inserted throughout the book are over sixty new inspiring illustrations of Saints. They are an invaluable aid to our readers in getting to know, love, and imitate the Saints.

By becoming familiar with the Saints, we cannot help but arrive at a fuller, deeper, and more practical knowledge of Jesus—a knowledge of Him as He is coupled with the desire to follow Him. In turn, this knowledge of our Lord is a knowledge also of God the Father: "If you had known Me, you would also have known My Father" (John 14:7).

It is this knowledge of God the Father and the Son that is the fulfillment of every Christian's life—the beginning as well as the end of everlasting life: "Now this is everlasting life, that they may know You, the only true God, and Him Whom You have sent, Jesus Christ" (John 17:3).

CONTENTS

7

CONTENTS 8

9   CONTENTS

CONTENTS

10

11   **CONTENTS**

CONTENTS

CONTENTS

CONTENTS

ST. FULGENTIUS OF RUSPE, Bishop
January 1

FABIUS Claudius Gordianus Fulgentius was born into a noble senatorial family of Carthage in 468. After receiving an excellent education including a thorough knowledge of Latin and Greek he was chosen lieutenant governor of Byzacena. But a reading of a sermon of St. Augustine convinced him to follow his long-cherished desire to be a monk.

In 508, he was elected Bishop of Ruspe (modern Kudiat Rosfa in Tunisia) but shortly afterward found himself exiled to Sardinia with some sixty other orthodox bishops by order of the Arian Thrasimund. The exiles built a monastery and devoted themselves to prayer, study, and writing.

In 515, Fulgentius was allowed to return to Carthage to dialogue with the Arians, but his effectiveness in doing so earned him a second exile in 518. Finally, in 523 King Hilderic succeeded Thrasimund and had the exiles returned home. Fulgentius won the people over to the true Faith by his wondrous gift of preaching and his inspirational example of humility. The people then prevailed upon the Saint to give up his desire to spend his last years in a monastery and to remain with them instead. He died at the age of sixty-five on January 1, 533.

Although Fulgentius lived in a time pervaded by persecutions and heresies, this holy man remained true to the Faith and propagated the authentic teaching, basing himself on the writings of St. Augustine. So well did he follow his master that he has been dubbed a "pocket Augustine."

REFLECTION   A new year suggests new beginnings. As we begin this year, let us be encouraged by St. Fulgentius' perseverance in faith to practice our Faith more openly and honestly so that our friends will truly know we are followers of Jesus.

PRAYER   *Lord, our God, as we renew ourselves in earthly resolutions, grant that, like St. Fulgentius, we may always do Your will. This we ask through Christ our Lord. Amen.*

ST. ADALHARD (ADELARD), Abbot

THE grandson of Charles Martel and first cousin to Charlemagne, St. Adalhard gave up court life in 773 at the age of twenty and entered the monastery of Corbie in Picardy as a gardener. His outstanding natural and supernatural gifts could not be hidden for long, however, and he was chosen abbot of the monastery. Shortly afterward, he was persuaded by Charlemagne to return to court and he became the Emperor's principal counselor, minister to his son Pepin, and tutor of the latter's son Bernard.

In 817, Bernard who had become King of Naples opposed Louis the Debonair, Charlemagne's successor. Adalhard was suspected of being implicated in the revolt and was exiled to the island of Héri, later known as Noirmoutier, off the coast of Aquitaine. In time, the Emperor realized Adalhard's innocence and recalled him home.

During his exile, Adalhard counseled the substitute abbot to dedicate himself to the evangelization of the Saxons, leading to the founding of a priory at Hethis. This was transferred to Hoexter giving rise to Corvey, the new Corbie. Such was Adalhard's eloquence and religious culture that he became known as the "Augustine of his time." But he also possessed a deep humility and a genuine concern for the spiritual good of his monks.

After the death of this man of God on January 2, 826, his relics were miraculously discovered and effected various healings, especially of paralytics and deaf-mutes. In 1026, Pope John XIX had his remains exhumed and transferred in solemn procession—which in accord with the canon law of the time was equivalent to official canonization.

REFLECTION As we resume our daily tasks, we are made aware of how quickly the world devours the spiritual realities of Christmas. Let us resolve, like St. Adalhard, to be constantly aware of our call to perfection through the renunciation of unnecessary material goods.

PRAYER   *God our Father, help us to put away the treasures of this earth and seek our happiness in You alone. This we ask through Christ our Lord. Amen.*

ST. ANTHERUS, Pope and Martyr

January 3

ST. Antherus was elected Pope on November 21, 235, and was martyred for the Faith forty-three days later on January 3, 236. He was put to death for attempting to preserve copies of the official proceedings against the martyrs. The site of his burial in the catacombs (Cemetery of St. Callistus) was discovered in 1854.

REFLECTION Ever sensitive to the demands of the Gospel, we acknowledge our debt to the Saints who have gone before us, especially the martyrs. When we encounter ridicule for living Gospel lives, let us recall the martyrs, especially St. Antherus.

PRAYER *God our Father, through the intercession of Pope St. Antherus, grant us the courage and grace to stand fast for principles of justice and truth in public life. This we ask through Christ our Lord. Amen.*

———◆●◆———

BL. CYRIAC ELIAS CHAVARA, Priest

The Same Day—January 3

BORN in Kainkay, India, in 1805, Bl. Cyriac had a pious childhood and was ordained a priest in 1829 as a member of the Syro-Malabar Catholic Rite. In 1855, he was instrumental in getting the Church's approval of a new religious community of priests called the Carmelite Brothers of Mary Immaculate. He governed this Congregation throughout his whole life and adapted it to his era and to his region of the world.

Cyriac also founded a Congregation for women and organized both contemplative and active apostolates so that the Congregation became the largest in India. He died on February 3, 1871, and was beatified by Pope John Paul II on February 8, 1986.

REFLECTION Bl. Cyriac guided his Congregation through all the problems that afflict new undertakings and saw it have missions in Tanzania, Somalia, Sudan, and Europe. He was spurred on by the heights of Carmel to give heroic service.

PRAYER   *God, our Father, let us be inspired by the life and actions of Bl. Cyriac to place our life in Your service as he did. This we ask through Christ our Lord. Amen.*

BL. ANGELA OF FOLIGNO, Religious

January 4

A NGELA of Foligno was born in Umbria around the year 1248. After a life of pleasure and misuse of the Sacraments, this young woman, wife, and mother turned to a life dedicated to God. Shortly afterward, she endured the successive deaths of her mother, her husband, and all her children.

Angela then joined the Third Order of Penance of St. Francis and drew many women to follow her example. She was conspicuous for her fervent love of God and human beings, especially the poor, and for her humility, patience, and poverty.

Angela was blessed by God with heavenly favors, and she had a special devotion to the mysteries of the life of Christ. She left remarkable writings on spiritual subjects, which gained for her the title "Teacher of Theologians." She died at Foligno on January 4, 1309.

REFLECTION   Strengthened by the Sacraments, we are called to live exemplary Christian lives. Like Blessed Angela let us strive to so imitate Christ that we may generously live the virtues of humility, patience, and poverty.

PRAYER   *God, loving Father, You call Your wayward children to contrition. Through the intercession of Bl. Angela, may we turn to You with hearts filled with sorrow. This we ask through Christ our Lord. Amen.*

ST. GERLAC OF VALKENBURG, Hermit

January 5—*Patron of Domestic Animals*

ST. Gerlac was born in Valkenburg, near Maastricht in Holland in the twelfth century. Addicted to feats of derring-do, he entered the military and led a completely worldly life. However, the tragic death of his young wife opened his eyes to the true nature of that life and he renounced the world as well as his former mode of living.

The troubled youth made a fervent pilgrimage to Rome and then to Jerusalem, where he remained for seven years doing penance and toiling unrelentingly to help the poor and the sick in hospitals. Returning to his own city, Gerlac gave away all his goods to the poor. Donning the habit of St. Norbert, he lived a hermit's life in a cave carved out of a tree on his previous estate. Every week he journeyed to Maastricht to venerate the relics of St. Gervase and every Saturday he went to Aachen to venerate the Blessed Virgin.

Toward the end of his life, Gerlac is said to have corresponded with St. Hildegard of Bingen. A contemporary biography (1222-1228) also indicates that St. Gerlac was favored with a vision of St. Gervase before his death, which took place on January 5 around 1165. Still in our day this holy man is invoked in many parishes as the special protector of domestic animals who become ill.

REFLECTION   Subject as we are to temptation and sin even as we try to live Christian lives, let us resolve to turn our thoughts and deeds to the welfare of others. Like St. Gerlac, we hope to continue good works until we are called to glory.

PRAYER   *Loving Father, Your Son Jesus Christ came that we might share everlasting life with You. May we, like St. Gerlac, mend our ways and return with faith and hope to Your house. This we ask through Christ our Lord. Amen.*

ST. DEOGRATIAS, Bishop
The Same Day—January 5

DEOGRATIAS was a priest of the city of Carthage. The city, seized by the Vandals in 439, had been without a bishop for fourteen years after St. Quodvultdeus had been driven into exile. Then Genseric, the Vandal king, decided to allow the consecration of another bishop.

Deogratias, who had won the respect of his people as well as of pagans and Arians, was named bishop. During the three years of his rule, he sold everything he had in order to ransom and build housing for Christians who had been taken to Africa by Genseric following his sack of Rome in 455. He also designated two of the largest churches in Carthage to be used to house those who were ransomed.

Such actions angered some of the Arians and they plotted to kill him but failed. However, worn out by his efforts, Deogratias died at Carthage in 457/458. His body had to be buried secretly to prevent people from seeking relics.

REFLECTION St. Deogratias through his priestly and pastoral care was well loved by his people as he expended his efforts to bring home individuals taken from their families and enslaved in Africa. For bishops and priests everywhere in the world today, the name of St. Deogratias should be a source of inspiration as they work for and among the people of God.

PRAYER *Almighty God, there is much to be accomplished in our world today especially among the outcasts, refugees, and disenfranchised. Through the intercession of St. Deogratias, may Christians be inspired to work tirelessly to bring justice to the rejected of society. This we ask through Christ our Lord. Amen.*

———◆◆———

ST. CHARLES OF SEZZE, Religious

January 6

CHARLES was born into a poor family of Sezze, Italy, in 1613. His pious parents wanted the priesthood for him, but Charles found learning difficult and was barely able to read and write. However, he was deeply concerned with the things of God and well versed in the science of the Saints.

Charles joined his brothers as a field hand, practiced strict penance, and took a private vow of chastity. Afflicted with a series of illnesses, he promised during one of them to become a religious if he was cured. Thus, at the age of twenty-two he entered the Franciscan Order as a lay brother.

A new illness thwarted his desire to shed his blood for the missions, and he was assigned to a community in Rome. Charles's outstanding spiritual wisdom attracted the attention of Pope Clement IX, cardinals, and many theologians. He composed a good many works of profound doctrinal theology despite his lack of formal theological education. Moreover, he was so consumed with strong devotion for the Eucharist and the Passion of Christ that his side bore—even after death—a visible open wound.

Charles died on January 6, 1670, and was beatified in 1882. Pope John XXIII added his name to the calendar of Saints in 1959.

REFLECTION The Magi found Jesus in His poverty-stricken home. Charles found Jesus in his penance, good works, and prayer. Like Charles let us share our spiritual and material goods with all people so that they may know the salvation of God.

———◆◆———

ST. LUCIAN OF ANTIOCH, Priest and Martyr

January 7

BORN at Samosata in Syria about the middle of the third century, Lucian received an intellectual education that gave him a great knowledge of all the ecclesiastical disciplines. He may also have led a hermit's life for a brief period. He soon entered the priesthood and his encyclopedic learning earned him a wide following. He became the head of a school of theology, and some of the pupils went on to hold the principal episcopal Sees in the East.

Lucian has sometimes been identified with another person (from Samosata) who incurred the excommunication of the Church. However, modern scholars have found no real evidence that such was the case. Lucian is justly famous for his Scriptural studies. The Saint was particularly interested in correcting the sacred texts of the Old and New Testaments from the faulty readings that crept into them and in arriving at their literal meaning. It is not clear whether he corrected the Old Testament text by checking it against the Hebrew text (since he knew the language) or by comparing it with the different editions of the famous Greek translation known as the *Septuagint*.

What is clear is that Lucian's edition of the Bible became widespread throughout the East before the end of the fourth century and developed into the customary text for a great number of Churches. It was used by St. Jerome in his magnificent Scriptural endeavors and is known by Bible scholars as the *Lucian Recension*.

Lucian was arrested in Nicomedia upon promulgation of Diocletian's edicts against the Christians in 303. For nine years he was subjected to imprisonment but remained steadfast in his faith. Finally, the saintly man was brought before the Emperor himself and presented an excellent apology or defense of the Christian Faith. He preached of the eternal Kingdom of Christ, first by words and then by his actions in prison. After fourteen days without food or water he was haled before the tribunal but answered all questions with the words: "I am a Christian." He was put to death for the Faith by starvation or by the sword in 312.

REFLECTION Lucian fed his faith on the Word of God. We benefit in our Scripture readings today from the work of scholar Saints like Lucian. May we grow in our faith through Scripture meditation.

PRAYER   *Lord our God, as a people of faith we look to You in heaven to fulfill our mission on earth and our destiny in Your Kingdom. May we be, like St. Lucian, strong in our faith till we come to You. This we ask through Christ our Lord. Amen.*

ST. SEVERINUS OF NORICUM, Abbot

Born of a noble Roman family about 410, Severinus was a singular individual, torn between his love for a completely contemplative life and his social mission among the Roman peoples of Noricum in Austria. After a stint as a monk in the East, he presided over a numerous monastic family for over thirty years.

Severinus became famous by prophesying correctly the destruction of Astura (in Austria) at the hands of the Huns, resulting from the people's infidelity to God, and by performing several miracles. He also came to the aid of a city on the Danube, Faviana, which was in the grip of a horrible famine. He preached penance among its people, and the ice of the Danube cracked, enabling barges to bring goods to the city and assuage the famine.

Severinus educated his monks in the precepts of the Lord, in the devotions of the Fathers, and in the veneration of the Martyrs. He showed great love for the poor and fearlessly confronted the heads of the barbarians. Odoacer on his march to Italy came to visit Severinus, who told the King that he would conquer the country. In gratitude Odoacer was ready to do whatever the Saint wanted—which turned out to be merely the restoration of a person who had been exiled.

Severinus constantly preached penance and piety, cured the sick, redeemed captives, aided the oppressed, warded off public calamities, and brought a blessing to all. He lived an ascetic life of penance—wearing only one tunic both in summer and in winter, going barefoot, eating but once a day at sundown, and sleeping on a sackcloth spread out on the ground.

After an illustrious life of miracles and prophecies, which gained for him the fame of a wonder-worker, Severinus foretold his death to the priest Lucillus. And he died on the appointed day, January 8, 482, while the monks were singing the words "Let everyone praise the Lord" from Psalm 150 that he himself had intoned.

REFLECTION God blessed His servant Severinus with many convincing qualities that led others to the Faith. Each of us has special gifts from God. We are called, like Severinus, to use them for the benefit of others.

PRAYER *God our Father, grant us the grace to live lives of faith and virtue, so that like St. Severinus we may bring many others to the Faith. This we ask through Christ our Lord. Amen*

———•———

ST. LAWRENCE JUSTINIAN, Bishop

The Same Day—January 8

LAWRENCE was born into the noble Giustiniani family of Venice in 1381. When his widowed mother suggested that he marry, Lawrence refused, and at the age of nineteen he joined the canons regular of St. George, who served on an island near Venice. He became known for his tremendous personal austerity as he went about the island begging for the poor.

In 1406, Lawrence was ordained. He preached in a number of places and became renowned as a teacher of religion. In 1433, Lawrence was named Bishop of Castello and gained a reputation as a man of holiness and charity as well as a negotiator of peace and a reformer. In 1451, Pope Nicholas appointed him Archbishop of Venice.

Known as the Patriarch of Venice, Lawrence became noted for prophecy and miracles, and his mystical treatises were well respected. He died in 1455, and was canonized in 1670 by Pope Clement X.

REFLECTION The good one can accomplish for others as an individual of prayer and deep spirituality is clearly shown in the life of St. Lawrence. Such a model should encourage us to become ever more serious about our relationship with God in a relaxed faith-filled and trusting manner.

PRAYER *Loving God, Your Bishop St. Lawrence responded wholeheartedly to Your invitation to become totally united with You in prayer and sacrifice. Through his intercession, enable us to imitate his example. This we ask through Christ our Lord Amen.*

ST. FILLAN, Abbot

January 9

A NATIVE of Ireland, Fillan (also spelled Foel-lan or Foilan) became a monk and accompanied his mother, St. Kentigerna, and a relative, St. Comgan, to Scotland during the eighth century. Fillan lived the life of a hermit near St. Andrew's Monastery and was later chosen abbot of the monastery.

After some time, Fillan resigned his position and returned to the eremitical life at Glendochart, Perthshire. He built a church and became renowned for his miracles. At his death, he was buried at Strathfillan.

Fillan was inscribed as a Saint in the earliest Irish and Scottish martyrologies. His bell and staff are still extant. So powerful was the healing power attributed to St. Fillan that it led to a practice that survived into the early nineteenth century. Those afflicted with mental illness were dipped in the pool of Strathfillan, then tied up and kept overnight in a corner of the ruins of the Saint's chapel. Those who were found loose in the morning were regarded as cured.

REFLECTION St. Fillan walked with Saints from childhood, and his example enabled others to walk with a Saint. We should realize that the habit of sanctity is like any other habit. In addition to dependence on God's grace, it is the result of careful repetition of good acts. Hence, we should begin today to cultivate good acts.

PRAYER   *Lord our God, You bestowed on St. Fillan the power to work miracles in Your name. Help the mentally ill, by his intercession, to be freed of their affliction and sing Your praises both in this world and in the next. This we ask through Christ our Lord. Amen.*

———◆•◆———

ST. PETER ORSEOLO, Religious

January 10

PETER Orseolo led a multifaceted life. Born in 928 into a noted Venetian family, he was commander of the city's fleet at the age of twenty and rid the area of pirates who had been preying on the ships.

In 976, when the Doge, Peter Candiani IV, was murdered and much of the city ravaged by fire, Peter Orseolo was chosen as the new Doge. In typical fashion, he applied himself to the situation and had the city peaceful and renewed inside of two years.

Then he suddenly relinquished his post to become a member of the Benedictine Abbey of St. Michael at Cuxa in Roussillon on the border between France and Spain. He and his wife of thirty-two years had lived as celibates after the birth of their only son Peter. Now he decided to embrace the religious life completely. He also went on to build a hermitage—probably at the suggestion of St. Romuald whom he had met at Cuxa and who had fostered hermitages among Benedictines.

After nine years of a dedicated life of prayer and penance, Peter died about 987/988, and many miracles were reported to have taken place at his tomb. Forty years later he was recognized as a Saint by the local bishop (which was then the usual custom for canonization in the Church).

REFLECTION In our world today, we Christians are called to holiness and leadership in the things of God. Peter Orseolo's public, beneficial life was sanctified through personal prayer and sacrifice. This message of prayer and sacrifice we preach in today's world.

PRAYER   *Heavenly Father, enable us to come close to You through prayer and penance. Like St. Peter Orseolo, may we spend our lives seeking Your will and Your Divine presence. This we ask through Christ our Lord. Amen.*

———◆———

ST. THEODOSIUS THE CENOBIARCH,
Abbot
January 11

THEODOSIUS was born at Garissus in Cappadocia in 423 and received an outstanding example of piety from his parents. His excelling knowledge of Scripture enabled him to be ordained a Lector at an uncommonly young age, and he then went to Palestine.

In the Holy Land he was surrounded by many possible means of sanctification. He chose the solitary life and settled in the desert of Judah where a host of hermits were already living. News of his surpassing holiness spread swiftly, bringing disciples flocking to him, and the holy man was obliged to build a monastery at Cathismus to house them.

In addition, three hospitals were attached to the monastery—one for the sick, one for the aged, and one for the insane. In time, St. Sabbas, a friend and compatriot of Theodosius, was appointed head of all those living in hermitages in Palestine, and St. Theodosius was placed over all those living in community. This accounts for his name of Cenobiarch—head of persons living a life in common.

Theodosius was removed from this office for a brief period by the Emperor Anastasius because he had remained faithful to the Council of Chalcedon and had fought against heretical doctrine. But he was recalled quickly when Justinian became Emperor and resumed his duties until his death at the age of 105 in 529.

REFLECTION   In his honest defense of Church teaching, Theodosius was publicly humiliated. His example calls us to resist the allures of a comfortable approach to life, while remaining steadfast in our faith and hope.

PRAYER   *God our Father, as followers of Christ Your Son, we are called to stand fast in the Faith. May we, like St. Theodosius, gladly accept the ridicule of those who would deny Your gifts and presence. This we ask through Christ our Lord. Amen.*

ST. MARGARET BOURGEOYS,
Virgin and Foundress
January 12

BORN at Troyes, France, in 1620, Margaret was twenty years old when she received a call to consecrate herself to the service of God. She followed it without hesitation. At first, she became a member of a congregation of Troyes made up of pious and charitable young women dedicated to the education of children in the poorest neighborhoods. In 1652, she left home and emigrated to Montreal, Canada, at the direct invitation of the governor of this new foundation to tutor the children of the French garrison.

Her hard work bore fruit and she opened the first school in 1657. Margaret also oversaw young women who came to the New French colony to marry and start families. Thus was born a school system and a series of social works that little by little extended to the whole country, gaining for Margaret the title "Mother of the Colony" and "Cofoundress of the Church of Canada."

The holiness of this dedicated servant of God attracted other women who wished to follow her life of prayer, heroic poverty, and indefatigable devotion to the service of others. This led to the formation of the Congregation of Notre Dame, which received its civil charter from King Louis XIV in 1671, its canonical approval from Bishop

Laval of Quebec in 1676, and the approbation of its religious constitutions in 1698.

Worn out by her unflagging labors in the cause of Christ, Margaret died in 1700. Her Congregation spread throughout Canada and entered the United States. Margaret was beatified in 1950 by Pope Pius XII and canonized in 1982 by Pope John Paul II, becoming the first Canadian Saint.

REFLECTION The life of St. Margaret was one of total readiness to follow God's call. In her desire to lead children to Christ, she started a new Congregation to add workers to the Lord's vineyard. We too should be prepared to follow the state of life to which we are called—no matter where it may lead.

PRAYER   *Lord, You chose St. Margaret Bourgeoys to form young people in the Christian life. Through her example and prayers, grant that we may lay hold of eternal blessings by our words and conduct. This we ask this through Christ our Lord. Amen.*

BL. YVETTE (or JUTTA) OF HUY, Widow

January 13

ENDOWED with extraordinary charisma, Yvette was a product of the development of mysticism in the Low Countries in the thirteenth century. In this she joined a select number of young women Christians such as Juliana of Cornillion, Eve of St. Martin, Isabelle of Huy, Mary of Oignies, Ida of Leau, Ida of Nivelles, Ida of Loviano, Christiana of St. Trend, Lutgard of Tongres, and Margaret of Ypres.

She was born of a wealthy family of Huy near Liège in 1158 and when very young was married off by her parents. Five years and three children later, she was a widow at the youthful age of eighteen. There was no dearth of suitors, drawn by her uncommon beauty, but Yvette would have none of them. She dedicated herself for eleven years to caring for lepers out of surpassing love for God.

For the last thirty-six years of her life, the holy woman lived as an anchoress and had many mystical experiences. Her prayers and miracles made her famous. She succeeded in bringing her father and one of her two remaining children back to the Faith and solicitously aided the countless people who flocked to consult her in her hermitage. She died on January 13, 1228.

REFLECTION As a mother and widow of great wealth, Bl. Yvette chose the mystical way rather than the ordinary path of a second marriage. Having served lepers with great dedication, she withdrew to a life of contemplation and spiritual direction. We should ask ourselves whether we are willing to "taste and see the goodness of the Lord."

PRAYER *Loving God, in calling Your servants to suffer illness in faith, You raised up Bl. Yvette to gently nurse the rejected leper. May we follow her heroic virtue and tend the sick poor. This we ask through Christ our Lord. Amen.*

ST. FELIX OF NOLA, Priest

January 14

V ERY little is known about Felix of Nola, and what we do know comes in great part from the poems that St. Paulinus wrote about him over a hundred years after his death. Paulinus built a church in the saintly priest's honor, and people came in droves to visit Felix's burial place.

Felix was the son of a Syrian soldier who had retired to Nola, near Naples, in Italy. During the persecution of Decius in 250, this priest was arrested and treated most brutally, but he escaped from prison with divine aid. He sought out Bishop Maximus who was sick and helpless and hid him in his own home, taking care of him.

Felix outfoxed his pursuers and successfully waited out the persecution. Upon the death of Maximus, the people wanted to make Felix bishop, but he refused. He remained in the high esteem of the people because of his goodness and his suffering in persecution.

Felix went to his heavenly reward about 260, and his praises were sung by the great St. Augustine as well as St. Paulinus.

REFLECTION Like St. Felix, we are called to suffer for our Faith. His was a brutal suffering; ours may be miniscule but of great length. Through Felix's example our resolution to persevere in good is strengthened.

ST. ARNOLD JANSSEN, Founder

January 15

ARNOLD Janssen, a modern-day apostle after the heart of St. Paul, was born in Goch, Germany, in 1837 and became a priest at Münster in 1861. He taught science for twelve years while acting as diocesan director of the Apostleship of Prayer for the last eight.

In 1873, Father Arnold became the editor of a journal about the missions, and two years later he established a Missionary Society in Steyl, Holland for that country as well as Germany and Austria. This became the Society of the Divine Word (SVD); its priest-members took simple vows, and it gained formal Papal approval in 1901. Its first missionaries were sent out in 1897—to Toga, New Guinea, North America, Japan, and Paraguay. The Society spread rapidly in the United States.

In 1889, the zealous priest founded the Holy Spirit Missionary Sisters to educate girls in mission lands. He also founded the cloistered Sister Servants of the Holy Spirit of Perpetual Adoration, whose purpose was to pray for success of the missionary effort. This indefatigable worker for God's Kingdom was called to his heavenly reward on January 15, 1909. He was beatified by Pope Paul VI in 1975 and canonized by Pope John Paul II in 2003.

REFLECTION   The temptation to fall back in our pursuit of good works is ever present. St. Arnold Janssen's good works enable us to see how much can be done with great zeal and vigor for God's Kingdom.

PRAYER   *Gracious God, hear the prayers of Your people as we strive to imitate the generous faith of St. Arnold. May we persevere in good and work diligently for the salvation of many. This we ask through Christ our Lord. Amen.*

ST. FURSEY, Abbot

January 16

BORN in Munster, Ireland, about 567, Fursey was educated by St. Brendan himself and became imbued with the great Saint's pioneering religious spirit. Entering the priesthood, he traveled throughout Ireland for twelve years, preaching and establishing a number of monastic houses.

Fursey then went on to England and France where he continued his apostolic work, founding more monasteries. At the same time, he was favored with visions that he related to his followers. They concerned the struggle between the forces of evil and the power of God, glimpses of heaven and hell. When they were set down in a book known as the *Visions of Fursey* they had a powerful impact on the vision accounts of the Middle Ages, especially Dante's *Divine Comedy*.

Worn out by zealous and unrelenting labor in the Lord's vineyard, Fursey died near Paris about the year 650 and was buried at Peronne. Many miracles were reported at his tomb and he is the Patron of the place. St. Bede spoke glowingly of Fursey in his *Ecclesiastical History* (731) and made him one of the best-known Irish Saints in England and France.

REFLECTION The Christian community is blessed with the good example of St. Fursey the Abbot. His life of dedication suggests we reexamine the living of our Faith and our zeal for the welfare of God's people.

PRAYER   *Father, help Your people to be zealous in spreading Your Word, and giving relief to those in need. May the virtues of Your holy Abbot Fursey mark our lives. This we ask through Christ our Lord. Amen.*

———◆———

ST. ROSALINA, Religious

January 17

BORN into a noble family of Villeneuve, Rosalina received a good Christian education and even as a child was devoted to the poor. An unverified story says that she was once bringing a poor person some food hidden under her apron when she was asked by her father what she had in the apron. The flustered child replied that she was bringing flowers—and opening the apron her father did indeed find a bunch of flowers.

Rosalina chose to give herself to God in the religious life. She relinquished the delights of her way of life and entered a Carthusian monastery in Bertrand in the diocese of Gap. Her devotion to the Lord and dedication to the Rule made her a model religious and she was soon named prioress of another Carthusian house at Celle Roubaud. Her brother became a benefactor of the monastery and built a church there.

On January 17, 1329, Rosalina went to meet the Lord she had served so unstintingly throughout her earthly life. Her tomb in the chapel became the site for many miracles. In 1607, her remains were transferred to a marble tomb in the chapel dedicated to her. Rosalina is the Patroness of the City of Draguignan.

REFLECTION The harshness of winter vividly reminds us of the desperation of the poor. St. Rosalina's complete devotion to the impoverished is a challenge for us to reach out to the desperate in the manner of Jesus.

PRAYER *Loving God, Your devoted servant St. Rosalina from her youth dedicated her life entirely to You. May her good example inspire all priests and religious to a deeper spirituality. This we ask through Christ our Lord. Amen.*

BL. CHRISTINA CICCARELLI, Virgin

MATTIA Ciccarelli was born in Abruzzi, Italy, on February 24, 1481, the youngest of six children of Domenico de Pericolo. From early childhood she experienced a strong attraction for the religious life and was devoted to prayer, fasting, and other practices of mortification. In June 1505, she entered the Augustinian monastery of St. Lucia in Aquila and took the name Christina.

Her great piety, complete obedience, and deep humility earned her the admiration of the other religious, and she was soon elected Abbess. Christina also became famous for her sanctity, for her visions, and for her ability to obtain miraculous cures. As a result, she was constantly visited by people from the highest to the lowest.

Two of her ecstasies are especially notable. On a feast of Corpus Christi, she was levitated from the ground, and a Sacred Host in a golden pyx radiated from her breast. On Good Friday, she experienced in great part the pains of our Lord's Passion during a vision that lasted until the following day. Christina died on January 18, 1543, and was buried to the right of the altar in the Church of St. Lucy.

REFLECTION   Bl. Christina's spirit of obedience suggests a lifestyle appropriate to the followers of the obedient Jesus. We live the very will of God as we obey His Commandments.

PRAYER   *God our Father, You asked Your Son Jesus to obey Your will so that we might be saved. May we always imitate the spirit of obedience of Bl. Christina so that we may become more like Jesus. This we ask through Christ our Lord. Amen.*

———◆•◆———

ST. GERMANICUS, Martyr
January 19

ALL that we know about St. Germanicus is found in a letter of the Christians at Smyrna, writing about the persecution that led to the arrest of St. Polycarp: "Thanks be to God, for He prevailed against all. The noble Germanicus [who was a disciple of St. Polycarp] encouraged the timidity of his companions by his constancy, and he fought with the wild beasts in a signal manner."

Condemned to death in Smyrna's amphitheater at the hands of wild beasts, the Saint provoked the animals to attack him when they hesitated and so won the admiration of the crowd and the crown of martyrdom. He was ground by the teeth of the beasts and merited to be one with the true bread, the Lord Jesus Christ, by dying for His sake in the middle of the second century.

REFLECTION   Buoyed by the love he had for Christ the Lord, St. Germanicus desired to emulate St. Ignatius of Antioch in the desire to be ground as the wheat of Christ. When his appointed time had come, he actually embraced martyrdom by instigating the beasts to take his life and so earned the martyr's crown.

PRAYER   *Lord God, St. Germanicus had such great love for You as to long for martyrdom. Help us to give our lives for You in diligently embracing the difficulties of everyday life. This we ask through Christ our Lord. Amen.*

———◆———

ST. HENRY OF FINLAND, Bishop and Martyr
January 20—*Patron of Finland*

HENRY was an Englishman of the twelfth century residing at Rome. In 1152, he was consecrated Bishop of Uppsala, Sweden, by the papal legate Nicholas Breakspear who later became Pope Adrian IV. In 1154, St. Eric, King of Sweden, led a punitive expedition against the Finns in retaliation for their marauding activity into Sweden, and Henry accompanied him.

Eric offered peace and the Christian Faith to the people of Finland, but they refused. A battle ensued and the Swedes won.

Henry baptized the defeated people in the Spring of Kuppis near Oslo. When Eric returned to Sweden, Henry remained behind, working to convert more of the Finns. To this end he built a church at Nousis, which became his headquarters.

In time, Henry met a violent death on account of his love of God. A converted Finnish soldier named Lalli had murdered a Swedish soldier. After careful consideration of the facts and assiduous prayer, Henry imposed the penalty of excommunication on the murderer. Lalli became enraged and slew the saintly bishop with an ax about the year 1157. Henry was buried at Nousis, and miracles were reported at his tomb.

REFLECTION In our quest for salvation, we are expected to lead lives of virtue. St. Henry of Finland was murdered for his quest for justice. With courage and through St. Henry's inspiration, may we lead good lives in the face of opposition and ridicule.

PRAYER   *God of mercy, justice, and love, through the intercession of St. Henry of Finland, may we be people of peace, law, and order. This we ask through Christ our Lord. Amen.*

———◆—◆———

ST. EUTHYMIUS THE GREAT, Abbot

The Same Day—January 20

BORN in the year 378 A.D. to wealthy parents in Melitine, Armenia, St. Euthymius was educated at the home of the Bishop of Melitine. After his ordination, St. Euthymius was made deputy of the monasteries in the Melitine diocese.

He was befriended by St. Polyeuctus, a hermit, and became attracted to a life of prayer and solitude. Accordingly, he left his birthplace and chose a cell near the monastery of Pharan. Here he made baskets to support himself, but gave most of his income to the poor.

After five years at Pharan, he joined one Theoctistus in his solitude near Jericho, coming out of his hermitage only on Saturday and Sunday to give spiritual direction. One day he cured an Arab's son with the Sign of the Cross, and many other Arabs were converted. When Juvenal, Patriarch of Jerusalem, heard of his reputation, Euthymius was made bishop and assisted at the Council of Ephesus in 431.

The Saint soon returned to his beloved solitude and was widely known for his charity and humility. He worked many miracles through the Sign of the Cross and as a result converted Empress Eudoxia and many of her followers. On the day he predicted, he died in 473 A.D., at the age of ninety-five.

REFLECTION Although a very talented individual, St. Euthymius sought the wisdom of God in solitude and prayer. His life serves to remind us of the true value of life and the care with which we should utilize our God-given gifts in the service of others.

PRAYER   *God, You ask us to live in wisdom and truth. Like St. Euthymius may we dedicate ourselves to living the Word of God in our lives. This we ask through Christ our Lord. Amen.*

ST. EPIPHANIUS OF PAVIA, Bishop
January 21

BORN about 439, Epiphanius was elected Bishop of Pavia, Italy, at the age of twenty-eight and developed into one of the most influential Italian leaders during the time of the collapse of the Western Empire. Venerated for his holiness and his great charity for all, he rebuilt the city of Pavia after Odoacer destroyed it.

This saintly bishop converted many to the Faith by the power of his eloquence, came to the aid of the hungry, and intervened for his people with the rulers of his day: the Emperor Anthemus, the Visigoth Euric, the Ostrogoth Theodoric, and the Burgundian Gonderbald.

Toward the end of his life, Epiphanius made the wearying journey to Lyons to intervene with King Gondebald for the release of 6,000 prisoners from Italy. Exhausted from his efforts, he died in 496 on his return from his errand of mercy. He was known as the "Peacemaker."

REFLECTION St. Epiphanius put forth herculean efforts to ensure the peace and well-being of his people in times of crisis. We should strive to spread peace among all with whom we come in contact every day and to maintain or restore peace between ourselves and God.

PRAYER   *O Lord, You bestowed on St. Epiphanius the wondrous power to work for peace among peoples. Grant us, through his intercession, to pursue peace avidly both in the spiritual and in the material realms all our lives. This we ask through Christ our Lord. Amen.*

BL. LAURA VICUÑA, Virgin
January 22

LAURA was born in Santiago, Chile, in 1891, during troublous times. Her soldier father took the family to the Andes for safety but died and left Mercedes his wife with two-year-old Laura and a baby sister Julia. Mercedes moved to the frontier town of Las Lajas and became the mistress of a well-to-do hacienda owner, Manuel Mora.

At eight years of age, Laura began to attend a boarding school run by the Daughters of Mary Help of Christians (Salesian Sisters). The example of the sisters led Laura to want to become one of them. Shortly after she made her First Communion at ten years of age, she asked the local bishop for permission to become a Salesian sister. He advised her to wait a few years. However, Laura knew she had a vocation, and her confessor shared this view.

In 1901, on a visit to the hacienda, Laura was horrified to be on the receiving end of Mora's improper advances. She fought him off and ran outdoors. She begged God to help her and to save her mother from the life of concubinage in which she was mired. The saintly girl also asked her confessor to allow her to offer her life for her mother's conversion. Because of her genuine spirituality, the confessor allowed her to do so.

In the winter of 1903, Laura became ill and returned to the hacienda. During the ever-worsening illness, the youth gave an example of perfect obedience to God's will, patience, fortitude, and a great desire for heavenly things. On January 14, 1904, Mora became drunk and demanded that Mercedes and the children come back to the house. Sick as she was, the young girl ran away but was quickly overtaken and beaten into unconsciousness by the frenzied man. Laura died a week later, on January 22, after confiding to Mercedes that she had offered her life for her.

The distraught Mercedes begged her daughter's forgiveness and promised to renew her life. That very night she came back to the Sacraments.

REFLECTION Young though she was, Bl. Laura gave a perfect example of holiness, offering her life for her mother's conversion. Her life indicates that each of us has a task to perform on earth, and with God's grace each of us can carry it out to the full.

PRAYER   *O God, in the young Laura Vicuña You wondrously combined strength of spirit and purity of innocence. Grant that, through her intercession, we too may overcome the trials of this life and show forth the beatitude promised to the pure of heart. This we ask through Christ our Lord. Amen.*

ST. EMERENTIANA, Virgin and Martyr

January 23

ST. Emerentiana was a Roman martyr originally buried in the great cemetery on the Via Nomentana. The early Christians celebrated her martyrdom on September 16 with that of Sts. Victor, Felix, and Alexander.

In time her remains were transferred to the Basilica of St. Agnes, which was located on the same Via Nomentana but a bit further on. This event led to the rise of a parallel story about St. Emerentiana that was found in the pre-Vatican II editions of the *Roman Martyrology* and the *Breviary.*

According to this later version, Emerentiana was the foster-sister of St. Agnes and of a similar young age. A catechumen, she went to pray at the grave of St. Agnes two days after her foster-sister's martyrdom. Confronted by an angry mob of pagans, she professed her faith and was stoned to death around 304. St. Emerentiana thus received a Baptism of Blood and joined her foster-sister in her heavenly home.

REFLECTION St. Emerentiana gave her life for Christ even though she was just in her teenage years and had not yet been formally received as a full member of the Church. We should strive to lead everyone to Christ.

PRAYER   *O Lord, by the merit of her chastity and by her confession of Your power, St. Emerentiana, Your Virgin and Martyr, was pleasing to You. May she now implore Your pardon for us. This we ask through Christ our Lord. Amen.*

ST. BABYLAS, Bishop and Martyr

January 24

ALTHOUGH little detail about the life of St. Babylas is known, he is considered to be the second most famous early Bishop of Antioch, after Ignatius. He was consecrated around 240.

It is believed that in 244 Babylas refused to allow Philip the Arabian to be admitted into the Church until Philip had performed public penance for having murdered Gordian, his predecessor. It is further believed that along with three young men, Urbanus, Prilidianus, and Epolonius, whom he had instructed in the Faith, St. Babylas was executed during a persecution under Decius, around 250. However, Eusebius claims St. Babylas died in prison. Nonetheless, at a later date, Babylas's relics were transferred with great solemnity from Antioch to Daphne. This great ceremony was held supposedly to combat the rising influence of the shrine of Apollo.

St. Babylas is further referred to in Aldhelm's treatise on *Virginity*, which in turn contributed much to the notoriety and enthusiasm for St. Babylas in England.

REFLECTION In carrying out the duties of one's state in life, it is very easy in our world to run into opposition. The example of St. Babylas's courage and determination in the face of great danger gives us reason and hope for being true to our Faith in the face of criticism and opposition.

PRAYER   *Loving God, through the intercession of Your holy Martyr Babylas, guide Your Church on the path of salvation. May his example of faith and courage help us to persevere in good. This we ask through Christ our Lord. Amen.*

ST. POPPO, Abbot

January 25

BORN in Flanders in 978, Poppo was reared by a devout mother who imparted to him a deep faith and spent the latter years of her life as a nun at Verdun. Poppo completed a short stint in the army and then decided to enter the religious life. He became a monk at St. Thierry's Monastery near Rheims.

About the year 1008, he teamed up with Abbot Richard of Saint-Vanne, a renowned monastic reformer. Together they restored the religious observance of several abbeys, among which were Saint-Vaast at Arras and Beaulieu. Later, Poppo went on to become an abbot general for a cluster of monasteries in Lotharingia. He maintained the high quality of their discipline and earned the great respect of his subjects as well as the people outside.

So great was Poppo's fame as a man of God that he became a kind of unofficial adviser to the Emperor, St. Henry II, even on political matters and affairs of state. After a life of total dedication to the things of God, Poppo died on January 25, 1048.

REFLECTION St. Poppo took pains to maintain his spiritual life at a high level even as he looked after the life and devotion of his monks. We should endeavor to monitor our own spiritual life daily so that it may remain vibrant and true.

PRAYER   *O Lord, You bestowed on St. Poppo the grace to lead others in the spiritual life. Through his intercession, enable us to follow his example and grow every day in depth of our devotion to You. This we ask through Christ our Lord. Amen.*

ST. ALBERIC, Abbot
Cofounder of the Cistercian Order

January 26

THERE is no evidence to indicate what circumstances led St. Alberic to embrace the eremitical lifestyle. We find him as a hermit at Collan, near Châtillon-sur-Seine, France. Other hermits in the area were invited by Alberic in 1075 to move to Molesmes, with one, Robert, as abbot and Alberic as prior. Here, living a monastic lifestyle, Alberic and his brothers attracted many others to their foundation.

As their numbers grew, some of the newer arrivals began to ignore the strict monastic rule. As a result, Robert left, and Alberic was imprisoned by his fellow monks. Soon thereafter, Alberic was released, but he returned to the monastery after a brief time. Alberic tried to instigate reform but was unsuccessful. In union with Robert and an Englishman, Stephen Harding, a new monastic venture was established at Cîteaux, near Dijon, in 1098.

Robert, Alberic, and Stephen Harding are considered the founders of the Cistercian Order. At the beginning, difficulties forced Robert to return to Molesmes, and Alberic was elected abbot. He established the original Benedictine Rule and called for its strict observance. At the same time, it appears Alberic played a role in the growth of the place of the lay brother in the monastery, as well as contributing to the use of the Romanesque artform characteristic of early Cistercian monasticism. Still, Alberic's successor, Stephen Harding, is usually associated with having fostered the characteristics of modern Cistercian lifestyle.

Remembered as a father figure, friend, and "fellow-soldier" in fighting the "Lord's battles," Alberic died on January 26, 1109, memorialized as one who truly loved his brother monks, Cistercianism, and the Word of God.

REFLECTION In coming out of his hermitage in order to establish a monastic community, St. Alberic generously followed the call of the Spirit. Yet he suffered many trials and tribulations in his efforts to establish a salvation-oriented lifestyle. As we journey through life seeking the guidance of the Spirit, let us be encouraged by St. Alberic's sense of fidelity to his call. May we be faithful to the duties of our state in life.

PRAYER *God, the Father of all who are faithful to You, Your servant Alberic followed Your will and left his solitude to do Your work. May we accept self-denial to bring Your Word to others. This we ask through Christ our Lord. Amen.*

———◆———

BL. JOHN OF WARNETON, Bishop

January 27

JOHN was born at Warneton in French Flanders. Little is known of his very early life or his family background. His parents saw to his schooling as a young man, and he was known to have been taught by such scholars as Lambert of Utrecht and St. Ivo of Chartres.

Shortly after his contact with St. Ivo, St. John became a monk at Mont-Saint-Eloi, near Arles. Eventually, he served as Archdeacon of Arles. He was well thought of in ecclesiastical circles, and much to his chagrin and against his wishes he was appointed Bishop of Thérouanne. Moreover, as bishop, he was so instrumental and zealous in furthering monastic reform that his life was threatened on many occasions.

Nonetheless, John could not be dissuaded from his course and continued through his personal piety and spirituality to be a moving force for monastic reform in the region of Arles. He died in the odor of sanctity on January 27, 1130.

REFLECTION John of Warneton from his earliest years was exposed to individuals of piety and spirituality to the extent that he literally followed in the footsteps of his teachers and became an individual of great piety. As we strive to walk in the footsteps of John, let us follow closely the example of our teacher, Jesus. May we always strive to be men and women of kindness and consideration for all people with whom we come in contact. Our daily lives can reflect the goodness of Jesus as long as we sincerely try to imitate His virtues.

PRAYER *Merciful Father, bless all Your people as You did Bl. John of Warneton with a deep spirit of piety, kindness, compassion, and consideration. This we ask through Christ our Lord. Amen.*

———◆•◆———

ST. JOHN OF REOMAY, Abbot

January 28

BORN at Dijon, France, in 425, John embraced the life of a solitary at Reomay. When disciples flocked to his way of life, his desire for solitude led him to emigrate to Lerins. He became a monk there and came in contact with the traditions of St. Macarius, one of the early practitioners of Eastern monasticism.

After some time, John was recalled by his bishop and founded the Abbey of Reomay, which later was named Mount St. John in his honor. He patterned his monastery after the Constitution of St. Macarius.

During his long rule, John gained renown for his holiness and his miracles. This holy man died about the year 554, and is regarded as one of the pioneers of monasticism in the West.

REFLECTION   In his desire for solitude with God, St. John fled to a different country and thereby encountered a new style of monachism that changed his life. We should remain ever open to the inspirations of the Spirit and follow them wherever they may lead.

PRAYER   *O Lord, You inspired St. John to pioneer a new way of religious life in the West. Grant us, through his intercession, to follow Your inspirations that constantly beckon us to a life of more devoted service to You. This we ask through Christ our Lord. Amen.*

ST. SULPICIUS SEVERUS, Bishop

January 29

WE know very little about the early life of St. Sulpicius Severus. He was appointed

Bishop of Bourges in 584. The following year he attended the Council of Mâcon.

Most of his life and influence is unrecorded. He is credited with having written a very popular life of St. Martin of Tours. Unfortunately, there was a writer of the same name who lived at the same time as Sulpicius who is also credited with writing the life of Martin. Nonetheless, Sulpicius's biography of Martin of Tours became one of the most popular of the Middle Ages and is credited with having done much to spread the cult of Martin, as well as having become a model medieval life of a Saint.

Sulpicius Severus died on January 29, 591.

REFLECTION St. Sulpicius Severus's concern for the things of God and his faithful service as Bishop of Bourges speak to us today of a hidden life well lived in the service of others. Sulpicius's scholarly work on Martin was accomplished through a true desire to imitate a holy Christian. May the lives of the Saints spur us on to a more spiritual life centered on the meaning and mystery of the life of Christ.

PRAYER *Lord God, You raised up Your servant St. Sulpicius Severus to lead Your people to salvation. May we imitate his great zeal for the salvation of souls. This we ask through Christ our Lord. Amen.*

ST. MUTIEN MARIE WIAUX, Religious

January 30

LOUIS Wiaux was born on March 20, 1841, at Mellet, Belgium. He was one of six children, and his Walloon family was noted for its piety. After attending a country school, Louis joined his father as a blacksmith. Following the advice of his parish priest, Louis entered the Brothers of the Christian Schools on April 7, 1852. He was given the name Brother Mutien Marie.

After his novitiate at Namur, he taught in elementary schools in Chimay and Brussels. In 1859, he was sent to St. Berthuin's School, at

Malonne. He would remain there for fifty-nine years. Owing to difficulty in controlling students in class, Brother Mutien was asked to teach art and instrumental music. This was so he would have fewer pupils at one time. Within a short time, he became a proficient teacher of the fine arts.

In his role as teacher, prefect of the boarding students and recreation supervisor, Brother Mutien's quiet but open manner was a source of encouragement for his students. He constantly prayed the Rosary, and his lengthy chapel visits earned him the nickname "the praying Brother." As he advanced in age his whole life seemed concentrated all the more on his work and prayer.

Following a short illness, Brother Mutien Marie died on January 30, 1917. Shortly thereafter his reputation for sanctity began to grow. He was beatified on October 30, 1977, by Pope Paul VI and canonized on December 10, 1989, by Pope John Paul II.

REFLECTION Brother Mutien's humility, obedience, kindness, and prayer-filled good example led many of his students to turn back to God. His simplicity and kindness won them over. Here is a modern Saint we can readily imitate.

PRAYER   *All-powerful God, help us follow the example of Brother Mutien Marie by showing in our lives the light of truth and love for all people. This we ask through Christ our Lord. Amen.*

ST. MARCELLA, Widow

S T. Marcella was a noble woman of Rome whose husband died only seven months after marriage. Marcella's widowhood became a cause of notoriety because she refused to marry the consul Cerealis. The latter did not take this rejection too well.

After her somewhat public encounter with Cerealis, Marcella gathered a group of distinguished ladies of Rome for the purpose of promoting a lifestyle of austerity and asceticism. Also, on a personal level, Marcella never ate meat or drank wine. Much of her time was spent in spiritual reading, prayer, and visiting the shrines of Martyrs.

When the invading Goths looted Rome in 410, Marcella was captured and tortured so that she would reveal the whereabouts of her wealth. The treasure had been given to the poor long before the Goths arrived. Eventually, the Goths freed Marcella and led her and her faithful companion, Principia, to the church of St. Paul, which Alaric the Goth had declared a place of sanctuary. However, a short time later, Marcella died in August 410.

During her lifetime Marcella carried on an extensive correspondence with St. Jerome in which issues of spirituality were discussed at length. She sometimes challenged his ideas and once scolded him for his hasty temper.

REFLECTION St. Marcella dedicated her widowhood to the service of God and the poor. She encouraged other women of means to seriously consider the direction of their lives and the necessity of good works. As we come near the Lenten Season, St. Marcella's life gives us substantial direction in the all-important questions of how we want to lead our lives and to what extent we should be generous to those in need.

PRAYER *Almighty and ever-living Lord, may we like St. Marcella dedicate our lives to the service of the poor. Grant us a spirit of detachment and generosity like that of Jesus. This we ask through Christ our Lord. Amen.*

ST. SIGEBERT III OF AUSTRASIA, King

February 1

IN 1638, when Sigebert was seven years old, his father, who was King of France, died, and the Saint took on the rule of Austrasia while his brother Cloris reigned over the rest of France. The young prince was educated by Bl. Pepin of Landers, who also instructed him in the Christian virtues.

Sigebert was devoted to prayer, to relieving the poor, and to endowing monasteries, churches, and hospitals. In 656, at the young age of twenty-five, he was called by God to enjoy the fruits of his earthly labors.

REFLECTION Although St. Sigebert was a prince of the world, he was not worldly. He preferred to carry out the good deeds of God, caring for the poor, the sick, and the Religious. We should follow his lead and at least pray daily for all who are in need of God's help.

PRAYER   *Heavenly Father, You led St. Sigebert, a prince of the world, to become a prince of Your Church. By his intercession, help us to follow his example and pursue the things of God first in our lives. This we ask through Christ our Lord. Amen.*

———◆◆———

ST. JOAN DE LESTONNAC, Abbess
February 2

S T. Joan de Lestonnac was born in Bordeaux, France, in 1556. She married at the age of seventeen. The happy marriage produced four children, but her husband died suddenly in 1597. After her children were raised, she entered the Cistercian monastery at Toulouse.

Joan was forced to leave the Cistercians when she became afflicted with poor health. She returned to Bordeaux with the idea of forming a new congregation, and several young girls joined her as novices. They ministered to victims of a plague that struck Bordeaux, and they were determined to counteract the evils of heresy promulgated by Calvinism.

Thus was formed the Congregation of the Religious of Notre Dame of Bordeaux. In 1608, Joan and her companions received the religious habit from the Archbishop of Bordeaux. Joan was elected superior in 1610, and her schools greatly prospered. She died on the Feast of the Purification in 1640, and many miracles occurred at her tomb. She was canonized in 1949 by Pope Pius XII.

REFLECTION   St. Joan's life was varied and full, but she never swerved from her determination to remain close to God. She prospered in good times and bad, and God finally took her to Himself, the reward of one who faithfully carried out His will.

PRAYER   *Lord God, You gave St. Joan a great capacity to love despite many disappointments and trials. Grant that, like her, we may follow Your will and one day share with her Your presence. This we ask through Christ our Lord. Amen.*

———◆◆———

BL. STEPHEN BELLESINI

The Same Day—February 2

BL. Stephen Bellesini was born at Trent on November 25, 1774. He entered the Order of Hermits of St. Augustine in 1790, at age sixteen. After pursuing studies at Rome and Bologna, he was unable to continue in the religious life inasmuch as the Augustinians fell victim to the excesses caused by the French Revolution.

Stephen thereupon devoted himself energetically to preaching, and especially the religious education of children, eventually being appointed by the government as inspector of schools in Trent. However, when the Augustinians were restored, Stephen returned to the religious life, becoming master of novices at Rome and later at Città delle Pieve. Several years later he became a parish priest at the Augustinian church at Genazzano, site of the famous shrine of Our Lady of Good Counsel.

Renowned for his piety and his devotion to his people, Stephen characteristically attended the sick without concern for his personal health when the cholera epidemic of 1840 struck. As a result, he contracted the disease and died on February 2, 1840. He was beatified by Pope Pius X in 1904.

REFLECTION Bl. Stephen's determination to serve God in His people enabled him to accept the challenge of perseverance in the midst of many obstacles, especially the French Revolution. In his zeal to minister to his parishioners in desperate times he cared little for the danger of cholera that eventually claimed his life.

PRAYER *Loving God, help us through the intercession of Bl. Stephen Bellesini to grow in zeal for reaching out to others in need, especially the sick. This we ask through Christ our Lord. Amen.*

———◆———

STS. SIMEON, a Just and Devout Man and ANNA, a Widow and Prophetess

February 3

SIMEON was a just and devout man who witnessed the Presentation of Jesus in the Temple (Luke 2:25-35). It had been revealed to him by God that he would not die before seeing the

Messiah. When the Infant Jesus was brought into the Temple by Mary and Joseph, Simeon now expressed his willingness to die and he prophesied a double effect of this Child's Messianic mission as well as the future suffering of Mary His Mother. Jesus was destined for the fall and rise of many in Israel and a standard that would be opposed.

Anna was a widow and prophetess who was also in the Temple at the Presentation of Jesus (Luke 2:36-39). She praised God and proclaimed the Infant to those who longed for the restoration of Israel. She was either 84 years old or 106 (15 years of virginity, 7 years of marriage, 84 years of widowhood). The word "prophetess" may be taken in the sense either of one who exhorts and consoles (1 Corinthians 14:3) or of one who knows and reveals future events (1 Corinthians 14:23).

REFLECTION Sts. Simeon and Anna led holy lives in the time of the Old Testament. They can be classed as the Poor of the Lord, the *anawim*, who awaited the coming of the promised Messiah and put their hope in the Lord alone. As a result, God found them worthy to greet Jesus as the Messiah and Savior, the blessed Hope and Redeemer of Israel.

PRAYER *Almighty God, Your devoted servants, Sts. Simeon and Anna, placed their trust in You and merited to announce the coming of the Redeemer. By their intercession, may we always accept Jesus as our Redeemer and deserve to merit eternal glory. This we ask through Christ our Lord. Amen.*

ST. JOHN DE BRITTO, Martyr

ST. John de Britto was born in Lisbon, Portugal, in 1647. His parents were part of the Portuguese nobility, and his father was the Governor of Brazil. John entered the Jesuit novitiate in Lisbon in 1662 at the age of fifteen. While studying at the University of Coimbra he became interested in India.

Once he was ordained in 1673, John was sent to the Indian Jesuit mission at Madura. He lived as did the Indians and hoped to convert people in the upper class in order to bring about greater influence for Christianity. In 1685, he was made superior of the mission, but because of his many conversions the Brahmins sought to kill him. Captured in 1687, he was released from prison and torture after one month.

Following a short visit to Portugal, John returned to Madura where, despite being threatened anew, he continued to preach. As a result, he was arrested and sentenced to death. On February 4, 1693, the holy man was brought before the executioner who hesitated to carry out the sentence. Father de Britto said: "My friend, I have prayed to God. I have done what I should do. Now do your part. Carry out the order you have received." He was beheaded and received the crown of Martyrs.

John de Britto was beatified by Pope Pius IX in 1853 and canonized by Pope Pius XII in 1947.

REFLECTION In his zeal to preach the Gospel and win souls for God, St. John de Britto willingly risked his life. His example encourages us not only to truly live the Gospel but also to willingly face challenges and difficulties in order that the Word may be effectively spread among those so much in need.

PRAYER   *Lord God, You sent Your Martyr St. John de Britto to preach the Gospel by word and example. Grant the grace of perseverance to those who steadfastly proclaim Your Word. This we ask through Christ our Lord. Amen.*

ST. ADELAIDE OF BELLICH, Abbess
February 5

ST. Adelaide of Bellich was the daughter of the Count of Guelder. Her father founded two nunneries, and Adelaide eventually ruled over both. First she presided over the convent at Bellich near Bonn. Later she became abbess of St. Mary's in Cologne.

Adelaide followed the Benedictine rule in both convents. She insisted that her nuns study Latin so that they could follow the Divine Office in choir more fittingly. The Saint loved the poor and provided for their needs. Moreover, she was an individual of great prudence, and St. Heribert, the Archbishop of Cologne, consulted her when he needed to make important decisions.

St. Adelaide died in the year 1015 at St. Mary's in Cologne. The nunnery she ruled there was eventually converted to a church of canonesses.

REFLECTION With the prospect of an easy life in her grasp, St. Adelaide turned aside from her good fortune to serve God. She was generous with both her material possessions and her personal talents. Her generosity and care speak eloquently to us.

PRAYER *God Almighty, in Your wisdom You have raised up St. Adelaide as an example of detachment and generosity. Through her example and intercession lift us out of the depths of selfishness and cupidity. This we ask through Christ our Lord. Amen.*

—————◆·◆—————

ST. VEDAST (or FOSTER), Bishop of Arras

February 6

S T. Vedast, whose English name is Foster, was born in France in the fifth century and emigrated to the diocese of Toul, where he was ordained by St. Remigius. He was selected to accompany King Clovis I to Rheims to prepare him for his Baptism. On the way he restored sight to a blind beggar, which confirmed the King in his new Faith.

After assisting St. Remigius in teaching the Faith to the Franks, Vedast was consecrated Bishop of Arras to reinvigorate the Faith that had waned there. He labored for forty years and succeeded in restoring the Christian Faith to that area. He died about 540.

REFLECTION Through the grace of God and the gift of miracles, St. Vedast brought back the Catholic

Faith to the people. This shows that when the Faith is presented in the right way, it will yield good fruits.

PRAYER   *God our Father, You enabled St. Vedast, Your Bishop, to give his life in leading people to Christ. By his intercession, help us to be faithful witnesses of the Christian Faith. This we ask through Christ our Lord. Amen.*

———◆◆———

ST. MOSES, Bishop
Apostle of the Saracens
February 7

AN Arab by birth, Moses is known as the Apostle of the Saracens. Saracen is the term used by the later Greeks and Romans when they were referring to the nomad tribes of the Syro-Arabian desert.

For a long period of time Moses lived the life of a hermit in the region between Syria and Egypt. The area was home to wandering groups of Saracens, and their queen, Mavia, agreed to have her followers evangelized, provided that they might have holy Moses the hermit as their bishop. However, Moses refused to accept consecration from Lucius, the Archbishop of Alexandria, because the latter was an Arian.

Eventually, Moses was consecrated bishop by an orthodox bishop, and he then spent his remaining days teaching and preaching. As a result he

converted a large proportion of the Saracen people to the Faith. He also succeeded in getting the
Romans and Saracens to live in peace with one
another. He died around the year 389.

REFLECTION St. Moses prepared himself for his
apostolate among the Saracens by prayer and fasting. It was his reputation for holiness that led the people to Moses. If we are to lead others to God, we must
be individuals of prayer first, and of good example
later.

PRAYER   *Lord God, through the intercession of
Your holy Bishop Moses, bring us nearer to You as
we pray and seek out others for salvation. This we
ask through Christ our Lord. Amen.*

———————◆•◆———————

ST. STEPHEN OF MURET, Abbot
February 8

S T. Stephen is thought to have been the son of
a nobleman of Thiers, Auvergne, where he
was born in the eleventh century. At the age of
twelve, he accompanied his father on a trip to
Italy and became ill at Benevento. Remaining
there, he received both his education and his religious vocation.

Returning home as an adult, Stephen founded
a monastery in the Muret Valley near Limoges,
France, and governed it for forty-six years until
his death in 1124. The community then moved to

Grandemont and was called the Grandemontines.

At first the new Congregation attracted many disciples because of its strict discipline, enclosure, and austere way of life, but within fifty years it suffered a decline, although it did manage to last until the end of the eighteenth century.

St. Stephen assigned saying the Divine Praises and contemplation to the clerics but entrusted the temporal concerns, such as administration, to the lay brothers of the Congregation. This new approach to monasticism enabled the Congregation to survive as long as it did.

King Henry II of England, a benefactor of Grandemont, asked Pope Clement II to canonize Stephen, which the latter did in 1189.

REFLECTION To St. Stephen is attributed a Rule and a collection of teachings containing his spiritual doctrine. His emphasis on *poverty,* inspired by St. Gregory the Great, paved the way for the poverty of the Mendicant Orders that would soon appear in the Church.

PRAYER   *Heavenly Father, Your Abbot St. Stephen brought a new Congregation into Your service. Through his intercession, grant that we may emulate its members in serving You no matter to what state of life we belong. This we ask through Christ our Lord. Amen.*

ST. MIGUEL CORDERO, Religious

February 9

FRANCISCO Febres Cordero Muñoz was born on November 7, 1854, to a prominent family in Cuenca, Ecuador. He was not able to stand till age five when he saw a vision of the Blessed Mother in his family courtyard. At age eight, he was miraculously preserved from a mauling by a wild bull.

In 1863, the Saint enrolled in a school run by the Christian Brothers who had only recently arrived in Ecuador. He was much impressed with the Brothers and when he was of age decided to join the Congregation despite some initial hesitation on the part of his parents. In 1868, he was accepted and became known as Brother Miguel.

Miguel's first assignment was in Quito, Ecuador, at the El Cebollar School, where he remained for thirty-two years. His year-end examinations of students became a celebrated event that attracted the presence and praise of many townspeople.

Brother Miguel was a prolific writer and outstanding pedagogue. He published his first textbook at age seventeen, and the government of Ecuador eventually adopted his texts for schools throughout the republic. In 1892, Brother Miguel was elected to the national Academy of Letters. In addition to books on education, he also published works that included odes, hymns, and occasional plays.

Despite his national notoriety in the field of education, Brother Miguel delighted in preparing the very young for their First Holy Communion. He also wrote manuals of piety, gave religious instruction, and conducted retreats. Later, Brother Miguel became director of novices for three years, a position he felt unworthy to hold.

In 1908, because of ill health, Miguel was sent to a Christian Brothers' school near Barcelona, Spain. He died on February 9, 1910, and his body was returned to Ecuador with great public ceremony. On the centenary of his birth, the Ecuadorian government issued postage stamps and erected a monument in his honor. Brother Miguel was beatified in 1977 by Pope Paul VI and canonized in 1984 by Pope John Paul II.

REFLECTION Despite his great learning and public acclaim, St. Miguel still preferred the simple tasks of preparing the young for First Holy Communion, giving retreats, and writing manuals of devotion. Clearly, his life calls us to stress the important things in our lives, those actions that lead to eternal salvation.

PRAYER   *Almighty and eternal God, through the exemplary dedication of St. Miguel Cordero may we always receive young people with kindness and thereby bring them more surely to You. This we ask through Christ our Lord. Amen.*

———◆◆———

BL. ALOYSIUS STEPINAC, Martyr

February 10

ALOYSIUS Stepinac, born in 1898 in Krasic, Yugoslavia, was in the military during World War I. Afterward, he studied for the priesthood, earning a Doctorate at the Pontifical Gregorian University, and was ordained in 1930. In 1934, he was made Coadjutor Archbishop of Zagreb and succeeded to the Archbishopric in 1937.

During World War II, the Archbishop strove mightily to save as many Jews as possible from being put to death. After the war, in 1945, he was arrested by the Communist government for protesting the murders of priests and for calling for freedom of the Church in Croatia.

In 1946, Aloysius was placed on trial for his strong defense of the Holy See and Church unity, and he was sentenced to sixteen years of hard labor. In 1951, because of ill health he was placed under house arrest. He was made a Cardinal by Pope Pius XII in 1953 but remained under house arrest until 1959. The saintly man died on February 10, 1960, as a result of his long and strenuous captivity. He was beatified in 1998 by Pope John Paul II.

REFLECTION Bl. Aloysius was unable to carry out the normal apostolate of a Bishop because of his long imprisonment, so he practiced an apostolate of the pen in caring for his flock. He wrote some 5000 letters in this respect, showing that there is always more than one way to do God's work.

PRAYER *Heavenly Father, Bl. Aloysius, Your Martyr, fought valiantly in the service of Your Church and those who are oppressed, such as the Jews. Through his prayers, help us to remove all bigotry and promote peace between peoples. This we ask through Christ our Lord. Amen.*

━━━━◆━━━━

ST. SOTERIS, Virgin and Martyr
February 11

ST. Soteris was born of a noble family in the third century. However, from an early age she held riches, power, and the trappings of personal beauty in low esteem. She consecrated her virginity to God, and in order to make herself less attractive, she refused to wear ornaments common to women of the day.

Soteris lived a simple and austere life. It is believed that she was arrested and suffered torture during the persecution of Decius. Legend says that despite terrible sufferings, she did not shed tears or cry out.

Her torture under Decius, around 249-251 occurred when Soteris was a young girl. About fifty years later, during the persecution of Diocletian, she was beheaded at Rome when she refused to sacrifice to pagan gods. She entered eternal glory on February 10, 304.

REFLECTION   Early in life St. Soteris recognized the true value of remaining close to God. Disdaining material possessions and a sensual lifestyle, she earned the admiration of many generations of courageous Christian women. She stands as an example to modern women of the beauty of a life lived in and for God.

PRAYER   *God, loving Creator, You have raised up St. Soteris to the glory of Your heavenly Kingdom. Through her intercession may we disown the sensuality, pride, and sin of our age and wait lovingly for Your coming to take us to eternal glory. This we ask through Christ our Lord. Amen.*

BL. HUMBELINE, Abbess

February 12

BORN in 1092 at Dijon, France, Humbeline was the sister of the great St. Bernard of Clairvaux. She married the nobleman Guy de Marcy and led a worldly life. One day St. Bernard gently exhorted her to change her ways.

Bernard's message stayed with Humbeline, and a few years later with her husband's consent she left the world behind. She entered the convent where her sister-in-law Elizabeth was Abbess. When Elizabeth left to found a convent near Dijon, Humbeline was appointed Abbess.

After a life dedicated to God, Humbeline died in 1136 at Jolly in the arms of St. Bernard. Her cult was approved in 1703 by Pope Clement XI.

REFLECTION A woman of nobility and wealth, Bl. Humbeline spurned the trappings of her life and followed Christ more closely. She exemplifies the Gospel suggestion to give up what one has in order to follow Christ. Her example remains valid in our day.

PRAYER   *Lord God, Your servant Bl. Humbeline chose Your love over that of this world's goods. Grant that we may follow You on the narrow road to detachment. This we ask through Christ our Lord. Amen.*

———◆———

BL. CHRISTINE OF SPOLETO, Tertiary

February 13

BL. Agostina Camozzi led a worldly life for a time, but after burying two husbands she decided to change her ways. Joining the Third Order of St. Augustine, she chose the name Christine since her one wish was to imitate Christ, the only physician who could calm her troubled spirit.

The holy woman chose a penitential life of prayer and devoted herself to the poor and the sick. She lived in various Augustinian convents but left as soon as the sisters began to treat her with special reverence.

In 1547, Christine decided to make a pilgrimage of reparation to Assisi, Rome, and the Holy Sepulcher. However, she did not get beyond Spoleto before she died on February 13, 1458, with the reputation of great holiness and many miracles. In 1834, Pope Gregory XVI confirmed her long-standing cult.

REFLECTION Bl. Christine went from a worldly life to one of complete imitation of Christ. Once she knew what God required of her, she lived only for Him and those who needed her help. Her Christian courage and faith move us to be more resolute in our faith as we meet the challenges of Christian living today.

PRAYER *Lord our God, You do not wish the sinner to die but to turn to You and live. May we be inspired by the example of Bl. Christine so that we may seek and find You, the fountain of everlasting life. This we ask through Christ our Lord. Amen.*

ST. AUXENTIUS, Priest and Archimandrite
February 14

ST. Auxentius was a member of the equestrian guard of Emperor Theodosius the Younger. He left the guard and lived as a hermit in the region around Mt. Oxia near Constantinople. Soon his reputation for holiness spread far and wide, bringing a ceaseless stream of people to him for his guidance.

During the fourth Ecumenical Council, Chalcedon in 451, Auxentius was cleared of having Eutychian sympathies (i.e., denying the two natures, human and divine, in Christ). Afterward, he lived in another place closer to Chalcedon on the mountain of Skopa.

The Saint spent the rest of his life there in prayer and austerity, instructing the disciples who came to him in droves. He also served as the spiritual director of a group of women who formed a community of nuns at the foot of the mountain known as "the nuns clothed in haircloth." He died on February 14, 473.

REFLECTION　Although St. Auxentius preferred the eremitical life, he still made time for those who came to him for guidance and help. We too should be ready to help others who look to us in their material and spiritual troubles.

PRAYER　*Loving Father, St. Auxentius spent his life entirely in Your service. May we seek out Your love and presence in all that we do. This we ask through Christ our Lord. Amen.*

ST. WALFRID, Abbot
February 15

WALFRID was born in Pisa in the eighth
century. He was prosperous and successful
as well as the loving father of six children. Later
he and his wife felt called to the religious life.

Walfrid and two married friends founded the
monastery of Palazzuolo and introduced the
Rule of St. Benedict. They also established a convent at some distance for their wives and Walfrid's daughter.

Both foundations flourished. The monastery
of Palazzuolo soon housed sixty monks, including one of Walfrid's sons, who became a priest
and eventually succeeded his father. After ten
years of rule over the abbey, Walfrid died
around the year 765. Public veneration of him
was approved in 1861.

REFLECTION We must take the circumstances of
our lives seriously, especially insofar as they affect
our spiritual lives. Personal spiritual growth and development is the true preparation for an eternity with
God.

PRAYER   O God, through the intercession of St.
Walfrid may we strive to be a people of prayer, work,
and fasting. This we ask through Christ our Lord.
Amen.

ST. MARUTHAS, Bishop

February 16—*Father of the Syrian Church*

ST. Maruthas, a Doctor of the Syrian Church in the fourth/fifth century, was Bishop of Maiferkat, Mesopotamia, near the Persian border. He carried out a diplomatic mission to King Yezdigerd of Persia for Emperor Theodosius and received permission from the King to restore the religious organization of Persia and build churches wherever he chose.

The Saint was famous for his knowledge of medicine. He also drew up a list of Christians martyred in Persia during the rule of King Sapor and brought so many relics of Martyrs to Maiferkat that it was renamed Martyropolis.

St. Maruthas composed several theological works and hymns used in the Syrian Liturgy. He died about the year 416 and is regarded as the Father of the Syrian Church.

REFLECTION   By his work and teaching, St. Maruthas kept the Faith alive in Persia and was much esteemed by St. John Chrysostom, among others. We should strive to learn ever more about our Faith, which was handed down to us by our Christian ancestors.

PRAYER   *Merciful God, You enlightened the Syrian people by the teaching of St. Maruthas, Your Bishop. Help us to assimilate the teachings of Your doctrine and perfect us as a people united in the true Faith and its expansion. This we ask through Christ our Lord. Amen.*

ST. FINTAN OF CLONEENAGH, Abbot

February 17

LEGEND has it that St. Fintan's mother, before his birth in the sixth century, experienced an angelic apparition predicting her future son's holiness. Moreover, in his childhood, Fintan seemed to have the gift of prophecy and knowledge of distant events. He was trained by St. Columba who suggested that Fintan go to Cloneenagh.

At first, when Fintan settled at Cloneenagh, he led the austere life of a hermit. Eventually he gathered disciples and established a monastery at Lix. It is claimed that the monks there ate nothing but herbs and drank only water. The monastery was of high repute, and Fintan, even though very severe with himself, was gentle and compassionate in dealing with others.

Even though he mitigated monastic rules for his subjects, Fintan made no changes in his personal practices of asceticism. Others testify that when he went off by himself to pray he was surrounded by light. The year of his death is generally believed to be 603, but the *Revised Martyrology* gives it as 440.

REFLECTION The widespread reputation of St. Fintan's personal holiness gives our generation the opportunity to reflect on the necessity of holiness in our lives. Moreover, although Fintan was severe on himself, he was gentle and compassionate with others. This kind of gentleness and compassion, along with personal holiness, can make over the world for Christ.

PRAYER　　*Almighty Lord, loving God, Your servant St. Fintan drew others to You by remaining close to You and detached from worldly goods. Help us to imitate St. Fintan's holiness and compassion in living with others. This we ask through Christ our Lord. Amen.*

ST. THEOTONIUS, Abbot

February 18

THEOTONIUS was an individual of holiness and austerity of life. Born in Spain in 1086 and educated at Coimbra in Portugal, his first assignment following ordination was at Viseu. His preaching gained him a great reputation. He was outspoken in attacking vice and did not hesitate to speak out against the worldly lives of rulers. Nonetheless, he was much loved by his king and queen.

Theotonius had a great love for the poor and the souls in purgatory. He used to sing Solemn Mass every Friday for the deceased. This was followed by a procession to the cemetery during which he received abundant alms that he in turn distributed to the poor.

Following a pilgrimage to the Holy Land, Theotonius decided to enter a monastery of the Canons Regular of St. Augustine at Coimbra. Soon thereafter he became prior, and he spent the last thirty years of his life in the monastery. He was a model prior and urged his monks to recite the Daily Office in choir without fail. He died at the age of eighty about the year 1162.

REFLECTION St. Theotonius, although he could have enjoyed the ease and splendor of the court, chose to serve God as a priest and monk. His holiness of life allowed him to preach the Gospel in all its purity. As followers of Christ, we can confront evil in the world only if we live the truth of the Gospel.

PRAYER   *Lord God, through the intercession of St. Theotonius grant Your people purity of heart, mind, body, and soul. This we ask through Christ our Lord Amen.*

BL. ALVAREZ OF CORDOVA, Priest

February 19

THE date and place of birth of Bl. Alvarez are uncertain, but it is known that he entered the Dominican convent at Cordova in 1368. He was a great preacher and was widely known in Andalusia and Italy. He became confessor and advisor to the Queen Mother Catherine, directed the early training of the young King John II, and was able to completely reform the court before returning to preaching.

Eventually Alvarez went to the mountainous region of Cordova to found a Dominican house of strict observance. His priory, Escalaceli (which means "Ladder of Heaven"), became a center for piety and learning. Working all day at preaching and teaching, Alvarez would spend entire nights in prayer. He and his brothers lived completely on the alms of the people. On the monastery grounds Alvarez erected several chapels dedicated to each of the stations of the Lord's Passion. Harsh disciplines for himself were the order of the day.

The date of Alvarez's death is unknown, but it is generally believed to have occurred some time around 1430. His public cult was confirmed in 1741.

REFLECTION   Bl. Alvarez of Cordova found his treasure in the strict observance of the Rule of St. Dominic. His powerful preaching and teaching led many to the Faith and his severity of life spoke to a Church taken up with worldly pursuits. Today his virtues are necessary for the preservation of individual faith and the Church as a whole.

PRAYER   *Loving Father, through the virtuous life and deep faith of Bl. Alvarez of Cordova Your Church was strengthened and glorified. Like Bl. Alvarez, may we staunchly defend the Church by unity and holiness of life. This we ask through Christ our Lord. Amen.*

BL. ELIZABETH OF MANTUA, Virgin

The Same Day—February 19

BORN in Mantua to wealthy parents in the year 1428, Bl. Elizabeth received a thorough religious education. Her father taught her Latin so that she was able to read the Little Office of the Blessed Virgin Mary. Her mother taught her the art of meditation.

Following her mother's death, Elizabeth and one of her sisters entered the third order of the Servites. Owing to her humility, gentleness, and reputation for supernatural gifts, many girls came under Elizabeth's direction and they formed a community of the third order Servites.

Elizabeth is said to have predicted her death one year before it happened. In 1468, at the age of forty, worn out by some unknown internal illness, she entered into the joy of the Lord. Extraordinary crowds attended her funeral, and many miracles were said to have been worked at her tomb. She was beatified in 1804 by Pope Pius VII.

REFLECTION   Bl. Elizabeth of Mantua was a woman of great personal sanctity. In order to more fully follow our Lord, she chose a life of virginity lived in the community tradition of the Servites. Elizabeth's servanthood is for us a beacon in a world that glorifies self-centeredness. Her life and its impact for good on others encourages us to follow her good example.

PRAYER   *Almighty, loving God, You raised Bl. Elizabeth of Mantua to the altar of sanctity after a humble and prayerful life. May we come to know the pure joys of serving You in others. This we ask through Christ our Lord. Amen.*

───◆─◆───

ST. TYRANNIO, Bishop of Tyre and Martyr

February 20

BISHOP Tyrannio of Tyre had been present at the martyrdom of a group of Egyptian Martyrs and had encouraged them during their torture and execution in that city around 304. The Christians gave outstanding proofs of their long-suffering and constancy in the Faith. After they had been cast before wild beasts without being touched, the Saints were put to death by the sword and their bodies were hurled into the sea.

Some time later, about 31, Tyrannio himself was arrested because of his faith. He was taken to Antioch together with St. Zenobius, a priest and physician of Sidon.

There Tyrannio was subjected to torture and then drowned in the Orantes River because he refused to sacrifice to pagan gods. Zenobius was subjected to the rack and died while enduring it.

REFLECTION The constancy of the Martyrs, like that of St. Tyrannio, in the face of the harshest of sufferings astounds us. We pray that if we should encounter persecution of this type, we may put all our trust in the Lord and remain faithful. Until then, we should gladly put up with the problems and sufferings of our ordinary lives.

PRAYER *Merciful God, our Father, be with Your people as they follow Mary's Son on the royal road of the Cross. Through the example and prayers of St. Tyrannio, give us the courage and grace to fully accept the challenges of the Christian life. This we ask through Christ our Lord. Amen.*

BL. NOEL PINOT, Priest and Martyr
February 21

BORN at Angers in 1747, Noel became a priest and excelled in ministering to the sick. In 1788, he was made pastor at a parish in Louroux Beconnais, which he revitalized spiritually through his piety and preaching.

In the wake of the French Revolution then in progress, priests were required to take an oath that went against the principles of the government of the Church. Father Noel refused to take it and was sentenced to be deprived of his parish for two years. Nonetheless, he continued to carry out his ministry in secret. Later, the holy priest even took clandestine possession of his parish and continued his pastoral work, managing to avoid capture for his defiance of the Revolutionary edict.

However, one day while fully vested for Mass, Father Noel was captured and dragged through the streets to the jeers of hostile spectators and soldiers. He remained in jail for twelve days and was given the death sentence for refusing to take the oath.

The holy priest went to the guillotine still vested for Mass and uttering the words that began the pre-Vatican II Mass: "I will go to the altar of God, to God Who gives joy to my youth." He joined his sacrifice to that of his Master on February 21, 1794, and was beatified in 1926 by Pope Pius XI.

REFLECTION   Confronted with the choice of taking a false oath or facing death, Bl. Noel placed his trust in Christ and His redemptive Sacrifice rather than in the leaders of the French Revolution. His action cries out for us to obey God rather than human beings.

PRAYER   *Almighty and eternal God, You endowed Bl. Noel with spiritual strength to choose death rather than renounce Your Church. Help us to love the Church and never do anything that harms her. This we ask through Christ our Lord. Amen.*

———◆•◆———

ST. MARGARET OF CORTONA, Penitent
February 22

MARGARET of Cortona was born in Loviana in Tuscany in 1247. Her father was a small farmer. Margaret's mother died when Margaret was seven. Her stepmother had little care for her high-spirited daughter. Rejected at home, Margaret eloped with a youth from Montepulciano and bore him a son out of wedlock. After nine years, her lover was murdered without warning.

Margaret left Montepulciano and returned as a penitent to her father's house. When her father refused to accept her and her son, she went to the Friars Minor at Cortona where she received asylum. Yet Margaret had difficulty overcoming temptations of the flesh. One Sunday she returned to Loviana with a cord around her neck. At Mass, she asked pardon for her past scandal.

She attempted to mutilate her face, but was restrained by Friar Giunta.

Margaret earned a living by nursing sick ladies. Later she gave this up to serve the sick poor without recompense, subsisting only on alms. Eventually, she joined the Third Order of St. Francis, and her son also joined the Franciscans a few years later. Margaret advanced rapidly in prayer and was said to be in direct contact with Jesus, as exemplified by frequent ecstasies. Friar Giunta recorded some of the messages she received from God. Not all related to herself, and she courageously presented messages to others.

In 1286, Margaret was granted a charter allowing her to work for the sick poor on a permanent basis. Others joined with personal help, and some with financial assistance. Margaret formed her group into tertiaries, and later they were given special status as a Congregation which was called the Poverelle ("Poor Ones"). She also founded a hospital at Cortona and the Confraternity of Our Lady of Mercy. Some in Cortona turned on Margaret, even accusing her of illicit relations with Friar Giunta.

All the while, Margaret continued to preach against vice and many, through her, returned to the Sacraments. She also showed extraordinary love for the mysteries of the Eucharist and the Passion of Jesus Christ. Divinely warned of the day and hour of her death, she died on February 22, 1297, having spent twenty-nine years performing acts of penance. She was canonized in 1728 by Pope Benedict XIII.

REFLECTION   St. Margaret of Cortona's conversion was truly an example of cooperating with grace in one's life. After early difficulties she turned her life into one of dedication to the service of others. Her reward was eternal joy in the midst of many who were converted through her efforts and example.

PRAYER   *God our Father, through the intercession of St. Margaret of Cortona we renew our resolve to fulfill the obligation of Lenten penance. Be with us as we turn from sin and hear the Good News. This we ask through Christ our Lord. Amen.*

ST. MILBURGA, Abbess

February 23

ST. Milburga lived in the eighth century. She was the daughter of Merenwald, King of Mercia, and Ermenburga, Princess of Kent, and the sister of Sts. Mildred and Mildgytha.

Milburga was the founding abbess of the nunnery of Wenloch, which was built with funds from her father or her uncle, King Wulfhere. Under her rule, the monastery flourished like a paradise.

The Saint received marvelous gifts from God such as the gift of healing, which she used to give sight to the blind. She also brought sinners to repentance through her words.

After a life of holiness and good works, St. Milburga wa afflicted with a painful and wasting disease, which she bore with equanimity. Her dying words were: "Blessed are the pure in heart" and "Blessed are the peacemakers." She died around the year 722.

REFLECTION A woman of nobility and wealth, St. Milburga nonetheless spurned the trappings of her state in order to imitate Christ more closely. Her life exemplifies the Gospel suggestion to sell what one has, give to the poor, and follow Christ. Her example remains appropriate in our day.

PRAYER *Lord God, Your servant St. Milburga clearly chose Your love over that of this world's goods. Grant that we may follow You on the narrow road of detachment. This we ask through Christ our Lord. Amen.*

———◆—◆———

BL. JOSEPHA NAVAL GIRBES, Laywoman

February 24

BORN in Valencia, Spain, in 1820, Josepha took charge of the family home at the young age of thirteen when her mother died. At eighteen, she made a vow of perpetual virginity and joined the Carmelite Third Order.

From her home, Josepha imparted the Faith to those who came to her, leading many of them to a full life of prayer. In time, she came to be regarded as a true mystic.

After having led many to God and fostered the vocation of countless others, this humble servant of the Lord died on February 24, 1893, and was beatified in 1988 by Pope John Paul II.

REFLECTION At her beatification the Pope acclaimed Bl. Josepha as "a secular virgin who dedicated her life to the apostolate in her hometown." She is a model for us as one who did the little things of life and offered them to the Lord. May we follow in her steps in transforming the world.

PRAYER   *Ever living God, as we recall the virtues of Bl. Josepha, grant us the wisdom to be conscious of the lures of worldliness so that we may in all simplicity serve others rather than ourselves. This we ask through Christ our Lord. Amen.*

———◆—◆———

ST. WALBURGA, Virgin
February 25

WALBURGA was born in Devonshire, England, around 710. She was the daughter of a West Saxon chieftain and the sister of St. Willibald and St. Winebald.

Walburga was educated at Wimborne Monastery in Dorset, where she became a nun. In 748, she was sent with St. Lioba to Germany to help St. Boniface in his missionary work. She spent two years at Bischofsheim, after which she became abbess of the double monastery at Heidenheim founded by her brother Winebald.

At the death of Winebald, St. Walburga was appointed abbess of both monasteries by her brother Willibald, who was then Bishop of Eichstätt. She remained superior of both men and women until her death in 779. She was buried first at Heidenheim, but later her body was interred next to that of her brother, St. Winebald, at Eichstätt.

REFLECTION   Although from the nobility, St. Walburga dedicated all her adult years to monastic life and the conversion of Germany. Her widespread reputation for holiness gave many in Germany the opportunity to seek out a fuller appreciation of the Faith. Her complete dedication to her Faith says much to all Christians today.

PRAYER   *Loving God, You invite us to be close to You in prayer and contemplation. May we follow St. Walburga's example in deepening our faith and prayer in the cause of salvation for all. This we ask through Christ our Lord. Amen.*

ST. VICTOR, Hermit

February 26

WE know very little about the life of St. Victor, and practically all of it comes from St. Bernard of Clairvaux. The great Cistercian Doctor collected local traditions about the Saint and thus kept his memory alive in the Church.

Victor was born near Troyes, France, in the seventh century. As a young man, his entire life seemed centered around the practice of prayer, fasting, and almsgiving.

Early in life, Victor was attracted to the religious life and was ordained. However, preferring a life of solitude, he became a hermit at Arcis-sur-Aube in Champagne. His holiness and life of virtue resulted in numerous conversions. Victor's remains were brought to the Benedictine monastery of Montiramey, and his feast was celebrated there by the monks. St. Bernard composed several hymns and an Office in his honor.

REFLECTION   As a young man, St. Victor turned his mind and heart to God. He was generous in his concern and care for the poor. As a hermit, his renowned holiness drew many pilgrims to his hermitage who accepted his direction toward conversion. Like St. Victor, may we lead others to Christ by our good Christian lives, reformed through Lenten penance and prayer.

PRAYER   *God, Almighty Lord, the generosity of Your servant St. Victor won many souls for You. May our generosity and virtue imitate his as we work toward the Kingdom. This we ask through Christ our Lord. Amen.*

———◆◆———

ST. ANNE LINE, Widow and Martyr
February 27

BORN about 1565 in Donmow (Essex), England, of ardent Calvinist parents, Anne Heigham became a Catholic together with her brother before the age of twenty. The children were both disowned by their parents, and in 1585 Anne married Roger Line, who was himself a disinherited convert.

Anne's husband was imprisoned for participating at Mass and was exiled to Flanders where he died in 1594. Penniless, Anne took a position as a housekeeper for Father John Gerard, S.J., who had a house of hospitality for priests in London.

Eventually, Fr. Gerard was arrested and then escaped from the Tower in 1597. Anne took vows of poverty, chastity, and obedience and moved to another house where she rendered hospitality to priests until 1601. On February 2 of that year, while a large number assembled for Mass at her house, the police arrived and arrested and imprisoned her.

On February 26, Anne was found guilty of harboring priests and hanged the next day. She was beatified in 1929 by Pope Pius XI and canonized in 1970 by Pope Paul VI.

REFLECTION St. Anne offers us a vivid reminder not only of love for God but also of love for country. She loved her country with all its faults and prayed for it and its rulers. We should strive to emulate her in both her loves.

PRAYER *Almighty God, You grant to all of us the virtue of love for country in addition to love for You. Through the example and intercession of St. Anne, Your Martyr, may we love You above all things and pray that our country and its rulers will remain faithful to Your teaching. This we ask through Christ our Lord. Amen.*

———◆◆◆———

BL. DANIEL BROTTIER, Priest
February 28

BORN in France on September 7, 1876, Bl. Daniel Brottier was ordained in 1899 for the diocese of Blois. However, desiring to be a missionary, he soon joined the Congregation of the Holy Spirit. In 1903, he was sent to Senegal and labored there for eight years, until ill health forced him to return to France.

At the Bishop's request, Daniel worked to raise funds for a cathedral at Dakur. He also served in the military as a chaplain during World War I and earned six citations for bravery plus the highest French awards.

After the war, the Saint administered an organization that cared for orphans. On February 2, 1936, thanks to his dedicated efforts, the cathedral in Senegal was consecrated by Cardinal Verdier of Paris. On that day, Daniel was overcome with illness and took to his bed. He died on February 28, 1936, and was mourned throughout France. He was beatified in 1984 by Pope John Paul II.

REFLECTION The saintly priest Daniel Brottier left us an example of a spirit of service, generosity, and true Christian courage that surmounted national borders and racial designations. We should strive to make that same spirit ours.

PRAYER *O Lord, You inspired Bl. Daniel, Your Priest, to seek out souls through a ministry to Senegal and as a worker for the good of orphans. Through his intercession, grant us the grace to have an unflagging missionary spirit all our days. This we ask through Christ our Lord. Amen.*

ST. HILARY, Pope

February 29

BORN in Sardinia, Hilary became a deacon and a trusted aide of Pope Leo the Great. In 449, he was present as one of the two papal legates at the so-called Robber Council of Ephesus. The followers of the heretical bishop Dioscorus feverishly backed the heresiarch Eutyches, founder of Monophysitism, and even physically attacked the legates who barely managed to escape with their lives.

On November 19, 461, Hilary was elected Pope to succeed Leo the Great. He confirmed the contents of the General Councils of Nicaea, Ephesus, and Chalcedon in an encyclical letter to the Eastern Church, rebuilt Roman churches, and held local Councils at Rome in 462 and 465. Hilary also ruled the Church wisely and well. He is renowned for vigorously defending the rights of all bishops while zealously eliminating the excesses of a few and for installing a library in the Church of St. Lawrence Outside the Walls.

Hilary made it clear that the Pope not the Emperor was the leader in spiritual matters. He even reproached the Emperor Anthemus in St. Peter's Basilica for supporting heretical teachers. The saintly pontiff died in 468.

REFLECTION St. Hilary's concern for solid doctrine and the good of the Church led him to reprove even the Emperor. His example should lead us to seek the things of God first in our lives and to follow the laws of God where they clash with man-made laws.

PRAYER *Loving God, St. Hilary Your Pope ruled Your Church with wisdom and charity. Teach us to reject the false teachings of the world and ever follow the teachings of Your Church. This we ask through Christ our Lord. Amen.*

ST. DAVID, Bishop

March 1—*Patron of Wales*

ACCORDING to tradition, St. David was the son of King Sant of South Wales and St. Non. He was ordained a priest and later studied under St. Paulinus. Later, he was involved in missionary work and founded a number of monasteries. The monastery he founded at Menevia in southwestern Wales was noted for extreme ascetism. David and his monks drank neither wine nor beer—only water—while putting in a full day of heavy manual labor and intense study.

Around 550, David attended a synod at Brevi in Cardiganshire. His contributions at the synod are said to have been the major cause for his election as primate of the Cambrian Church. He was reportedly consecrated archbishop by the Patriarch of Jerusalem while on a visit to the Holy Land. He also is said to have invoked a council that ended the last vestiges of Pelagianism.

David died at his monastery in Menevia around 601, and his cult was approved in 1120 by Pope Callistus II. He is revered as the Patron of Wales.

REFLECTION Undoubtedly, St. David was endowed with substantial qualities of spiritual leadership. What is more, many monasteries flourished as a result of his leadership and good example. His staunch adherence to monastic piety bespeaks a fine example for modern Christians seeking order and form in their prayer life.

PRAYER   *Lord God, Your faithful servant St. David evoked a positive response in his people of Wales. May we, like them, be inspired by his piety and attachment to goodness and truth. This we ask through Christ our Lord. Amen.*

———◆●◆———

BL. ANGELA OF THE CROSS GUERRERO,
Religious
March 2

ANGELA of the Cross was born at Seville, Spain, in 1846. From her earliest years she had a great devotion to Christ Crucified. She fostered this devotion along with the stark poverty of the Cross in her religious daughters in the Congregation of the Cross, an institute devoted to the poor, the most rejected, and the disenfranchised.

In this community members were to live with and like the poor. The community was to exist solely on free-will donations. The sisters were to consider themselves as pilgrims and receive alms with great humility.

In addition, the poverty that Angela's sisters embraced was to go beyond mere contemplative deprivation. They were called upon to work with poor families, orphans, and the sick and to educate both children and adults in fundamentals. All were to receive from the sisters money, housing, instruction, clothing, and medicine, and everything was to be given in love. Angela died on March 2, 1932, and was beatified in 1982 by Pope John Paul II.

REFLECTION   The poverty of the Cross shouts to us, especially when we are well off in the midst of so many hungry, poor, homeless, and marginalized people. As we move through Lent, may we resolve to imitate the poverty and the devotion to the Cross exercised by Bl. Angela.

PRAYER   *Merciful God, our Father, enable Your people to follow the example of Bl. Angela and imitate the poverty of Jesus Crucified. May we share generously with those who are most in need. This we ask through Christ our Lord. Amen.*

ST. ANSELM OF NONANTOLA, Abbot

March 3

ANSELM, the Duke of Friuli, Italy, enjoyed great early success in his military career in the service of his brother-in-law, the Langobard King Aistulf. In addition, however, he was a devout Christian, and he founded a hospital and two monasteries. Later, wanting to grow spiritually, he went to Rome and joined the Benedictines around 753.

When Anselm became abbot of the Benedictine community of Nonantola, Pope Stephen III gave Anselm permission to transfer Pope St. Sylvester's body there. King Aistulf richly endowed the monastery, and eventually Anselm's monks numbered more than one thousand.

When King Aistulf died, his successor Desiderius exiled Anselm to Monte Cassino. How

ever, after seven years, Anselm was sent back to
Nonantola by Charlemagne. He died in 803 after
serving fifty years as a monk.

REFLECTION   In life, even though we have the best
of intentions, our good works are misunderstood.
What is important, however, as we see in Anselm's
life, is that we remain faithful to the end no matter
what the opposition.

PRAYER   *God our Father, through Your holy Word
You call us to lives of prayer, penance, and good
works. Through the intercession of St. Anselm, may
we remain faithful to You and Your people. This we
ask through Christ our Lord. Amen.*

BL. PLACIDA VIEL, Virgin

March 4

VICTORIA Eulalia Jacqueline Viel was born
in the Norman village of Val-Vacher in 1815.
One of eight children, she had little schooling.
She lived on the family farm until she was seven-
teen years of age. At that time, she was accepted
by the St. Mary Magdalen Postel community at
Saint-Sauveur-le-Vicomte and took the name
Placida.

After pursuing her previously neglected education at a school in Argentan and returning to
the community, Placida was initiated by the
foundress into the duties of school administration. She founded some new convents, and was
eventually made mistress of novices.

In 1846, Placida was elected superior-general of the Sisters of the Christian Schools. For more than thirty years she directed the institute, opening orphanages, nursery schools, and free elementary schools. A woman of charm and good humor as well as inner strength and great determination, she wanted to accomplish for girls what St. John Baptist de la Salle had achieved for boys in Christian education. As a result, she was able to open thirty-six schools for the poor in Normandy. She died on March 4, 1877, at the age of sixty-two, and was beatified in 1951 by Pope Pius XII.

REFLECTION Bl. Placida lived a very simple life, yet her personal qualities and trust in God allowed her to establish many convents and schools during a short time. She prayed much, was unafraid to ask for fiscal help, and brought much enthusiasm to her work. The object of her many endeavors was that young girls would be well trained in their Faith in pleasant and positive circumstances and surroundings.

PRAYER *Lord God Almighty, You did not hesitate to reveal through Your Son Jesus the necessity of bringing children to You. Through the witness of Bl. Placida, may we always show good example to youth and enthusiastically support Christian education so that we too may shine like stars for all eternity. This we ask through Christ our Lord. Amen.*

ST. VIRGIL, Bishop
March 5

VIRGIL was born in Gascony in the sixth century and educated in the monastery at Lérins on the isle of Saint-Honorat, where he became a monk. Later he was chosen to be abbot there as well as of Saint-Symphorien at Autun.

Eventually Virgil was called from monastic life to become the Archbishop of Arles by Pope St. Gregory I. Gregory also designated Virgil to consecrate St. Augustine as Archbishop of Canterbury.

Virgil won considerable renown as a bishop. He was responsible for the construction of many churches in Arles, and after his death around 618 several miracles were attributed to his intercession.

REFLECTION   St. Virgil proved to be a great leader and initiator. His concern for souls in his diocese led him to work tirelessly in building many centers of worship. In an age of widespread fear, he displayed great courage and trust in God, leading his people to see the importance and power of prayer.

PRAYER   *Heavenly Father, Your servant St. Virgil was skilled in using his talents to bring others to the knowledge of the Faith. May our zeal for Your glory match Virgil's enthusiasm for the triumph of good over evil. This we ask through Christ our Lord. Amen.*

ST. CHRODEGANG, Bishop
March 6

ST. Chrodegang, an individual of great intellect, was born near Liège in 712. After serving as the chief minister to Charles Martel, he was appointed as Bishop of Metz in 742, even though he was still a layman.

Outstanding for his personal holiness, justice, and charity, Chrodegang possessed great concern for the common good. Eventually he became Pepin's ambassador to the Holy See and worked assiduously to establish the papacy on a firmer basis.

In his diocese Chrodegang undertook a reform of the diocesan clergy modeled on the Rule of St. Benedict. His reform movement was so successful that he is considered to be the founder of the Canons Regular. Backed by Charlemagne, his reform was well established in France, Italy, Britain, and Germany.

Besides building and restoring many charitable institutions, churches, and monasteries, Chrodegang founded the school of music at Metz, which was the first area in the north to stress the Roman Liturgy and Gregorian Chant. He died on March 6, 766.

REFLECTION   A quality lifestyle rooted in prayer, justice, peace, and charity can be a very effective means of evangelization. As did the life of St. Chrodegang, it can bring many blessings to the Church and can lead to the conversion of many people of good faith.

PRAYER   *O Lord, in Your care and concern for Your people You invite us to be individuals of peace and justice. Through the intercession of St. Chrodegang, may our lives of virtue bring people of all convictions to an openness to and an enthusiasm for peace and justice. This we ask through Christ our Lord Amen.*

———————◆◆———————

ST. TERESA MARGARET REDI, Virgin

March 7

ANNE Mary Redi was born in the Tuscan city of Arezzo in 1747 and belonged to a noble family. At the age of ten she was sent to St. Apollonia Convent in Florence to be educated.

After spending seven years there, Anne Mary returned home, only to return to Florence in 1764 to become a Discalced Carmelite nun at the convent of St. Teresa. Granted a special grace of contemplative insight, she felt called to a hidden life of love and self-sacrifice. Taking the religious name Teresa Margaret of the Sacred Heart, she progressed rapidly, fulfilling her vocation through heroic charity toward others.

St. Teresa died in Florence in 1770 at the age of twenty-three, renowned for her life of sanctity. Pope Pius XI canonized her in 1934.

REFLECTION The grace of God works wonders even among the young. Brief as it was, St. Teresa Margaret Redi's whole life may be regarded as one continued ascent of her guiltless soul to God. She could hardly speak of God without her face becoming suffused with joy. Her life encourages us to show young people the joys and graces of a life lived in the depths of God's perfect love.

PRAYER   *Father, You enabled St. Teresa Margaret Redi to draw untold sources of humility and charity from Jesus. Through her prayers may we never be separated from the love of Christ. This we ask through Christ our Lord. Amen.*

———◆—◆———

ST. STEPHEN OF OBAZINE, Abbot

March 8

STEPHEN was born in the Limousin area of France around the beginning of the twelfth century. From his earliest days he proved to be an individual of great devotion, piety, and works of charity, and eventually he was ordained a priest.

Following ordination, Stephen was determined to live a life of mortification and penance. This led him, along with another priest, to embrace solitude in the forest of Obazine. Stephen and his companion distributed all their possessions to the poor before their departure. Shortly thereafter, many expressed a desire to follow the two priests into the solitary life. Therefore, they obtained permission from the Bishop of Limoges to open a monastery consisting of a number of small huts for one or two monks.

The monks under the gentle Stephen practiced extreme austerities. They ate only at evening and spent the rest of the time in prayer, reading, and manual labor. And Stephen did exactly what all did. Later, Stephen founded a convent of 150 nuns, and their way of life was equally austere.

Before he died, and since there was no written Rule for his monastery, St. Stephen requested that his monks be allowed to become affiliated with the Order of Cîteaux. In 1142, Stephen himself received the Cistercian habit, and he became an Abbot. He died twelve years later in 1159.

REFLECTION The holiness of St. Stephen was such that others were quick to follow him. Separating themselves from the world, Stephen and his companions lived a joy-filled life of prayer and austerity. In our Lenten program of reform, we must ever be mindful of the necessity of prayer and penance in all that we do.

PRAYER *Heavenly Father, You blessed the French people and the world with the pious presence of St. Stephen and his companions. Through our Lenten prayer and penance may we draw others away from sin and the world. This we ask through Christ our Lord Amen.*

ST. THEOPHYLACT, Bishop

The Same Day—March 8

THEOPHYLACT was born in Asia in the eighth century. As a youth he migrated to Constantinople where his education was supervised by St. Tarasius, the devout Patriarch of Constantinople.

Later, recognizing that Theophylact had a vocation, St. Tarasius sent him and another youth, St. Michael the Confessor, to a recently established monastery near the Bosphorus Sea. There the two young men led thoroughly Christian lives.

Theophylact became noted for his goodness to the poor, his care of widows, orphans, and the mentally ill, his kindness to the blind, the lame, and the sick, and his solicitude for travelers for whom he established hospices.

After some years of success in monastic life, Theophylact was consecrated Bishop of Nicomedia by St. Tarasius. He resolutely opposed the iconoclasm of Emperor Leo V and vigorously defended the Church's doctrine. As a result, Leo banished him to the fortress of Coria in Asia Minor where he died about the year 840 after enduring imprisonment for thirty years.

REFLECTION Although a very devout monk, St. Theophylact was well aware of the needs of the poor and the indigent. His Christian response to the most needy of God's people won many souls to God. Our

Church and our age today call each of us to extend ourselves on behalf of the poor and those in need.

PRAYER   *Loving Lord of the poor and outcast, Your servant St. Theophylact was outstanding in his care of the marginalized in this world. May our Lenten sacrifices focus on our need to respond to the most desperate of Your loved ones. This we ask through Christ our Lord. Amen.*

ST. CATHERINE OF BOLOGNA, Virgin

March 9—*Patroness of Artists*

BORN in 1413, Catherine de Vigri was the daughter of a diplomatic agent of the Marquis of Ferrara. At the age of eleven she was appointed maid of honor to the daughter of the marquis and shared her training and education. When the daughter eventually married, she wanted Catherine to remain in her service, but Catherine left the court and became a Franciscan tertiary at the age of fourteen.

Catherine had determined to live a life of perfection, and she was admired by her companions for her holiness. Eventually her community became part of the Poor Clares, and through her efforts with Pope Nicholas V, the Poor Clare convent at Ferrara erected an enclosure, and Catherine was appointed superioress. The reputation of the community for its holiness and austerity became widespread. She then was appointed superioress of a new convent in Bologna.

In Lent of 1463, Catherine became seriously ill, and she died on March 9. Buried without a coffin, her body was exhumed eighteen days later because of cures attributed to her and also because of the sweet scent coming from her grave. Her body was found to be incorrupt and remains so today in the church of the Poor Clare convent at Bologna. Patron of artists, she was canonized in 1712 by Pope Clement XI.

REFLECTION Despite the opportunity to live a noble life at court, St. Catherine eagerly responded to her call to lead the religious life. Her piety, charity, and kindness attracted many to follow her along the road to perfection. The beauty of her life and death encourages us to resolve to live in perfect charity as a Lenten goal.

PRAYER *Lord God, You call each of us to perfect charity both here and in the Kingdom. Through the intercession of St. Catherine of Bologna, may we deny ourselves the pleasures of an uncharitable tongue so as to be more faithful to Your commands. This we ask through Christ our Lord. Amen.*

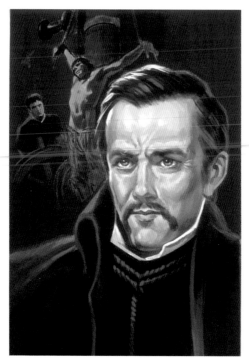

ST. JOHN OGILVIE, Martyr

March 10

BORN in 1579, John Ogilvie belonged to Scottish nobility. Raised a Calvinist, he was educated on the continent. Exposed to the religious controversies of his day and impressed with the faith of the Martyrs, he decided to become a Catholic. In 1596, at age seventeen he was received into the Church at Louvain.

Later John attended a variety of Catholic educational institutions, and eventually he sought admission into the Jesuits. He was ordained at Paris in 1610 and asked to be sent to Scotland, hoping some Catholic nobles there would aid him given his lineage. Finding none, he went to London, then back to Paris, and finally returned to Scotland. John's work was quite successful in bringing back many people to the Faith.

Some time later he was betrayed by one posing as a Catholic. After his arrest he was tortured in prison in an effort to get him to reveal the names of other Catholics, but he refused. After three trials, John was convicted of high treason because he converted Protestants to the Catholic Faith as well as denied the king's spiritual jurisdiction by upholding the Pope's spiritual primacy and condemning the oaths of supremacy and allegiance. Sentenced to death, the courageous priest was hanged at Glasgow in 1615 at the age of thirty-six.

REFLECTION The life of St. John Ogilvie prompts us to be faithful to our elected leaders in things secular and political, while, at the same time, remaining faithful to God's Word in all matters spiritual. As followers of Jesus we must use every legitimate means to counteract injustice in the world.

PRAYER *O Lord, You are our hope and salvation. Through the intercession of St. John Ogilvie, may we remain steadfast in all matters of faith and justice. This we ask through Christ our Lord. Amen.*

ST. PIONIUS, Martyr
March 11

ST. Pionius was a priest and a native of Smyrna, Turkey, who lived in the second century. Renowned for his learning as well as for the numerous conversions he had achieved, he was imprisoned along with fifteen companions during the persecution of Decius.

Pionius and his companions suffered horrible tortures as a result of their steadfast refusal to offer worship to pagan gods. Finally the proconsul Quintilian, on a visit to Smyrna, ordered that they be executed if they would not submit.

Pionius was stretched out on a rack and his body was torn with hooks. When even this failed, Quintilian ordered Pionius to be burned alive. As the flames consumed his body, Pionius cried out his final words on earth: "Lord, receive my soul."

REFLECTION As we open ourselves in faith to the daily martyrdom of temptation, may we, like St. Pionius, accept the pains necessary to overcome temptation so that, should death take us unaware, we too may say: "Lord, receive my soul."

PRAYER *God our Father, you are honored in Your holy Martyrs. May we, like St. Pionius, resist the temptation to turn away from You. This we ask through Christ our Lord. Amen.*

BL. SERAPHINA (or FINA), Virgin

March 12

SERAPHINA (also known as Fina) was born in the thirteenth century at San Geminiano, in Tuscany, of impoverished parents. She was a pretty and attractive girl, but despite her poverty she always saved half her food for the poor. Moreover, she lived as a recluse at home, sewing and spinning, and spent most of her nights in prayer.

At an early age, soon after her father's death, Seraphina was stricken with a painful paralysis. In order to be more like Christ, she asked to be placed on a plank where she was unable to move or turn. In her pain she often prayed, "It is not my wounds but Yours, O Christ, that hurt me." Although she was not a nun, she seems to have followed the Benedictine way of life.

After her mother's death, few wanted to help Seraphina because of the repulsive sores on her body. She prayed to St. Gregory the Great who had also suffered from disease, and it is believed that Gregory revealed the day of her death in a vision. She died on March 12, 1253, venerated as a holy person, and many miracles were reported through her intercession.

REFLECTION Bl. Seraphina had an extraordinary sense of resignation to the difficulties of life. Poverty, pain, and paralysis did not dampen her intense devotion to Christ Crucified. As we move toward Good Friday, her life reminds us of the need to be open to suffering in our lives, and that this pain and difficulty can accomplish much good if we accept it in union with Christ Crucified.

PRAYER   *Loving God, as we offer our little sacrifices during this Lenten time, may we, through the intercession of Bl. Seraphina, become more open to our call to holiness as followers of the Crucified Christ. This we ask through Christ our Lord. Amen.*

ST. LEANDER OF SEVILLE, Bishop

March 13

LEANDER was born at Cartagena, Spain, of Severianus and Theodora, illustrious for their virtue. St. Isidore and St. Fulgentius, both bishops, were his brothers, and his sister, Florentina, is also numbered among the Saints.

He became a monk at Seville and then the bishop of that See. He was instrumental in converting the two sons—Hermenegild and Reccared—of the Arian Visigothic King Leovigild. This action earned him the king's wrath and exile to Constantinople, where he met and became close friends with the papal legate—the future Pope Gregory the Great. It was Leander who suggested that Gregory write the famous commentary on the Book of Job called the *Moralia*.

Once back home, under King Reccared, St. Leander began his life-work of propagating Christian orthodoxy against the Arians in Spain. The third local Council of Toledo (over which he presided in 589) decreed the consubstantiality of the three Persons of the Trinity and brought about moral reforms. Leander's unerring wisdom and unflagging dedication led the Visigoths and the Suevi back to the true Faith and obtained the gratitude of Gregory the Great.

The saintly bishop also composed an influential Rule for nuns and was the first to introduce the Nicene Creed at Mass in the West. Worn out by his many activities in the cause of Christ, Leander died around 600 and was succeeded in the See of Seville by his brother Isidore.

The Spanish Church honors Leander as a Doctor of the Faith.

REFLECTION   St. Leander's most driving force was to spread the true Faith among the Arians in Spain. With God's grace and by dint of hard work and unrelenting prayer, he was able to achieve this exalted goal. His struggle and victory tell us once more that nothing is impossible with God.

PRAYER   *God our Father, by the teaching of St. Leander, Your Bishop, You uprooted the Arian heresy from Spain. Through his merits and intercession, keep us free from all stain of vice or error. This we ask through Christ our Lord. Amen.*

ST. LEOBINUS, Bishop

March 14

THE son of peasants, St. Leobinus was born near Poitiers in France and labored in the fields as a youth. He wanted to study, so he sought work in the monastery at Noailles. After working all day, he would study in the evening. St. Avitus was impressed with the youth, and suggested that Leobinus join his hermitage after gaining greater monastic experience.

During a war between the Franks and the Burgundians, Leobinus was captured and tortured by marauders who wanted to learn where any monastic treasures had been hidden. Left for dead, he later recovered and went to Le Perche where St. Avitus readily accepted him into his community.

Some time afterward Bishop Aetherius of Chartres ordained Leobinus and appointed him as Abbot of Brou. Later Leobinus succeeded Aetherius as Bishop of Chartres. He instituted a variety of reforms there before his death on March 14 around the year 557.

REFLECTION The life of St. Leobinus reminds us that God in His wisdom decides how He will use His creatures, even those in the most difficult circumstances. And so we too must be willing to be open to all people no matter what their state in life. Status and personal spirituality do not reflect one another.

PRAYER *Loving God, send Your Spirit upon us as You enlightened St. Leobinus. Help us to follow where the Spirit leads us in doing Your will. This we ask through Christ our Lord. Amen.*

ST. LAZARUS, Bishop
The Same Day—March 14

AROUND 439, St. Lazarus became Bishop and later Archbishop of Milan. At the time the Ostrogoths were ravaging Italy, and they controlled Milan. Despite the difficult times and incidents of suffering, he ruled prudently and faithfully.

Lazarus is believed to have developed the Rogationtide litanies, which he is said to have been the first to introduce. In order to invoke God's protection during the Ostrogoths' invasion, he ordered three days of fast with processions, litanies, and visits to various churches, from Monday to Wednesday within the Octave of the Ascension. The First Council of Orleans (511) ordered that this observance should be general throughout France, and it spread quickly to England and elsewhere. St. Lazarus died on March 14, about the year 450.

REFLECTION Despite the unsettled situation caused by marauding Ostrogoths in his See, St. Lazarus never lost sight of his duty to lead and serve his people. His trust in God and faith in public prayer exemplified his deep personal faith, one which was emulated by his followers. We too are called upon to live our faith so as to draw others to Christ.

PRAYER *Loving God, may we have the faith and courage of St. Lazarus, so that, having lived according to the dictates of the Gospel, we may lead others to salvation. This we ask through Christ our Lord. Amen.*

ST. CLEMENT MARY HOFBAUER
March 15—*Apostle of Vienna*

CLEMENT Mary Hofbauer was born at Tasswitz, Moravia, on December 26, 1751, the ninth child of a butcher. He worked as an apprentice baker in the Premonstratensian monastery at Bruck and later became a hermit.

When hermitages were abolished by Emperor Joseph II, Clement went to work as a baker in Vienna. Later he went to Italy and lived as a hermit in the company of a friend, Peter Kunzmann.

Eventually Clement joined the Redemptorists after studies at the University of Vienna and in

Rome and was ordained in 1785. At first, he was sent to Vienna but could not establish a house there because of Emperor Joseph II's ban on religious foundations.

At the request of the papal nuncio, Clement and his companions went to Warsaw and engaged in missionary work there. Clement worked among the poor, built orphanages and schools, and sent Redemptorist missionaries to Germany and Switzerland.

When Napoleon suppressed religious orders in his territories, Clement and his companions were imprisoned in 1808, and each was expelled to his native country. Clement settled in Vienna and began to attract attention by his sermons, holiness, and spiritual direction. He founded a Catholic college in Vienna and was influential in revitalizing the religious life of the German people.

Clement defeated efforts to establish a German national Church. He fought strenuously against Josephinism, which sought the secular domination of the Church and the hierarchy. He died in Vienna on March 15, 1820, and was canonized by Pope Pius X in 1909. He is called the "Second Founder of the Redemptorists."

REFLECTION Frustrated by civil authorities in his desire to live as a hermit, St. Clement joined the Redemptorists where his zeal for the Kingdom proved an obstacle to the very authorities who brought him out of seclusion. A man of prayer, zeal, and holiness, he built up the Kingdom of God when the forces of secularism were trying to negate the influence of the Church.

PRAYER   *Gracious God, You blessed St. Clement Mary Hofbauer with a burning sense of zeal for the spread of Your Word. May we be generous in imitating his courage in the face of civil opposition in working for the spread of the Kingdom. This we ask through Christ our Lord. Amen.*

ST. EUSEBIA, Abbess

March 16

EUSEBIA was the daughter of St. Adalbald and St. Rictrudis. After her father was murdered in 652, she was sent by her mother to the abbey of Hamage near Doudi, France, where Eusebia's great-grandmother, St. Gertrude, was abbess.

When Gertrude died, Eusebia was only twelve years of age, but even so she was elected abbess. For it was customary for the head of a religious house to be of noble birth so that the community would be protected by the noble family. However, her mother Rictrudis, who was abbess of Marchiennes, felt that Eusebia was too young and inexperienced to be abbess. Therefore, Rictrudis merged the communities of Hamage and Marchiennes and ordered Eusebia to come to her with all her nuns.

Eusebia and some of her companions from Hamage were not too happy when they arrived at

Marchiennes with St. Gertrude's body, because they had been unable to carry out Gertrude's last requests. After consultation with bishops and other devout persons over a period of time, Eusebia and her companions were allowed to return to Hamage.

Eusebia proved quite capable in her reestablished role as abbess, successfully following the example and precedents established by St. Gertrude. She died around 680 at the age of forty.

REFLECTION   St. Eusebia from a very early age was exposed to the devout life. No other lifestyle seemed to hold any interest for her. Eventually she proved herself capable of governing a flourishing convent. Hers was a life totally dedicated to God.

PRAYER   *Loving God, in her complete devotion to You, St. Eusebia beckons to us over the centuries to place our trust in You. May we, like her, persevere in the good we have resolved to do in our Lenten observance. This we ask through Christ our Lord. Amen.*

———◆◆———

ST. GERTRUDE OF NIVELLES, Virgin
March 17

GERTRUDE, born in Landen in 626, was the daughter of Bl. Pepin and Bl. Itta. Her early native piety was fostered by her parents. Even though she had a chance to marry well, she refused, proclaiming herself a spouse of Christ.

When Pepin died, Gertrude's mother later built a double monastery at Nivelles, and Gertrude was made abbess even though she was only twenty years old. However, when her mother died in 652, Gertrude delegated most of the monastic administrative duties to others. She was then free to spend much of her time in the study of Scripture and also to increase her penances.

Gertrude's fasting and mortifications had caused a severe deterioration in her health by the time she was thirty. Therefore she appointed her twenty-year-old niece to succeed her as abbess. She died on March 17 in the year 659.

REFLECTION St. Gertrude was surrounded by individuals of faith. Spurning the married state, she devoted herself entirely to her personal spiritual growth and that of those who came under her care in the monastery. In this season of penance, her life calls us to a more complete observance of Lent.

PRAYER   *Almighty God, as we travel the perilous road through the world to Your Kingdom, we ask, through the intercession of St. Gertrude of Nivelles, for the means necessary to complete the most important journey—namely, that to Your heavenly Kingdom. This we ask through Christ our Lord. Amen.*

ST. ALEXANDER, Bishop and Martyr

March 18

ALEXANDER was a student with Origen at the famous Christian school of Alexandria in the late second century. He became Bishop of Cappadocia and during the persecution of

Severus was imprisoned for several years (204-211). Following his release from prison, he made a pilgrimage to Jerusalem and was proclaimed coadjutor bishop there in 212.

Demetrius, the Bishop of Alexandria, censured Alexander for participating in the ordination of Origen and for encouraging Origen to teach in churches while still a layman. Despite this, Alexander received Origen in exile.

Meanwhile, in Jerusalem Alexander developed a great theological library. During the persecution of Decius, he was seized and again imprisoned. After making a public confession of faith, he was condemned to be thrown to the wild beasts, but they refused to attack him. Alexander was then taken to Caesarea where he died in chains about the year 250. The Church recognizes him as a martyr.

REFLECTION   St. Alexander, despite his wealth of learning and important ecclesiastical positions, was known as an individual of great mildness, especially in his sermons. When put to the test during two persecutions, he remained steadfast, and was willing to suffer death for the Faith. Today when we are criticized by friends and society for the moral tenets of our Faith, St. Alexander is a prime example of how we should stand fast in the face of ridicule and ostracism.

PRAYER   *Loving Father, Your servant St. Alexander was willing to suffer prison and death for the Faith. May we always rejoice in our great gift of faith and persevere in good in a hostile world. This we ask through Christ our Lord. Amen.*

ST. JOHN OF PINNA, Abbot

JOHN of Pinna was a Syrian by birth who lived in the sixth century. He left his native land when it was torn by the Monophysite controversies.

John settled at Pinna, near Spoleto, where he built a monastery and served as its first abbot. He later founded another abbey near Pesaro.

Legend has it that John was regarded with awe and reverence in the Spoleto area owing to a series of unnatural phenomena that took place where he was to build his monastery. For example, a tree under which John was told to sit by an angel bloomed in December, causing the Bishop of Spoleto and the people of the town to give fervent praise to God. John remained as abbot at his monastery for forty-four years, until his death.

REFLECTION St. John of Pinna withdrew from his homeland so as not to be caught up in the Monophysite heresy. He then established a monastery in a foreign land and persevered to the end of a holy life dedicated to God. We are coming near to the end of our Lenten resolves. Like St. John we should eagerly anticipate the peace and joy of the accomplishment of goals sought and achieved.

PRAYER *Almighty, living God, as we approach the end of the Lenten season, may we, like St. John of Pinna, remain faithful to the end so that, having lived up to our commitment, we may share the joy of the*

Lord's faithful servants. This we ask through Christ our Lord. Amen.

———◆◆———

BL. SIBYLLINA OF PAVIA, Virgin
The Same Day—March 19

SIBYLLINA was orphaned at an early age toward the end of the thirteenth century and had to become a servant before reaching the age of ten. Unable to read or write, she suffered complete blindness by the age of twelve and was given shelter by some Dominican tertiaries of Pavia.

At first Sibyllina believed that if she prayed hard enough to St. Dominic her sight would be restored. When she failed to regain her sight, she accepted this as God's will. Thereafter she became a recluse, living in a small cell next to the Dominican church. In her solitude she led a life of severe austerity until the age of eighty.

People of all walks of life came to seek Sibyllina's direction and counsel. She shared her great devotion to the Holy Spirit with many who sought her help. When she died in 1367, she had lived in her hermit's cell for sixty-five years. When she was beatified in 1853, her body was still incorrupt.

REFLECTION Bl. Sibyllina accepted the difficulties of her life with resignation to the will of God. Without complaint, she persevered in her great mortifications until she entered into eternal light. Like Sibyllina, during this season of Lent let us throw off the blinding attraction of sensuality and embrace the living light of love of God and neighbor.

PRAYER   *Loving Father, Your poor and humble servant Sibyllina was deprived of the light of day for most of her life. May we use our sightedness to bring others to Your honor and glory. This we ask through Christ our Lord. Amen.*

ST. CUTHBERT, Bishop
March 20

ALTHOUGH there is some confusion as to whether St. Cuthbert was born in Ireland, Scotland, or England, we know that he was orphaned at an early age, for a time was a shepherd, and eventually became a monk at Melrose Abbey. In 661, Cuthbert went to Ripon Abbey for a short time but returned to Melrose when King Alcfrid turned Ripon Abbey over to St. Wilfrid. In a short time, St. Cuthbert became abbot at Melrose.

Later, because of a dispute between St. Colman and the Council of Whitby over Roman liturgical practices, Cuthbert, with most of the monks of Lindisfarne, migrated to Ireland. Still later, St. Eata appointed Cuthbert prior of Lindisfarne.

St. Cuthbert continued his missionary activities and attracted large crowds. He then asked

permission to become a hermit. His wish having been granted, Cuthbert lived on a nearby island, and in 676 moved to one of the Farnes Islands near Bamborogh. In 685, against his will, St. Cuthbert was chosen Bishop of Hexam. He arranged with St. Eata to switch Sees, and Cuthbert thus became Bishop of Lindisfarne but without the monastery.

The last two years of his life were spent in ministering to his flock, caring for those who were sick with the plague, and working numerous healings. He is also said to have been gifted with prophecy. Cuthbert died at Lindisfarne on March 20, 687.

REFLECTION   St. Cuthbert's many and varied positions as a monk contributed to the welfare of the Church. As an individual of learning and piety, he sacrificed his life of contemplation to shepherd the See of Lindisfarne. His personal manner and lack of concern for his own health enabled Cuthbert to be the Good Shepherd to many outcasts of his flock. Cuthbert's selfless example reminds us of our responsibility for bringing others to Christ.

PRAYER   *Almighty God, You blessed the people of Lindisfarne with the presence of Your Bishop St. Cuthbert. May our concern for our more desperate brothers and sisters reflect the generosity of this holy man. This we ask through Christ our Lord. Amen.*

ST. ENDA, Abbot
March 21

ST. Enda was the son of Ainmire in Meath. He became a soldier and was celebrated for his military feats. He then felt the call to be a monk and entered the Monastery of Whithorn in Galloway.

Ordained at Rome, the Saint returned to Ireland and built churches at Drogheda. He also founded monasteries in the Boyne Valley. After asking for and receiving the island of Aran from his brother-in-law King Oengus of Munster, he built the Monastery of Killeaney there (as well as ten subsidiary foundations).

The Saint brought many disciples to this monastery, including St. Kieran of Clonmacnoise. Together with St. Finnian of Clonard, Enda is regarded as the founder of monasticism in Ireland, contributing to Ireland being dubbed the "Island of Saints" and having a great effect on the whole of Europe. After a life lived entirely for God, Enda died around the year 542.

REFLECTION   Such was the reputation of St. Enda for sanctity and austerity that many were inspired to join him in the monastic life. There they saw firsthand the Saint's penitential practices and were led to join him in them. We would do well to practice penance in our lives and especially during the time of Lent.

PRAYER   *Almighty God, You enabled Your Abbot, St. Enda, to inaugurate the monastic life in Ireland as well as all of Europe. By his intercession, help us to embrace a life of holiness and do penance. This we ask through Christ our Lord. Amen.*

———◆◆◆———

ST. NICHOLAS OWEN,
Religious and Martyr
March 22

ST. Nicholas Owen was a mason and carpenter by trade, and he made wondrous use of those talents in the service of the persecuted Church in sixteenth-century England. For over twenty years he built hiding places for priests within mansions.

The Saint became a Jesuit lay brother in 1580. In 1594, he was arrested with Father John Gerard but was set free upon the payment of a ransom by a well-to-do Catholic. Then in 1597 he is believed to have brought about Father Gerard's escape from the Tower of London.

In 1606, Brother Nicholas was arrested together with Father Henry Garnet (whom he had served for eighteen years), Father Oldcorne, and Brother Ralph Ashley. Imprisoned in the Tower of London, he endured terrible tortures that eventually led to his death on March 2 of that year. He was beatified in 1929 by Pope Pius XI and canonized in 1970 by Pope Paul VI.

REFLECTION The building genius possessed by St. Nicholas enabled the Church to reap the benefits of the Sacraments for her members in England when

Catholics were being hunted down because of their religion. Known as "Little John" and "Little Nicholas," he used his talent to the full and never gave away any hiding places, thus saving the lives of scores of priests and people.

PRAYER   *O Lord, You chose St. Nicholas Owen to be made like Christ, Who died to save the world. Through his intercession, strengthen Your Church with the same faith and love that strengthened him and bless her always with Your gift of unity. This we ask through Christ our Lord. Amen.*

ST. WALTER OF PONTOISE, Abbot

March 23

WALTER Gautier was born in Picardy, France, in the eleventh century. A well-educated individual, he became a professor of Philosophy and Rhetoric. Later, he entered the Benedictine abbey of Rebais-en-Brie.

When King Philip I appointed Walter as the first abbot of a new monastery at Pontoise, Walter reminded Philip that God was the one who conferred such honors, not the king. Seeking solitude, he fled Pontoise on two occasions, but both times he was forced to return.

Walter then went to Rome to ask Pope Gregory VII for release from his position so that he could follow a life of solitude. However, the Pope told Walter to use the talents God had given him, and thus Walter resigned himself to staying at

Pontoise. When he spoke out against simony and the evil lives of the secular clergy, this caused great outrage, and on one occasion he was beaten and thrown into prison.

After his release, Walter continued to live a life of mortification, spending entire nights in prayer. After establishing the foundation of a convent in honor of Mary at Bertaucourt, Walter died on Good Friday around the year 1095.

REFLECTION Having given up the honors and esteem of an academic career, St. Walter opted for the hidden life of a monk. However, his talents were widely recognized, and he was forced into leadership roles he never sought. Through obedience he remained in an active monastery, maintaining his practices of mortification and prayer. When he spoke the truth he suffered for it, but despite failing health he remained steadfast in his dedication to God.

PRAYER   *Merciful Lord, we are encouraged by the exemplary life of St. Walter of Pontoise. May we, like him, seek always to live up to the demands of the Gospel and speak out against injustice and evil in our society. This we ask through Christ our Lord Amen.*

———◆●◆———

ST. SECUNDULUS, Martyr

March 24

ALL that we know of St. Secundulus is that he was a member of a group of catechumens in Carthage who were martyred around 203 in the persecution of Septimius Severus. Their Acts are completely authentic and influenced other accounts of martyrdom. They were written by Saturus, the group's instructor, and completed by an eyewitness thought to have been Tertullian.

The Emperor had forbidden conversions to Christianity, thus rendering catechumens liable to the death penalty. The other members of the group were Perpetua (a married woman of noble family), Felicity (a slave girl), Saturninus, and Revocatus (a slave), and the above-mentioned Saturus, who were thrown to the wild beasts on March 7, then slain by the sword, and are commemorated on that date.

At the time of the Martyrs' arrest, all of them were still catechumens. They were baptized while under "house arrest," then transported to the common prison. At their trial, they were all condemned to death and returned to prison to await execution.

Secundulus was one of them during their imprisonment. He gave his life for Christ, suffering and dying while imprisoned for the Faith.

REFLECTION St. Secundulus was a catechumen, one who had learned about Christ and chosen to be a Christian. Although he faced great obstacles at this particular time in Carthage, he did not draw back or deny Christ but remained steadfast in the Faith. May we too ever cling to the Faith no matter what we may have to endure.

PRAYER   O Lord, inspired by Your love, St. Secundulus was able to disregard persecution and over-

come the torment of death. Aided by his prayers, may
we make constant progress in our love for You. This
we ask through Christ our Lord. Amen.

ST. LUCY FILIPPINI, Virgin

March 25

LUCY Filippini was born in Tarquinia in Tuscany, about sixty miles from Rome. Shortly
after her birth in 1672, she was orphaned, and
when she was still quite young, her evident piety
brought her to the notice of Cardinal Marcanto-
nio Barbarigo. The cardinal persuaded Lucy to
go to Montefiascone to engage in the work of
training schoolmistresses. She worked under Bl.

Rose Venerini, who had founded the same kind of school in Viterbo.

Lucy, through her modesty, charity, and spirituality, won many people over to her. She founded numerous new schools, and in 1707 Pope Clement IX asked her to found a school in Rome. Although she spent only six months in Rome, her schools prospered, and she continued to work with great zeal and enthusiasm.

However, in 1726, Lucy became seriously ill, and she never regained normal health thereafter. She died a saintly death on March 25, 1732, the day she had predicted. She was canonized in 1930 by Pope Pius XI.

REFLECTION St. Lucy, an individual of many talents and deep piety, devoted her entire life to Christian education. She was tireless in her efforts to open more and more schools. As we move to meet the challenge of Catholic education in the United States today, we can be encouraged by St. Lucy's enthusiasm and zeal for good Christian teaching.

PRAYER *Almighty Father, as Your servant St. Lucy shines like a star for all eternity, may we leave no effort undone to bring the light of Christ to Your neediest children. This we ask through Christ our Lord. Amen.*

———◆◆◆———

ST. LUDGER, Bishop
March 26

L UDGER was born at Zuilen near Utrecht in the Netherlands. He studied at Utrecht under

St. Gregory and later went to England and continued his studies for three and a half years under Alcuin at York. When he returned to the Netherlands he worked as a missionary and was ordained in 777 at Cologne. Then he spent seven years as a missionary in Friesland until invading Saxons expelled all priests.

After a pilgrimage to Rome in 785, Ludger spent two years at Monte Cassino. While there he met Charlemagne who sent Ludger back to Friesland charged with the spiritual welfare of five provinces. He experienced considerable success in that assignment and built monasteries at Werden and Münster. In 793, he refused Charlemagne's offer to become Bishop of Trier, but in 804 he was consecrated the first Bishop of Münster.

Despite his many activities, Ludger allowed nothing to interfere with his public or private prayers and devotions. Toward the end of his life he suffered considerable pain, but he followed his work and prayer routine unfailingly. He celebrated two parish Masses on his last day on earth, Passion Sunday, March 26, 809. That evening he died peacefully surrounded by family and friends.

REFLECTION Despite the many offices held and good works accomplished by St. Ludger, he was exacting with himself and others in prayer and spiritual exercises. He never neglected private or public praise of God. St. Ludger stands as a model for busy Christians living in a modern, frenetic society.

PRAYER   *Heavenly Father, as we work in Your vineyard may we bring Your Good News to others with zeal and energy. Like St. Ludger, may we always remain faithful to Your presence in our lives. This we ask through Christ our Lord. Amen.*

———◆—◆———

BL. PEREGRINE OF FALERONE, Priest

March 27

B L. Peregrine of Falerone was born into a noble and wealthy family in the diocese of Fermo, Italy. In 1200, he happened to be studying Philosophy and Theology at Bologna when St. Francis of Assisi came to preach there. So impressed was Peregrine by the Saint that he decided to become his follower. He became an early member of the Franciscan Order.

Peregrine was ordained but, despite his great learning, preferred to carry out the simplest tasks. He thus attained the ideal of Christian perfection and became one of the most exemplary disciples of St. Francis.

In imitation of St. Francis, Peregrine wished to save unbelievers and so went to the Holy Land among the Muslims as Francis had done. His time there was peaceful as he reverently visited the holy places with the book of Gospels in his hand and tears streaming from his eyes.

On returning to Italy, Peregrine made his way to the most modest and out-of-the-way convents.

Yet the more he hid his feats and the more humble he was, the greater his holiness shone forth and the more people were attracted to him. In the last years of his life, though still young, he retired to the Convent of St. Severian and died there in 1232.

REFLECTION Bl. Peregrine was called to imitate Jesus by imitating St. Francis of Assisi. His one desire was to preach Christ to all peoples both in word and in deed. Nothing else really mattered to him. May we strive to follow Christ in everything we do and say.

PRAYER   *God our Father, You called Bl. Peregrine to the religious life and enabled him to reach spiritual perfection. By his prayers, help us to follow Christ in accord with our state in life. This we ask through Christ our Lord. Amen.*

ST. PROTERIUS, Bishop and Martyr
March 28

ST. Proterius was ordained (sometime in the fifth century) by St. Cyril, the Patriarch of Alexandria, and he became the leader of the orthodox party in that city. Later, Proterius was appointed archpriest by Dioscorus, Cyril's successor. However, when Dioscorus became openly heretical and supported Eutyches at the so-called Robber Council of Ephesus in 449, Proterius opposed him.

Dioscorus was denounced and condemned at the Council of Chalcedon in 451, and Proterius was elected Patriarch to replace him. As a result, Alexandria became divided into two opposing camps, one supporting Proterius, the other backing Dioscorus. When Dioscorus died, his supporters chose Elurus as his successor.

Elurus was subsequently driven from the city by the imperial commander, and thereupon his followers rioted. Proterius took sanctuary in a church but he was stabbed to death there in the year 454.

REFLECTION   In maintaining the Faith and tradition of the early Church, St. Proterius exposed himself to grave danger. Nonetheless, he met the challenge and put Church doctrine ahead of personal accommodation. He stands as an exemplar for all ages of unflinching devotion to the teaching of the Church, to truth revealed and practiced.

PRAYER   *Almighty God, our Father, Your servant St. Proterius was faithful to Your inspired Word and the tradition of the Church in the face of grave danger to his life. As Proterius shed his blood for the Faith, may we discipline ourselves to uphold the teaching and tradition of the Church. This we ask through Christ our Lord. Amen.*

———◆–◆———

ST. MARK, Bishop

March 29

S T. Mark was Bishop of Arethusa in Lebanon in the fourth century. One day he destroyed a pagan temple and angered the people in the surrounding area. In 361, Julian the Apostate became Roman Emperor and ordered those who had destroyed pagan temples to replace them. The saintly Bishop refused to do so and was obliged to flee. However, when he heard that more of his flock had been arrested, he returned and gave himself up.

The Bishop was dragged through the streets, stripped, scourged, cast into the city sewer, and then given over to schemes of schoolboys. Nonetheless, he remained totally calm, and his attitude greatly inspired the pagans. As a result, the people's anger toward him was replaced by admiration, and they set him free.

In fact, the people asked the Bishop to be instructed in his Faith and many of them became Christian. The Saint was left in peace to the end of his life, which occurred in 364.

REFLECTION   The way St. Mark conducted himself in adversity amazed the pagan people in his region and eventually led many of them to the Faith. His renunciation of striking back at those who attacked and humiliated him made them desire to know what accounted for such a stance. When they found out that it stemmed from the teaching of Jesus, they were on the way to becoming Christian themselves.

PRAYER   *Lord, You enabled St. Mark, Your Bishop, to refrain from striking those who struck him and so win over the pagans of his city. Through his intercession, enable us to practice true Christian restraint in every circumstance. This we ask through Christ our Lord. Amen.*

———◆◆———

ST. ZOZIMUS, Bishop
March 30

ZOZIMUS'S parents were landowners in Syracuse, Sicily. When Zozimus was born around 570, they dedicated him to the service of St. Lucy. At the age of seven he was placed in St. Lucy's Monastery near Syracuse.

Zozimus remained at Syracuse for thirty years. When the abbot of St. Lucy's died, Zozimus was appointed abbot and a few days later was ordained. He ruled the monastery with much love, wisdom, and prudence.

In 649, the See of Syracuse became vacant, and Zozimus was elected bishop by the people, despite his unwillingness to accept the position. As bishop, he was zealous in teaching the people and in his generosity for the poor. He died around 600.

REFLECTION Although the monastic life was imposed on him from early childhood, St. Zozimus eventually became a faithful member of the community.
When he was called to monastic leadership, his good
qualities and holiness of life prompted the people of
Syracuse to have him elected bishop. His episcopacy,
focused on the temporal and spiritual good of his people, gave great glory to God.

PRAYER   *Heavenly Father, look with favor on the
young people who seek to serve You. May they, like
St. Zozimus, lead lives of zeal for the spread of Your
Word and loving concern for the poor. This we ask
through Christ our Lord. Amen.*

BL. JOAN OF TOULOUSE, Virgin

March 31

AROUND 1265, when St. Simon Stock paused
in Toulouse on his way to Bordeaux, a
woman named Joan asked to be affiliated with
the Carmelites. St. Simon agreed. She was given
the Carmelite habit and permitted to take a vow
of perpetual chastity.

Bl. Joan followed closely the rule of St. Albert
of Jerusalem. Thus she is considered to be the
first Carmelite tertiary as well as the founder of
the Carmelite tertiary order.

Joan deprived herself of life's necessities in
order to relieve the sick and the poor. She lived a
life of penance, while, at the same time, training
young boys in lives of holiness preparatory to

their entering the Carmelite Order. Her cult was confirmed in 1895.

REFLECTION Despite the lack of accurate facts about Bl. Joan's life, her cult has been of such magnitude as to indicate an individual of great piety, holiness, and love and concern for the sick and poor. She wanted only to serve and to live a life wholly dedicated to God. Once given the opportunity, her cooperation with God's grace brought many blessings to the Church.

PRAYER *Loving Father, as we move through life we are aware of the Saints who have gone before us. Through the intercession of Bl. Joan of Toulouse, grant us the favor of desiring nothing other than to serve in Your Name. This we ask through Christ our Lord. Amen.*

———◆◆———

ST. CELSUS OF ARMAGH, Bishop

April 1

CELSUS (Cellach Mac Aodh) was born in 1079. We know little of his early life, but as a layman he succeeded to the hereditary bishopric of Armagh in 1105 and remained in that position for the remainder of his life.

Only twenty-six years old at the time of his appointment, Celsus developed a reputation as a reformer and was likewise known as an able and effective administrator. He traveled much of Ireland, preaching reform and reminding clergy and laity alike of Armagh's jurisdiction. In 1111, with the papal legate, Gilbert of Limerick, Celsus presided over the Synod of Rath Bresail. The fifty bishops present worked zealously to bring the Irish Church into line with the other Churches of Europe.

Celsus likewise rebuilt the Armagh cathedral, and frequently served as a mediator between warring Irish kings. On his deathbed, the holy prelate appointed his Archdeacon, St. Malachy, as Archbishop of Armagh, thus breaking the hereditary succession to that See. Celsus died at Ardpatrick in Münster on April 1, 1129.

REFLECTION Reform of the organizational Church is always a challenging task, and it seems as though reformer Saints surface when they are needed. However, although good example and exhortation are abundant in the case of individual self-reformation, the same kinds of grace, prayer, fasting, and determination are required.

PRAYER *Lord, through the merits and prayers of Your saintly Bishop Celsus keep us faithful to our Lenten spiritual progress. This we ask through Christ our Lord. Amen.*

ST. MARY OF EGYPT, Anchoress
The Same Day—April 1

ONE day, in the fifth century, St. Cyriacus and his companions found a woman named Mary living as a hermitess in the Jordanian desert. Mary told them that she had been a famous actress and singer but had sinned, and that she was therefore doing penance. When they returned to look for Mary, they found her dead.

In the Middle Ages an elaborate legend about St. Mary of Egypt developed. It was said that Mary was an Egyptian who at the age of thirteen went to Alexandria and was an actress for seventeen years. Once, while praying before an icon of the Blessed Virgin, she came to her senses and withdrew to the desert east of Palestine, where she lived in prayer and penance for forty-seven years. During this time she was troubled with many temptations and found relief only in prayer, especially her devotion to the Blessed Virgin.

Eventually Mary was discovered about 430 by a holy man named Zosimus. The following Lent Zosimus went to see Mary again but found her dead. Zosimus told the story to his fellow monks, and the tradition of St. Mary of Egypt was preserved.

REFLECTION St. Mary of Egypt at first apparently lived a very worldly life. Through the intercession of the Blessed Virgin Mary, she obtained the grace of conversion and retired to live a holy life for forty-seven years. She never returned from the desert, persevering in good until the end. Lent is a time of grace and repentance, and St. Mary's response to the grace of conversion is a model for all people in all ages.

PRAYER *Lord God, during this holy season of Lent we acknowledge our sinful lives. Through the inter-*

*cession of St. Mary of Egypt, may we turn from evil to
live lives without sin. This we ask through Christ our
Lord. Amen.*

———◆———

ST. JOHN PAYNE, Priest and Martyr

April 2

ST. John Payne (also spelled *Paine*) was born
in Peterborough, England, and became a
Catholic as a convert. He received his theological
training at Douai, France, and was ordained in
1576. He was then sent back to the English mission together with St. Cuthbert Mayne.

St. John's efforts met with immediate success.
He acted as the steward for Lady Petre at Ingate-
stone Hall, which was a hiding place for priests.
A year later he was arrested and released; leaving England he returned in 1579.

The Saint was falsely accused of plotting to
assassinate Queen Elizabeth I; the accuser was
John Elliot, who made a living by denouncing
priests. After the saintly priest was cast into the
Tower of London and tortured for nine months,
he was condemned to death. He was hanged,
drawn, and quartered at Chelmsford on April 2,
1582, and canonized in 1970 by Pope Paul VI.

REFLECTION   So great was St. John's love for bringing people to the true Faith that he constantly risked
his life to proclaim it to his countrymen. Convicted by
a trumped-up charge of treason, the Saint followed
the road of his Lord Jesus Christ in dying for the peo-

ple. His life should teach us to render witness to the Faith day after day.

PRAYER   *God, our Father, You enabled St. John, Your Priest and Martyr, to imitate the life of Your only-begotten Son by being falsely accused and condemned to death. May his intercession help us to bear true witness to the Faith and lead others to Christ. This we ask through Christ our Lord. Amen.*

———◆—◆———

ST. NICETAS, Abbot

April 3

ST. Nicetas lost his mother when he was one week old, and his father entered a monastery a few years later. So Nicetas was raised there. Upon coming of age, he entered the Medikion Monastery in Bithynia, and was ordained in 790, eventually becoming its Abbot.

Along with other Abbots, Nicetas refused to go along with Emperor Leo the Armenian who wanted them to embrace iconoclasm, i.e., opposition to the use of sacred images in the Church. Accordingly, the saintly Abbot was exiled to Anatolia and was brought back only when he agreed to Leo's wishes.

Once he was back in Constantinople, however, Nicetas publicly repudiated iconoclasm. This brought him exile in Glyceria in 813. After years of living in a dungeon filled with darkness, he was released in 820 (when Michael the Stammerer became Emperor) and returned to the eremitical life until his death in 824.

REFLECTION   St. Nicetas paid heavily for his fidelity to the Church's teaching about the good use of sacred images. Leo the Armenian put great pressure on the religious leaders to back the iconoclastic Patriarch Theodotus, whom Leo had set over the Church in place of St. Nicephorus. When Nicetas withdrew allegiance to this Patriarch and denounced iconoclasm, he was exiled to a life of darkness. His food was hard bread and his drink stagnant water. Yet the Saint remained steadfast and finally was freed to return to his eremitical life.

PRAYER   *O Lord, You enabled St. Nicetas, Your Abbot, to withstand prison and exile while defending the proper use of sacred images in the Church. By his intercession, help us to make good use of these images so as to increase in knowledge and love of our Faith. This we ask through Christ our Lord. Amen.*

───◆─◆───

ST. BENEDICT THE BLACK, Religious

April 4—*Patron of Blacks*

ST. Benedict the Black, also known as Benedict the Moor, was born a slave near Messina, Italy, in 1526. Freed by his master, he became a recluse in union with other hermits at Montepellegrino. Eventually he was appointed superior of the community.

However, when Pope Pius IV ordered in 1564 that communities of hermits be disbanded, St. Benedict became a Franciscan lay brother at St. Mary's Convent in Palermo. At first he served as

the cook, but eventually he was appointed superior, and later he became novice-master. But preferring a life of service, he asked to be relieved of such responsibilities and became the cook again.

Benedict had a reputation for holiness, miracles, and generosity. He was also a skillful counselor, and many people came to seek his help. He died in 1589 and was canonized by Pope Pius VII in 1807. He is the Patron of Blacks in the United States.

REFLECTION As a slave who was given his freedom, St. Benedict the Black devoted his entire life to God. His hard work for the community and his reputation for holiness led him to positions of honor, but he kept his focus on the true wisdom of all life, namely, the love of God and love of neighbor. Refusing to allow his humble origins to keep him from his life's goal, he pursued God's love and was richly rewarded. The sting of slavery was turned into the glorious victory of unending love and light.

PRAYER   *Almighty Father, we are all enslaved by the burden of sin. Through the intercession of St. Benedict the Black, may we share the freeing wisdom of the love of God in our lives and bring others out of the bondage of oppression, guilt, and sin. This we ask through Christ our Lord. Amen.*

ST. JULIANA OF MOUNT CORNILLON,
Virgin
April 5

JULIANA was born at Retinnes, near Liège, Flanders, in 1192. Orphaned at the age of five, she was placed in the care of the Augustinian nuns of Mount Cornillon. When very young, she experienced visions of the Lord Who indicated there was no feast day in the Church in honor of the Most Blessed Sacrament.

St. Juliana later became a nun at Mount Cornillon and in 1225 was elected prioress. When she began proposing a feast of the Most Blessed Sacrament, the lay directors of the convent drove her out, claiming that she had mishandled funds. She was exonerated by the Bishop of Liège, and was recalled to the convent in 1246, the very year that the bishop introduced the feast of Corpus Christi to his diocese.

When the bishop died in 1248, Juliana was again driven out, and she took refuge in the Cistercian convent of Salzinnes near Namur. However, Salzinnes was burned down when Henry II of Luxembourg laid siege to Namur. Juliana then retired to Fosses for the remainder of her life, passing away on April 5, 1258. Eventually Pope Urban VI established the feast of the Most Blessed Sacrament. Juliana's cult was confirmed in 1869. The *Revised Roman Martyrology* lists her as a Saint.

REFLECTION   St. Juliana of Mount Cornillon led a very holy life from a young age. Her visions confirmed her in her devotion to the Most Blessed Sacrament, although her obedience to the vision directive cost her dearly. Nonetheless, she persevered till the end. Like Juliana we ought to reflect on the role of the Holy Eucharist in our lives and bring a profound respect and joy to our time before the Most Blessed Sacrament.

PRAYER   *Loving God, You directed Your people through St. Juliana to honor the Blessed Sacrament left by Your Son as His memorial. May we, like St. Juliana, extend ourselves in our own devotion to the Most Blessed Sacrament and in our efforts to spread this devotion to others. This we ask through Christ our Lord. Amen.*

———— ◆ ————

ST. CATHERINE OF PALMA, Virgin

The Same Day—April 5

CATHERINE Tomàs was born on the island of Majorca in 1533. An orphan, she felt called to the religious life at the age of fifteen, but her confessor cautioned her to wait for a while. Meanwhile he arranged for her to enter the service of a family in Palma, where she was taught to read and write.

Finally, Catherine joined the Canonesses of St. Augustine at St. Mary Magdalene Convent in Palma. From the outset, her sanctity, humility, and desire to serve others was clearly evident. On occasion, she would go into a trance for as long as fifteen days at a time, and she was endowed with supernatural gifts, including visions, prophecy, and the ability to withstand the assaults (both physical and spiritual) of the powers of darkness. At the same time, she maintained her inner spiritual joy.

Catherine foretold the date of her death, which occurred in 1574 at the age of forty-one. She was beatified by Pope Pius VI in 1792 and canonized by Pope Pius XI in 1930.

REFLECTION St. Catherine entered the convent, and after some years of quiet growth and development, she was subjected to positive and negative phenomena that could have been a source of great distress for her. She remained serene and fulfilled her duties while waiting for the coming of the Lord to take her home forever. Let us call upon St. Catherine of Palma to sustain us in difficult times.

PRAYER *Loving God, You ask us to serve You for a time on this earth. We take up our cross in Your name. Through the intercession of St. Catherine of Palma, may we patiently live and work for good until You send Your messenger to receive us. This we ask through Christ our Lord. Amen.*

ST. IRENAEUS OF SIRMIUM,
Bishop and Martyr
April 6

IRENAEUS was the Bishop of Sirmium, about forty miles west of Belgrade. He was arrested in the year 304, during Diocletian's persecution, taken before Probus, governor of Pannonia, and subsequently put on the rack for refusing to sacrifice to the gods.

After the torture on the rack, St. Irenaeus was imprisoned and subjected to additional physical torments. Then he was examined publicly a second time, but he would not give in. Accordingly, he was sentenced to be drowned in the river.

St. Irenaeus protested this form of death, indicating that a true Christian could face his executioner and accept the most cruel torments. As a result, the Saint was beheaded, and then his body was thrown into the river.

REFLECTION　St. Irenaeus was an example of strong faith in the early Church. Despite excruciating torture he refused to bend to the demands of the governor. His fortitude reminds us of the necessity of living up to the demands of our Faith and to accept its challenges even though we are not faced with the threat of martyrdom.

PRAYER　*Almighty God, Your Bishop and Martyr Irenaeus willingly gave his life for Your great gift of faith. Like him may we persevere to the end strong in our faith and convictions. This we ask through Christ our Lord. Amen.*

ST. GALLA, Widow

The Same Day—April 6

GALLA was the daughter of a noble patrician who had been a Roman consul in 485. After he was unjustly executed, she married, but a

year later she was widowed. Shortly thereafter, though young and wealthy, Galla was determined to devote herself to Christ. She thereupon joined a community of women who lived near St. Peter's Basilica, and she remained there until her death from cancer in the sixth century, possibly around the year 550.

Galla spent most of her time caring for the poor and infirm. She is mentioned in St. Gregory's *Dialogues*, and it is also believed that St. Fulgentius of Ruspe wrote *Concerning the State of Widowhood* for her.

REFLECTION Following the unexpected death of her husband, St. Galla set aside self-pity and devoted herself to the admirable labor of working for others. She remained faithful to her charges until illness took her to her eternal reward.

PRAYER *O God, we ask Your help as we make our way to You. As followers of Your Son we are rejected by the world. Through the intercession of Your servant St. Galla, help us to persevere in good until we go to meet You. This we ask through Christ our Lord. Amen.*

———◆———

ST. WILLIAM OF ESKILSOË, Abbot
The Same Day—April 6

WILLIAM was born around 1125 at Saint-Germain in France. He became a canon of St. Genevieve collegiate church in Paris, and when Pope Eugenius II decreed the establishment of canons regular at St. Genevieve's in 1148, William adopted the severe lifestyle almost immediately.

William's reputation for holiness and austerity became widespread, and eventually the bishop of Roskilde in Denmark invited him to restore discipline in the monasteries of his diocese. William agreed and started with the canons regular of Eskilsoë. He encountered much opposition, but after great difficulty, he proved successful, ruling Eskilsoë as abbot for thirty years.

William also established the monastery of St. Thomas in Zeeland and continued his work of reform. Although he then left Denmark for a short time, he eventually returned to his abbey, and he died there on April 6, 1203. He was canonized by Pope Honorius III in 1224.

REFLECTION God raised up His servant William for the reformation of monastic life in Denmark. William met this call with a great deal of courage and leadership, while leading a life of great personal holiness. William's answer to God's challenge is a good example of what every Christian is called to do to spread God's Word in a hostile world. Living the Gospel is the essence of the challenge, and a substantial call to holiness is part and parcel of a positive response.

PRAYER   *Loving God, the joy of Easter is a foretaste of eternal life. May we, through the intercession of St. William, lead lives of virtue and holiness so as to bring others to an appreciation of the Word. This we ask through Christ our Lord. Amen.*

ST. PETER OF VERONA, Martyr
The Same Day—April 6

PETER was born at Verona, Italy in 1205. Both of his parents were Catharists, a heresy that denied God created the material world. Even so, Peter was educated at a Catholic school and later at the University of Bologna.

While in Bologna, Peter was accepted into the Dominican Order by St. Dominic. He developed into a great preacher, and was well known for his inspiring sermons in the Lombardy region. In addition, around 1234, he was appointed by Pope Gregory IX as inquisitor of northern Italy, where many Catharists lived.

Peter's preaching attracted large crowds, but as inquisitor he made many enemies. In 1252, while returning from Como to Milan, he was murdered by a Catharist assassin at the age of forty-six. The following year he was canonized by Pope Innocent IV.

REFLECTION   Although his parents were members of an heretical sect, St. Peter of Verona was strong in his Catholic Faith. However, his faithfulness to the Gospel message in his preaching as a Dominican brought about much opposition, and eventually Peter paid with his life for preaching the truth. One of the hazards of preaching and living the Gospel is that we must be considered undesirable according to worldly values. With faith in the Father, and as His children, we are called to stand firm and never waver from the truth even in the face of death.

PRAYER   *Lord God, as we seek to live the Gospel we become different from those who reject Your Word. Grant that like St. Peter of Verona we may live our Gospel lives with courage and complete trust in You. This we ask through Christ our Lord. Amen.*

ST. GEORGE THE YOUNGER, Bishop

April 7

L ITTLE is known of the early life of St. George the Younger. He was a native of Mitylene, the capitol of Lesbos in Greece, who lived in the eighth century. A very wealthy man, George used his worldly goods for the relief of the sick and poor and then entered a monastery. He was called from the monastery to become Bishop of Mitylene. As bishop the Saint continued his generosity and became known for his severe fasts and profound humility.

When persecution came under Emperor Leo the Armenian, George stood firm for the Catholic Church and spoke against the destruction of statues. Accordingly, George was sent into exile at Chersonese, and he died there in 816.

When the Saint's relics were returned to Mitylene, many miracles were recorded. George was known as the healer of disease and effective in saving the possessed. He was called "the Younger" to differentiate him from two of his predecessor bishops of Mitylene who had the same name.

REFLECTION   The Images of the Trinity, the Blessed Virgin, and the Saints have from time to time been the object of great dispute in the Church. We preserve these Images as a reminder that we should imitate the lives and virtues of the people honored and remembered. Our goal is to join them in the presence of God forever.

PRAYER   *God our Father, in the midst of troubled times You hear the prayers of Your people. Like St. George, grant us the wisdom and courage to stand fast in the Faith. This we ask through Christ our Lord. Amen.*

———◆◆———

ST. AGABUS, Prophet

April 8

AGABUS was a prophet of the Apostolic Church. He came to Antioch with some prophets from Jerusalem and, through the Holy Spirit, prophesied that a severe famine was coming over the entire Roman world. The famine took place during the reign of Claudius probably in 42-44, and the Antiochian Christians sent help to their brethren in Jerusalem (Acts 11:27-30).

Years later, the same prophet Agabus came down from Jerusalem to Caesarea when Paul was there. By symbolic actions in the manner of the Old Testament prophets, he foretold Paul's captivity. However, this prophecy did not deter Paul from going to Jerusalem, where he was imprisoned as had been foretold (Acts 21:10-13, 33).

Tradition includes Agabus among the seventy-two disciples.

REFLECTION The prophets of the New Testament fulfilled a very important task together with the apostles and teachers (1 Cor 12:28-29). They were itinerant preachers who imitated the life of Jesus and visited the communities to remind them of the Lord's teachings. St. Agabus carried out his task to the letter. May we all do the same with our task in life.

PRAYER *O God, You enabled St. Agabus to be a prophet of the New Testament and ensure that the teachings of Your Son would be carried out fully. Through the prayers of this prophet, may we always remain steadfast to the teachings of our Lord, Who lives and reigns with You and the Holy Spirit forever. Amen.*

———◆———

ST. HUGH OF ROUEN, Bishop

April 9

BORN in the late seventh century, St. Hugh was the son of Drogo, Duke of Burgundy, grandson of Pepin de Herstal, and nephew of Charles Martel. At an early age, he became a monk at the abbey of Fontenelle or that of Jumièges.

Hugh was soon named Abbot of Metz and shortly afterward became Bishop of Rouen (722) as well as Paris and Bayeux. At the same time he was also Abbot of Fontenelle and Jumièges. Multiple offices were the norm in those days and he received them through the influence of his relatives, especially his uncle Charles.

The Saint used the revenues from his posts to foster learning and piety. In time, he resigned from all of them and chose to live at Jumièges as a choir-monk. He died around the year 730 with a great reputation for holiness.

REFLECTION St. Hugh was elevated to positions of wealth and power in the Church and assured of much revenue. He consistently used his wealth for the good of others, e.g., endowing abbeys and building churches for the people. His life teaches us the right usage of money and power.

PRAYER *God our Father, You enabled St. Hugh, Your Bishop, to amass wealth and power but use them for good. By his intercession, teach us how to remain humble in the midst of any wealth and power we might attain. This we ask through Christ our Lord. Amen.*

———◆———

ST. MICHAEL DE SANCTIS, Priest
April 10

MICHAEL de Sanctis was born in Catalonia, Spain, around 1591. At the age of six he informed his parents that he was going to be a monk. Moreover, he imitated St. Francis of Assisi to such a great extent that he had to be restrained.

After the death of his parents, Michael served as an apprentice to a merchant. However, he continued to lead a life of exemplary fervor and devotion, and in 1603 he joined the Trinitarian friars at Barcelona, taking his vows at St. Lambert's Monastery in Saragossa in 1607.

Shortly thereafter, Michael expressed a desire to join the reformed group of Trinitarians and was given permission to do so. He went to the novitiate at Madrid and, after studies at Seville and Salamanca, he was ordained a priest and twice served as superior of the house in Valladolid. His confreres considered him to be a Saint, especially because of his devotion to the Most Blessed Sacrament and his ecstasies during Mass. After his death at the age of thirty-five on April 10, 1625, many miracles were attributed to him. He was canonized in 1862 by Pope Pius IX.

REFLECTION St. Michael de Sanctis is noted as being remarkable for innocence of life, wonderful penitence, and love for God. He seemed from his earliest years to have been selected for a life of great holiness, and he never wavered in his great love of God or his vocation. As our young people look for direction in a world that seems not to care, St. Michael stands out as worthy of imitation as well as of the prayers of both young and old alike.

PRAYER   *Loving God, You raised up Your servant St. Michael de Sanctis to the holiness of Your Saints. In a short life he earned a heavenly reward. May St. Michael become a living guide for the youth of the world today. This we ask through Christ our Lord. Amen.*

————◆————

ST. ISAAC OF SPOLETO, Monk

April 11

ALL that we know about St. Isaac comes from the *Dialogues* of Pope St. Gregory the Great. Isaac was a Syrian who left his homeland because of the Monophysite persecution and took up residence at Spoleto, in Umbria, Italy. There he immediately cast out a devil from one of the custodians of the local church building.

The people realized that they had a holy man in their midst and offered to give him gifts and even build a monastery for him. Isaac refused to accept anything. He simply retired to a cave on Mount Luco.

Several years later, he had a vision of our Lady who urged him to instruct disciples. He then became the head of a "laura," a kind of monastery consisting of a number of monks leading a communal life yet inhabiting separate cells grouped around a church.

The Saint advised his monks not to accept offerings from the faithful, saying to them, "A monk who desires earthly possessions is no monk at all!" St. Isaac is said to have possessed the gifts of prophecy and miracles.

REFLECTION St. Isaac lived the life of a true monk and led others to do the same. Theirs was a life free from the world and lived for God alone. May his example show us how to offer our daily life to the Lord, no matter what state we embrace.

PRAYER   *Heavenly Father, You called St. Isaac to the life of a monk bereft of most earthly goods. By his prayers, help us never to hanker for the things of this world but to offer them for Your glory. This we ask through Christ our Lord. Amen.*

———◆———

ST. ALFERIUS, Abbot
April 12

ALFERIUS was born of the noble Pappacarboni family in Salerno, Italy, in 930. While on a mission to the French court for Duke Gisulf of Salerno, he contracted a serious illness, and he made a vow that if he were cured of his illness he would enter the religious life.

After his recovery, Alferius became a monk at Cluny. However, Duke Gisulf recalled him to Salerno so that he might reform the monasteries in Gisulf's jurisdiction. Unfortunately, the Saint had little success in his attempts to do so.

In the year 1011, Alferius became a hermit outside Salerno. Many were attracted to him, and eventually he selected twelve individuals and founded the world-renowned Benedictine abbey of La Cava. Alferius died in 1050 at the age of one hundred and twenty.

REFLECTION St. Alferius, having made a vow to enter the religious life if he were cured of a serious illness, was faithful to his promise. Nonetheless, de-

spite his reputation for holiness and virtue, he was unable to carry forward the reform movement in Salerno requested by Duke Gisulf. Later, when Alferius founded La Cava, he was a model religious and his foundation was successful, particularly in the number of foundations that grew out of the original abbey.

PRAYER   *Loving God, You planted the seed of religious life through Your devoted servant St. Alferius. May we always be open to Your call to lives of holiness and virtue. This we ask through Christ our Lord. Amen.*

———◆———

ST. HERMENEGILD, Martyr
April 13

HERMENEGILD was the son of Leovigild, an Arian Visigoth king of Spain in the sixth century. Leovigild raised his children in the Arian heresy. However, when Hermenegild married Indegundis, the daughter of King Sigebert of Austrasia, he gave up Arianism and returned to orthodox Catholicism, whereupon his father disinherited him.

Hermenegild then led a revolt against his father. He thought he would be able to get help from either the Romans or the Eastern emperor in his revolt, but such was not the case. As a result, King Leovigild defeated Hermenegild at Seville, but then a reconciliation was effected, and

Hermenegild regained some of his former court privileges.

However, when Leovigild asked his son to return to Arianism, Hermenegild refused and was imprisoned. While in prison he clothed himself in sackcloth and practiced great mortifications so that he would not give in to his father's blandishments to give up the Faith. At Easter in 586, when he refused to receive Communion in jail from an Arian bishop, he incurred the wrath of Leovigild who sent soldiers to the prison to kill Hermenegild with an axe.

REFLECTION　In an age when the true Faith is subject to so many confrontations in so many different ways, St. Hermenegild is a model of staunch faith in the face of prison and death. Deprived of his courtly rights and privileges, he withstood the test and refused to bend to the demands of his father that he embrace Arianism. In order to avoid the temptation of denial of the Faith, Hermenegild had recourse to prayer and mortification. His adherence to the Faith won him a martyr's crown.

PRAYER　*Almighty God, You have created us in Your image and likeness. As we endure the challenges of our faith in You here on earth, may we follow the example of Your servant St. Hermenegild by persevering in prayer and faith until Your coming. This we ask through Christ our Lord. Amen.*

ST. LYDWINA, Virgin
April 14

L YDWINA was born in the year 1380 at
Schiedam, Holland, one of the nine children
of a workingman. At the age of sixteen she was
injured in an ice skating accident and became an
invalid for the remainder of her life, with increasing pain as the years passed. However, she
accepted the pain in reparation for the sins of
others. She often meditated on Christ's Passion
and had great devotion to the Eucharist.

As time passed, Lydwina's reputation for
piety became widespread. Around 1407, she
began to experience ecstasies and visions in
which she participated in the Passion, saw Purgatory and Heaven, and visited with the Saints.
During the last nineteen years of her life the only
food she consumed was Holy Communion, and
in the last seven years of life she became almost
completely blind.

Lydwina's sufferings, ecstasies, and resignation to God's will were declared valid by an ecclesiastical commission before her death. After
her death in 1433, Thomas à Kempis wrote her
biography, and her cult was formally confirmed
by Pope Leo XIII in 1890. The *Revised Roman
Martyrology* calls her a Saint.

REFLECTION   St. Lydwina, an active teenager when
she suffered her accident, accepted the great burden
of being an invalid in an era when there was little or

no medical relief available. As her infirmities increased, she continued to resign herself to her condition and to be at peace with God while offering the merits of her terrible sufferings for the welfare of others. Lydwina today is a model for young people whose careers are cut short and who still have much to offer in the way of prayer and good works.

PRAYER Almighty God, through the intercession of St. Lydwina may we be open to those events in our lives that bring suffering and disappointment. Like her may we turn misfortune and suffering into good for others. This we ask through Christ our Lord. Amen.

BL. CESAR DE BUS, Priest and Founder

April 15

CESAR de Bus was born in 1544 at Cavaillon, France, and joined the army at eighteen, ultimately waging war with the Huguenots. After his war service he wrote poetry, tried his hand at painting, and led a worldly life in Paris for three years.

Upon the death of his brother, Cesar renounced his worldly ways, went back to school, and became a priest in 1582. His preaching and charitable works gained him wide recognition. In 1592, he founded the secular order of Christian Doctrine, composed of priests dedicated to catechetical instruction.

Later, Bl. Cesar founded an order of women dedicated to the same purpose, which ultimately became part of the Ursulines. Cesar went to his eternal reward on April 15, 1607, and was beatified in 1975 by Pope Paul VI.

REFLECTION   Bl. Cesar de Bus saw the problems of the world as a soldier and ne'er-do-well. then once he was committed to Christ, he set about alleviating some of those problems. We should strive to bring help to the world in our own little way—by praying first of all and then by doing what is in our power to do.

PRAYER   *Almighty God, You raised up Bl. Cesar, Your Priest, to enhance the Church with a new group of religious. By his prayers, help us to see what is needed to be done and to do it for You. This we ask through Christ our Lord. Amen.*

ST. TURIBIUS, Bishop of Astorga
April 16

S T. Turibius became Bishop of Astorga, Spain, in the fifth century when the Priscillianist heresy was making great inroads in that country. This heresy was a type of Manicheanism that appealed to both clergy and laity.

St. Turibius championed the true Catholic Faith, exposing the falsity of the new doctrines and opposing the leaders who had strayed from the truth. He also wrote to Pope Leo the Great about what he was doing and asked for his aid. The Pope backed the bishop and condemned the teachings of the Priscilliansits.

As a result, the heresy lost its power over the people and was practically eliminated in Spain. Turibius was able to rule his diocese in peace, while maintaining discipline among the clergy and good morals among the people. He died in 450 with a reputation for holiness.

REFLECTION   St. Turibius came to the defense of the Church when a heresy threatened to undermine the true Christian teaching. He used well the weapons at his disposal to combat this false teaching and even called upon the Roman Pontiff to join in the fight on behalf of his flock. In the end, the true Faith prevailed. We should strive always to defend the teachings of the Church whenever they are attacked by anyone.

PRAYER   *O Lord, You raised up St. Turibius, Your Bishop, to defend the teachings of the Church against a pernicious heresy. By his prayers, help us to learn the Faith so well that we may be able to defend it in our daily life. This we ask through Christ our Lord. Amen.*

ST. FRUCTUOSUS OF BRAGA, Bishop
The Same Day—April 16

BORN into a Spanish military family of the seventh century, Fructuosus of Braga determined at an early age to devote his life to the service of God. Since his parents died when he was young, he was free to follow his inclination. He gave much of his inheritance to the poor and to his freed slaves and then founded several monasteries.

Later he went into the wilderness and led an austere life as a hermit. Many people flocked to him, including entire families, and he built convents for both men and women, generally adopting the Benedictine Rule.

Later, in order to pursue his desire for solitude, Fructuosus planned to go to Egypt as a hermit but was forbidden to do so by his king, and soon afterward he became Bishop of Dumium. In 656, he was made Archbishop of Braga in Portugal. There he experienced confrontation, but he eventually won over those who were opposed to his administration. He died in the year 665.

REFLECTION When we are called by the Spirit to draw closer to God, our response should be as generous as that of St. Fructuosus. Through his zeal and personal holiness he attracted many to serve God in the fullness of their faith.

PRAYER *We turn to You, God our Father, in our need. Help us through the intercession of St. Fructuosus to listen carefully to Your Spirit in our lives. This we ask through Christ our Lord. Amen.*

———◆◆———

BL. MARY ANN OF JESUS NAVARRO,
Virgin
April 17

MARY Ann of Jesus Navarro was born on January 17, 1565, in Madrid, Spain. From her earliest days she was known to have led a virtuous life. At the age of twenty-three she refused an offer of marriage and dedicated herself completely to God under the direction of the Mercedarian Fathers.

In 1614, having taken the habit of the Third Order of Mercy, Mary Ann professed her vows. The remainder of her life was taken up with works of mercy.

Mary Ann had a deep devotion to the Holy Eucharist, and her prayer life, humility, and mortification were an inspiration for many. As a result, she was commanded under obedience to write her biography. She died on April 17, 1624, in Madrid, where her incorrupt body is preserved.

REFLECTION Bl. Mary Ann responded openly and fully to the grace of God. Ever faithful to her prayer life and self-imposed penances, she spent her entire life in serving the needs of others, especially the poor. That life was one of complete cooperation with the grace of God.

PRAYER   *O God, You taught Bl. Mary Ann, model of penance and faithful devotee of the Eucharist, to serve Christ in her brothers and sisters. Help us, through her intercession, to share in the Divine Mysteries and to answer Your call to serve the needs of Your people, our neighbors. This we ask through Christ our Lord. Amen.*

BL. MARY OF THE INCARNATION,
Widow
April 18

MARY of the Incarnation was born in Paris on February 1, 1565, and baptized Barbe Aurillot. At the age of sixteen, she married Peter Acarie, and they had six children, three of whom entered the Carmelite Order and one of whom became a priest.

In spite of her household duties and many hardships, Barbe attained the heights of mysticism. She was deeply influenced by the writings of St. Teresa of Avila and had mystical contact with the Saint. Moreover, she was mainly responsible for introducing the Discalced Carmelite Nuns into France.

After Barbe's husband died in 1613, she asked to be admitted to the Carmelites as a lay sister. She took the name Mary of the Incarnation and was professed in 1615 at the Carmel in Amiens. Her reputation for sanctity was widespread, and she was distinguished for her spirit of prayer and the spread of the Catholic Faith. Mary was highly esteemed by many holy men of her day, particularly St. Francis de Sales. Mary died at Pontoise on April 18, 1618, and was beatified in 1791 by Pope Pius VI.

REFLECTION Having led a full life as a faithful wife and mother to six children, Mary, through prayer and devotion, was able to reach the state of mystical prayer. Once her husband died, and her children were raised, Mary became a Carmelite Nun, seeking only the lowly position of a lay sister. Despite her desire merely to serve, her reputation for spirituality was widespread, and other mystics sought her out for direction. Her zeal and prayer for the Faith are worthy of imitation by all Christians, both lay and religious.

PRAYER   *Heavenly Father, You gave Bl. Mary of the Incarnation heroic strength in the face of adversities and zeal for the extension of the Carmelite Order. May we courageously endure every trial and persevere to the end in Your love. This we ask through Christ our Lord. Amen.*

_____◆●◆_____

ST. ATHANASIA, Abbess

The Same Day—April 18

ATHANASIA was born on the island of Aegina in Greece in the eighth century. At an early age she was married to an army officer, but after only sixteen days of marriage her husband was killed in a battle against invading Arabs.

Later Athanasia married a very religious man. After some time, this second husband wanted to become a monk. She consented and converted her home into a convent, of which she was named abbess, and eventually moved her community to Timia.

Later, Athanasia, while living in a cell in Constantinople, served as advisor to Empress Theodora for about seven years. After that she returned to Timia, where she died shortly there about 860.

REFLECTION When God calls His servants in a special way, there is no set pattern. As St. Athanasia's life demonstrates, no matter what our calling, God's grace is sufficient for us. It is always there for the taking.

PRAYER *O God, in all walks of life You call us to holiness of life in conformity with Your will. Through the intercession of Your Abbess St. Athanasia, may we always be joyful in living out Your plan for us. This we ask through Christ our Lord. Amen.*

ST. LEO IX, Pope

April 19

LEO IX was born in Alsace on June 21, 1002, and given the name Bruno. After his studies, he was ordained a deacon. Despite that, he commanded troops under Emperor Conrad II during the invasion of Italy in 1026. Bruno was elected Bishop of Toul while in Italy, and he ruled there for twenty years, introducing reforms among the secular clergy and the Cluniac reform in the monasteries.

In 1048, with the support of his relative, Emperor Henry III, Bruno was elected Pope, succeeding Pope Damasus II, and he was consecrated February 12, 1049. As Pope Leo IX, he called a synod at Rome and started many reforms, traveling throughout Western Europe to ensure that the reforms were carried out. He was called the Apostolic Pilgrim. Among other things, Leo condemned Berengarius of Tours for denying transubstantiation and brought peace to Hungary when it was in the throes of war.

In 1053, Leo led an army against Norman invaders, but he was defeated and captured and later imprisoned at Benevento. St. Peter Damian emphatically denounced him for leading an army. Leo also opposed some proposals of Patriarch Michael Cerularius of Constantinople, which marked the beginning of the separation of Rome from the Eastern Churches.

It was Leo who proposed that Popes be elected only by cardinals, a policy that was formally established five years after his death on April 19, 1054. He was canonized by Pope Victor III in 1082, owing in part to many miracles attributed to his intervention.

REFLECTION Pope St. Leo IX was very active in gaining acceptance of his proposals by direct personal intervention. A reform-minded Pope, he used his office as well as his personal piety to convince prelates, priests, religious, and laity to become active in bringing the Church into conformity with the dictates of the Gospel. Through a sense of dedication and personal conviction, he was effective in mounting reform in the Western Church.

PRAYER   *Lord God, You gave Pope St. Leo IX to Your Church at a time when reforms were greatly needed. Leo's devotion to the Church and her teachings gives us hope during these difficult times that the Church currently endures. May we always remain faithful to the Gospel as St. Leo did and work courageously for unity among Your people. This we ask through Christ our Lord. Amen.*

ST. AGNES OF MONTEPULCIANO,
Virgin
April 20

AGNES was born in 1268 in the Tuscan village of Gracchiano-Vecchio. When she was nine years old she requested admittance to an austere convent at Montepulciano and made remarkable progress there.

Eventually the nun in charge of Agnes was appointed head of a new convent in Procena, and she took Agnes with her. Agnes's reputation attracted others to Procena, and she was elected abbess in a short time, although she was only fifteen years of age. Pope Nicholas IV dispensed Agnes from the canonical age requirement.

After being elected abbess, Agnes increased the austerity of her life, and for fifteen years she subsisted simply on bread and water, meanwhile sleeping on the ground with a stone for a pillow. After seventeen years the people of Montepulciano convinced her to return, and they built her a new convent, which she placed under the auspices of the Dominicans. She was finally installed as prioress, and remained there until her death in 1317 at the age of forty-nine after a prolonged and painful illness. Reported to have been blessed with the gifts of visions, levitation, and miracles, she was canonized in 1726 by Pope Benedict XIII.

REFLECTION St. Agnes was blessed from her earliest years with an intense desire to serve God in the religious life. After entering the convent she was a constant source of edification for the other community members. In response to being placed in a position of leadership and responsibility, she increased her penance and prayer, while at the same time attracting other young people into God's consecrated service.

PRAYER   *Loving God, through the intercession of St. Agnes of Montepulciano, may many young men and women be attracted to Your service in the religious life and priesthood. May they be generous in meeting the needs of others through personal prayer and sacrifice. This we ask through Christ our Lord. Amen.*

ST. ANASTASIUS II, Martyr

The Same Day—April 20

ANASTASIUS II was born in the sixth century. In the year 599, he succeeded Anastasius I as Patriarch of Antioch.

After Anastasius notified Pope St. Gregory the Great of his election, the Pope urged him to rid his jurisdiction of simony. Selling of religious offices and benefices was rampant there at the time.

In 609, the emperor Phocas was forcing Syrian Jews to convert to Christianity. They rose in rebellion, and in the conflict Anastasius was killed during that year.

REFLECTION Like Joseph, who accepted the responsibility for Mary as she was about to give birth, St. Anastasius had a strong sense of Christian responsibility. This virtue enabled him to die for the Faith. This kind of example makes us pause and examine the roots of our Faith.

PRAYER   *Loving Father, Your people cry out to You in faith. Through the intercession of Your servant St. Anastasius II, be with Your Church as we bring Your Word to those most in need. This we ask through Christ our Lord. Amen.*

———◆◆———

ST. CONRAD OF PARZHAM, Religious
April 21

CONRAD Birndorfer was born in Parzham, Bavaria, on December 22, 1818, the youngest of nine children. In 1849, at the age of thirty-one, he became a Capuchin lay brother. After taking his solemn vows in 1852, he was assigned to the shrine of Our Lady at Altötting, where he served as porter for more than forty years.

Many of the pilgrims to the shrine remembered his great devotion to Mary, as well as his generous charity for all who came to the monastery. Moreover, he was gifted with the ability to prophesy and to read people's hearts. Many demands were made on him by individuals who were in need of spiritual help.

Conrad died at Altötting on April 21, 1891, and was canonized in 1935 by Pope Pius XI.

REFLECTION   St. Conrad spent his entire religious life in the humble post of porter. Yet through his personal holiness he managed to call many back to God with a renewed lifestyle. St. Conrad's life ably demonstrates that one sincere and holy Christian can make a tremendous difference in the world. The possibilities for good are endless.

PRAYER   *Loving God, You call us to the state of perfection. Through the intercession of St. Conrad, may we respond with humility, generosity, and detachment to the call of the Gospel to holiness. This we ask through Christ our Lord. Amen.*

ST. OPPORTUNA, Virgin and Abbess

April 22

OPPORTUNA was born in the eighth century in Normandy, France. At a very early age she entered the Benedictine convent near Almenèches. Her brother Chrodegang, the Bishop of Séez, gave her the veil.

As an ordinary nun, and later as abbess, Opportuna was a great source of edification for the community, particularly because of her piety and austerity. However, when her brother the bishop was murdered, she was deeply affected, and she died shortly thereafter, around 770.

After her death, many legends developed about Opportuna, and numerous miracles were attributed to her. She has always been a very popular Saint in France.

REFLECTION All Christians are called to holiness. One's state of life largely determines the means by which holiness is achieved. For St. Opportuna it was the monastic life, but for many others it is the chosen way they exercise God's gifts. Any state of life can constitute the road to salvation if we accomplish God's will and embrace our vocation.

PRAYER *O God, may we, like St. Opportuna, remain faithful to Your will in our regard. Ever attentive to the demands of the Gospel, we seek You in our workplace and our homes. Keep us always in Your care. This we ask through Christ our Lord. Amen.*

BL. HELEN OF UDINE, Widow
April 23

HELEN of Udine was a member of the Valen-
tini family of northeast Italy. At the age of
fifteen she married a knight named Anthony dei
Cavalcanti. For twenty-five years Helen and An-

thony had a very happy marriage and raised several children.

Her husband's death was a tragedy for Helen. Following his burial, she decided to become a tertiary of the Hermits of St. Augustine. For the remainder of her days she devoted herself to prayer, mortifications, and works of charity.

Later Helen took a vow of perpetual silence, speaking only on Christmas night. She also endured many trials and temptations but at the same time she experienced spiritual delights and ecstasies. Many people were cured through her intercession. For the last three years of her life she was bedridden on her pallet of stones and straw. She died on April 23, 1458, at the age of sixty-two. Pope Pius IX approved public devotion in honor of Helen in 1848.

REFLECTION Bl. Helen of Udine, widowed after twenty-five years of a very happy marriage, turned her time and attention to spiritual growth and works of charity. Despite the physical and emotional abuse she suffered through satanic interventions, she nevertheless remained steadfast in her devotion to God and the welfare of the poor and indigent. The pain of her husband's death never left her, but she turned her sorrow into joy in the service of God and His people.

PRAYER   *Almighty God, many of Your daughters suffer the devastating separation from their beloved spouses caused by death. May all widows take heart in the courage and devotion of Your servant Bl. Helen of Udine. Grant them courage to come closer to You in service to others. This we ask through Christ our Lord. Amen.*

———◆◆———

STS. MARY OF CLEOPHAS AND SALOME

April 24

MARY of Cleophas, also known as Mary of Clopas, was the mother of the Apostle St. James the Less and Joseph (Matthew 27:56; Mark 15:40), the wife of Clopas, and very likely the sister of the Blessed Virgin Mary (John 19:25).

Salome was the wife of the Galilean fisherman Zebedee and the mother of the Apostles Sts. James and John. She is mentioned in the Gospels sometimes by name (Mark 15:40; 16:4) and sometimes by the phrase "the mother of the sons of Zebedee" (Matthew 20:20; 27:56, 58).

Both of these Saints were members of the group of women that followed Jesus. They were present at His Crucifixion (Matthew 27:56; Mark 15:40; John 19:25) and both went with St. Mary Magdalene to the tomb of Jesus on Easter Sunday (Mark 16:1; Luke 24:10).

Little else is known of the life of St. Mary and practically nothing about St. Salome. According to one legend, St. Mary traveled with St. James the Greater to Spain and died in that country. Another legend states that she accompanied Lazarus, Mary Magdalene, and Martha to Provence.

REFLECTION Sts. Mary of Cleophas and Salome were present with Jesus when He was crucified and they discovered the empty tomb with Mary Magdalene on the first Easter Sunday. Thus their lifetime encompassed the Incarnation and the Redemption of the world. Their courageous following of Jesus and belief in His Word are demonstrated in the fact that on Calvary they stood by the Mother of Jesus in her great travail. Their courage in the face of ridicule and danger is a significant memorial and model for all Christians, especially women, in following Jesus unstintingly in a hostile environment.

PRAYER *Loving God, You have redeemed Your people through the Death and Resurrection of Jesus. Through the intercession of Sts. Mary of Cleophas and Salome, may we ardently seek the Risen Jesus in our lives. This we ask through Christ our Lord. Amen.*

———◆◆———

ST. MARY EUPHRASIA PELLETIER,
Virgin
The Same Day—April 24

ROSE Virginia Pelletier was born in 1796 on the island of Noirmoutier off the coast of Britanny. While at school in Tours, she determined to devote her life to God.

Rose became attracted to the Institute of Our Lady of Charity of the Refuge, founded by St. John Eudes in 1641. Its purpose was to rescue "fallen" women and to protect those in danger. In 1814, she joined the convent as a novice and was professed in 1816 under the name of Mary Euphrasia. In 1825, at the age of twenty-nine, she was elected superior and established a new foundation at Angers.

In time, Mother Mary Euphrasia came to the conclusion that all the convents should be under one organization. Unable to do this in her Congregation, she created the Institute of Our Lady of the Good Shepherd to work with wayward girls. In 1835, papal approbation was obtained, and many new convents were established with great effect. When St. Euphrasia died in 1868, the Good Shepherd nuns were 2,760 in number and known throughout the world. She was canonized in 1940 by Pope Pius XI.

REFLECTION St. Mary Euphrasia Pelletier was struck by the good example of those who worked in Tours for the welfare of women of the streets. Like Jesus, St. Mary Euphrasia reached out to the most rejected of society. Her conviction about the need for central organization was an inspired one given the number of foundations that sprang up under her direction. St. Mary Euphrasia's trust in God in the face of opposition was a blessing for thousands of women who otherwise may never have gotten a chance in life or heard the Word of God and known of His love for them.

PRAYER   *Loving God, Your children are sometimes forced into grave circumstances in a world that has thrown aside Your Word. Through the intercession of St. Mary Euphrasia Pelletier, may we always energetically move to attack evil and injustice in our society. This we ask through Christ our Lord. Amen.*

ST. FRANCA VISALTA, Virgin
April 25

FRANCA Visalta was placed in the Benedictine convent of St. Syrus at Piacenza in 1177, when she was seven years of age. She was professed at the age of fourteen and was notable for her prayer, obedience, and mortifications. Later she was elected abbess, but because of the strictness of her rule she was deposed.

The ensuing calumnies and interior trials were a true hardship for Franca. However, one of her followers, Carentia, entered the Cistercian novitiate at Rapallo and then persuaded her parents to erect a Cistercian house at Montelana, which Carentia entered. Franca was appointed as abbess of the new community, which was later moved to Pittoli.

Despite her failing health, Franca continued to live a life of severe austerity, spending most of her nights in the chapel absorbed in continuous prayer. She died in 1218. Pope Gregory X, a relative of Carentia, confirmed Franca's cult for Piacenza.

REFLECTION As St. Franca grew in perfection, she demanded of others that they be more faithful to their commitments, especially in the matter of self-denial. Ousted from office because of her insistence on austerity, she willingly suffered the public humiliation of having been removed yet still continued to live in the convent. She did not spare her own health in keeping her night vigils, inspiring others by her holiness of life and mortifications, prayer, and fasting.

PRAYER   *Heavenly Father, You ask us to commit ourselves to You in prayer, fasting, love, and works of charity. May we, like St. Franca, overcome all obstacles in our lives and remain faithful to Your call to greater perfection. This we ask through Christ our Lord. Amen.*

———◆———

BL. ROBERT ANDERTON AND BL. WILLIAM MARSDEN, Martyrs

The Same Day—April 25

ROBERT Anderton and William Marsden were both born in Lancashire, England, in the sixteenth century. They were ordained priests in Rheims, France, and assigned to return to the English missions. However, their ship was driven off course and they landed on the Isle of Wight.

The two young men immediately were regarded with suspicion and brought before a magistrate. When they did not deny that they were priests, they were imprisoned. During their trial, despite their valid defense that they had not been on English soil for the period of time required for a legal arrest, they were found guilty of treason and sentenced to death.

Eventually their conviction was upheld, and Bl. Robert and Bl. William were executed on the

Isle of Wight on April 25, 1586, impressing many of the onlookers by their cheerful bearing on the scaffold. They were beatified in 1929 by Pope Pius XI.

REFLECTION Bl. Robert and Bl. William, filled with zeal for their persecuted countrymen, did not hesitate to return to England to bring the consolation of the Sacraments to their brothers and sisters in the Lord. A happenstance of nature cut short their apostolate, and they eagerly embraced martyrdom by openly admitting their priesthood. Having accepted the call to the priesthood, they eagerly followed Jesus to Calvary on the scaffold when they offered themselves joyfully and willingly for the honor and glory of the Father. Their open love for God and His people is a living model for all Christians, particularly priests who are called to embrace the Cross of Jesus.

PRAYER *Loving God, You call each of us to perfection according to our state in life. Like Bl. Robert and Bl. William may we willingly embrace the Cross in union with Jesus and so proclaim Your work in a hostile world. This we ask through Christ our Lord. Amen.*

———◆–◆———

ST. CLETUS, Pope

April 26

ST. Cletus, also known as Anacletus (from the Greek word for "blameless"), was an early bishop of Rome who became Pope. He followed St. Linus (66-78), the successor of St. Peter, and preceded St. Clement of Rome (91-101), ruling the

Church from 79 to 91 as the second Pope from St. Peter. He is commemorated in the ancient Canon of the Mass (i.e., Eucharistic Prayer I).

Cletus was a Roman, son of Emiliano, born in a quarter not far from the house of Pudentus, the host of St. Peter. During his pontificate, the destruction of Jerusalem by Titus took place. Many Jews were led away as slaves to Rome, and Cletus comforted them and lightened their misery.

There is also a tradition that Cletus appointed twenty-five presbyters for Rome, erected a monument over St. Peter's burial place, and died a martyr, but it has no foundation. During his time, the monarchical episcopate had not yet come to power in Rome.

REFLECTION   St. Cletus was Pope at the time when the position was still in a state of flux. However, it is doubtless true that he did all he could to solidify the new post of Roman Pontiff—builder of bridges between Christians and others. May we always remember to pray for the Pope, who has the good of the Church and the world in his hands, a huge task for any human to fulfill.

PRAYER   *Almighty God, You chose St. Cletus to be the second Pope after St. Peter and aided him in bringing about the position of Roman Pontiff. By his intercession help us to revere the Pope as the Vicar of Your Son on earth and pray for him in his onerous duty. This we ask through Christ our Lord. Amen.*

ST. PETER ARMENGOL, Martyr

April 27

PETER Armengol was born around 1238 in Catalonia, Spain. His early life left much to be desired, since it is believed that he ran away from home and joined a group of bandits. At one time Peter met his father's entourage, which his group intended to plunder. But when Peter recognized his father, he begged to be forgiven.

Peter then decided to change his lifestyle to one of repentance and mortifications. He entered the Order of Mercedarians and devoted his life to the redemption of captives. On one occasion, when there was insufficient money to redeem eighteen young boys, Peter gave himself as a hostage for their freedom. Shortly thereafter he was hanged, but when his body was taken down, he was discovered to still be alive.

Peter remained with the Mercedarians for the remainder of his life, suffering continually as the result of tortures inflicted during his captivity. He died in 1304. In 1686, Pope Innocent XI allowed public devotion to Peter.

REFLECTION Although he roamed and plundered the countryside with a pack of bandits as a young man, St. Peter Armengol eventually entered the Order of Mercedarians and went so far as to offer himself to the Moors in order to win the freedom of young boys from slavery, fulfilling the Gospel dictum that the greatest act of love is to lay down one's life for another. Spared an early death at the hands of the

Moors, he remained faithful to the end. Peter's life is a glowing example of the grace of God at work and the effective results of cooperation with God's love for His people.

PRAYER   *Merciful Lord, You raised St. Peter Armengol to the perfection of love. Fill our hearts with the same spirit that moved him to offer himself to You as a pleasing victim for the defense of the Christian Faith and the freedom of captives. This we ask through Christ our Lord. Amen.*

ST. PAMPHILUS, Bishop of Sulmona
April 28

S T. Pamphilus was Bishop of the united dioceses of Sulmona and Corfinium located in the Abruzzi, Italy, during the last part of the seventh century. In this capacity, he lived a holy and austere life, diligently educated his people, and took care of the poor.

The saintly Bishop also had a custom of celebrating Mass after the singing of Night Offices at midnight. Afterward he distributed alms and at dawn provided a meal for the poor and sat down and ate with them.

This manner of acting on the part of the Bishop was displeasing to some of his clergy. They objected to this early schedule, claiming that no other Bishop in Italy celebrated Mass before three or six o'clock in the morning. In frustration, they leveled charges of heresy against Pamphilus before Pope Sergius I.

The Saint was completely vindicated by Sergius, who also presented him with a hefty donation for his poor. St. Pamphilus died about the year 700.

REFLECTION St. Pamphilus was a lover of the Liturgy and of the poor. Despite the objections of some clergy, he did what he thought was good for his people. His life calls us to strive for full, active, and conscious participation at each Eucharist.

PRAYER   *Lord God, through the intercession of St Pamphilus, help us to love the Liturgy, especially the Eucharist, and to put it into practice in our lives. We ask this through Christ our Lord. Amen.*

ST. HUGH OF CLUNY, Abbot
April 29

BORN at Samur in 1024, Hugh entered the Benedictine Monastery of Cluny at the youthful age of fifteen. He was ordained at twenty and elected Abbot at twenty-five. As such he undertook the leadership of the Benedictine confederation that depended on Cluny.

During the sixty years of his rule, Hugh raised Cluny to the greatest heights. He became the advisor to nine Popes, was often consulted by the heads of Western Europe, and had the ultimate control over 200 monasteries.

This great Saint was blessed with keen para-psychological insight and diplomatic ability, and his generosity and integrity were apparent to all who came in contact with him. One of his monks declared: "He read much and prayed more. It is difficult to say which was greater, his prudence or his simplicity. . . . He was never angry, except against sin." Hugh died in 1109 and was canonized by Pope Callistus III in 1120.

REFLECTION   Few men have been so universally esteemed or so influential as St. Hugh. Yet he was not averse to waiting upon lepers with his own hands at a hostel that he founded. This is but one indication of how he was able to promote revival of the spiritual life in the eleventh century and to exercise a preeminent influence on the political and ecclesiastical affairs of his time.

PRAYER   *Almighty God, You endowed St. Hugh, Your Abbot, with outstanding spiritual gifts, which enabled him to enhance the life of the Church in his day. By his intercession, help us to have a spiritual life that will lead to the good of others. This we ask through Christ our Lord. Amen.*

ST. JOSEPH COTTOLENGO, Priest

April 30

BORN near Turin, Italy, St. Joseph became a canon of the Church of Corpus Domini ("The Body of the Lord"). In 1827, he opened a little house near his church dedicated to housing the sick and the derelict. It later became the Little House of Divine Providence at Valdocco.

This Little House developed into a kind of township, with asylums, orphanages, hospitals, schools, and workmen of all types. The Saint depended solely on alms to meet the large daily expenses to maintain all these institutions.

Furthermore, St. Joseph kept no accounting books and made no investments. He trusted completely in Divine Providence to see him through—and that trust was never in vain. Above all, this saintly priest was a man of assiduous prayer, which helped him to continue his care of a great many people, especially the most abandoned and needy. He died in 1842 and was canonized by Pope Pius XI in 1934.

REFLECTION St. Joseph is also known as the founder of the Societies of the Little House of Divine Providence. He insisted that it was through the prayers of those who entered into the Congregations he founded that his work went forth. The Saint knew that it was God Who provided the help he needed to take care of the poor souls to whom he administered. We should strive to cultivate a similar trust in God in our lives.

PRAYER   *God our Father, You enabled St. Joseph, Your Priest, to have an abiding trust in Your Providence amid the great charitable works he performed in the world. By his prayers, help us to attain a great trust in Your Divine Help in all our trials and undertakings. This we ask through Christ our Lord. Amen.*

ST. PEREGRINE LAZIOSI, Priest

May 1

PEREGRINE Laziosi was born of a wealthy family at Forli, Italy, in 1260. As a youth he was active in politics as a member of the antipapal party. During one uprising, which the Pope sent St. Philip Benizi to mediate, Philip was struck in the face by Peregrine. When Philip offered the other cheek, Peregrine was so overcome that he repented and converted to Catholicism.

Following the instructions of the Virgin Mary received in a vision, Peregrine went to Siena and joined the Servites. It is believed that he never allowed himself to sit down for thirty years, while as far as possible observing silence and solitude.

Some time later, Peregrine was sent to Forli to found a new house of the Servite Order. An ideal priest, he had a reputation for fervent preaching and being a good confessor. When he was afflicted with cancer of the foot, and amputation had been decided upon, he spent the night before the operation in prayer. The following morning he was completely cured. This miracle caused his reputation to become widespread. He died in 1345 at the age of eighty-five, and he was canonized by Pope Benedict XIII in 1726.

REFLECTION St. Peregrine Laziosi, like St. Paul, was in open defiance of the Church as a youth. Once given the grace of conversion, he became one of the great Saints of his time. His great fervor and qualities as a confessor brought many back to the true Faith.

Afflicted with cancer, Peregrine turned to God and was richly rewarded for his faith, enabling him over many years to lead others to the truth.

PRAYER　*Loving God, may the afflictions we suffer as we await the Kingdom lead us to bring others the Good News of salvation. May we imitate the fervor and piety of St. Peregrine Laziosi so as to become more visible instruments of Your message. This we ask through Christ our Lord. Amen.*

———◆◆———

ST. JEREMIAH, Prophet and Figure of the Messiah

The Same Day—May 1

THE son of Hilkiah the Prophet, Jeremiah was born about 650 B.C. in Anathoth, three miles northeast of Jerusalem. He received his vocation when he was still very young, a vocation that included renunciation of marriage and family. He prophesied for some forty years (626-586 B.C.), becoming one of the four Major Prophets of the Old Testament.

This "Prophet of the Eleventh Hour" had the unpleasant task of foretelling the destruction of the Holy City and the Southern Kingdom—and of witnessing the fulfillment of his prediction. He also foretold the return from the Babylon Exile and uttered the great oracle of the New Covenant (31:31-34), sometimes called "the Gospel before the Gospel." This passage contains his most sublime teaching and is a landmark in Old Testament theology.

The figure of Jeremiah is an image of the suffering just person and holds a very special importance. The figure is a prefiguration of Jesus, "the man of sorrows" acquainted with infirmity and grief (Isaiah 33:3) because of the sins of His people. Hence, Jeremiah predicts the coming of the Messiah and His kingly mission by his life and works as well as by his deeds (23:5-6).

REFLECTION Jeremiah appears as Preacher, Prophet, and Theologian of Messianism and as the type of the suffering Messiah of the Songs of the Servant of the Lord. He manifests His humanity so that we will seek holiness in conjunction with our own humanity. He calls us in times of trial to rely not on the Temple, the Law, circumcision, sacrifices, or any other human source but on God alone, for He saves His people. To rely on God, we must put on a new heart and manifest love and service toward Him.

PRAYER   *O God, in Your wisdom You called Your Prophet St. Jeremiah to prefigure Christ the Messiah by his own person. Through his intercession, help us learn to put on Christ every day of our lives. This we ask through Christ our Lord. Amen.*

ST. WIBORADA, Virgin and Martyr

May 2

WIBORADA was born of a noble family in Aargau, Switzerland, in the ninth century. Her brother Hatto was ordained a priest, and when he became provost of St. Magnus Church, she turned her home into a hospital and would tend the patients her brother would bring to her.

After a pilgrimage to Rome, Hatto took the Benedictine habit at St. Gall Monastery. Wiborada remained for a while in the world and suffered many calumnies. Then she withdrew to a life of solitude near St. Gall Monastery and later moved to a cell next to the Church of St. Magnus, where she practiced extraordinary penance. Her miracles and prophecies attracted many people, including other recluses.

Wiborada foretold her death at the hands of invading Hungarians. The clergy of St. Magnus and St. Gall escaped thanks to her warning, but she refused to leave her cell and was axed to death in 926. She was canonized in 1047 by Pope Clement II.

REFLECTION   St. Wiborada, as a companion to her priest brother, maintained a close relationship with the Church. Eventually she sought the Lord in solitude. Even so her holiness of life attracted others to her. Blessed with the gift of prophecy and miracles, she nevertheless exhibited great humility and did everything for God's honor. She did not fear death and remained in her hermit's cell even though she knew she would be murdered there.

PRAYER   *Lord God, in the midst of many trials and temptations may we, like St. Wiborada, remain faithful to You through lives of prayer, virtue, and good works. This we ask through Christ our Lord. Amen.*

STS. TIMOTHY AND MAURA, Martyrs

May 3

TIMOTHY and Maura were a young Christian couple who lived in Upper Egypt in the third century. Both of them had a fervent love for Scripture, and Timothy served as a lector at the church at Penapeis, near Antinöe.

Timothy and Maura were married only twenty days when Timothy was taken before the governor and asked to turn over his Scripture books to be burned. When Timothy refused, he was forced to endure brutal tortures, including the insertion of red-hot iron instruments into his ears and the cutting off of his eyelids.

When Timothy still would not give in, Maura was arrested in the hope that this would cause

him to yield, but Maura declared herself willing
to die with her husband. Then both Timothy and
Maura were nailed to a wall where they were left
to die over an excruciating nine days. Their martyrdom took place around 286 during the reign
of Diocletian.

REFLECTION   Sts. Timothy and Maura, who in the
worldly sense had everything to live for in their
young married lives, stand today as staunch models
of faith and devotion to the Word of God. Their love
for each other did not stand in the way of their love for
God and Scripture. The whole order of things
was clear for them. Despite the threat of tortures too
horrible to imagine, they together gave their lives
for the Faith, suffering nine days and nights of torment and abuse before entering into the glory of
God.

PRAYER   *Lord God, Your Martyrs Sts. Timothy and
Maura give us hope and courage in the midst of life's
trials. May we like them hold out to the end, ever
faithful to Your Word in both thought and action. This
we ask through Christ our Lord. Amen.*

───────◆•◆───────

ST. ANTONINA, Martyr

May 4

ST. Antonina is commemorated on this day by
the *Revised Roman Martyrology* as a woman
who suffered martyrdom under the governor
named Priscillian during the persecution of Diocletian in the third/fourth century.

The Saint was severely tortured and afflicted with various torments. For three days she was suspended by one arm and then imprisoned for two years. Finally, she was burnt at the stake because of her love for the Lord.

The pre-1970 *Roman Missal* had the following short history: A soldier named N. tried to save St. Antonina, who had been condemned to death during the persecution of Maximian in Constantinople. He changed clothes with her and took her place. However, the ruse was discovered, and both were tortured and then burnt to death.

REFLECTION Whatever was the actual manner of death of St. Antonina's martyrdom, the Church believes that she died a Martyr for Christ and for her Christian Faith. Therefore, she has enrolled Antonina in the Calendar of Saints. We should glorify her and pray that we too may remain steadfast in faith to the end.

PRAYER   *Lord, You enabled St. Antonina, Your Martyr, to overcome all tortures and atrocities and so remain true to her Faith. By her prayers, grant us the grace to remain ever faithful to You all our lives and attain the crown she received. This we ask through Christ our Lord. Amen.*

◆━━━●◆●━━━◆

ST. ANGELO, Priest and Martyr
May 5

ANGELO was born in Jerusalem, the son of Jewish parents who were converts to Christianity. He and his twin brother joined the Carmelites at the age of eighteen.

For five years Angelo lived as a hermit on Mount Carmel. Then he went to Sicily, where he experienced great success in making converts among the Jews, especially in the areas of Palermo and Leocata.

It was in Leocata that he was stabbed to death in 1225 by an individual named Berengarius whom Angelo had denounced for his wicked ways. As he lay dying, Angelo prayed for the people who had been listening to him, but especially for Berengarius who had just stabbed him.

REFLECTION   Called by God to the religious life, Angelo entered into his spiritual journey with great zeal and devotion, first as a hermit and then as a preacher among the people of Sicily. His eloquence in preaching, along with his good example, led many to seek entrance into the Church. Eventually one of the sinners whom he had denounced killed Angelo, giving him the great gift of a martyr's crown. Angelo received life everlasting while asking forgiveness for his murderer.

PRAYER   *Loving God, You ask us to follow Your Son's example in bringing Your Word to others. May we, like St. Angelo, be filled with love for Your Gospel and by our good lives preach it fearlessly. This we ask through Christ our Lord. Amen.*

———◆———

BL. NUNTIUS SULPRIZIO, Layman

The Same Day—May 5

NUNTIUS Sulprizio was born at Abruzzi in 1817. Little is known of his family, but at an early age he was apprenticed as a blacksmith. He was to spend his entire short life in this occupation.

Nuntius was not gifted with good health and his earnings were meager, but he accepted such hardships as God's will for him. In addition, in contrast to the times in which he lived, Nuntius was known for his chastity of life. He overcame the social immorality of his day and became both a model and a challenge to his young companions and those with whom he worked.

Nuntius's contemporaries attest that there was always something special about him. The graces of his baptism were preserved in his life and he refused to become involved in the ways of the world. His good example was such that many of his friends were able to avoid the pitfalls of sin. Today his life continues to bespeak the dignity of God's creation, especially in the individual person. He died at the age of nineteen in 1836 and was beatified in 1963.

REFLECTION Given the conditions of our day and the role of Mary whom we honor this month, the life of Bl. Nuntius exhorts all to redoubled efforts to maintain or recapture the ideal of chastity. A chaste and holy life can be marked with great happiness and joy both here and hereafter.

PRAYER *Father of the lowly, in Your goodness You endowed Your servant Bl. Nuntius with great joy and purity of heart. May we follow You as he did in our search for the pearl of great price. This we ask through Christ our Lord. Amen.*

ST. EDBERT, Bishop
May 6

EDBERT was born in England in the seventh century. There seems to be no information about his early years. St. Bede the Venerable notes that he was a monk who had a reputation for an extensive knowledge of the Bible as well as for personal sanctity.

Edbert showed great generosity to the poor, distributing to them one-tenth of all his goods. Eventually he was appointed as bishop of the See of Lindisfarne in England as successor to St. Cuthbert. He remained at Lindisfarne for eleven years, until his death. Twice yearly he withdrew into solitude in order to fast and pray.

When St. Cuthbert's body was found to be intact, Edbert had the body placed above ground for veneration. Shortly thereafter, he himself fell sick and was buried in St. Cuthbert's former grave after his death in 698. His relics were transferred to Durham in 875.

REFLECTION It is interesting to note that St. Edbert's familiarity with Scripture moved him to be exceedingly generous to the poor. As receivers of God's great gift of His Word, we should ask ourselves about our conviction from the Bible as regards our individual responsibility toward the poor.

PRAYER   *Almighty Father of our Lord Jesus Christ, Your Son came that we might live with You forever. Through the merits and intercession of St. Edbert, may we, like Jesus, have as our primary care and concern Your beloved poor. This we ask through Christ our Lord. Amen.*

———◆━◆———

ST. PETER NOLASCO, Priest

The Same Day—May 6

P ETER Nolasco was born of a noble family around the year 1180 at Languedoc, France. When he was fifteen years of age, his father died, leaving him a substantial fortune, which he used in Barcelona to rescue Christian slaves from the Moors.

Eventually, Peter decided to found a religious congregation whose object would be the ransoming of Christian slaves. He and St. Raymond of Peñafort, his spiritual director, founded the Order of Our Lady of Ransom, also known as the Mercedarians.

Diocesan approval of the Order was given in 1223, and papal approval followed in 1235 during the reign of Gregory IX.

As master general, Peter traveled frequently into Moorish Spain. Once while in Algeria he was imprisoned for a short time. He died on May 13, 1249.

REFLECTION   St. Peter Nolasco's lively faith and piety bolstered his zeal for freeing those enslaved by the Moors. He carried out several redemptions and was always ready to give his own life for the freedom of captives in danger of denying the Faith. Like Peter, our faith and zeal should lead us to lives of holiness dedicated to the welfare of and concern for those enslaved by sin and excess. Our good example will free them for eternal salvation.

PRAYER   *O God, You clothed St. Peter Nolasco, Your priest, with the love of Christ; and through the Blessed Virgin Mary You made him a messenger of love and liberty for Christians held in captivity. Help us to imitate him by working for the redemption of all the oppressed and for the building up of Your Church. This we ask through Christ our Lord. Amen.*

ST. DOMITILLA, Martyr

May 7

ST. Domitilla was the daughter of the sister of St. Flavius Clemens, a Roman consul who became a convert. During the persecution of Domitian (85-96 A.D.), she was accused of refusing to sacrifice to the gods and of bearing witness to Christ. She was exiled to the island of Ponza and endured a long martyrdom there.

Some hagiographers believe that there were two Christian women who had the name Flavia Domitilla. The elder was the daughter of a sister of Emperor Domitian and Titus and was herself the wife of St. Flavius Clemens. The second Domitilla was a niece of this woman—and the Saint commemorated this day.

REFLECTION   Nobility was in the family of St. Domitilla, but she did not cling to earthly honors. She chose instead to follow the only real nobility, that of Christ—to give her life in His service. By her martyrdom she attained that nobility forever.

PRAYER   *Almighty God, You called St. Domitilla, Your Martyr, to follow Your Son and give up the nobility of earth. By her prayers, help us to renounce the pleasures of this world and serve You every day of our lives. This we ask through Christ our Lord. Amen.*

ST. VICTOR MAURUS, Martyr

May 8

VICTOR Maurus was a native of Mauretania, born in the third century, and was called Maurus to distinguish him from other confessors named Victor. He is believed to have been a soldier in the Praetorian guard.

Victor was a Christian from his youth, but it was not until he was an elderly man that he was arrested for the Faith. After severe tortures, including being basted with molten lead, he was decapitated under Maximian in Milan around 304. Later a church was erected over his grave.

According to St. Gregory of Tours, many miracles occurred at the shrine. In 1576, at the behest of St. Charles Borromeo, Victor's relics were transferred to a new church in Milan established by the Olivetan monks. The church still bears St. Victor's name today.

REFLECTION   After a life of adherence to the Faith during perilous times, St. Victor Maurus was taken prisoner and tortured as an old man. Despite age, infirmity, and declining health, he remained steadfast in the Faith, gladly giving up his life for the Kingdom. His generous response to the call to martyrdom stands as a solemn sign to the modern Church of the folly of the things of this world.

PRAYER   *Loving God, like Your Martyr St. Victor Maurus, may we set aside the things of this earth and keep our minds and hearts set clearly on the ways of salvation. This we ask through Christ our Lord. Amen.*

———◆◆———

ST. ACACIUS, Martyr

The Same Day—May 8

ORIGINALLY from third-century Cappadocia, St. Acacius became a centurion in the Roman army and a Christian. When the persecution of Diocletian and Maximinus was in full sway early in the fourth century, Acacius was denounced by a tribune at Perinthus in Thrace.

The Saint was subjected to severe tortures but steadfastly refused to deny the Faith. In the end, he was taken to Byzantium (i.e., Constantinople) and endured a public scourging. Then he was beheaded.

So well known did St. Acacius become as a Christian Martyr that Constantine the Great built a church in his honor in Constantinople. It is said to have housed the walnut tree on which the Saint had been hung while being scourged.

Other forms of his name are: Acaro, Achatius, and Agario, and he is listed as one of the Fourteen Holy Helpers.†

REFLECTION   No matter by what name we call him, St. Acacius is a man who died for Christ and who imitated Christ. He reminds us that we too must live for Christ every day so that in the end we will also die for Him and attain the glory of Heaven.

PRAYER   *Lord God, You enabled St. Acacius to give up his life as he followed Your Son and then gained the Martyr's crown. By his prayers, help us to remain steadfast in faith throughout life and come to heavenly glory upon death. This we ask through Christ our Lord. Amen.*

---

† A group of Saint-Martyrs regularly invoked during the Middle Ages for emergencies or afflictions, and particularly at the hour of death. Although the names of the Saints as well as their special intercessions varied from place to place, the most common listing was: Sts. *Acacius* (May 8: for headaches and pain); *Barbara* (Dec. 4: for lightning and sudden death); *Blase* (Feb. 3: for ailments of the throat); *Catherine of Alexandria* (Nov. 25: for diseases of the tongue); *Christopher* (July 25: for hurricanes and accidents to travelers); *Cyriacus* (Aug. 8: for possession by the devil); *Denis* (Oct. 9: for headaches and demonic possession); *Erasmus or Elmo* (June 2: for epilepsy, insanity, and sterility); *Eustachius* (Sept. 20: for diseases of the intestines); *George* (April 23: for danger from fires); *Giles* (Sept. 1: for infections of the skin); *Margaret or Marina* (July 20: for help with pregnancy); *Pantaleon* (July 27: for consumption); and *Vitus* (June 15: for hydrophobia, snake bites, and "St. Vitus Dance").

BL. THERESA OF JESUS GERHARDINGER,
Virgin
May 9

CAROLINE Gerhardinger was born on June 20, 1797, near Regensberg, Germany, the daughter of working class parents. Little is known of her childhood. At the age of six she attended school under the Canonesses of St. Augustine. In 1809, she witnessed the nuns being expelled from their convent by government decree.

Later, Caroline was tutored by Bishop Michael Wittmann, and his counsel convinced her to devote her life to God and Christian education. The bishop suggested that she and her companions might live under a mitigated rule.

In 1828, Bavaria and the Holy See signed a concordat under which convents were permitted to open. Caroline and her companions then committed themselves to God and Christian education by vow. The group was invited to Munich to establish schools, and King Ludwig financed the remodeling of the former Poor Clare convent.

This group eventually became the School Sisters of Notre Dame. Caroline took the name Theresa and because of her devotion to Jesus in the Blessed Sacrament came to be known as Theresa of Jesus. She set about establishing the group and had much to suffer in the process.

On January 23, 1854, the Holy See approved Bl. Theresa's Rule and Constitutions. She died on May 9, 1879, and was beatified on November 17, 1985, by Pope John Paul II.

REFLECTION Bl. Theresa of Jesus Gerhardinger spent her entire adult life in the cause of Christian education. She gathered a group of dedicated women around her to share in this goal, and despite great obstacles and much opposition, she persevered and was rewarded for her efforts as she lived to see her fledgling Congregation of the School Sisters of Notre Dame receive papal approval. The immeasurable contribution of Bl. Theresa's perseverance to Christian education cannot be overestimated.

PRAYER *God our Father, You assure us that those who teach shall shine like stars for all eternity. Like Bl. Theresa of Jesus Gerhardinger, may our lives be a timely lesson in Christian education and living. This we ask through Christ our Lord. Amen.*

———◆—◆———

ST. ISAIAH, Prophet
The Same Day—May 9

ISAIAH was the greatest of the Prophets and one of the major witnesses of the Messianic hope in Israel. His ministry began in the second half of the eighth century B.C., which saw the collapse of the Northern Kingdom (722) and the constant peril of the Southern Kingdom at the hands of her foes.

The Saint was a man of great vision, ability, and political influence whose message is

MAY 9

the Lord and the pettiness and sinfulness of
human beings.

Isaiah's prophecies concerning Immanuel
have earned him the title of the Fifth Evangelist
because of their Messianic character and their
influence on Christian revelation. Isaiah also attacked social injustices as the most indicative
sign of Judah's tenuous relationship with God.

The Saint exhorts his hearers to trust in their
omnipotent God and to live accordingly. Justice
and righteousness, teaching and word, and assurance of Divine blessing upon the faithful and
punishment upon the faithless are recurrent
themes in his message from the Holy One of Israel to a proud and stubborn people.

REFLECTION St. Isaiah reminds us that God is just
and holy. He abhors sin and has set in motion a Divine plan to overcome it centering around the teachings and deeds of His incarnate Son. All who adhere
to faith in Him and live according to the Covenant
made in His Son Jesus will escape sin—for Jesus
came in the flesh to be the sole bringer of salvation.

PRAYER *O God, in Your wisdom You called St.
Isaiah, Your Prophet, to prepare the world for the
coming of Your Son and His Kingdom. By his prayers,
teach us how to read his wonderful words and take
them to heart. This we ask through Christ our Lord.
Amen.*

ST. JOHN OF AVILA, Priest

May 10—Apostle of Andalusia

JOHN was born of wealthy parents at Almodóvar del Campo in New Castile, Spain, on January 6, 1499. At the age of fourteen he was sent to the University of Salamanca to study law.

However, John was attracted to the religious life and left the university to live in austere circumstances. Later he studied at Alcalà and was ordained a priest.

Upon the death of his parents, John inherited much wealth, but he gave most of it to the poor. He had a reputation as an outstanding preacher and served as a missionary in Andalusia. He is often called the Apostle of Andalusia.

John's popularity as a preacher continued to grow. Eventually he became the spiritual director of St. Teresa of Avila, St. John of the Cross, St. Francis Borgia, and St. Peter of Alcantara. He died on May 10, 1569, at Montilla, Spain.

John's ascetical writings, especially his letters, are Spanish classics. He was beatified by Pope Leo XIII in 1894 and canonized by Pope Paul VI in 1970.

REFLECTION   The wonders, works, and conversions that St. John was able to accomplish in his lifetime he attributed to his close relationship with God. When one considers the austerities practiced by Saints like John, one can only imagine the joys they experienced. If we want to see true peace, joy, and happiness, we must look to holiness of life.

PRAYER   *God our Father, You call Your children to find their happiness here and hereafter in Your loving presence. Through the merits and prayers of St. John of Avila, may we learn the true meaning of prayer and fasting in our lives. This we ask through Christ our Lord. Amen.*

———◆—◆———

ST. JOB, Exemplar of Patience

The Same Day—May 10

JOB is the main character of the Biblical Book of Job and a faithful servant of the Lord. Without warning he suddenly becomes afflicted with the loss of his family and contracts a devastating sickness. However, he bears all this with uncommon patience. Three friends come to dialogue with him and try to make sense out of his misfortune.

The friends put forth the common Old Testament belief that his afflictions are the result of some sin on his part. Although accepting his fate, Job steadfastly refuses to accept the idea that he has sinned.

Ultimately, God speaks from the tempest, and Job finds peace in His presence. Job is declared to be in the right against the belief of his friends. In the end, Job receives a new family and greater prosperity than before. Accordingly, Job is the leading exemplar of patience and trust in God when misfortunes come to human beings.

REFLECTION Even though Job is shown to be in the right, God points out to him the many things that he does not know. It is God—and not any human being—Who runs the world. Therefore, in time of adversity, we should not complain but always place our trust in Him alone.

PRAYER   *O God, in Your wisdom You raised up St. Job, Your servant, to be an example of true patience and trust in You. By his prayers, teach us to remain ever trusting in Your Divine Providence and so be patient until the trials disappear. This we ask through Christ our Lord. Amen.*

———◆━◆———

ST. IGNATIUS OF LACONI, Religious

May 11

BORN on December 17, 1701, in Laconi on the island of Sardinia, the second of nine children, Ignatius lived in dire poverty. As a youngster he worked in the fields. Eventually, in 1721, at the age of twenty, he entered the Capuchin monastery of St. Benedict at Buoncammino, despite the objections of his father, and in 1722 he took his vows.

Thus Ignatius began his life as a lay brother that would last over sixty years. He worked for many years in the monastery weaving-room, and for the last forty years of his life he would beg from door to door and in the streets.

Rumors of Ignatius's holiness began to circulate. He was loved by the street children, and people seemed to regain their health after he spoke with them. When he came in from his begging rounds, Ignatius would spend nearly the entire night in prayer. Eventually, worn out by his labors, his health began to fail and he died on May 11, 1781. He was canonized by Pope Pius XII in 1951.

REFLECTION   The hidden life of the lay brother St. Ignatius of Laconi reveals to us the necessity of rooting pride from our minds and hearts. Much of the good Ignatius accomplished sprang from his humble acceptance of God's will in doing the most menial tasks.

PRAYER   *Gracious God, pour down upon us the humble spirit of St. Ignatius. May we have the grace and courage to root out pride from our lives. This we ask through Christ our Lord. Amen.*

———◆———

ST. EPIPHANIUS OF SALAMIS, Bishop

May 12

EPIPHANIUS was born at Besanduk, Palestine, around 315. Eventually he became a monk and was well versed in five languages in his pursuit of knowledge of Holy Scripture. For a while he lived in several communities in Egypt, but he returned to Palestine around 333, was ordained, and built a monastery at Eleutheropolis, of which he was superior.

Epiphanius was well known for his scholarship, spirituality, practice of self-denial, and ability as a spiritual director. In 367, he was chosen Bishop of Constantia and then Metropolitan of Cyprus, while at the same time he remained head of his monastery.

Although Epiphanius preached against Arianism, the Arian emperor Valens did not restrain him. Hardly a model of diplomacy, Epiphanius did not hesitate to confront those with whom he disagreed, including the Bishop of Jerusalem and St. John Chrysostom. He died in 403 while traveling from Constantinople to Salamis. An authority on devotion to Mary, he wrote many theological treatises.

REFLECTION   The roots and tradition of devotion to Mary extend beyond the time of St. Epiphanius. Nonetheless, we see in him a significant mind who marked the importance of devotion to Mary. In this month of Mary let us renew our personal devotion to her while at the same time imitating her desire to do God's will.

PRAYER   *Lord, when Your Son Jesus hung on the Cross He gave His Mother to the Church. Through the example and intercession of St. Epiphanius, may we honor her with lives of truth, virtue, humility, chastity, and obedience. This we ask through Christ our Lord. Amen.*

———◆—◆———

BL. JULIANA OF NORWICH, Anchoress

May 13

JULIANA (also known as Julian) was born around 1342. Little is known of her early life. However, her reputation became widespread as one who recorded sixteen revelations she experienced in a state of ecstasy. They are found in her book *Revelations of Divine Love*, also called "The Shewings."

Juliana's writings are considered to be some of the most deeply spiritual of her age. She wrote about the power of love versus evil, the Trinity, and Christ's Passion. Much of her work is transcendentally doctrinal, with little or no effort at methodological direction.

At the age of sixty-one, Juliana shut herself up in seclusion at a church in Conisford, Norwich. Little is recorded about her after her leave-taking. Her death is placed around 1423.

Why Juliana chose Norwich is unclear, and whether or not she was a native of Norwich is another unanswered question. Although she is almost universally recognized as Blessed, there has never been any formal ceremony of beatification. She is not listed in the *Revised Roman Martyrology*.

REFLECTION   Sometimes God in His own way communicates with individuals. Apparently that is the case with Bl. Juliana. Much was revealed in her relationship with God that has remained worthwhile over the centuries. Such revelations assure us that Jesus came to call all people to holiness and salvation.

PRAYER   *Almighty Father of our Lord Jesus Christ, we praise and worship You for the many holy people You send into our midst. May we strive to imitate the virtue, trust, and faith of Bl. Juliana in You. Amen.*

ST. SERVATIUS (or SERVAIS), Bishop

The Same Day—May 13

BORN in the fourth century, St. Servatius (also known as Servais) was probably an Armenian and in time he was made Bishop of Tongres, Belgium. In this position, he came to the defense of St. Athanasius and offered him refuge upon the latter's exile.

After the murder of Constans, Servatius was sent by the usurper Magnentius together with another prelate to plead the usurper's cause before Emperor Constantius II. In 359, Servatius actively opposed the Arians at the Council of Rimini.

The Saint foretold the invasion of Gaul by the Huns (which came to pass seventy years after his death) and strove to ward off this evil by fasting and prayer as well as a pilgrimage to Rome. On his return home, St. Servatius contracted a fatal fever and died about the year 384.

REFLECTION St. Servatius strove mightily to spare his flock the two evils: the Arian heresy and the invasion of the Huns under Attila. He was able to slow down the first, but the second was out of his hands since he was long dead when it occurred. His life reminds us that we too should do everything we can to form the right idea about the teachings of the Church and pray to ward off evil.

PRAYER *Almighty God, You made St. Servatius, Your Bishop, the defender of the Christian Faith and his flock. By his prayers, help us to remain true to the*

Faith and pray daily for the Church and clergy. This we ask through Christ our Lord. Amen.

———◆•◆———

ST. MARY MAZZARELLO, Virgin

MARY Mazzarello was born in 1837 at Mornese, near Genoa, Italy. The child of peasants, she worked in the fields, and when she was seventeen she joined a sodality of the Daughters of Mary Immaculate founded by a disciple of St. John Bosco.

In 1860, Mary was stricken with typhoid and was unable to work in the fields any longer. She then started dressmaking with a friend named Petronella. Like Don Bosco, Mary and Petronella became interested in working with youth.

In 1872, Don Bosco founded a group of nuns with Pope Pius IX's permission. Mary was appointed superioress of the Daughters of Our Lady Help of Christians, also known as the Salesian Sisters. The congregation spread quickly and expanded its goals to charitable works as well as teaching. Mary died at the motherhouse in Nizza Monferrato in 1881. She was canonized by Pope Pius XII in 1951.

REFLECTION St. Mary Mazzarello from her earliest years worked hard and lived the simple peasant lifestyle. Always fervent in her prayers, she was active in pious organizations. Eventually, with her companion Petronella and through the efforts of Don Bosco, she

became superioress of the Salesian Sisters, a group of dedicated women that numbered over eight hundred foundations by 1900. Her example is a vivid reminder that a lifestyle lived in cooperation with God's grace can work wonders.

PRAYER   *Loving God, You raised up St. Mary Mazzarello for the Christian education of youth. May her virtue and goodness inspire other women to dedicate themselves to Christian education and works of charity. This we ask through Christ our Lord. Amen.*

———◆–◆———

ST. SEVERINUS, Bishop of Septempeda
May 15

ST. Severinus and his brother St. Victorinus came from a well-to-do family. In time, they distributed their wealth among the poor and needy and lived as hermits at Montenero.

The two brothers were highly regarded as holy men, and Pope Vigilius chose them to be Bishops of the Church. Victorinus ruled Camerino, and Severinus presided over Septempeda in the Marshes of Ancona, Italy.

Such was the reverence in which Severinus was held by all the people that the name of Septempeda was changed to San Severino in his honor. The holy man died around 550 shortly before Septempeda was destroyed by the Ostrogoths under Totila.

REFLECTION   St. Severinus was a man who longed to live the life of a hermit in profound communication with God. However, he was needed to help spread the Faith. So he led the busy life of the early bishops who worked indefatigably to build the Church of God. He did it so well that his name lives on in the city that he served most of his life.

PRAYER   *Almighty God, You called St. Severinus from the eremitical life to shepherd the Church at Septempeda. Through his intercession, help us to discover Your will for us and to do it willingly and well. This we ask through Christ our Lord. Amen.*

———◆———

ST. ANDREW BOBOLA, Priest and Martyr

May 16

ANDREW Bobola was born of an aristocratic Polish family in Sandormir, Poland, in 1591. He entered the Jesuits in 1611, at Vilna, Lithuania. Ordained in 1622, he began his parish ministry in Vilna, and, in 1630, he was appointed superior of the Jesuit community at Bobrinsk, where he became renowned for his heroic charity during a plague.

From 1636 until 1656, Andrew was a successful missionary to the Orthodox, reconciling entire villages of separated Orthodox with Rome. Meanwhile Cossack, Russian, and Tartar raids on Poland forced the Jesuits into hiding. In 1652, Prince Radziwill gave Andrew a house in Pinsk to serve as a refuge for Jesuits.

In 1657, Andrew was captured during a Cossack raid on Pinsk. He was severely beaten, but when he refused to renounce his Faith, he was subjected to the most barbaric tortures, and finally was beheaded at Janow on May 16, 1657. He was canonized by Pope Pius XI in 1938.

REFLECTION St. Andrew Bobola, a very successful preacher and a holy religious, was eventually caught up in the politics and religious hatred of his day. Despite the dangers involved, he continued to work for the good of souls. Once captured, he maintained his Faith in the midst of the most unspeakable tortures until he was finally beheaded. His life contributed to the firm establishment of the true Faith in Poland.

PRAYER   *Loving God, in Your wisdom You raised St. Andrew Bobola to the altar of sanctity and blessed him with the crown of martyrdom. May we imitate his faith-filled courage in fulfilling the duties of our state in life. This we ask through Christ our Lord. Amen.*

ST. RESTITUTA, Virgin and Martyr

May 17

AT the height of the Roman Empire in the third century, according to whoever ruled at the moment, the followers of Christ were sometimes allowed to practice their Faith somewhat openly, but on occasion they were the object of the most harsh persecution.

In the case of St. Restituta she was a victim of the persecution of either Valerian or Diocletian.

An African maiden, she apparently lived in Carthage. As a result of her dedication to the Christian religion, she was sought out and martyred about the year 304.

It is believed that Restituta's relics are enclosed in a reliquary in the Cathedral of Naples.

REFLECTION The seven swords that pierced the heart of the Blessed Mother stand in stark contrast to the brutal murder of St. Restituta. Yet what Mary accomplished for the Church as the suffering Mother of Jesus, St. Restituta sustained in shedding her blood for the Church. Mary's "fiat" and St. Restituta's life given for the Faith speak volumes to the Church on earth. The important thing is that we learn to listen.

PRAYER *O God, You preserve Your Church through the blood of Your holy Martyrs. Through the prayers of St. Restituta, make us worthy inheritors of the Faith, willing to accept the challenges from both within and without. This we ask through Christ our Lord. Amen.*

———◆———

ST. ERIC OF SWEDEN, Martyr

May 18—*Patron of Sweden*

IN 1150, Eric was recognized as king in most parts of Sweden. He was responsible for the spread of Christianity in upper Sweden, and at Old Uppsala he built the first large church to be erected in that country. He also codified the ancient laws of his kingdom.

Eric next had to deal with the Finns who were raiding his lands. After he defeated the Finns, he asked the Englishman, St. Henry, Bishop of Uppsala, to evangelize the people of Finland. However, some of Eric's nobles were opposed to the Faith, and they conspired against him with Magnus, the son of the king of Denmark.

Around Ascension time, the Danish army marched on Sweden. As Eric went out from church to meet the Danish army, the conspirators pulled him down from his horse and cut off his head. The date of his martyrdom was May 18, 1161. Until the Protestant Reformation, St. Eric was regarded as the principal Patron of Sweden.

REFLECTION Although never formally canonized, St. Eric was a layperson of extraordinary zeal for the Faith. Not only did he spread the Faith in his realms but he also built substantial places of worship. Moreover, in his zeal for the Faith, he sponsored St. Henry's evangelization of the Finns. As a result he gained the crown of martyrdom. His life elicits admiration for his courage and determination to spread the Faith and calls for our imitation.

PRAYER O God, You have given us the great gift of faith. Like the Mother of God, may we be open to Your will in our lives, and live according to Your Word so that others may share our Faith. This we ask through Christ our Lord. Amen.

STS. CALOCERUS AND PARTHENIUS,
Martyrs

IN the third century, Calocerus and Parthenius were brothers who were eunuchs in the palace of Tryphonia, the wife of the emperor Decius. They were Armenians who had come to Rome with a consul named Aemilian. When Aemilian died, they were left in charge of his daughter Anatolia.

Calocerus and Parthenius were summoned before Decius on the dual charge of being Christian and of wasting Anatolia's inheritance. The two brothers made a courageous defense of their Faith, but they were condemned to be burned alive in 304.

Miraculously Calocerus and Parthenius emerged from the flames unscathed. Thereupon they were beaten on the head with flaming sticks until they were dead. Anatolia had their bodies buried in the cemetery of Callistus.

REFLECTION Despite the rather wretched condition of their lives, St. Calocerus and Parthenius were individuals of deep spirituality. When asked to renounce the Faith, they refused to do so despite the certainty of death for their refusal. In the end they gained a martyr's crown and willingly planted the seeds of the Faith in the Roman Empire.

PRAYER *Loving God, in faith we turn to You as we make our way through a hostile world. Like Sts. Calo-*

cerus and Parthenius, may we willingly profess our Faith through lives of peace and virtue. This we ask through Christ our Lord. Amen.

───◆◆───

ST. THEODORE OF PAVIA, Bishop

May 20

LITTLE is known of the early life of St. Theodore of Pavia. We are first introduced to him as Bishop of Pavia.

Theodore headed the See of Pavia from about 750 to 785. During his thirty-five year service in Pavia, he was subject to great opposition. Several times he was banished from his diocese by the Arian Lombard kings.

Undoubtedly Theodore preached against the Arian heresy and was thus punished. Nonetheless, he remained faithful to the end and achieved the goal of Sainthood.

REFLECTION Just as was true in the life of St. Theodore, Church leaders today are experiencing great obstacles to their teaching and preaching the truth of the Gospel. The bishops' pro-life stance for all individuals and their attempts to stem the tide of egotistical sexuality have won for Church leaders threats, hate expressed in the media, and a strong undercurrent of opposition among some Church members. Our times call for a strong faith and perseverance in virtue.

PRAYER *God our Father, through the intercession of Your Bishop St. Theodore, strengthen the faith of*

*the Church as she condemns the murder of innocent
children and the desecration of human sexuality. This
we ask through Christ our Lord. Amen.*

———◆●◆———

ST. EUGENE DE MAZENOD, Founder
May 21

EUGENE de Mazenod was born on August 1,
1782, at Aix-en-Provence in France. Early in
life he experienced the upheaval of the French
Revolution. Nonetheless, he entered the seminary, and following ordination he returned to
labor in Aix-en-Provence.

That area had suffered greatly during the revolution and was not really a safe place for a
priest. Eugene directed his ministry toward the
poorest of the poor. Others joined his labors, and
this became the nucleus of a religious community, the Missionaries of Provence.

Later Eugene was named Bishop of Marseille.
There he built churches, founded parishes, cared
for his priests, and developed catechetics for the
young. Later he founded the Oblates of Mary Immaculate, and in 1841 the Oblates sailed for missions in five continents. Pius XI said, "The
Oblates are the specialists of difficult missions."

After a life dedicated to spreading the Good
News, Eugene died on May 21, 1861. He was be-
atified by Pope Paul VI in 1975 and canonized by
Pope John Paul II on December 3, 1995.

REFLECTION   The Oblates of Mary Immaculate continue to carry on the work initiated by St. Eugene de Mazenod. His strong faith, spirit of detachment, and total acceptance of direction of the Holy Spirit is responsible for bringing the Faith and Sacraments to untold numbers in difficult mission lands. As we celebrate St. Eugene's memory, let us open ourselves completely to the Holy Spirit and the support of our missionaries.

PRAYER   *Father of our Lord Jesus Christ, through the merits and intercession of St. Eugene, send us the fullness of the Holy Spirit so that in whatever way possible we may participate in the good works of our missionaries. This we ask through Christ our Lord. Amen.*

ST. HUMILITY, Abbess

May 22

HUMILITY was born at Faenza, Italy, in 1226. She was baptized Rosanna by her well-to-do parents. At age fifteen, she married a nobleman named Ugoletto. Their happy marriage produced two children, both of whom died in infancy.

After nine years of marriage, Ugoletto narrowly escaped death. Thereupon both Rosanna (still only twenty-four) and Ugoletto decided to enter the dual monastery of St. Perpetua near Faenza. Ugoletto entered as a lay brother, and Rosanna as a nun, taking the name Humility. For twelve years she lived as a recluse in a cell near the church of St. Apollinaris, practicing great austerities under the direction of St. Crispin.

Later, at the suggestion of the abbot of the Vallombrosans, Humility became the founding abbess of Santa Maria Novella Convent at Malta, the first Vallombrosan convent for nuns. Later, the Saint founded a second convent at Florence, Italy, where she died on May 22, 1310, at the age of eighty-four.

REFLECTION St. Humility's life with her husband Ugoletto was such that both could have worked out their eternal salvation in their married state. However, events in their lives convinced them to enter the religious life in a dual monastery. After twelve years in seclusion, prayer, and mortification, Humility was chosen to found two convents. Her personal spirituality contributed much to making both houses successful foundations. Her holiness and detachment are models for all couples who experience challenges in their marriage relationships.

PRAYER *O God, through the intercession of St. Humility may we be faithful to our commitments in life, particularly in our relationships with one another. This we ask through Christ our Lord. Amen.*

ST. DESIDERIUS, Bishop and Martyr

May 23

ST. Desiderius is said to have been originally from Genoa. He went to preach the Faith in

France and became Bishop of Langres. He was there when the fierce Vandals, who were Arians, invaded France in the fifth century. The Vandals besieged the city and could have captured it only with great difficulty because its inhabitants fought with indomitable valor.

As a result, the aggressors resorted to sacking the city with unmitigated fury. At that point, Bishop Desiderius sought to end the carnage and bring peace. He made his way to the head of the barbarians, presented him with a Gospel, and pleaded for his people.

However, the Vandal leader was unmoved. He ordered the Bishop to be beaten and put to death. The Book of the Gospel was stained with the Saint's blood as he offered himself for his flock.

REFLECTION St. Desiderius made a desperate attempt to bring peace to his city and ended up following Christ's example by giving his life for his flock. His life is a reminder that we must always seek peace and be ready even to die for it.

PRAYER   *Lord God, You gave St. Desiderius, Your Bishop and Martyr, the strength to strive for peace in the face of a fierce invader. By his prayers, help us to seek peace and justice for our family, for our country, and for the world. This we ask through Christ our Lord. Amen.*

ST. SIMEON STYLITES THE YOUNGER,
Hermit
May 24

BORN in Antioch in 521, St. Simeon at the age of five went to the nearby hill country after the death of his father and came under the protection of a monk named John. Both Simeon and John lived on platforms on top of columns in order to ensure solitude. Simeon ascended his platform at seven years of age.

At the age of twenty, in order to avoid pilgrims, Simeon retired to a more inaccessible mountain refuge. After ten years, he established a monastery, and at the same time, he had a column built there for himself. He lived on this column for the last forty-five years of his life.

When Simeon was thirty-five, he was ordained, with the bishop ascending the column to impose hands. Simeon would celebrate Mass on his platform and the monks would climb a ladder to receive the Eucharist from him. Many cures and miracles were attributed to him. He died in 592, having spent the final sixty-odd years of his life upon a pillar.

REFLECTION   In reflecting upon the unusual holiness, lifestyles, mortifications, and supernatural phenomena associated with St. Simeon, we assure ourselves that conversion of life is well worth pursuing. We need not look for special interventions but should accept the rigors of fulfilling the duties of our state in life.

PRAYER   *Father in Heaven, as we await the Second Coming of Your Son, You bid us draw closer to You in prayer, virtue, and good works. Through the intercession of St. Simeon Stylites the Younger, grant us the grace always to keep in mind our personal salvation and the evangelization of others through well-lived lives. This we ask through Christ our Lord. Amen.*

———◆———

ST. MADELEINE SOPHIE BARAT, Virgin
May 25

MADELEINE Sophie Barat was born on December 12, 1779, at Joigny in Burgundy, France. Her older brother, who was studying for the priesthood, saw to Madeleine's early education and discipline. Since she was a very attractive young lady, her priest-brother was afraid that she would be led astray, and thus he moved her to Paris where he lived.

Since she had great interest in the Christian education of young ladies, on November 21, 1800, Madeleine entered religious life, and one year later she went to Amiens to found the first school and convent of her new congregation of nuns, the Society of the Sacred Heart of Jesus. She was appointed superioress at the age of twenty-three and she held that office for sixty-three years.

Many other branches continued to open, and in 1818, Rose-Phillippine Duchesne was sent with four companions to work in North America. In 1826, with the approval of Pope Leo XII, the Society of the Sacred Heart was formally established.

Madeleine died on May 25, 1865, at the age of eighty-six. She was canonized in 1925 by Pope Pius XI.

REFLECTION Although possessed of great natural beauty and a multiplicity of talents, St. Madeleine Sophie Barat responded to the call for the Christian education of youth. She gathered a small group to begin the religious life, and in a short time she was appointed superior of the fledgling organization. Under her very capable leadership, Madeleine's congregation opened foundations in twelve countries on two continents, and she continued in her office as superi-

oress for sixty-three years, until her death. The good that her congregation and its schools have accomplished throughout the years speaks eloquently of her love for and devotion to her Lord.

PRAYER   *O God, You raised up Your servant St. Madeleine Sophie Barat for the Christian education of youth. May we always be open to and supportive of dedicated teachers. Bless their work with Your loving presence. This we ask through Christ our Lord. Amen.*

———◆—◆—◆———

ST. MARIANA OF QUITO, Virgin
May 26

MARIANA was born in 1618 in Quito, Ecuador. Her parents were of the Spanish nobility, but she was orphaned as a child, and she was raised with loving care by her sister and her sister's husband.

Early in life Mariana was attracted to religion, and at the age of twelve she became a recluse in her sister's house, under the direction of a Jesuit. She never left that house for the rest of her life, except to go to church. She ate very little, slept only three hours a night, and was reputed to have had the gifts of prophecy and miracles.

In 1645, Quito was ravaged by an earthquake and epidemic. Mariana offered herself publicly as a victim for the sins of the people. The earthquake immediately ended, and as the epidemic began to subside, Mariana was taken ill and died on May 26, 1645, at the age of twenty-six. Known

as the "Lily of Quito," she was canonized in 1950 by Pope Pius XII.

REFLECTION St. Mariana of Quito was attracted to things religious from a very early age, and she dedicated herself completely to God. Her severe mortifications and extended prayer life were accompanied by seemingly miraculous powers. Ever open to the welfare of others, Mariana offered herself in expiation for the sins of the people of Quito. As a result, her union with God was effected and many of her contemporaries were gained for Heaven.

PRAYER *Loving God, we are aware of sin in our lives despite the many graces You send us. May we, through the intercession of St. Mariana of Quito, make reparation for our sinful lives. This we ask through Christ our Lord. Amen.*

———◆◆◆———

ST. BRUNO OF WÜRZBURG, Bishop

May 27

BRUNO was the son of Duke Conrad of Carinthia and Baroness Matilda. He was ordained at an early age and eventually became the Bishop of Würzburg in 1033.

As bishop, Bruno built several churches in his diocese as well as St. Kilian's Cathedral. Moreover, he was a noted scholar of his day and authored several books. At one time he served as an advisor to Conrad II, in which role he was able to effect the end of the siege of Milan.

In 1045, Bruno joined the forces of Emperor Henry III on a campaign against the Hungarians. He died during that year in Austria when a building in which he was staying collapsed.

REFLECTION   Some Saints achieve eternal glory by a life of seclusion. Others like St. Bruno are people of action. He combined administrative expertise, scholarship, and a fervent desire to advance the growth of the Church. In all of these gifts he gave glory to God.

PRAYER   *God our Father, the achievements of St. Bruno did much to strengthen Your Kingdom here on earth. May we live so worthily as to share with him Your Kingdom in Heaven. This we ask through Christ our Lord. Amen.*

BL. MARGARET POLE, Martyr
May 28

MARGARET Plantagenet was born in Farley Castle, near Bath, England, on August 14, 1471, the daughter of the Duke of Clarence and the niece of Kings Edward IV and Richard III of England. In 1491, she married Sir Richard Pole, but eventually she was left a widow with five children. King Henry VIII regarded her highly and made her Countess of Salisbury as well as governess to his daughter Mary.

Margaret incurred Henry's wrath when she disapproved of his intention to marry Anne Boleyn. She was forced out of court, and when her son, Reginald Cardinal Pole, wrote against the Act of Supremacy, Henry swore to destroy the Pole family. Two of her sons were executed in 1538 for being brothers of the cardinal, and ten days later Margaret herself was arrested. In 1539, with the approval of Parliament, Henry had Margaret imprisoned in the Tower of London for supposed complicity in a revolt.

In April 1541, when another uprising occurred, Margaret was beheaded at once. Without benefit of trial or proof of guilt, she suffered martyrdom for the Faith at the age of seventy. She was beatified in 1886 by Pope Leo XIII.

REFLECTION Today Christians are becoming increasingly aware of challenges to their beliefs in rulings imposed upon them by the governing powers in their homelands. We in the United States will not be subjected to martyrdom for upholding the teachings of the Church, as was Bl. Margaret Pole, but we are constantly being opposed for our stands regarding abortion, euthanasia, and moral standards. Bl. Margaret's life gives courage to all Christians in the face of challenge, innuendo, and slander.

PRAYER   *Loving God, through Your Word You have given us the means to justice and peace in this life and eternal salvation in the next. May we, like Bl. Margaret Pole, stand firm in our belief and willingly embrace the barbs and ridicule that others heap upon us. This we ask through Christ our Lord Amen.*

BL. RICHARD THIRKELD, Priest and Martyr

May 29

RICHARD Thirkeld was born in Durham, England, and educated at Oxford. At a very advanced age, after completing studies for the priesthood at Douai and Rheims, he was ordained in 1579 and prayed constantly for the privilege of suffering martyrdom for the Faith.

After ordination, Richard was sent to the area around York. A nighttime visit to a Catholic prisoner aroused suspicion, and shortly thereafter he was arrested. When he admitted that he was a priest, he was placed in Kidcote Prison in York. Two months later he was tried for having heard confessions and was condemned to death.

That night in the prison he ministered to others who had been condemned to death. The Saint accepted his sentence with evangelical joy and was hanged, drawn, and quartered. However the death sentence was carried out in secret because Richard was so greatly venerated by the people. He died in 1583 and was beatified by Pope Leo XIII in 1886.

REFLECTION Having been called to the priesthood at a very late age, Bl. Richard was likewise called to martyrdom, a favor for which he prayed for many years. He ministered to the Catholics of York at great risk, but he did not falter. When he was arrested and condemned to death, he was filled with great joy. What great faith this man of God displayed! His joy in the service of the Lord knew no bounds.

PRAYER   *Loving God, You vested Your servant Bl. Richard Thirkeld with the robe of eternal salvation. May we live our lives for You in the fullness of joy and expectation of sharing Your glory. This we ask through Christ our Lord. Amen.*

ST. FERDINAND III OF CASTILE, King

May 30

FERDINAND was the son of the King of Léon, and his mother was the daughter of the King of Castile. Born in 1198, Ferdinand became King of Castile in 1217 and the King of Léon in 1230. He was strict in the administration of justice, but was quick to forgive personal affronts.

Ferdinand founded the University of Salamanca. However, he is most remembered for his successful twenty-seven-year campaign against the Moors in Spain. He rebuilt the cathedral of Burgos and turned the mosque at Seville into a church. He said that his purpose in fighting the Moors was to rescue Christians from the rule and domination of the infidels.

The father of three children by his wife Joan of Ponthieu, Ferdinand died on May 30, 1252, and was buried in the Cathedral of Seville in the habit of the Friars Minor. In 1671, he was canonized by Pope Clement X.

REFLECTION St. Ferdinand III of Castile ruled his realm with a strong sense of responsibility to God, the source of all power. At the same time, he did not use his power and prestige to destroy individuals who may have disagreed with him. As a good Christian, he fulfilled the demanding responsibilities of his leadership role according to the dictates of the Gospel, using his political and economic power for the good of his people.

PRAYER *O God, we ask You to keep all world leaders aware of their responsibility to You and to their people. Through the intercession of St. Ferdinand, may they ever be mindful that they serve in Your Name and so bring peace and justice to their nations. This we ask through Christ our Lord. Amen.*

ST. PETRONILLA, Virgin and Martyr

May 31

ACTUALLY very little is known of St. Petronilla's life. She lived in the first century, but most scholars consider the story that St. Petronilla was the daughter of the Apostle Peter to be unfounded. However, it is possible that she did minister to him.

There is a generally accepted story that a nobleman named Flaccus proposed marriage to Petronilla. When Petronilla refused, Flaccus gave her three days to reconsider. Petronilla spent those three days in prayer and fasting. Then, continuing to be resolute in her refusal, she was put to death.

It is believed that Petronilla's body was laid to rest in the cemetery of Domitilla, where a fresco exists that clearly depicts her martyrdom.

REFLECTION The lives of the Martyrs can be a great help in moving us to make the kinds of decisions that can be quite positive yet challenging. To love one's enemies, to do good to those who persecute us, to remain chaste in a sexual revolution, to be faithful to commitments made—all these are ways and means of not only strengthening our faith but also sharing in the sufferings of Christ.

PRAYER *Merciful God, our Father, through the intercession of Your Martyr St. Petronilla, may we always strive to be strong in our dedication to follow Your Son Jesus Who lives and reigns forever with You and the Holy Spirit. Amen.*

ST. IÑIGO, Abbot

June 1

IÑIGO, also known as Eneco, born in the eleventh century, was a native of Bilbao, Spain. Early in his life he became a hermit. Next he went to Aragon where he became a monk at San Juan de Peña, and eventually he was elected prior.

When his term was completed, Iñigo again took up the life of a hermit in the Aragon Mountains. However, in 1029, King Sancho the Great convinced Iñigo to become abbot of a group of monks in a monastery at Oña. The monastery, founded by Sancho's father-in-law, was in need of reform, and he wanted Iñigo to lead the process.

Iñigo was very successful in the reform movement, and he developed a reputation as a peacemaker. Moreover, some attributed miracles to his intercession. He died at Oña about the year 1060, and was canonized by Pope Alexander IV in 1259.

REFLECTION St. Iñigo from his earliest years was drawn to both the contemplative and the eremitical life. A man of God, he was able to bring peace and harmony to the monastery at Oña, and he won over others to the reasonableness and satisfaction of leading the monastic life to its fullest. What is more, the good example of the monks helped the people who lived in the area to become convinced of the beauty and satisfaction of a life lived in God's presence and love.

PRAYER   *Almighty Father, may we be open to the Spirit in our lives so that we may imitate the virtues of*

Your servant St. Iñigo. May our lives bring peace to our neighbors. This we ask through Christ our Lord. Amen.

———•—•———

ST. STEPHEN OF SWEDEN,
Bishop and Martyr
June 2

VERY little is known of the early life of St. Stephen of Sweden who lived in the eleventh century. We find him first as a monk at the New Corbie monastery in Saxony. After his ordination, he was sent to Sweden as a missionary bishop.

St. Stephen's work in Sweden was crowned with success, and many were converted. He was the first to establish the Christian Faith on the shores of the Sound that lies between Denmark and Sweden.

As he moved about Sweden, he came into conflict with a group in Uppsala who worshiped the pagan god Woden. Because of his efforts to put a stop to this pagan worship, he was murdered around the year 1075.

REFLECTION   In St. Stephen of Sweden we have an example of one who was full of zeal for the Kingdom of God. Shortly after ordination he was sent to the Swedish missions, and his success in spreading the Word of God eventually led to his martyrdom. A man of prayer and courage, St. Stephen beckons to young people today to follow the challenge of the Gospel and to walk in the footsteps of Jesus.

PRAYER   *Loving God, in Your Covenant with Your people You grant us a share in Your everlasting life. Through the merits and intercession of Your Bishop and Martyr St. Stephen, may we always be full of zeal for living and spreading Your Word. This we ask through Christ our Lord. Amen.*

ST. ERASMUS (or ELMO),
Bishop and Martyr
The Same Day, June 2—Patron of Sailors

WHEN we remove all the later legendary additions from the life of St. Erasmus, our knowledge of him is reduced to the following three facts: (1) he was Bishop of Formiae in Campania, Italy, (2) suffered martyrdom for the Faith under Diocletian around the year 303, (3) and his relics were transferred to Gaeta in 842.

This Saint is also known as Elmo (as well as Erarmo, Ermo, and Telmo). He was one of the Fourteen Holy Helpers (invoked for emergencies or afflictions)† and the Patron of Sailors. The blue lights that are sometimes seen on mastheads before and after storms were regarded by Neapolitan sailors as signs of their Patron's protection and came to be called "St. Elmo's Fire" (or "Lights").

---

† See p. 223.

REFLECTION   St. Erasmus was invoked very often in the past as one of the Fourteen Holy Helpers, i.e., Saints who could be counted upon to come to the aid of their suppliants in their trouble. He is an apt reminder that when we encounter difficulty in life, we should confidently call on the Saints to intercede with God in our behalf.

PRAYER   *Almighty God, You enabled St. Erasmus, Your Bishop and Martyr, to become the Patron of Sailors and to be invoked for diseases such as epilepsy, insanity, and sterility. Through his prayers, may we always be protected from evil on earth and reach our true home in Heaven with You. This we ask through Christ our Lord. Amen.*

ST. CLOTILDA, Queen

June 3

CLOTILDA was born at Lyons, France, around 474. The daughter of King Chilperic of Burgundy, as a young girl she married Clovis, King of the Franks, in 492.

Clotilda sought to convert Clovis to Christianity, and he was officially received into the Christian community on Christmas Day in 496, after successfully appealing to "Clotilda's God" for success in a battle.

After Clovis died in 511, Clotilda's life was marked with great sorrow as her three sons, Clodimir, Childebert, and Clotaire, fought with each other over their inheritance. So intense was

this conflict that on one occasion two of Clodimir's children were murdered by their uncle
Clotaire.

Overcome by grief, Clotilda left Paris to go to
Tours, where she remained for the rest of her life
devoting herself to the service of the sick and poor.
A widow for thirty-four years, she died in 545.

REFLECTION We see in St. Clotilda a woman of
virtue and piety. Ever faithful to God in prayer and
good works, she was able to bring her husband to the
Faith through her good example. After his death, her
faith was put to the test by the internecine struggle
among her sons. Finally she devoted her life to work
among the rejected of society, and she remained with
them until she was taken into the loving presence of
the Father.

PRAYER *O God, You call us to a life of prayer and
virtue. As we struggle to meet the demands of our
Faith, may we be helped by the merits and intercession of Your servant St. Clotilda and become, above
all, people of peace and charity. This we ask through
Christ our Lord. Amen.*

ST. METROPHANES, Bishop

June 4

METROPHANES, a bishop of the Eastern
Church in the fourth century, is believed to
have been the son of Dometius, the brother of
Emperor Probus. After Dometius was converted

to Christianity, he moved to Byzantium, where he was ordained by Bishop Titus.

Dometius later succeeded Titus as Bishop of Byzantium. Dometius in turn was succeeded by his two sons, first by Probus in 301 and then by Metrophanes in 313.

During Metrophanes's tenure, Byzantium was declared independent of the See of Heraclea. Metrophanes had a reputation for holiness, and it is believed that his widespread renown for a virtuous life convinced the emperor Constantine to make Byzantium the capital of the Empire. Metrophanes died about the year 325.

REFLECTION Holiness of life is a requirement for the follower of Christ. In the case of St. Metrophanes, his personal holiness led secular rulers to react in a favorable manner. Personal holiness and striving after individual goodness can be and often is a significant contribution to the welfare of society. One's personal holiness can truly change the world.

PRAYER *O God, You call us to holiness of life and the practice of virtue. Through the intercession of Your Bishop St. Metrophanes, may we truly follow Your Son to eternal salvation. This we ask through Christ our Lord. Amen.*

——◆◆——

ST. DOROTHEUS OF TYRE, Martyr

June 5

ACCORDING to legend, Dorotheus of Tyre was a scholarly individual and the author of several books. He was a priest of Tyre who suffered greatly for the Faith and was driven into exile during the persecution of Emperor Diocletian.

Some time later, Dorotheus returned to Tyre where he was consecrated bishop of the city. In that role he attended the Council of Nicaea in 325.

However, under the persecution of Julian the Apostate 361-363, Dorotheus was forced to flee to Odyssopolis in Thrace. While there he was arrested and beaten to death. It is believed that he was over one hundred and seven years old.

REFLECTION   When we make a commitment to our Faith, there is no way of knowing what will be required of us during a lifetime. Persecution, beatings, imprisonment, slander, betrayal, and discrimination are a few of the challenges one may have to suffer for the Faith. However, like St. Dorotheus, we can accept this with the knowledge that God is always with us.

PRAYER   *O God, come to our aid in time of trial and challenge to our Faith. Through the intercession of Your servant St. Dorotheus, grant Your people the favor of perseverance. This we ask through Christ our Lord. Amen.*

ST. JARLATH, Bishop
June 6

JARLATH is regarded as the founder and principal patron of the Archdiocese of Tuam in

Galway, Ireland. He belonged to the Conmaicne family, perhaps the most important and powerful family in Galway during that period.

Jarlath was trained by a holy man and ordained a priest along with his cousin. He then founded the monastery of Cluain Fois, just outside Tuam, and presided over that monastery as abbot-bishop.

Later, Jarlath opened a school attached to the monastery, one which soon became renowned as a great center of learning. St. Brendan of Clonfert and St. Colman of Cloyne were among his pupils at the school. Jarlath died around 550.

REFLECTION An individual of learning must frequently weigh evidence on both sides of an issue. This can be difficult when dealing with matters pertaining to the Faith. Yet, through this kind of exercise, the Faith is strengthened and advanced. We praise God for talented individuals like Jarlath who devoted their lives to scholarship and piety.

PRAYER   *Loving God, as we study the Faith may we be always open to the Spirit. Through the intercession of Your Bishop St. Jarlath, help us to grow in wisdom and learning and come to know You better. This we ask through Christ our Lord. Amen.*

BL. ANNE OF ST. BARTHOLOMEW, Virgin

June 7

ANNE OF St. Bartholomew was born in 1549 at Almeneral, Spain. Until the age of twenty she was a shepherdess. At that time, she joined the Carmelites under the direction of St. Teresa of Avila.

Anne was a lay sister. For six years she served as secretary to St. Teresa and was her constant companion. It was in her arms that St. Teresa breathed her last.

A few years later Anne was sent with a group of nuns to Paris to begin the Carmelite reform in France. At both Tours and Pontoise she served as prioress. In 1612 she founded a Carmelite house in Antwerp, where her reputation for holiness, miracles, and prophecies was widespread. She died at Antwerp in 1626 and was beatified in 1917 by Pope Benedict XV.

REFLECTION The simplicity and holiness of Bl. Anne's life enabled her to make a significant contribution to the reform of the Carmelite Order, a process that has been the source of rich blessings for the Church since the sixteenth century. Simplicity and holiness of life can change the world!

PRAYER   *O God, as we make our way in this life to You, we are burdened with worldly cares. Through the intercession of Your servant Bl. Anne, help us to free ourselves of selfishness and greed for the sake of the Kingdom. This we ask through Christ our Lord. Amen.*

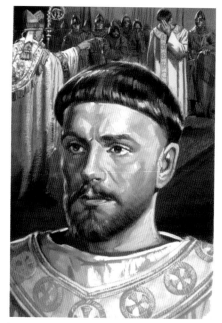

ST. WILLIAM OF YORK, Bishop

June 8

WILLIAM of York was the son of Count Herbert, treasurer to Henry I. His mother Emma was the half-sister of King William. Young William became treasurer of the Church of York at an early age and was elected Archbishop of York in 1140.

William's election was challenged on the grounds of simony and unchastity. He was cleared by Rome, but later, a new Pope, the Cistercian Eugene III, suspended William, and in 1147, he was deposed as Archbishop of York.

William then retired to Winchester where he led the austere life of a monk, practicing much prayer and mortification. Upon the death of his accusers and Eugene III, Pope Anastasius IV restored William to his See. However, after one month back in York, the saintly prelate died in the year 1154. Some claimed he was poisoned by the archdeacon of York, but no record of any resolution in the case remains extant. Pope Honorius III canonized William in 1227.

REFLECTION St. William of York's life clearly demonstrates the great harm that gossip, slander, and revenge can do not only to individuals but also to those faithful who admire and respect the slandered. When we are slandered or detraction is spread about us, we must remain steadfast in our love of God and determine never to indulge ourselves in revenge.

PRAYER *O God, when Jesus walked this earth, He was subjected to much verbal abuse. Through the example and intercession of Your Bishop St. William, may we always imitate Your Son's calming forgiveness toward those who malign us. This we ask through Christ our Lord. Amen.*

ST. COLUMBA, Abbot

June 9

ABOUT 521, St. Columba or Colum-cille was of illustrative Irish descent and grew up in the company of a host of Saints at the school of St. Finian of Clonard. After his ordination to the priesthood, he founded many churches in Ireland.

In 563, with twelve companions he journeyed to Scotland and founded the monastery of Hy on Iona, which went on the become the greatest monastery in Christendom as well as the nursery of Saints and apostles and the most powerful factor in the conversion of Picts, Scots, and Northern English.

The Saint's holiness, austerity, and reputation for miracles attracted all types of visitors to the monastery. After a most active life in God's service, Columba died on June 9, 597, at the foot of the altar, at Iona, while blessing people, and was buried—like St. Bridgid—beside St. Patrick at Downpatrick in Ulster.

REFLECTION A wonderful picture of St. Columba is provided by a few words of his biographer: "He had the face of an Angel, and he was of a wonderful nature—refined in speech, holy in works, remarkable in counsel . . . and loving toward everyone." It is no wonder then that he had such an enormous effect on Western Christianity and that his monastic rule held sway until the Rule of St. Benedict ultimately became the norm almost everywhere.

PRAYER   *Almighty God, You chose Your Abbot St. Columba to bring the Faith to the peoples of Ireland, Scotland, and Northern England. By his prayers, help us to bear witness to the Faith to all those whom we encounter. This we ask through Christ our Lord. Amen.*

ST. ITHAMAR, Bishop of Rochester

June 10

ST. Ithamar was the first Anglo-Saxon to occupy an English episcopal See. Upon the death of St. Paulinus, St. Honorius, Archbishop of Canterbury, consecrated Ithamar Bishop of Rochester.

The eminent Church historian, St. Bede the Venerable, states that St. Ithamar was equal in devotion and knowledge to his predecessors in the episcopate, St. Justus and St. Paulinus, who had come to England as Italian missionaries with St. Augustine of Canterbury in 597.

Later, in 655, Ithamar consecrated his countryman St. Deusdedit (or Frithonia) as Archbishop of Canterbury. The date of the Saint's death was unknown previously, but the *Revised Roman Martyrology* puts it at 666, and he was buried at Rochester.

REFLECTION Although we have very little knowledge about St. Ithamar, we know that praise given him by Bede the Venerable is our guarantee that he was a devoted and learned shepherd of his countrymen. In so doing, Ithamar served both God and his country. May we too strive to serve God and country in every way.

PRAYER *O Lord, You made St. Ithamar Your Bishop an outstanding exemplar of Divine love and the faith that conquers the world and added him to the role of saintly pastors. By his prayers, grant that we may persevere in faith and love and so become shar-*

*ers in his glory. This we ask through Christ our Lord.
Amen.*

———◆———

ST. PAULA FRASSINETTI, Virgin

PAULA Frassinetti was born in Genoa, Italy, on March 3, 1809. Later she was sent to Quinto, a neighboring village, to live with her brother who was a parish priest there. Despite her poor health, she began to teach poor children at Quinto.

Eventually Paula gathered a group of women to help with the teaching. Later they were organized into an institute called the Sisters of St. Dorothy. The sisters eventually opened many foundations all over Italy and then went to Portugal and Brazil to establish other convents.

In 1863, Paula's congregation received formal papal approval. After suffering several strokes, she died on June 11, 1882. She was beatified by Pope Pius XI in 1930 and canonized by Pope John Paul II in 1984.

REFLECTION Despite poor health, St. Paula took up the noble work of teaching the poor. Her followers joined in this demanding but virtuous work. Today the Church looks to the laity to help with the evangelization of her children, especially the poor. Like St. Paula, those who elect to join in this important work will shine in glory for all eternity.

PRAYER   *Loving God, You have entrusted the followers of Your Son with Your Word. Through the example and intercession of St. Paula, may we be open
to the challenge of bringing that Word to those most
in need through teaching and good example. This we
ask through Christ our Lord. Amen.*

———◆—◆———

ST. JOHN OF SAHAGUN, Priest

The Same Day—June 11

JOHN was born in Sahagún, Spain, in the fifteenth century. He was educated by the Benedictine monks at San Fangondez Monastery in
Sahagún. At the age of twenty he received a
canonry from the Bishop of Burgos, despite the
fact that he had several other benefices.

Ordained in 1445, John surrendered every
benefice except that of St. Agatha in Burgos.
After extended study at the University of Salamanca, he became renowned both as a preacher
and as a spiritual director.

In 1463, John joined the Augustinians and
eventually served as a novice master and prior at
Salamanca. He was a staunch defender of the
rights of workers and deeply devoted to the
Blessed Sacrament. Reportedly he performed
miracles and was able to discern the condition of
souls. Because John inveighed against corruption in high places, he endured several death
threats. This saintly priest died in 1479, allegedly

poisoned by the mistress of a man he had convinced to leave her. Pope Alexander VIII canonized him in 1690.

REFLECTION   In many ways the life of a Christian calls for both faith and courage. Like St. John of Sahagún, we must expect to be treated with scorn if we speak out in favor of peace, justice, truth, generosity, and concern for the poor, according to Gospel principles.

PRAYER   *God our Father, in Your wisdom you raised up St. John of Sahagún as an example of faith and courage. Grant us the courage to imitate his love for Your Word. This we ask through Christ our Lord. Amen.*

ST. LEO III, Pope

June 12

ST. Leo was a Roman priest of honorable birth and blameless character who was unanimously elected Pope in 795. In 799, he attempted to suppress the unruly factions of Rome but was himself seized and beaten. He recovered from his wounds at a monastery and went to seek the help of Charlemagne, the King of the Franks, who brought him safely to Rome and reestablished order there.

On Christmas Day, 800, Leo crowned Charlemagne Emperor of the West, thereby founding the Holy Roman Empire and laying the foundation of the Middle Ages and inaugurating a new age in Europe.

Leo did much to defend the Divine Sonship of Christ against the Adoptionist heresy in his day, although he decided against adding the word "Filioque" in the Nicene Creed in order not to alienate Greek Christians. This Latin word (ultimately added to the Creed in 1013 by Pope Benedict VIII) means "and from the Son" and was added by the Latin Church after the phrase "the Holy Spirit . . . Who proceeds from the Father." It was intended to eliminate the heretical idea that the Son was adopted in His human nature.

Leo was also much concerned with the affairs of the Church in England. Assisted by Charlemagne's rich gifts, he also adorned many churches in the cities of Italy. He died in 816 and was canonized by Pope Clement X in 1673.

REFLECTION   Pope Leo's symbolic act of crowning Charlemagne in St. Peter's on Christmas Day inaugurated the Christian Empire of the West, thus realizing St. Augustine's ideal of the City of God. Each of us in our small way is still called to build the City of God in our country, obeying all good civil laws as well as Church laws every day.

PRAYER   *O Lord, You raised up St. Leo to lead and shepherd Your Church at a critical time in the world. By his prayers, send us great Church leaders who can guide us unerringly in the difficult days of our time. This we ask through Christ our Lord. Amen.*

———◆◆◆———

ST. EULOGIUS, Bishop

June 13

A SYRIAN by birth, St. Eulogius became a monk at a young age in the Monastery of the Mother of God at Antioch and later its abbot. Upon the death of John the Patriarch of Alexandria, Eulogius succeeded to that office.

A few years later, on a trip to Constantinople, Eulogius met St. Gregory the Great who was at that time a papal representative at the Byzantine court. The two became immediate friends and went on to exchange letters even after Gregory became Pope.

Although St. Eulogius wrote against heresies, especially Monophysitism, very few of his writings are extant. When one of his writings was submitted to St. Gregory before publication, the Pope approved it with the words: "I find nothing in your writings except what is admirable." In one of his letters Gregory seems to imply that St. Eulogius had some influence in originating the mission to England given by Gregory to St. Augustine of Canterbury. Eulogius died at Alexandria in 607.

REFLECTION   St. Gregory wrote about the friendship he had with St. Eulogius, saying: "He is not far from me who is one with me." This shows how close the two friends really were while still living far apart. We should dwell on what Sacred Scripture says about true friendship: "A true friend is a strong refuge; anyone who has found one has found a treasure. A true friend's value is priceless; his worth cannot be measured. A faithful friend is a lifesaving remedy" (Sirach 6:14-16).

PRAYER   *O Loving God, You enabled St. Eulogius, Your Bishop, to be united, in Your friendship, with St. Gregory the Great. By his prayers, help each of us to find a true friend and be a true friend ourselves. This we ask through Christ our Lord. Amen.*

———◆———

STS. VALERIUS AND RUFINUS, Martyrs

June 14

VALERIUS and Rufinus were Christians who lived at Soissons in Gaul at the end of the third century. They fled during the persecution of Diocletian, but eventually they were captured.

After making a bold confession of their Faith, Valerius and Rufinus were scourged, tortured, and beheaded. Little else is known about them. They may have been missionaries sent from Rome to evangelize in Gaul, or they may have been minor officials in charge of local granaries.

After their martyrdom, which took place in the fourth century, a church was erected over their graves in the town of Bazoches.

REFLECTION   To live one's Faith is to live the Word of God. This lifestyle may indeed provoke opposition, challenge, persecution, and even death. Like Sts. Valerius and Rufinus, when we are challenged to renounce our Faith, we must boldly confess it no matter what the consequences.

PRAYER   *O God, through the intercession of Your Martyrs Sts. Valerius and Rufinus, come to our help in time of difficulty. Aware of the weakness of our faith, we rely on Your grace to persevere in good in the face of evil. This we ask through Christ our Lord. Amen.*

ST. ELISHA, Prophet
The Same Day—June 14

ST. Elisha was a Prophet from Abel-meholah who succeeded Elijah in the ninth century B.C. He had a lengthy ministry during the reigns of Jehoram, Jehu, Jehoahaz, and Joash as kings of Israel.

The Saint performed many miracles, among which were the following. He saved a poor widow from financial troubles by the miraculous multiplication of her oil supply (2 Kings 4:1-7). He brought a child back to life (2 Kings 4:8-37). During a famine in Gilgal, he saved a school of prophets from death when they had eaten poisonous vegetables (2 Kings 4:38-41). By obeying his word, Namaan the Syrian captain was cleansed of leprosy (2 Kings 5).

The prophet also aided the king of Israel in his Syrian wars (2 Kings 8:7ff), incited Hazael to seize the throne of Damascus (2 Kings 6:8ff; 7:1ff), and Jehu to seize the throne of Samaria (2 Kings 9:1ff). And on his deathbed, he promised Jehoash victory over the Syrians (2 Kings 13:14ff). He was known as the Wonderworker.

REFLECTION Elisha completed the work of Elijah, destroying the system of Baal worship in the land and anointing Hazael and Jehu. Then the crowning work of his career—cleansing Namaan the Syrian—gave him an influence with the Syrian king that enabled him to help Israel.

PRAYER *O God, in Your wisdom You called St. Elisha to be Your Prophet and enabled him to perform miraculous works. By his prayers, help us to discern the true prophets in our time and work with them for the good of the world. This we ask through Christ our Lord. Amen.*

ST. VITUS (or GUY), Martyr

June 15—Patron of Actors and Dancers

THE cult of St. Vitus (a boy of twelve) was in the past intertwined with those of St. Modestus, his tutor, and St. Crescentia, his nurse. In 1969, the cult of St. Vitus alone was confirmed while Modestus and Crescentia were stricken from the catalogue of Saints. They do not appear in the *Revised Roman Martyrology.*

All that we know for certain about St. Vitus is that he was martyred for the Faith in the Roman province of Lucania in the fourth century.

During the Middle Ages, St. Vitus was one of the Fourteen Holy Helpers† and was invoked for hydrophobia, snake bites, and "St. Vitus Dance." He is the Patron of Actors and Dancers.

REFLECTION The first important thing we know about St. Vitus is that he gave his life for Christ. The second important thing we know about him is that Christ gave him the power to intercede in heaven for those who are threatened by diseases on earth. If we concentrate on those two facts, we do not have to know anything else in order to have recourse to his help in time of need.

PRAYER *Loving Father, You strengthened St. Vitus to offer his life for You and empowered him to come to the aid of Your people on their earthly pilgrimage. By his prayers, save us from evils of body and soul. This we ask through Christ our Lord. Amen.*

† See p. 223.

ST. AMOS, Prophet

The Same Day—June 15

AMOS was a shepherd and a tender of sycamore fruit. He was from Tekoa in Judah about six miles south of Bethlehem. The Lord called him to be a prophet to the Northern Kingdom of Israel (Amos 7:12-13) during the reign of Jeroboam (784-744 B.C.), a period of peace and well-being. He was to vindicate God's justice and holiness against the prevarications of the people.

Amos strongly condemned various abuses (e.g., the buying and selling of justice), and for that reason he was expelled from Israel (Amos 7:10-13).

Amos is celebrated above all for his attacks on the rich who oppose the poor and on formalistic worship as well as for his invitation to seek God and his announcement of the hunger for the Word of God.

REFLECTION Amos's message was rejected, but his words would not die. When Israel fell to her enemies, his prophecy provided the explanation as to why God would allow the disaster to occur—it was a punishment for sin that would ultimately bring the people back to God.

PRAYER *O God, in Your wisdom You made St. Amos, Your Prophet, the herald of social justice and love for the poor. By his prayers, raise up new prophets in our day. Let every land be bathed in the healing power of Your justice. This we ask through Christ our Lord. Amen.*

ST. LUTGARDIS, Virgin

June 16

LUTGARDIS was born in 1182 at Tangres in the Netherlands. At the age of twelve she was placed in the Benedictine convent of St. Catherine near Saint-Trond. Originally she felt no inclination whatsoever toward the religious life, but one day she had a vision of Christ that changed her outlook.

At the age of twenty, Lutgardis entered the Benedictines. For more than a decade she experienced ecstasies during which she had visions of our Lord and the Blessed Mother.

Lutgardis later went to a Cistercian convent at Aywières, where she spent the final thirty years of her life and became renowned as a mystic with the gifts of healing and prophecy. She died on June 16, 1246, having suffered blindness the last eleven years of her life.

REFLECTION Although not all are called to the degree of mystical union that St. Lutgardis experienced, nonetheless God's invitation to intimate union is universal. Our openness to God working in our lives, no matter who we are, is the first step down the road of perfect union with Him.

PRAYER *Loving God, be with us as we make our way to You. Through the example and intercession of Your Virgin St. Lutgardis, help us come to an understanding of Your great desire to engulf us in Your rapture and love. This we ask through Christ our Lord. Amen.*

ST. THERESA OF PORTUGAL,
Queen and Religious
June 17

THERESA of Portugal was the eldest daughter of King Sancho I. Later she married her cousin, King Alfonso IX of León, Spain. Before the marriage was declared invalid because of close blood ties, Theresa had given birth to several children.

After the marriage was dissolved, Theresa returned to Portugal and converted a Benedictine monastery at Lorvão into a convent to house three hundred nuns who would follow the Cistercian rule. She herself took up permanent residence there, although she continued to live in the lay state.

In 1231, Theresa settled a bitter dispute among her children over succession to the throne of León. She then returned to the convent, took the veil, and remained there until her death in 1250. Her cult was approved by Pope Clement XI in 1705.

REFLECTION All too often in life our best intentions encounter difficult obstacles. Where goodwill is involved, we try to make the best of circumstances. St. Theresa, after having been separated from her children, made the best of her life by fostering a religious foundation and unselfishly settling a family dispute.

PRAYER *O God, You ask us to follow Your Son Jesus in an ordinary way. Through the example and intercession of Your servant St. Theresa of Portugal, help us to effectively deal with the complexities of life in a calm and charitable manner. This we ask through Christ our Lord. Amen.*

———◆◆———

ST. ELIZABETH OF SCHÖNAU, Virgin

June 18

ELIZABETH was born in Germany in the year 1126. She entered a Benedictine convent at Schönau, near Bonn, Germany, at the age of twelve and was professed in 1147.

Some years later Elizabeth began to experience visions, along with ecstasies and prophecies. Sometimes these were counterbalanced with diabolical interventions that often left her bruised and beaten. She described some of her visions in three books authored by her brother Egbert, a monk and later an abbot.

In 1157, Elizabeth became abbess at Schönau, and seven years later, on June 18, 1164, she died at the age of thirty-eight. She does not seem to have been formally beatified or canonized, but she is referred to as a Saint in the *Revised Roman Martyrology.*

REFLECTION In our efforts to join ourselves to God, as long as we are veiled from eternity, we are, like St. Elizabeth, subjected to the possibility of evil afflictions. Although wickedness can take many confusing and alluring forms, our faith in God will see us through these difficult struggles.

PRAYER   *O God, in Your creative wisdom You know our weakness in the face of temptation. Through the prayers of St. Elizabeth of Schönau, remain with us as we make our way back to You. This we ask through Christ our Lord. Amen.*

———◆•◆———

BL. OSANNA OF MANTUA, Virgin

The Same Day—June 18

OSANNA Andreasi was born on January 17, 1449, at Mantua, Italy. Her parents were of the noble class. She reportedly had her first mystical experience at the age of five—a vision of paradise.

After rejecting her father's plans for her to marry, she became a novice as a Dominican tertiary when she was seventeen. However, she was not professed until thirty-seven years later, probably because of the responsibility she felt to care for her brothers and their families after the death of her parents.

Between the ages of seventeen and twenty-two, Osanna had a series of more particularized mystical experiences. She received the favor of participating physically in the Mysteries of the Passion of Christ. She shared in the Crowning with Thorns, the Piercing of Our Lord's side, and the wounds on His hands and feet. Although the wounds did not appear on her body, she suffered physical pain as if they were there.

However, Osanna was not a mystic who turned her back on the world. She expended much time and money to help the poor. She also made it a daily practice to visit the sick, comfort the afflicted, and dispense spiritual advice to all who flocked to her. All the while, she led an austere life and experienced many visions of Christ and the Blessed Mother.

Osanna joined Savonarola in deploring the lack of morality in Italian society. Moreover, a record of her spiritual conversations with Girolamo de Monte Oliveto has been preserved. She died in 1505, and her cult was approved by Popes Leo X and Innocent XIV.

REFLECTION From time to time certain individuals are blessed with a variety of visions and ecstasies. When one cooperates with this special kind of invitation for the greater honor and glory of God, one in effect performs the will of God, as did Bl. Osanna. It is important to remember that ordinary events well lived also constitute the will of God.

PRAYER *Loving God, may we be always ready to respond to Your invitation to holiness. Through the example and intercession of Your servant Bl. Osanna, may we openly acknowledge Your will in our lives. This we ask through Christ our Lord. Amen.*

ST. JULIANA FALCONIERI, Virgin
June 19

JULIANA Falconieri was born of a wealthy Florentine family in 1270. When she was very young her father died, and thus she was raised by her mother and an uncle named Alexis who was one of the founders of the Servites.

At the age of fifteen Juliana refused her family's plan for her marriage. She became a Servite tertiary a year later, although she continued to live at home until 1304 when her mother died.

Immediately thereafter Juliana gathered together a group of women dedicated to prayer and good works. Later she drew up a rule of life and was appointed superioress of the group.

Since her rule was approved by Pope Martin V one hundred and twenty years later, she is considered to be the foundress of the Servite nuns. She died about 1341 at the age of seventy-one and was by canonized by Pope Clement XII in 1737.

REFLECTION   Although we are not in touch with canonized Saints in our daily lives, nonetheless there are many people around us who are striving after sanctity. Like St. Juliana Falconieri, we must be open to their good example and imitate their virtues in our lives.

PRAYER   *Loving God, You call us to a life of perfection according to Your Word. Through the intercession of St. Juliana Falconieri, may we draw others to lives of virtue. This we ask through Christ our Lord. Amen.*

ST. METHODIUS, Bishop and Martyr

June 20

ST. METHODIUS was Bishop of Alypius in Lyca and of Tyre in Phoenicia in the third and fourth centuries. He died a martyr at Chalcis in 312.

We have no information about his life or martyrdom, and his fame rests on his writings, especially his treatise on virginity entitled *Banquet of the Ten Virgins* (which is written on the style of Plato's *Symposium*) and his *Dialogue about the Resurrection.*

The *Symposium* ends with a hymn to our Lord as the Bridegroom of the Church, and the maiden Thecla sings a series of strophes that are answered by others with a refrain. Hence, this forms one of the earliest Christian hymns. St. Methodius died about 312.

REFLECTION Methodius is honored as a Saint despite the fact that in his *Symposium* he inadvertently gave support to the error of Millenarianism (i.e., Christ's temporal reign of a thousand years before the general resurrection). We should always strive to avoid error in our knowledge of the Faith.

PRAYER   *Almighty God, You chose St. Methodius to shepherd Your Church and inspire her through his wonderful writings. By his prayers, grant us good leaders who will teach and inspire us in the Faith. This we ask through Christ our Lord. Amen.*

ST. LEUTFRIDUS (or LEUFROY), Abbot

BORN into a Christian family from Evreux in Normandy, St. Leutfridus studied there and at Condat and Chartres. Then he returned to Evreux and devoted himself to the instruction of boys.

Later, the Saint felt called to the religious life and made his way to the monastery of Cailly. Moving on to Rouen, he followed the guidance of St. Sidonius and received the religious habit.

Returning home, St. Leutfridus found the ideal spot to end his wandering ten miles from Evreux, on the River Eure. In 690, he built a monastery and a church there, dedicated to the Holy Cross. It attracted many disciples and he ruled it for forty-eight years. After a life of great holiness, Leutfridus died in 738.

REFLECTION   So greatly did St. Leutfridus honor his religious vows that he once refused Christian burial to a monk who had died with money in his purse. His life should teach us not to become attached to the passing things of this world and to look earnestly for our heavenly home.

PRAYER   *O Lord, You called St. Leutfridus, Your Abbot, to the religious life for his own good and that of those who flocked to him. By his prayers, teach us to lead the life of our state to the nth degree. This we ask through Christ our Lord. Amen.*

ST. EUSEBIUS, Bishop
June 22

EUSEBIUS was the Bishop of Samosata and a defender of orthodoxy in the fourth century. Active in the synod of Antioch in 361, he was instrumental in the election of St. Meletius as Bishop of Antioch. The Arians at the synod expected Meletius to favor them, but when Meletius proved to be orthodox, Emperor Constantius demanded that Eusebius surrender the voting records of the synod. When Eusebius refused, even when threatened that his right hand would be amputated, Constantius, impressed with his courage, released him.

Over a long period Eusebius worked to settle the Arian question, but he was unsuccessful. Later he traveled throughout Syria and Palestine encouraging Christians during the persecution of Valens.

In 374, Eusebius was exiled to Thrace by Valens, but when Valens died in 378, Eusebius returned to Samosata. In 379, he was killed by a tile thrown from a roof by an Arian woman in Dolikha where he had gone to install a Catholic bishop.

REFLECTION Sometimes in living out the demands of the Gospel we may be subjected to ridicule, abuse, or even assault. Like Christ and His Saints, especially Eusebius, let us place our trust in God and seek courage in our personal awareness of God's presence in our lives even in the most difficult times.

PRAYER   *O God, You called Your people to a life of goodness and perfection in the midst of an unaccepting world. Through the example and intercession of Your Bishop St. Eusebius, grant us the grace of perseverance in good in the face of contradiction. This we ask through Christ our Lord. Amen.*

———◆━◆━◆———

BL. MARY OF OIGNIES, Virgin
June 23

MARY of Oignies was born of a wealthy family at Nivelles, Belgium, in the twelfth century. Her parents gave her in marriage at the age of fourteen, although she really wanted to be a religious. Therefore she convinced her husband to live in perfect continence and to transform their home into a refuge for lepers.

In addition to nursing the lepers, Mary led a very austere life. Most of her substance she lavishly distributed as alms to the poor. Her holiness of life led others to seek her counsel and direction.

Later, with the permission of her spouse, Mary moved to a hermit's cell near the Augustinian house at Oignies, where she died on June 23, 1213. In her great devotion to the Eucharist and the Passion, she had many visions and ecstasies, along with the gift of prophecy, and she possessed psychic powers as well.

REFLECTION   Sometimes God reveals His plans for us in different ways. Through her husband's consent,

Mary was able to dedicate her life and possessions to the welfare of others in the person of the leper. We are all called to a sense of detachment and dedication. Mary's life challenges us to seriously come to grips with the Gospel values in our personal lives.

PRAYER   *Loving Father, many faithful share Your generous gifts with those most in need. Through the example and intercession of Your Virgin Bl. Mary of Oignies, enlighten our minds and hearts so that we may be clearly identified with Gospel values. This we ask through Christ our Lord. Amen.*

ST. SIMPLICIUS, Bishop of Autun
June 24

ST. Simplicius was born into a distinguished fourth-century Gallo-Roman family and married a young woman of similar condition. The two of them agreed to live in continence and dedicated themselves to good works.

Because of his integrity and charity, Simplicius was elected Bishop of Autun. However, since he and his wife continued to live under the same roof, they had to undergo the ordeal by fire to prove that they were truly celibate—and they were proven right.

The vindication won by these two holy people led over one thousand pagans to seek Baptism. More conversions occurred at the bishop's miraculous destruction of a statue of the goddess

Berecynthia, which spawned orgies. Simplicius died around 375 with a reputation for sanctity.

REFLECTION   St. Simplicius and his wife chose to live their marriage celibately as an offering to the Lord. They are a good example of what St. Paul urged all Christians to do—to offer themselves to the Lord. May we too offer ourselves to the Lord each day.

PRAYER   *O Lord, You called St. Simplicius, Your Bishop, to shepherd Your people at at time when Church law did not yet impose celibacy on all the clergy. By his prayers, send us more vocations to the religious life and the priesthood so that Your people may not lack the means of sanctification that You obtained by Your Passion, Death, and Resurrection. This we ask through Christ our Lord. Amen.*

———◆◆———

ST. WILLIAM OF VERCELLI, Abbot
June 25

WILLIAM of Vercelli was born of noble parents at Vercelli, Italy, in 1085. Orphaned as an infant, he was raised by relatives.

At the age of fourteen, William made a pilgrimage to Compostela in Spain. Later he spent two years as a hermit at Monte Solicoli, where he cured a blind man, and then went to live as a hermit on Monte Virgiliano.

At Monte Virgiliano William attracted many disciples who were eventually formed into a community in 1119, known as Hermits of Monte

Vergine. The success of this community eventually led him to establish five other houses during his lifetime. He also served as advisor to King Roger I of Naples before dying at Guglietto on June 25, 1142.

REFLECTION The idealism of youth is well served when it is guided through the Spirit. Age is not a determining factor in mounting a deeply affective spirituality. Like St. William of Vercelli, young people especially should be given the opportunity to explore the Word of God in all its wonder and challenge.

PRAYER *O God, You call all Your people to holiness of life. Through the prayers of Your servant St. William of Vercelli, help us to bring Your message of love and forgiveness into the world through good example and virtuous lives. This we ask through Christ our Lord. Amen.*

———◆•◆———

ST. PELAGIUS, Martyr
June 26

PELAGIUS was born at Asturias, Spain, around the year 912. At the age of ten he was left with the Moors as a hostage for his uncle.

At that time Abd-ar-Rahman III was the ruler of Cordova, Spain. When Pelagius had not been ransomed after three years, Abd-ar-Rahman told Pelegius that he would set him free and grant him great rewards if he would deny Christ and become a Mohammedan.

When Pelagius refused to deny his Faith, Abd-ar-Rahman subjected him to the cruelest of tortures. Eventually he died at the hands of his torturers in 925, and his body was dismembered. In 985, his relics were moved to Oviedo.

REFLECTION   At a very tender age St. Pelagius was confronted with the choice of life or death for his Faith. Despite the significance of the choice and his knowledge of the kinds of tortures practiced at the time, he chose to sustain his faith in Jesus Christ. The world tempts us to choose between Christ and its charms. Through the youthful courage of St. Pelagius, may we be inspired to choose Christ.

PRAYER   *O God, You have raised up for us a wonderful example of faith in the person of Your Martyr St. Pelagius. May we always willingly defend our Faith against all challenges. This we ask through Christ our Lord. Amen.*

BL. MADELEINE FONTAINE, Virgin and Martyr,
AND COMPANIONS, Martyrs
The Same Day—June 26

MADELEINE Fontaine was born at Etepagny, France, in 1723. In 1748, she became a Sister of Charity of St. Vincent de Paul.

Eventually Madeleine was appointed superior at the community convent in Arras in 1767. While there she and three other sisters (Frances Lanel, Térèse Fantous, and Joanna Gérgard) were arrested by French revolutionaries in 1794. Madeleine and her companions refused to take the Oath of the Constitution, and they were accused of counterrevolutionary activities.

Madeleine was tried by a tribunal at Cambrai and convicted. The other three sisters were convicted as accomplices. All four were then guillotined. Pope Benedict XV beatified them in 1920.

REFLECTION In desperate times radicalized individuals attack religious institutions and their social stability. The French revolutionaries were no exception. In the face of death, Madeleine and her companions would not deny the Church or their Faith. Like them we must learn unswerving fidelity to our beliefs and our Christian community.

PRAYER *O God, the forces of desperation and death promote significant challenges for young people today. Through the intercession of Bl. Madeleine Fontaine and her Companions, may the fidelity of our youth be preserved. This we ask through Christ our Lord. Amen.*

—◆—

ST. JOSEMARIA ESCRIVA DE BALAGUER, Priest

The Same Day—June 26

BORN in Barbastro, Spain, in 1902, Josemaria decided to become a priest, and while still a seminarian in 1921 he was inspired to start the society of *Opus Dei* (Latin for "Work of God") to promote holiness among both men and women in the world.

In 1943, Josemaria founded the Society of the Holy Cross for priests, He also saw to it that in its mission Opus Dei made use of publishing houses and radio stations to serve the Church. All the while, the Saint lived by the motto: "To hide and disappear so that only Jesus may shine."

After a life dedicated to the works of the Lord, Josemaria died of a heart attack on June 26, 1975. He left the society in good hands: 60,000 members in 80 countries and 1000 priests.

In 1983, John Paul II granted to the society something the Saint had sought: the protection of a personal prelature of the Holy Father so that it would be placed under the Pope and not under the authority of the local bishops. The same Pope beatified Josemaria in 1992 and canonized him in 2002.

REFLECTION St. Josemaria's fidelity allowed the Holy Spirit to lead him to the heights of personal union with God, which resulted in an extraordinarily fruitful apostolate. The Saint took no credit for this, attributing it all to the Divine goodness. May we all strive to follow his example of humility.

PRAYER   *Almighty God, You called St. Josemaria, Your Priest, to found a new society in Your Church to lead men and women to holiness in the world. By his prayers, teach us how to reach holiness in the world. This we ask through Christ our Lord. Amen.*

BL. MARGUERITE BAYS, Virgin

June 27

BORN in Switzerland in 1915, Marguerite was raised in the Faith and became a dressmaker. She lived at home as a member of the Franciscan Third Order and worked for her parish as a catechist and as a member of the Society for the Propagation of the Faith.

When Marguerite was 38, she developed cancer of the intestines. She was miraculously cured by the next year (1854) and received the Stigmata, the wounds of Christ, in her body, and for the next twenty-five years relived Christ's Passion each Friday.

Crowds flocked to Marguerite's house, and she always greeted them lovingly with courage, faith, and grace. After having suffered willingly for Christ and others, she went to her reward on June 27, 1879. She was beatified by Pope John Paul II in 1995.

REFLECTION   Bl. Marguerite lived a religious life in the world. She became a sign of God for all to see. Simply by being herself, she brought many back to the Faith. May we all strive to bear witness to the Faith by our lives.

PRAYER   *God our Father, You called Bl. Marguerite to be a sign of Your Divinity in the world. By her prayers, help us to become signs of the Faith to all who come in touch with us. This we ask through Christ our Lord. Amen.*

ST. PAUL I, Pope
June 28

PAUL was educated at the Lateran school with his brother, the future Pope Stephen III. Paul was ordained at Rome, and he was known for his kindness and clemency. Always ready to help people in trouble, he never indulged in revenge. Moreover, he was very good to the poor.

Later Paul served on diplomatic missions for Pope Stephen III. He was elected to succeed his brother as Pope on April 26, 757. During his pontificate of ten years he was on friendly terms with King Pepin. He resisted attempts by the Byzantines to dilute temporal power, and in 765 he came to an agreement with the Byzantine Desiderius over their respective boundaries.

During his pontificate, Paul built several churches and monasteries in Rome and strongly opposed the iconoclastic Emperor Constantine Coproynmus. He died at St. Paul's Outside the Walls in Rome on June 28, 767.

REFLECTION   When one is selected for a position of power, the Gospel demands that one remain simple, open, and just in dealing with others. Despite his background and connections, St. Paul I lived a life of compassion and simplicity, a life worthy of our imitation.

PRAYER   *O God, through the intercession of Pope St. Paul I, may we live simple, virtuous lives in the service of Your Word. This we ask through Christ our Lord. Amen.*

ST. VINCENTIA GEROSA, Virgin

The Same Day—June 28

CATHERINE Gerosa was born at Lovere, Italy, in 1784. In her youth she was orphaned, and after that she devoted her life to the poor in a lay capacity until she was forty.

Around 1824 Catherine met St. Bartholomea Capitanio, and together they organized a congregation for the welfare and support of the sick poor and for the education of children. This group was known as the Sisters of Charity of Lovere, and Catherine took the name Vincentia.

In 1833, St. Bartholomea died. Vincentia succeeded her and carried on the work of the fledgling group. Following an extended illness, she died on June 28, 1847, at the age of sixty-three. She was canonized in 1950 by Pope Pius XII.

REFLECTION In recalling the life of St. Vincentia Gerosa, one is convinced that individuals who in their generosity fully cooperate with the grace of God can accomplish great wonders on this earth while at the same time bringing many to salvation.

PRAYER *O God, through the intercession of St. Vincentia Gerosa, may we imitate her love, concern, and generosity for the poor. This we ask through Christ our Lord. Amen.*

ST. CASSIUS, Bishop of Narni

OUR knowledge of St. Cassius comes to us from Pope St. Gregory the Great, in his *Dialogues*, which delineate his exemplary life, his care for his flock, and his generosity to the poor. He was Bishop of Narni in Umbria, Italy, from 537 to 558.

One day, St. Cassius was told by one of his priests that he would die in Rome on the Feast of Sts. Peter and Paul. Hence, the Saint made it his custom to journey on pilgrimage to Rome annually on the eve of June 29. For six years, he returned from his pilgrimage, but on the seventh the priest's prediction came to pass.

In 558, after St. Cassius had celebrated Mass and given Communion to the people, he went peacefully to his eternal reward.

REFLECTION St. Cassius daily offered the Holy Sacrifice of the Mass with tears and doled out whatever he had to the poor. We should never forget that the Mass is a call to put our faith into practice in every way that we can—by giving generously of time, money, love, and instruction to our neighbor.

PRAYER *Lord, You called St. Cassius, Your Bishop to shepherd Your Church by word and deed. By his prayers, help us to be subservient to our shepherds and pray for them every day. This we ask through Christ our Lord. Amen.*

ST. BERTRAND, Bishop

June 30

BERTRAND was born at Autun, France, around 553. As a young man he was ordained in Paris by St. Germanicus. Later he served at the cathedral school in Paris, where he became an archdeacon.

In 587, Bertrand was appointed Bishop of Le Mans. In that position he was occasionally forced to take sides in factional disputes, and as a result he was several times driven into exile, but finally he was reinstated by King Clotaire II in 605.

As bishop, Bertrand was known for his generosity to the poor and his agricultural abilities, particularly in the cultivation of grapes. He also founded a monastery, a hospice, and a church. He died on June 30, 623.

REFLECTION   One of the blessings of a life lived according to the dictates of the Gospel is that the interests of the poor and the sick are served. This in turn contributes to the general welfare of society. Like St. Bertrand, we must cherish the opportunity to serve Christ in His poor and rejected.

PRAYER   *O God, in our hour of greatest need You promise to be with us. Through the example and intercession of Your Bishop St. Bertrand, enable us always to reach out to those who call upon us for service in Your Name. This we ask through Christ our Lord. Amen.*

ST. OLIVER PLUNKET, Bishop and Martyr

July 1

OLIVER Plunket was born on November 1, 1629, at Loughcrew in County Meath, Ireland. His family was of noble lineage and supported King Charles I and the cause of national freedom. After studies in Dublin and Rome, Oliver was ordained a priest in 1654 and then remained in Rome for the next fifteen years as a professor of Theology. During that period he also served as consultor to the Sacred Congregation of the Index and procurator for the Irish Bishops.

In 1669, Oliver was consecrated at Ghent as Archbishop of Armagh and Primate of Ireland. He instituted many reforms in his archdiocese and put an end to many abuses that had cropped up because of the absence of bishops owing to persecutions.

Oliver himself was forced into hiding when all Catholic priests and bishops were expelled from Ireland, and in 1679 he was jailed in Dublin. Later removed to Newgate Prison in London, he spent nine months in solitary confinement. Convicted of treason for having spread the Catholic Faith, Oliver was hanged, drawn, and quartered at Tyburn on July 1, 1681. He was canonized in 1976 by Pope Paul VI.

REFLECTION Sometimes those who have gone before us speak eloquently of their Faith through the memory of their lives. Such is the case of St. Oliver Plunket. Despite false accusations and imprisonment, along with a horrible death, he remained true to his Faith to the very end.

PRAYER *Loving Father, Your servant St. Oliver Plunket loved us so much that he gave up his life for the Faith. Let us share that saving Faith today. This we ask through Christ our Lord. Amen.*

ST. AARON, First High Priest
of the Old Law

AARON was the son of Amran and Jochebed and the brother of Moses and Miriam. In the Old Testament, he is described as Moses' associate, i.e., his spokesman (Exodus 4:14), aide (Exodus 7:19), replacement (Exodus 24:14), or companion (Exodus 7:10, 22). He was also the first high priest and founder of the priestly line (Exodus 28:1-2; Leviticus 8:1—9:24).

Aaron was associated with Moses in every enterprise (Exodus 6:23). He is mentioned in the early narratives in connection with the Exodus, the building of the golden calf, and the complaint against Moses' marriage to a Cushite woman.

Later, the people murmured against Aaron and Moses (Numbers 14:2; 16:41), but he was vindicated by God making his rod to sprout (Numbers 17:8). His rod was preserved "before the testimony" (Numbers 17:10) and in the New Testament it is said to have been placed in the Ark (Hebrews 9:4).

Aaron, like Moses, did not get to enter the Promised Land because he doubted God's ability to cause water to spring from the rock at Meribah (Numbers 12:20). He died at Mount Hor (Numbers 20:28), near Moserah (Deuteronomy 10:6). He is the ancestor of St. Elizabeth, the mother of St. John the Baptist (Luke 1:5).

REFLECTION St. Aaron served God faithfully in very difficult conditions and helped Moses deliver the people from bondage and founded a priesthood that helped them worship the Lord and become his chosen people. He thus contributed to getting the people into the Promised Land and enabled them to serve the Lord.

PRAYER *O God, in Your wisdom You raised up Your servant St. Aaron to help free Your people and give them a country of their own. Through his prayers, help us be ever grateful that we can be Your people and enjoy freedom in our day. This we ask through Christ our Lord. Amen.*

———◆—◆———

ST. MONEGUNDIS, Widow

July 2

MONEGUNDIS was born at Chartres, France, in the sixth century. Little is known of her childhood. As a young lady she married and later gave birth to two daughters.

After the deaths of her children, Monegundis asked her husband to allow her to become an anchoress and to build a cell for herself at Chartres. He agreed, and Monegundis lived on oat bread and water while walled up in her cell.

Some years later, Monegundis moved to Tours and built another cell, near the tomb of St. Martin, where she remained for the rest of her life. Many women were drawn to her, and some of her followers organized the convent of St.

Pierre-le Puellier in Tours. Monegundis died after 557. Following her death, many miracles were attributed to intercessions at her tomb.

REFLECTION   We never know when tragedy will enter our lives. A resolute faith and an extensive prayer life filled with mortification, like those of St. Monegundis, will enable us to see the true way when all seems dark.

PRAYER   *O God, in Your goodness You have given us the courageous example of Your servant St. Monegundis as a beacon on our journey home. Through Your infinite kindness, help us to walk without fear. This we ask through Christ our Lord. Amen.*

———◆———

ST. HELIODORUS, Bishop

July 3

HELIODORUS was born at Altino, Italy, around 332. As a young man he served as a soldier.

In the year 372, Heliodorus met St. Jerome at Aquileia and became one of his disciples, helping to finance Jerome's translation of the Bible into Latin, which became known as the *Vulgate*. However, although he followed Jerome to the East, Heliodorus refused to join him in a life of seclusion in the Palestinian desert. Jerome was upset with this refusal and rebuked Heliodorus in a very strong letter.

When Heliodorus eventually returned to Italy he was appointed Bishop of Altino, a small town

near Venice. In that role he was a staunch oppo-
nent of Arianism while continuing his financial
support of Jerome. He died at Altino around the
end of the fourth century and the beginning of
the fifth.

REFLECTION   St. Heliodorus was a young man of
courage and devotion. Yet, when his instincts did not
lead him into the desert lifestyle, he maintained the
Faith and continued to sustain his personal efforts in
spreading God's Word.

PRAYER   *O God, Your servant St. Heliodorus gave
his life and work for the glory of Your Word. May we
imitate his generosity in living for the spread of the
Gospel. This we ask through Christ our Lord. Amen.*

ST. BERTHA, Abbess

July 4

BERTHA was born in France in the seventh
century. The daughter of Count Rigobertus
and Ursanna, she was married at the age of
twenty and became the mother of five daughters.

Having built a convent at Blangy in Artois,
Bertha went there to live following her husband's
death, accompanied by two of her daughters, and
assumed the role of abbess.

Once Bertha was satisfied that the convent
had been established on a firm religious foundation, she placed one of her daughters in charge.
Then she retired to a cell in the convent and de-

voted the remainder of her life to contemplation and prayer. She died around the year 725.

REFLECTION There comes a time in everyone's life when things have to be put in order. After the example of St. Bertha, we must examine our aims and objectives in order to make sure we are on the correct path to God.

PRAYER *Loving Father, we acknowledge Your abiding presence with us. Through the example and intercession of Your servant St. Bertha, help us always to measure and perform our actions with an awareness of Your being with us in a very special way. This we ask through Christ our Lord. Amen.*

BL. MATTHEW LAMBERT, ROBERT MEYLER, EDWARD CHEEVERS, AND PATRICK CAVANAGH, Martyrs

July 5

THESE four Blesseds are some of the Irish Martyrs who were killed during the English persecution of Catholics in Ireland from 1579 to 1654. They remained steadfast in the Faith and refused to renounce the authority of the Pope.

Matthew Lambert was a baker, martyred with several companions in 1581 at Wexford. He professed the Faith to the end.

Robert Meyler was a Catholic sailor who professed his Faith and died with Matthew Lambert.

Edward Cheevers was another Catholic sailor who kept the faith to the end and died with Matthew Lambert.

Patrick Cavanagh was a third Catholic sailor who remained faithful to the end and died with Matthew Lambert.

These martyrs were beatified on September 27, 1992, by Pope John Paul II as part of the 17 Martyrs of Ireland.

REFLECTION During the reign of King Henry VIII (1509-1547) and Queen Elizabeth I (1558-1603), it was a crime to speak out on Catholicism or to be reconciled to the Catholic Church or to celebrate the Mass or to harbor Catholic priests. Practicing the Faith brought death to a host of Catholics at that time. Pope John Paul II said: "We thank [these Martyrs] for the example of their fidelity . . . which is a heritage of the Irish people and a responsibility to be lived up to in our age."

PRAYER   *O Lord, You strengthened these Martyrs of Ireland so that they chose death rather than deny the Faith. By their prayers, may we have the strength to practice our Faith daily and never deny it. This we ask through Christ our Lord. Amen.*

ST. PALLADIUS, Bishop
July 6

S T. Palladius was a deacon in Rome who was responsible for having St. Germanus of Auxerre sent to Britain in 429 to combat the error of

Pelagianism that had cropped up there. In 431, he was consecrated by Pope Celestine I and sent to Ireland as the first Irish bishop.

The Saint labored in Leinster, meeting a great deal of opposition, especially on the part of the local chieftains. Still, he managed by dint of effort to make some converts and succeeded in building three churches. However, because of the meager harvest, inside of one year Palladius decided to cross over into Scotland.

Unfortunately, the Saint died in 432 (soon after leaving Ireland), at Fordun, near Aberdeen. His reputation for holiness followed him, and in the Middle Ages his relics were venerated there.

REFLECTION St. Palladius strove mightily in the Lord's work but his harvest was little. He met only opposition on the part of the people he went to instruct. He suffered greatly in trying to evangelize an opposed people. But he was able to prepare the ground for better results when St. Patrick came to Ireland soon afterward. As the dictum found in St. Paul says, "I planted the seed, and Apollos watered it, but it is God Who caused it to grow" (1 Corinthians 3:6).

PRAYER *O Lord, You sent St. Palladius to prepare the ground in Ireland and Britain for the Faith. By his prayers, help us to do what we can to spread the Faith to others by our prayers and the witness of our lives. This we ask through Christ our Lord. Amen.*

ST. ETHELBURGA, Abbess

July 7

E THELBURGA was the daughter of Anna, the King of the East Angles. Very little is known of her childhood.

At an early age, Ethelburga went to Gaul with her half-sister St. Sethrida. There both entered the convent at Faremoutier, where at that time St. Burgundofara was abbess.

Around 600, St. Burgundofara died and was replaced as abbess by Sethrida. When Sethrida passed away, Ethelburga became abbess. She died at Faremoutier around 695. After seven years her body was found to be incorrupt. In France, St. Ethelburga is known as St. Aubierge.

REFLECTION   One of the most important decisions young people are called upon to make is what they are going to do with their lives. St. Ethelburga was faithful to her vocation to the religious life. The most important thing for each of us is to be faithful to our own calling—whatever it may be.

PRAYER   *God our Father, in Your wisdom You have created all people as individuals, with different gifts. Through the example and intercession of Your Virgin St. Ethelburga, enable us to reflect the beauty of Your creation by returning our gifts and talents to You in working for the salvation of others. This we ask through Christ our Lord. Amen.*

ST. KILIAN, Bishop and Martyr
July 8

S T. Kilian was an Irish monk who was consecrated bishop and journeyed to Germany
with eleven companions to proclaim the Faith
and converted the local ruler of Wurzburg called
Gozbert.

Kilian then went to Rome and received permission from Pope Conon (687-688) to evangelize Franconia (i.e., Baden and Bavaria). On returning from Rome, Kilian saw that Gozbert had
married his brother's widow, Geilana, and he
persuaded him to separate from her because
such a marriage was forbidden by the Church.

While Gozbert was away on military duty,
Geilana in retaliation had St. Kilian murdered together with two of his fellow missionaries,
Colomon a priest, and Totnan a deacon. This
took place around the year 689.

REFLECTION St. Kilian gave up his home and country to travel to those who had not heard of Christ or
His Church. He thus took his life in his hands as he
tried to teach the Faith to pagans. And in the end he
was rewarded by being beheaded. We should pray
often for our own modern-day missionaries who put
their lives on the line in order to preach Christ to people who do not know Him.

PRAYER *Almighty Father, You called St. Kilian,
Your Bishop and Martyr, to preach the Faith to those
who had no knowledge of it. By his prayers, send
forth workers into the vineyard, for there are many*

people still without Christ in our world. This we ask through Christ our Lord. Amen.

ST. NICHOLAS PIECK, Priest, AND COMPANIONS, Martyrs

ST. Nicholas Pieck (1538-1572), a Franciscan priest, and eighteen companions form part of the group of Martyrs of Gorkum. They number nine Franciscan priests and two lay brothers plus eight priests from the diocesan and regular clergy.

After his ordination in 1558, St. Nicholas began his mission of converting the Calvinists. He evangelized the principal towns of Belgium and Holland, and became superior of the monastery at Gorkum.

At the time, the Calvinists were part of the Dutch struggle to overthrow the Spanish rule in the Low Countries. In time, the Calvinists captured that town, and the Saint and his companions were sentenced to death. They were subjected to various tortures to make them deny the Real Presence of Christ in the Eucharist and the primacy of the Pope. All the Martyrs remained steadfast and were hanged, earning an eternal crown. They were canonized in 1867 by Pope Pius IX.

REFLECTION   The Martyrs were caught in the battle between the anti-Spanish Calvinist forces who captured the town of Gorkum and the Spanish rulers of the Low Countries. In spite of torture of all kinds, the Martyrs, led by St. Nicholas, remained true to the Faith till the end.

PRAYER   *Almighty God, You enabled Your Priest St. Nicholas and his Companions to remain true to the Faith and earn an eternal crown. By their prayers, help us to live our Faith every day out of love for You. This we ask through Christ our Lord. Amen.*

ST. AMALBURGA, Widow
July 10

B ORN in Brabant in the seventh century, St. Amalburga was married to Count Witger. From this marriage there were three children. All three became Saints: Gudula, Reineldis, and Emerbert of Cambrai.

After their children were raised, Count Witger became a Benedictine monk at Lobbes, while Amalburga joined the Benedictine convent at Maubeuge, where she was professed by St. Aubert, Bishop of Cambrai.

St. Amalburga died in the eighth century after a life of asceticism. She was buried beside her husband at the monastery of Lobbes.

REFLECTION   In the modern age, we can imitate the lives of Amalburga and her husband in a variety of ways not available to them. In our day, lay ministry can be a great opportunity for individuals who have raised their children and have retired. Many works of charity, mercy, and ministry are in need of generous volunteers.

ST. OLGA, Widow
July 11

OLGA was born at Pskov, Russia, around 879. Also known as Helga, in 903 she married Igor, Duke of Kiev.

When Igor was assassinated in 945, Olga reacted with vengeance on his murderers, ordering that they be scalded to death and murdering many of their followers. After his assassination, Olga ruled the country for the rest of her life.

In 957, Olga became a Christian and was baptized in Constantinople. Turning from her former ways, she devoted the remainder of her life to the spread of Christianity. In this endeavor she did not achieve great success, but her grandson, St. Vladimir, evangelized Russia. She died at Kiev on July 11, 969, at the age of ninety.

REFLECTION Many times conversion brings with it an abundance of grace. The life of St. Olga calls all of us to serious conversion of life, becoming examples of virtue and charity for others.

PRAYER *O God, You are ever ready to welcome us back to Your fold. Through the example and intercession of Your servant St. Olga, grant us the grace to remain always open to Your invitation to a life of grace, virtue, and peace. We ask this through Christ our Lord. Amen.*

ST. JOHN JONES, Priest and Martyr

July 12

ST. John Jones was born in 1559 into a Catholic family in England. He joined the Order of Friars Minor and was forced to go into exile in France where he was ordained a priest. After a brief sojourn in Rome, he returned to his homeland and remained in London, secretly exercising his priestly office.

In 1596, the Saint was arrested and imprisoned for two years. Then he was convicted of being a Catholic priest guilty of treason for having been ordained abroad and having returned to England.

In the end, St. John was hanged, drawn, and quartered at Southwick in London on July 12, 1598. He was canonized by Pope Paul VI in 1970 as one of the Martyrs of England and Wales.

REFLECTION   Although St. John was well aware that he was in great danger when he returned to bring the Faith to the people in England, he never wavered but preached the Faith to one and all. In this light, the troubles we endure in life seem small compared to those that he and other Martyrs endured.

PRAYER   *Almighty God, You made Your Martyr John a distinguished defender of the Faith. Through his intercession, may all those who glory in the Name of Christ return to the unity of the true Faith. This we ask through Christ our Lord. Amen.*

———◆◆———

ST. CLELIA BARBIERI, Virgin
July 13

CLELIA Barbieri was born at Bundrie, Italy, on February 13, 1847. From the very beginning she appeared to have all the characteristics of an unusually precocious child. She seemed never to be interested in the things of this world, and was faithful to the practice of the supernatural virtues.

During her very short life, Clelia's holiness was recognized by local Church officials. Her strong belief in God convinced her of the need to respect all people, to live soberly, with modesty, goodness, and a great sense of devotion. She was known to be a very simple and open person, of delicate demeanor, humble, simple, sensitive to the demands of morality, and possessed of a deep spirituality.

Eventually, Clelia gathered her followers into a religious group called Our Lady of the Seven Dolors. Their object was to pray for and give service to the poor. She died on July 13, 1870, was beatified by Pope Paul VI in 1968, and was canonized by Pope John Paul II in 1989.

REFLECTION Prayer, love, openness, simplicity, joy, charity, and concern for the poor are the ideals and virtues of youth. When young people are able to maintain and foster their ideals, as St. Clelia Barbieri was able to do, this leads inevitably to a life with God. The challenge for modern youth is to taste and see the goodness of the Lord.

PRAYER *Lord God, walk with our young people as they seek the ideals of Your Word. Through the intercession of Your servant St. Clelia Barbieri, guide them away from distractions that will turn them from Your loving presence. This we ask through Christ our Lord. Amen.*

ST. EZRA, Priest and Scribe

The Same Day—July 13

ST. Ezra was a priest and scribe who is the protagonist of the Book of Ezra, the coworker of Nehemiah, and one of the leading figures in the restoration of the Jewish community after the Babylonian Exile.

In 458 B.C. or 428 B.C., he received permission from Artaxerxes, King of Persia, to return from the Exile to Jerusalem and to carry out a religious reform. He joined with Nehemiah in fashioning the Jewish community after the Exile and is regarded by the Talmud as a second Moses—for restoring the Law to the people.

Upon arriving in Jerusalem, Ezra called the people together and ordered that the Law be proclaimed in their midst. This public reading was a type of promulgation of the Law so that all who heard it and affirmed it would be bound to live according to its precepts.

Ezra then set up a court to decide what to do about those who had married foreign women. After three months the work was finished and the foreign wives were divorced. Ezra called upon the people to make hard choices. He saw that too many compromises could lead to a weakening of commitment to the point that people are no longer what they claim to be. In doing so he helped Israel remain God's people.

REFLECTION Ezra's example is a powerful reminder to us today that we must, at times, reject the messages that our permissive society gives. We cannot live selfishly, thinking only of our pleasure or success or money. We must rather live a life of love and self-sacrifice. We must be willing to pay the price of fidelity, no matter how high it might be.

PRAYER *O God, in Your wisdom You raised up Your Priest and Scribe St. Ezra to keep Your people faithful to You after the Exile. By his prayers, help us to remain faithful to You all our lives. This we ask through Christ our Lord. Amen.*

ST. FRANCIS SOLANO, Priest

July 14—Apostle of South America

BORN in Cordova, Spain, in 1549, St. Francis joined the Franciscan Friars in 1569 and was ordained in 1576. He became well known by his preaching and conversions. A decade later he asked to go to the New World.

Arriving there in 1589, he labored for the rest of his life on behalf of the well-being of the Native Peoples as well as the Spanish colonizers of South America and became known as the Wonderworker of the New World. A single word from his lips would cause an attacking army to fall back. When his companions were hungry, a command uttered by him brought in fish from the sea. The simple movement of his hand caused a raging bull to become tranquil at his feet.

About the year 1600, St. Francis returned to Peru where he taught the catechism to the Native Peoples and preached repentance to the Spanish until his death at Lima in 1610. He was canonized in 1726 by Pope Benedict XIII.

REFLECTION   St. Francis Solano ranged far and wide in the regions of Central America and brought the Faith to the Native Peoples by words, healings, and signs. He wore himself out by his continuous exertions and penance, working in the vineyard of the Lord. He reminds us to pray daily for those who do not yet know Christ.

PRAYER   *God our Father, through St. Francis You brought many nations of America into the Church. Through his prayers, join our hearts more closely to You and lovingly implant reverence for Your Name in the nations who do not know You. This we ask through Christ our Lord. Amen.*

ST. VLADIMIR OF KIEV, King

July 15—*Apostle of Russia*

VLADIMIR of Kiev was born into a noble family around 975. Reared in idolatry, he was known for his barbarity and loose morals. However, around 989, Vladimir was converted to Christianity. How this came about is fairly speculative. Apparently his marriage to Anne, the daughter of Emperor Basil II of Constantinople, preceded his conversion. Some said that he married because of political and economic motives.

Whatever the reason, his conversion signaled the advent of Christianity in Russia.

Following his conversion, Vladimir abandoned his former wives and mistresses and destroyed pagan idols in his realm. He determined to lead a virtuous life and invited Greek missionaries to evangelize Russia. At the same time he provided them with almost excessive support, sometimes forcing people to accept Baptism.

Known as the Apostle of Russia and revered as a notorious sinner who had mended his ways, Vladimir was held with great respect throughout Russia. Although he was under the ecclesiastical jurisdiction of the Byzantine Church, he sought to maintain friendly relations with Rome. Before his death in 1015, the Saint gave away all his personal possessions to his friends and to the poor.

REFLECTION The process of conversion can be a difficult one. When turning to God means giving up a life of sensuality and debauchery, the fullness of God's grace and love comes clearly into focus. St. Vladimir's life is a beckoning to all who feel separated from God to confidently accept His invitation to reform together with the discipline involved.

PRAYER *Lord our God, look with favor on the people of Russia as they struggle with newfound freedom. Through the intercession of Your servant St. Vladimir, may they respond generously to Your grace. This we ask through Christ our Lord. Amen.*

ST. MARY-MAGDALEN POSTEL, Virgin

July 16

MARY-MAGDALEN Postel was born in Barfleur, France, on November 28, 1756. Educated by the Benedictines at Valognes, she returned to Barfleur at the age of eighteen and opened a girls' school. When the school was closed during the French Revolution, she used it to shelter fugitive priests.

After the Concordat of 1801, Mary-Magdalen resumed her work in Catholic education. In 1807, she and three other companions took vows of religion at Cherbourg. This was the beginning of the Sisters of the Christian Schools of Mercy, with Mary-Magdalen appointed as superior.

The newly formed institute experienced many grave difficulties. However, once Mary-Magdalen and her companions acquired the abbey of Saint-Sauveur-le-Vicomte, which had been abandoned during the Revolution, the group began to grow and develop. St. Mary-Magdalen died on July 16, 1846, at the Saint-Sauveur Abbey at the age of ninety. She was canonized in 1925 by Pope Pius XI.

REFLECTION From the outset St. Mary-Magdalen Postel dedicated her life to Christian education. Her efforts continue today to bring God's Word and peace to many young people. She is a model of Christian dedication and holiness.

PRAYER   *O God, through the example and interces-sion of St. Mary-Magdalen Postel may we dedicate our*

lives and talents for the welfare and benefit of Your peo-
ple. This we ask through Christ our Lord. Amen.

———◆◆———

ST. MARCELLINA, Virgin
July 17

MARCELLINA was the daughter of the prefect of Gaul and the sister of St. Ambrose.
Born at Trier, Gaul, around the year 330, Marcellina, when very young, moved to Rome with her
family and was entrusted with the care of her
two brothers.

In the year 353, Marcellina was consecrated
as a virgin to the religious life by Pope Liberius.
She had a reputation for leading a life of great
austerity, to such an extent that St. Ambrose encouraged her to follow a less strict regimen in
her later years.

St. Ambrose was so inspired by her holiness,
detachment, and mortification that he dedicated
his famous treatise on virginity to her. St. Marcellina is believed to have died around 398.

REFLECTION   St. Marcellina knew that prayer, fasting, and detachment from material things put us in
touch with our true selves. They help us focus on the
true reason for our having been born, for our destiny
in both life and death.

PRAYER   *God our Father, Your servant St. Marcellina has shown us the way to a good and holy life. Grant
us the grace to imitate her great love and attachment
for You. This we ask through Christ our Lord. Amen.*

ST. BRUNO, Bishop

July 18

Bruno was born of a noble family at Solero in the Piedmont section of Italy in 1049. He studied at Bologna and became a canon at Siena in 1079.

In 1080, having become renowned for his defense of Church teaching about the Blessed Sacrament against Berengarius, Bruno was appointed Bishop of Segni. Outstanding in his knowledge of Scripture, he preached against simony and lay investiture, and ceaselessly devoted himself to Church reform.

In 1095, Bruno resigned his bishopric and became a monk at the Abbey of Monte Cassino. However, the people of Segni objected so strongly that he had to reverse his decision, although he continued to live at Monte Cassino. He was elected abbot there in 1107. Later Pope Paschal II ordered Bruno to resign that position and return to Segni. The saintly abbot died in 1123 and was canonized in 1183 by Pope Lucius III.

REFLECTION St. Bruno stood squarely behind the Church against secular rulers who wanted to bend the rules somewhat. For this he was in some eyes punished. Nonetheless, his holy and dedicated life won not only the hearts of his people but also the crown of Sainthood.

PRAYER *O God, may we always be true to our Faith. Through the example and intercession of Your*

Bishop St. Bruno, may we stand firm against those people of power and wealth who would undermine the Faith for the sake of their own prestige. This we ask through Christ our Lord. Amen.

———◆———

ST. MACRINA THE YOUNGER, Virgin
July 19

MACRINA the Younger, the daughter of St. Basil the Elder and St. Emmelia, was born in Caesarea in Cappadocia around 330. Her mother provided her early education, and she could read from a very early age, especially the Book of Wisdom and the Psalms.

Macrina was likewise instructed in household affairs and was betrothed at the age of twelve. However, her fiancé died suddenly, and she refused any further offers of marriage. She dedicated her life to God and turned her efforts to helping educate her three brothers in the ways of God: St. Basil the Great, St. Peter of Sebaste, and St. Gregory of Nyssa. After the death of her father, she and her mother retired to the family estate in Pontus. Other women were invited to live there and follow a community rule of prayer and asceticism with St. Emmelia as abbess.

After her mother's death, Macrina became abbess. She gave everything she owned to the poor and supported herself by manual labors, sleeping on a bed of two boards. She died in 379. St. Gre-

gory's account of his sister's life speaks of cures both received and worked through St. Macrina.

REFLECTION   In an age when the accumulation of material possessions is highly esteemed, the example of St. Macrina's embracing poverty, along with her great devotion to prayer and a life of virtue, stands as a sign from God of the invitation He extends to all in every age. To dispose of unneeded goods in favor of the poor is to give full respect to God's invitation to everlasting life.

PRAYER   *God of love and mercy, turn toward Your people who cry out in a desert of worldliness. Through the example and intercession of Your Abbess St. Macrina, help us to overcome the desire for goods and wealth. This we ask through Christ our Lord. Amen.*

ST. MARGARET (or MARINA),
Virgin and Martyr
July 20—Patroness of Women in Childbirth

MARGARET (known as Marina in the East) was a young Christian martyred for the Faith. However, both the time and the place of her martyrdom are unknown. She went on to become one of the most popular Saints of the Middle Ages and was numbered among the Fourteen Holy Helpers.†

Her legendary Acts state that she was a convert to Christianity. As a result, her father, a pagan priest of Antioch in Pisidia, cast her out of the family home. Later, she tended sheep and caught the eye of the prefect Olybrius, who became infatuated with her. However, when she spurned his advances, he charged her with being a Christian.

In prison, Margaret had an encounter with the devil in the form of a dragon. Supposedly, he swallowed Margaret, but the Cross she carried irritated his throat, and Margaret was regurgitated. She became venerated as the Patroness of Women in Childbirth.

When attempts at execution failed, many who witnessed what took place were converted. Eventually, Margaret was beheaded, probably during the persecution of Diocletian around 304.

---

† See p. 223.

It is said that one of the voices St. Joan of Arc heard was that of St. Margaret.

REFLECTION   Difficult decisions based on principle or religious conviction can sometimes be hard to sustain. St. Margaret's life shows the wisdom of sustaining oneself through God's love in one's own convictions, reached under the guidance of an experienced spiritual director.

PRAYER   *Loving God, come to our aid in times of difficulty and temptation. Through the example and intercession of Your Virgin and Martyr St. Margaret, enable us to remain faithful to You. This we ask through Christ our Lord. Amen.*

ST. ELIJAH, Prophet

The Same Day—July 20

ST. Elijah from Tishbe in Gilead was the dramatic ninth-century B.C. Prophet of the Lord in the days of kings Ahab (875-853 B.C.) and Ahaziah (853-852 B.C.), in Israel. During that time he vindicated the rights of the one God against the faithless people with such strength of soul that he prefigured not only St. John the Baptist but also Christ Himself. He did not leave any written oracles, but his memory was preserved especially on Mount Carmel.

Elijah challenged the prophets of Baal to a contest on Mount Carmel, and the Lord vindicated Himself against Baal there. While Elijah was threatened by Jezebel, Ahab's wife, he received comfort and direction from God. During the drought, Elijah was fed by ravens and by a widow of Zarephath, whose son he raised to life.

The Prophet condemned the house of Ahab because of Jezebel's murderous seizure of Naboth's vineyard and also condemned Ahaziah, Ahab's son, for appealing to a pagan god during his illness. After working many wonders, Elijah anointed Elisha as his successor and was taken up in a fiery chariot.

REFLECTION   It was the belief that Elijah would return before the coming of the Messiah. This is why John the Baptist is called another Elijah and why Elijah appeared along with Moses during Jesus' Transfiguration on Mount Tabor. The God of Elijah sides with the poor and the weak and frustrates the hopes of those who like to grow in power through contact with Him.

PRAYER   *O God, in Your wisdom You raised up St. Elijah to be a Prophet for Your people and keep them faithful to You. By his prayers, send new prophets into the world in our day to keep Your people completely faithful to You. This we ask through Christ our Lord. Amen.*

———◆———

ST. ARBOGAST, Bishop

July 21

ARBOGAST was born in Aquitaine, France, in the sixth century, although some legends record his birthplace as Ireland or Scotland. Little or nothing is known of his childhood. However, sometime later, after he had developed a hermitage in Alsace, his reputation for holiness spread.

When King Dagobert's son was killed from an attack by a wild boar while hunting, St. Arbogast's prayers restored the lad to life. In gratitude the king appointed Arbogast as Bishop of Strasbourg.

Arbogast was known to be an individual of great humility who was wholeheartedly devoted to his flock. When he died in the sixth century, a church was erected over his burial site.

REFLECTION   In the life of St. Arbogast, what is quite clear for us is the necessity of profound prayer in order to be able not only to meet the temptations in our everyday experience but also to acquire the virtues for a good life.

PRAYER   *O God, we cry out to You in our hour of need. Through the intercession of Your Bishop St. Arbogast, help us to turn away from worldly desires and turn completely toward You. This we ask through Christ our Lord. Amen.*

———◆◆———

ST. WANDRILLE (or WANDREGISILUS),
Abbot
July 22

BORN around 1600, near Verdun, France, Wandrille came of a noble family, possibly related to Merovingian royalty, and was brought up at the court of Dagobert I. He entered into an arranged marriage with a young noblewoman, but after a pilgrimage to Rome, he and his wife decided to join the monastic life. He had some monastic training and also lived as a hermit.

The Saint went on to Bobbio and then to Romain-Motier Abbey on the Isère, where he spent the next ten years and where he was given minor orders and the diaconate by St. Ouen. He was ordained a priest by St. Omer.

Afterward, St. Wandrille founded the Abbey of Fontenelle in Normandy and developed it into a missionary and spiritual center. He also founded a school there and took care of the people in the surrounding area. He died around the year 688 with a reputation for holiness.

REFLECTION   St. Wandrille gave up the world when he left the court and became a monk, but he came back to save the people, especially through the abbey he founded. His kindness transformed bitter lives. His humility led the proud to return to their homes. His teaching and preaching brought back many souls to the Lord. We should not forget to pray for those who are estranged from the Church in our day.

PRAYER   *O Lord, You called Your Abbot St. Wandrille from the king's court to the monastic life, and he founded an abbey that attended to the needs of both monks and laity. By his intercession, remind us to pray for religious vocations that will bring workers into Your vineyard. This we ask through Christ our Lord. Amen.*

ST. JOHN CASSIAN, Abbot
July 23

JOHN Cassian, usually referred to simply as Cassian, was born around 360, probably in Dobruje, Romania. Around 380, he and his friend Germanus went to visit the Palestinian holy places. While in Bethlehem, they decided to become monks, but eventually they migrated to Egypt where monasticism was better developed. They sought out various hermits, including those in the desert of Skete, to learn about the monastic life.

Around 400, Cassian went to Constantinople and studied under St. John Chrysostom. Chrysostom ordained Cassian a deacon. Later when Chrysostom was condemned, Cassian went to Rome to defend him before Pope St. Innocent I. Some believe that Cassian was ordained in Rome, but he dropped from sight for a time after his Rome experience.

When Cassian later surfaced in Marseilles, he founded a monastery for men and another for women. His communities were clearly characterized by the monastic style of Egypt. Moreover, his writings on monastic life had a great influence in France. St. Benedict recommended Cassian's works as authoritative resources on the training of monks. Cassian died in Marseilles around 435.

REFLECTION The attraction for things of God can sometimes be so overwhelming that some individuals, like St. John Cassian, follow every means possible to secure a lifestyle that emphasizes the supernatural. Monks shut away in monasteries are so filled with peace and joy in the knowledge of God's presence that we are encouraged to find a solitude of some kind in the midst of our workaday world.

PRAYER   *Father of all people, You sent Your servant St. John Cassian in search of You in the desert and in monastic life. Through his example and intercession, may we too withdraw from the world to the degree that we may be refreshed by Your holy presence. This we ask through Christ our Lord. Amen.*

ST. EZEKIEL, Priest and Prophet

The Same Day—July 23

ST. Ezekiel was both priest and prophet, and he ministered to his fellow exiles from 593 to 563 B.C. He is the Prophet of the Temple and the Liturgy as well as of the Absolute Majesty of God and of the New Life.

Like Jeremiah, Ezekiel denounces the false illusions of his people, their moral corruption, and especially the idolatry of their worship. He preaches a religion of the heart, announces a New Covenant, and insists on the personal responsibility of every member of the people.

Called the "Father of Judaism," Ezekiel announces the restoration of Israel and the coming of God to reign over His people like a shepherd. He fosters the people's hope by his vision of dry bones coming to life again. He also makes use of symbolic actions; for example, when his wife died he refrained from mourning as a sign to his people of the coming liberation.

REFLECTION   St. Ezekiel imparts a strong sense of sin, seen as an abomination before God. At the same time, he inculcates in all an equally vivid sense of the gratuity of salvation: human beings cannot merit forgiveness; it is God Who grants it beyond the boundaries of strict justice and thus heaps confusion upon unrepentant sinners.

PRAYER   *O God, in Your wisdom You sent St. Ezekiel Your Prophet to console Your people and speak to them about new life and the coming restoration. By his prayers, help us to remain filled with hope in all circumstances since it is on Your promises that we rely. This we ask through Christ our Lord Amen.*

STS. BORIS AND GLEB, Martyrs

July 24—St. Boris: Patron of Moscow

BORIS and Gleb were the younger sons of St. Vladimir of Kiev in the tenth century. When their father died, his eldest son and their stepbrother, Svyatopolk, plotted to take the entire inheritance for himself by having Boris and Gleb murdered.

Boris and Gleb were thoroughly imbued with the teaching of Christ. Although they learned of Svyatopolk's sinister plan and were urged to take up arms against him, they refused to do so because of their Faith. Boris was slain in 1015 while he was at prayer and asked forgiveness for his brother and his slayers before he died.

That same year, Gleb undertook a sea journey to meet Svyatopolk at Kiev, but he never got there. He was slain aboard his boat on the Dnieper River by his step-brother's henchmen.

Another brother, Yaroslav, managed to bury the bodies of the Martyrs five years later in St. Basil's Church at Vyshgorod. From the first, the two brothers were revered as voluntary Martyrs for Christ and regarded as Saints of God. Their burial place became a popular shrine, and miracles were attributed to the prayers of the Martyrs.

In time, Boris was named the Patron of Moscow, and their cult was confirmed in 1724. They are sometimes referred to by the names Romanus and David.

REFLECTION   In His Sermon on the Mount, Jesus urged His followers to accept ill-treatment for His sake without retaliation. Sts. Boris and Gleb, spurred on by a great faith, followed this dictum to the letter. In this violent world of ours, we should frequently reflect on adhering more closely to the peaceful principles of our Lord.

PRAYER   *God of peace, You desire that all Your children live at peace with one another. Through the example and intercession of Your Martyrs Sts. Boris and Gleb, enable us to cultivate the peace of Christ within ourselves and to bring it to others—especially in times of stress. This we ask through Christ our Lord. Amen.*

ST. EUPHRASIA, Virgin

The Same Day—July 24

EUPHRASIA'S father Antigonus was a relative of Emperor Theodosius I who completed the transformation of the Roman Empire into a Christian state. When Antigonus died, the emperor assumed responsibility for the care of Euphrasia and her mother at Constantinople.

When Euphrasia was five years of age, Theodosius arranged for her future marriage with a senator. While waiting for Euphrasia to reach a suitable age, her mother took her to Egypt, and they settled near a convent of nuns. At the age of seven, Euphrasia asked to enter the convent and, with the permission of her mother, was allowed to do so.

When she was twelve, Arcadius, who had succeeded his father Theodosius as emperor, ordered Euphrasia to return to Constantinople and marry the senator to whom she was betrothed. In reply, Euphrasia wrote and asked to be excused, requesting that her parents' property be distributed to the poor and used to ransom slaves. Realizing that Euphrasia had a religious vocation, the emperor acceded to her request, and she remained in the convent for the rest of her life.

Euphrasia carried out meticulously all the duties of her state. She added to them continuous prayer and much fasting as well as equanimity in the face of false accusations. After a life totally dedicated to God, she went to her eternal reward some time in the fifth century.

REFLECTION   St. Euphrasia was attracted to a life of piety from an early age. Although she could have led a life of ease as wife to a senator, she chose to remain in the convent where, for most of her life, she performed the most menial tasks. Like Euphrasia, let us live out Lent in a true spirit of humility.

PRAYER   *Gracious God, You looked with favor on Your servant St. Euphrasia and enabled her to follow You in poverty and humility. May we have the courage to imitate her virtues as we live up to our Lenten goals. This we ask through Christ our Lord. Amen.*

———◆◆———

ST. MAGNERICUS, Bishop

July 25

ST. Magnericus was born in the sixth century. As a youth he lived at Trier in Bishop Nicetius's residence. Later Magnericus was ordained by Nicetius, and he accompanied the bishop when Nicetius was exiled by King Clotaire I in retaliation for his excommunication on charges of corruption and licentiousness.

About one year later, Magnericus returned to Trier, and in 566, he became Bishop of Trier. Magnericus offered sanctuary to Bishop Theodore of Marseilles when he had been banished by Guntramnus of Burgundy, going so far as to plead with King Childebert II on behalf of the bishop.

Magnericus built several monasteries and churches dedicated to St. Martin of Tours to whom he had great devotion. St. Gregory of Tours was a close friend and great admirer of Magnericus, who died about the year 596.

REFLECTION   Truth sometimes has a way of bestirring others to anger. This is all the more true regarding the truth of the Gospel. Like St. Magnericus, we can expect confrontation if we live or preach God's Word.

PRAYER   *O God, You graciously revealed to us the Good News through Your Son. By the example and intercession of Your Bishop St. Magnericus, grant us the will and courage to always live the truth You give us in Your Word. This we ask through Christ our Lord. Amen.*

ST. BARTHOLOMEA CAPITANIO, Virgin

July 26

BARTHOLOMEA Capitanio was born at Lovere, Italy, in 1807. She wanted to become a nun, but when her parents refused permission, she took a vow of perpetual chastity and began to work with youth.

Later, with Catherine Gerosa (now known as St. Vincentia), St. Bartholomea founded the Sisters of Charity of Lovere, based on the Rule of the

Sisters of Charity of St. Vincent de Paul. Their object was to educate the young and care for the sick poor. In its early days the institute experienced some grave difficulties, but eventually it won papal approval.

As the congregation spread, St. Bartholomea wrote many letters on the subject of spirituality. Eventually some were published. She died at the age of twenty-nine on July 26, 1833, and was canonized in 1950 by Pope Pius XII.

REFLECTION In a very short time, St. Bartholomea accomplished much. Since we never know how much time we will have to pursue our salvation, it is important that we take our spiritual life seriously.

PRAYER *O God, You call us to holiness of life. May we, through the intercession of St. Bartholomea, respond with zealous generosity. This we ask through Christ our Lord. Amen.*

———◆◆———

BL. TITUS BRANDSMA, Priest and Martyr
The Same Day—July 26

ANNO Sjoera Brandsma was born on a farm near Oegeklooster in the Netherlands on February 23, 1881. A good student, he earned a Doctorate at the age of twenty-eight and developed into a young man of devotion and piety. Three of his four sisters became nuns, while a brother was a Franciscan priest, and he himself joined the Carmelites, taking the name Titus and becoming ordained.

Titus taught philosophy at the Catholic University of Nijmegen and traveled widely speaking for many causes. Moreover, Titus was a journalist and author. In 1935, Titus wrote a public protest condemning new marriage laws against the Jews. Later, he said a Catholic newspaper could not accept Nazi propaganda and still be considered Catholic.

The courageous priest refused to hide from the Nazis and was arrested, hurled into several prisons, and ultimately brought to the concentration camp at Dachau. He remained there only five weeks. Titus was beaten nearly every day, given extra work time, and harassed by the guards, yet he urged his fellow prisoners to pray for the guards. Eventually the ill-treatment made him so weak that he was sent to the prison infirmary, where doctors performed inhumane experiments on him. In pain he would cry out: "Not my will but Yours be done!"

On July 26, 1942, Titus gave his Rosary to his nurse who had left the Church. She administered poison by injection, and Titus died in ten minutes. His body was cremated at Dachau.

Titus's writings were approved on April 2, 1964, his cause was introduced on December 10, 1973, and he was beatified by Pope John Paul II on November 3, 1985.

REFLECTION   The joy of the Lord marked the life of Bl. Titus Brandsma. It gave him courage to stand fast in the face of the great untruth that was National Socialism. We too must be firm in our concerns to remove the evil of racism from our midst.

PRAYER   *All-powerful Father, You created us in Your image and likeness and charged us to love all our brothers and sisters no matter what their race or nationality may be. May our individual lives, through the example and intercession of Your Martyr Bl. Titus Brandsma, be a crusade against the sin of racism. This we ask through Christ our Lord. Amen.*

BL. MARY-MAGDALEN MARTINENGO,
Virgin
July 27

MARY-MAGDALEN Martinengo was born of a noble family at Brescia in northern Italy, in 1687. Her mother died when she was an infant, and perhaps as a result her childhood was marked by intense religious devotion.

At the age of eighteen Mary entered the Capuchinesses of Santa Maria della Neve in Brescia. Elected prioress twice, she also served as mistress of novices.

During her lifetime of fifty years, Mary practiced severe mortifications and had great devotion to our Lord Crucified. She died in 1737 and was beatified by Pope Leo XIII in 1900.

REFLECTION   The life of Bl. Mary-Magdalen Martinengo reminds us that we must take all the means necessary to fulfill the duties of our state in life. As we are filled with God's grace, we are called to share His goodness with others.

PRAYER   *O God, in Your wisdom You call each of us to a life of holiness and perfection. Through the intercession of Bl. Mary-Magdalen Martinengo, may we imitate her holiness. This we ask through Christ our Lord. Amen.*

———◆◆———

ST. PANTALEON (or PANTELEIMON),
Martyr

The Same Day, July 27—Patron of Physicians and Invoked against Consumption

ST. Pantaleon is one of the Fourteen Holy Helpers† and is honored by the Greeks as the "Great Martyr and Wonderworker" and one of the

---

† See p. 223.

Holy Moneyless Ones who treated the sick without payment. He is also known as Panteleimon (the Greek form of his name), meaning "The All-compassionate One." He was martyred about 305.

However, the legends that have come down to us about him are suspect. He was supposedly the son of a pagan father, Eustorgius of Nicomedia, brought up in the Faith by his Catholic mother, Eubula. He studied medicine and became the physician to Emperor Galerius Maximian at Nicomedia.

After straying from the Faith for a time, he returned to it. Then, during Diocletian's persecution, he distributed all his possessions to the poor and was arrested as a Christian and put to death. Relics of his blood are preserved at Constantinople as well as Madrid, Spain, and Ravello, Italy, and they are said to liquefy on his feast day like the blood of St. Gennaro at Naples. He is invoked against consumption and is the Patron of Physicians.

REFLECTION For a time, St. Pantaleon lapsed from the Faith. However, once converted, he applied that Faith in full measure to everything that he did. He cured people without demanding payment. Then when persecution broke out, he willingly gave up his life. We should be determined to keep the Faith in all circumstances and even be prepared to give up our lives for it.

PRAYER *Heavenly Father, You inspired St. Pantaleon Your Martyr to heal the sick out of love for You without any payment and to give up his life for the*

Faith. By his prayers, give us the grace to keep the Faith all our lives and be ready to die for it. This we ask through Christ our Lord. Amen.

STS. NAZARIUS AND CELSUS, Martyrs

July 28

NAZARIUS is believed to have been born in Rome in the first century. His mother was a Christian and his father was a pagan Roman army officer. Nazarius was raised as a Christian and personally instructed by St. Peter.

Later in life, Nazarius and a companion, Celsus, preached Christianity in Milan. During Nero's first persecution, Nazarius and Celsus were beheaded in Milan, sometime around the year 68.

Legend has it that Nazarius' blood was both liquid and red when his tomb was discovered by St. Ambrose in 395. Both Saints have been enshrined at Milan. Nothing more is known of them.

REFLECTION   When one lays down one's life for the Faith, it bespeaks a bold and beautiful belief in Jesus and His Father. As we take up our cross daily, we surely tread in the footsteps of Jesus and His Holy Martyrs, like Sts. Nazarius and Celsus.

PRAYER   *O God, You have brought us to the fullness of life in grace through Your Death and Resurrection. Through the intercession of Your Martyrs Sts. Nazarius and Celsus, help us so to live as to always reflect Your image in our lives. This we ask through Christ our Lord. Amen.*

ST. OLAF OF NORWAY, King and Martyr

July 29—Patron of Norway

OLAF Haraldsson, the son of a Norwegian lord, was born in 995. Much of his youth was spent as a pirate. Later, leaving his piratical ways, he was baptized.

After recapturing most of Norway from the control of the Danes and Swedes in 1015, Olaf became king in 1016. He then tried to unify and Christianize Norway. However, his subjects rose in rebellion in 1029, and he was forced to flee to Russia.

Returning to Norway in 1030, Olaf attempted to win back his kingdom but was slain in the process on July 29, 1030. Miracles were later reported at his shrine, which eventually became the Cathedral of Trondheim and a place of pilgrimage for Scandinavians. Olaf was canonized in 1164 by Pope Alexander III and is regarded as the Patron of Norway.

REFLECTION   Through our efforts to bring others to God we are sometimes required to take grave risks, as St. Olaf was called upon to do. It is our knowledge that God is truly with us that sustains us in our quest.

PRAYER   *Lord our God, through the intercession of St. Olaf of Norway, may we always have the courage of our convictions and staunchly defend the rights of all peoples to honor You. This we ask through Christ our Lord. Amen.*

ST. LEOPOLD MANDIC, Priest

BOGDAN Mandic, the last of twelve children, was born at Castelnovo, in Dalmatia, on May 12, 1866. A very frail young man, he was given over to much silent prayer at a very early age. It is said he was a lad of angelic purity.

On November 16, 1882, Bogdan entered the Capuchin seminary in Udine. He studied hard and advanced rapidly in the way of perfection. On April 20, 1884, Bogdan entered the Capuchin novitiate at Bassaoso del Groppa and took the name Brother Leopold. Later he studied Philosophy at Padua and Theology in Venice. He was ordained on September 20, 1890.

Leopold labored in Capuchin convents for nineteen years before being sent to Padua, where he was to remain until his death except for one year spent in a prison camp during World War I for refusing to renounce his Croat nationality.

The major portion of his life at Padua was spent in the confessional, sometimes more than twelve hours a day. The zealous priest froze there in winter and sweltered in the heat of summer. Moreover, he was afflicted with terrible arthritis. This was his apostolate for forty years. People of all ages and ranks came to him. Many were converted and others sent on the road to perfection.

On the last day of his life, July 30, 1942, Leopold rose at 5:30 a.m. and spent an hour in prayer. Then while vesting to celebrate Mass, he collapsed. A few hours later, he passed away reciting the *Hail Holy Queen*. He was canonized by Pope John Paul II in 1983.

REFLECTION St. Leopold Mandic from his earliest years was attracted to prayer. Although he held many offices during the first nineteen years of his ministry as a Capuchin priest, he always remained faithful to solitude and prayer. St. Leopold's apostolate in the confessional at Padua exacted much physical suffering, but his gentleness, patience, and kindness led many back to God.

PRAYER *Loving God, You call us to a life of perfection, yet we fall into sin. You have given us the promise of forgiveness through Confession. Through the example and intercession of Your Priest St. Leopold, may we turn to You in gentleness and kindness, always ready to forgive those who offend us. This we ask through Christ our Lord. Amen.*

———◆•◆———

STS. ABDON AND SENNEN, Martyrs

The Same Day—July 30

ABDON and Sennen were Christian noblemen from Persia who lived in the third century. Despite the fact that the persecution of the Emperor Diocletian was in force, they placed their trust in God and continued to practice their Faith.

The two saintly noblemen were soon reported to the authorities and arrested. They were then transported to Rome in chains.

Once in Rome, Abdon and Sennen were ordered to sacrifice to pagan gods. When they steadfastly refused, they were tortured and thrown to the wild beasts—but the beasts did them no harm. Thereupon they were beheaded by gladiators and earned the crown of martyrdom.

REFLECTION Sts. Abdon and Sennen gave up fame, riches, and even their very lives for the Faith. They remind us that each of us must be prepared to do the same. Though we may not be called to martyrdom, we are all called to offer ourselves daily to the Father in union with Christ.

PRAYER   *O God, You endowed Your Martyrs Sts. Abdon and Sennen with abundant grace to bring them to their present glory. Grant that, through their merits and intercession, we may deserve to be delivered from all adversities. This we ask through Christ our Lord. Amen.*

ST. HELEN OF SKÖVDE, Widow and Martyr

July 31

HELEN of Skövde was born in Västergötland, Sweden, in the twelfth century. She belonged to a noble family. However, after the death of her husband, she gave all her possessions to the poor.

Following this, Helen made a pilgrimage to Rome. When she returned home, she found herself accused of involvement in the death of her son-in-law. It was later proved that the deed had been perpetrated by mistreated servants, but by that time Helen had been executed.

Following Helen's death, many miracles were reported at her tomb, and public devotion to her was approved under Pope Alexander III in 1164, just four years after her death.

REFLECTION Like Jesus the innocent Lamb, St. Helen was put to death. Her goodness was preserved through the manifestation of God's power at her tomb. Although we may be suspect but innocent here in this life, God will provide sure justice hereafter.

PRAYER *O God, we too sometimes stand falsely accused. Through the intercession of Your servant St. Helen of Skövde, may we place our trust in You and accept Your care in times of stress. This we ask through Christ our Lord. Amen.*

———◆———

ST. JUSTIN DE JACOBIS, Bishop
The Same Day—July 31

JUSTIN was born in San Fele, Italy, on October 9, 1800. At the age of eighteen he entered the Vincentians and was ordained a priest in 1824. He labored zealously in Naples, especially during the cholera epidemic.

Later Justin was chosen by the Congregation for the Propagation of the Faith as Prefect Apostolic for Abyssinia and asked to establish a mission in Ethiopia. He went to Africa in 1839 and remained there for twenty years where he worked strenuously for his people, founding missions and establishing a native clergy.

Consecrated a bishop on January 7, 1849, he bravely endured persecutions and imprisonment. Finally worn out by his labors, he died on July 31, 1860. He was beatified on June 25, 1939, by Pope Pius XII and canonized on October 25, 1975, by Pope Paul VI.

REFLECTION From time to time individuals are blessed with the gift of an ardent zeal for souls and the welfare of others. The life of St. Justin de Jacobis can be for others an energizing model to reinvigorate oneself in the service of the Gospel.

PRAYER   *Lord God, through the example and inter-cession of Your Bishop St. Justin de Jacobis, may we bring the Gospel to our neighbor with an ardent zeal and an abundant charity. This we ask through Christ our Lord. Amen.*

ST. ETHELWOLD, Bishop of Winchester

August 1

BORN in Winchester around 912, St. Ethelwold became a priest. In 943 St. Dunstan
restored the Benedictine observance in the
Abbey of Glastonbury, and Ethelwold joined the
Order and became one of the deans.

In 955 he was made Abbot of Abingdon and in
963 Bishop of Winchester. He went on to become
a leader in the monastic revival in that century,
founding or restoring abbeys and earning the
name "Father of Monks."

During the period of this skilled craftsman the
Winchester School of Illumination flourished,
and he highlighted the musical and liturgical as-
pects of worship. He died on August 1, 984.

REFLECTION St. Ethelwold was instrumental in en-
hancing the spirituality of his day by revitalizing
monasticism and beautifying the Liturgy. We should
strive to appreciate our Christian heritage, which can
revive our spirituality in a host of ways.

PRAYER *Lord God, through the intercession of St.
Ethelwold, help us grow in our spiritual life. Enable us
to worship You in spirit and in truth all the days of our
life. We ask this through Christ our Lord. Amen.*

THE SEVEN HOLY MACCABEES AND ST. ELEAZAR, Martyrs

The Same Day—August 1

THE Seven Maccabean Brothers are regarded as the first martyrs to suffer for their Faith before the advent of Christ.

The actual names of these Seven Martyrs and the place of their death are not known. *Maccabee* was the name of the Jewish dynasty that began in 168 B.C. with a revolution led by Mattathias against the Syrian King, Antiochus IV Epiphanes, who was attempting to force paganism upon the Jews; this name was then conferred upon the entire family of Mattathias as well as upon all of his followers.

Among these adherents were Seven Holy Brothers, each of whom successively endured the cruelest of tortures with incredible courage before being put to death. Immediately after their execution, the mother of these Seven Martyrs who had witnessed their suffering and still had encouraged them to persevere in their fortitude also suffered martyrdom rather than betray her Faith.

St. ELEAZAR was a ninety-year-old Israelite who refused to save his life by eating pork that was forbidden by the Mosaic Law but commanded by Antiochus IV Epiphanes (175-164 B.C.).

Eleazar was a prominent person and chief of the scribes. His friends begged him to dissimulate and eat lawful meat that they would substitute out of consideration for his age. However, he preferred a glorious death rather than a shameful life (2 Maccabees 6:18-31).

This splendid instance of courage probably occurred in Syrian Antioch where the seven Maccabees were martyred with their mother (2 Maccabees 7:1-41).

REFLECTION   The holy Maccabees and Eleazar provide us with a powerful example of remaining faithful to our Faith under the most difficult of circumstances. Like them, we should be convinced that the greatest treasure we have is our Faith and remain determined never to lose it.

PRAYER   *Heavenly Father, may the fraternal crown of Your Martyrs gladden us. May it increase virtue in us who believe and, by their manifold prayers, bring us consolation. This we ask through Christ our Lord. Amen.*

———◆—◆———

ST. STEPHEN I, Pope

August 2

STEPHEN, a Roman by birth, became Pope on May 12, 254, and reigned until August 2, 257. His pontificate is especially important for the light it throws on the development of the Holy See. It provides early evidence of the Roman See's exercising primacy over other Churches.

Stephen condemned the practice of rebaptizing heretics carried out by the Church of Carthage whose head was St. Cyprian. In accord with the previous Church tradition also followed by the Sees of Alexandria and Palestine, Rome recognized the Baptisms administered by heretics.

This Supreme Pontiff is also known for explicitly appealing to Christ's words to Peter in Matthew 16:18 as the basis for the primacy of the Roman Church: "You are Peter, and upon this rock I will build My Church."

Stephen died soon afterward (today he is no longer thought to have been a martyr) and was buried in the papal crypt of Callistus on the Appian Way.

REFLECTION St. Stephen reminds us that we must always be in tune with the teaching of the Church. Despite the fact that Bishop Cyprian of Carthage was a holy man who went on to give his life for the Faith, Stephen let him know that his view on rebaptism of heretics was erroneous. Stephen thus showed that it is by following the mind of the Church that we will be saved.

PRAYER   *Heavenly Father, Your Son Jesus established the Church and chose St. Peter and his successors to rule and guide her throughout the ages. Through the intercession of Your servant St. Stephen I, help us to love the Church and follow her teachings all our lives. This we ask through Christ our Lord. Amen.*

ST. PETER OF ANAGNI, Bishop
August 3

BORN in the eleventh century at Salerno, Italy, St. Peter became a Benedictine monk in his native city. In 1062, he was consecrated Bishop of Anagni by Pope Alexander II, at a time when the Pope found himself in Anagni because he had been chased out of Rome. This consecration was recommended by another monk, Hildebrand, the future Gregory VII.

A few years later, Pope Gregory sent St. Peter to Constantinople as his legate. Upon returning to Anagni, the Saint undertook the construction of a great church that was to become the city's new cathedral. The work was interrupted when the Bishop left Europe with the First Crusade, which he followed to its triumphant conclusion.

Upon returning to his diocese, St. Peter was able to complete the construction of the new church before his death in 1105. He was canonized in 1109 by Pope Paschal II.

REFLECTION St. Peter lived in turbulent times, marked by conflict between the Empire and the Papacy. The Saint did his best to follow the will of God in spite of all earthly occurrences. We too should remember always to give to God what is God's and to give earthly sovereigns what belongs to them.

PRAYER   O Lord, You called Your servant St. Peter to shepherd Your people in a time of special problems. By his intercession, may we always strive to give You what is Yours and to earthly rulers what be-

longs to them. This we ask through Christ our Lord. Amen.

———◆—◆———

ST. IA, Martyr

August 4

G IVEN the lack of sources concerning the events of St. Ia's life, it is difficult to formulate an accurate biography of this fourth-century martyr.

According to the most reliable sources, Ia was Greek. Some say she was a slave. Apparently she enjoyed success in converting Persian women to Christianity. As a result, she was arrested during a persecution by King Sapor II of Persia.

For the next several months, Ia was imprisoned and subjected to the cruelest of tortures in an attempt to get her to deny the Faith, but it was all to no avail. Eventually, her torturers gave up, and Ia was beaten to death and then beheaded about the year 362. Some nine thousand Christians also suffered martyrdom during this persecution.

REFLECTION To give up one's life for the Faith, as St. Ia did, could be a great source of consolation, affording the assurance of eternal salvation. However, to persevere in the Faith under the daily duress of temptation and ridicule is a similar though longer path to eternal bliss, a journey most are called to make.

PRAYER *O God, in Your great wisdom and goodness You have created us to be with You for all eternity. Through the example and intercession of Your*

Martyr St. Ia, help us so to live our Faith that we may overcome with love those who would have us deny You. This we ask through Christ our Lord. Amen.

ST. NONNA, Widow
August 5

NONNA was a Christian who later married a magistrate named Gregory from Nazianzus in Cappadocia. Gregory was a member of a Jewish-pagan sect.

Nonna's deep religious faith and observance was responsible for Gregory's conversion to Christianity. Later, he became a priest and eventually a bishop. Today he is known as St. Gregory Nazianzen the Elder.

Nonna and Gregory had three children and all were canonized: St. Gregory Nazianzen, St. Caesarius of Nazianzen, and St. Gorgonia. Nonna survived her husband by a few months, and also two of her children, passing away at a venerable age in 374.

REFLECTION   In an age when the sacred character of the family seems to be under attack from many facets of society, St. Nonna and her entire family achieved what every family is called upon to do. To strive for sanctity within the context of family would go far in reducing the tragic decline of family life today.

PRAYER   *Lord our God, in the Nazianzen family we see great hope for married people and their children.*

Through the example and intercession of Your servant St. Nonna, may parents lead their children to holiness of life and perseverance in good. This we ask through Christ our Lord. Amen.

ST. OSWALD OF NORTHUMBRIA, King

The Same Day—August 5

OSWALD was born in Northumbria, England, around 605. When his father was killed in battle, Oswald had to flee to Scotland, where, at Iona, he was converted to Christianity.

In 634, Oswald formed an army and defeated Cadwallon and thus became King of Northumbria. He attributed his victory to a vision of St. Colman, which he experienced, and to the fact that he had erected a large Cross the night before the battle.

Oswald then asked St. Aidan to come to Northumbria to preach Christianity and evangelize his kingdom. To this end he built churches and monasteries and asked monks from Scotland to help in this work. As a king, Oswald was known for his personal spirituality and piety. He was killed in battle at the age of thirty-seven in 642.

REFLECTION St. Oswald's life leads us to contemplate the great advantages we have in our gift of the Faith and to be motivated to share it with others. This can be done effectively by living God's Word.

PRAYER *O God, come to our aid as we seek to spread the Good News of Your Kingdom. Through the example and intercession of Your servant St. Oswald, help us to remain steadfast in the face of opposition. This we ask through Christ our Lord. Amen.*

STS. JUSTUS AND PASTOR, Martyrs

August 6—*Patrons of Madrid and Alcalá*

JUSTUS and Pastor were brothers who were born in Spain at the end of the third century, in the midst of the persecution of Diocletian.

Dacian, the governor of Spain, ordered them to be arrested because they boldly proclaimed the Faith while he was questioning suspected Christians. Accordingly, Dacian sentenced the two youths to be brutally scourged.

When Justus and Pastor refused to retract their confession of faith, Dacian ordered them to be beheaded. At the time they were respectively thirteen and nine years old. Their martyrdom took place at Alcalá in the year 304. Today Justus and Pastor are honored as the Patrons of Madrid and Alcalá.

REFLECTION   The hatred of the Evil One for those who proclaim the Faith extends even to children. Yet the forces of evil seem unaware of the prominence of God's grace when one's faith is put to the test. Like Sts. Justus and Pastor, we must consider seeking out trials for our Faith.

PRAYER   *O God, the world rejects Your Word and Your ways. Through the example and intercession of Your Martyrs Sts. Justus and Pastor, may we who have been so wonderfully gifted in the Faith always be faithful in proclaiming Your message, even in the face of threat and bodily harm. This we ask through Christ our Lord. Amen.*

———◆———

ST. HORMISDAS, Pope

The Same Day—August 6

ST. Hormisdas was a widower and a deacon of the Church at Rome, who was chosen to be

Pope in 514 and ruled till 523. His son Silverius was also later chosen to be Pope (536-537).

The Saint spent most of his pontificate dealing with the delicate situation brought about in the East by the Acacian Schism (484-519), which was caused by the attempt of Acacius of Constantinople to placate the Monophysites. And he brought it to an end by the confession of faith known as the "Formula of Hormisdas."

At the Pope's accession, the East was succumbing more and more to the Monophysite heresy. Through his efforts, Pope Hormisdas had the Formula drawn up and accepted by the Church of East and West. It affirms that the perfection and wholeness of the Catholic Religion has always been preserved in all its purity by the Apostolic See and that those who do not agree with it are out of its communion.

The Formula insists on the "Tome of Leo I" and the definitions of the Council of Chalcedon (451), and condemns Nestorius, and Eutyches, Dioscoros, Acacius, and other Monophysite leaders by name. The Formula was eventually made ecumenical by the signatures of all the fathers of the Fourth Council of Constantinople in 869. It is regarded as one of the most important pieces of evidence of the recognition of Papal authority in the first six centuries.

REFLECTION By his efforts (some of which can be found in the one hundred of his letters that are extant), St. Hormisdas brought peace to the Church between East and West and saw to it that the rights of the Church were protected by new peoples in the West. Indeed, he was a man of peace, and he should serve to remind us of the peace of Christ that we should always bear with us.

PRAYER   *Father of peace, You raised up Your Pope St. Hormisdas to bring about peace in the whole Church. By his prayers, help us to pray for peace and to pursue peace in our lives. This we ask through Christ our Lord. Amen.*

ST. ALBERT OF TRAPANI, Priest
August 7

ALBERT was born at Trapani, Sicily, in the thirteenth century. It is believed that Albert's parents promised that if they were blessed with a son, he would be dedicated to Our Lady of Mount Carmel.

Therefore, Albert entered the Carmelites at a very early age. After his ordination he was stationed at the priory in Messina where he became renowned for his preaching, especially among the Jewish people.

In 1296, Albert was elected provincial in Sicily. Toward the end of his life he lived as a hermit, and he died at Messina around 1306/1307. Although he was never formally canonized, his cult was approved in 1476 during the reign of Sixtus IV.

REFLECTION The life of St. Albert demonstrates that, in meeting the challenges and choices of life, a certain openness to the grace of God is needed. This cooperation with grace opens the way for a deeply spiritual life, one that becomes attractive to others.

PRAYER *Lord God, You made St. Albert of Trapani a model of purity and prayer and a devoted servant of Your Mother. May we practice these same virtues and thus be worthy always to share the banquet of Your graces. This we ask through Christ our Lord. Amen.*

———◆———

ST. ALTMAN, Bishop

August 8

ALTMAN was born at Paderborn, Westphalia, around 1020. After studies in Paris, he was ordained and became head of the cathedral school at Paderborn and later chaplain to Emperor Henry III.

On a pilgrimage to the Holy Land, Altman, along with seven thousand other Christians, was captured by the Saracens. After their eventual release and return home, nearly half of them had perished.

In 1065, Altman became the Bishop of Passau. He was especially interested in education and care for the poor. However, when he attempted to enforce Pope Gregory VII's rules on simony and celibacy, most of his clergy refused to obey. And when he tried to enforce the decree on lay investiture, Emperor Henry III drove him from his diocese.

Appointed apostolic delegate to Germany, Altman was again driven out of his diocese of Passau when he returned there in 1081. His last years were spent at the Abbey of Göttweig, Austria, where he died in 1091.

REFLECTION St. Altman's life reminds us that although obedience to Church leaders can be difficult at times, it is necessary to listen carefully to and cooperate with the Holy See. When this is done, God's will is accomplished.

PRAYER *Loving Father, You called upon Your Son Jesus to live in obedience to Your will for the salvation of the world. Through the example and intercession of Your Bishop St. Altman, may we share in that same spirit of obedience. This we ask through Christ our Lord. Amen.*

STS. CYRIACUS, LARGUS, SMARAGDUS, AND COMPANIONS, Martyrs

The Same Day—August 8

ST. Cyriacus was one of a group of martyrs, including Largus and Smaragdus, who suffered in Rome under Diocletian about the year 304. He was a deacon who headed the group and later gave his name to a church. The Acts of these martyrs are dubious and all that we know for sure is that Cyriacus's name was given to a church and that the martyrs were buried near the seventh milestone on the Ostian Way.

St. Cyriacus is one of the Fourteen Holy Helpers invoked for emergencies or afflictions (against demonic possession).†

REFLECTION   Although we know very little about St. Cyriacus and his companions, we know that they all remained firm in the Faith till the end and gave their lives for Christ. St. Cyriacus was then made part of the Fourteen Holy Helpers to aid his adherents in time of trouble. We should pray to him and to all the Saints for help in remaining true to our Faith.

PRAYER   *O Lord, You gladden us by the annual feast of Your Holy Martyrs Cyriacus, and his Companions. Through their prayers, help us to imitate the fortitude that they showed in suffering for You. This we ask through Christ our Lord. Amen.*

———◆———

BL. JOHN OF SALERN0, Priest
August 9

JOHN Guarna was born at Salerno, Italy, about the year 1190. While studying at Bologna, he met St. Dominic and became a Dominican priest. In 1219, he was made the superior of a group of thirteen friars sent to preach in Etruria.

The group started their mission at Ripoli outside of Florence, then moved to San Pancrazio, which adjoined the walls of the city. In 1221, Bl.

† See p. 223.

John became the founder of the Dominican Friary Santa Maria Novella.

Bl. John preached to the Petarines, who resembled the Albigensians in their heretical beliefs, and eventually brought many of them back to the Faith. The saintly man was blessed with the ability to read minds and hearts. After a life spent wholly in God's work, he went to his eternal reward in 1242, and his cult was approved under Pope Pius VI in 1783.

REFLECTION   On his deathbed, Bl. John reminded his fellow Dominicans that the reception of Communion requires more care, devotion, and purity than any other action they might perform in life. We would do well to dwell on this thought whenever we are to receive this holiest of Sacraments and take steps to do so in the best possible manner.

PRAYER   *God our Father, You called Bl. John Your Priest to enter the religious life and preach the Faith to Catholics and heretics alike. By his prayers, help us to get to know and love our Faith better every day. This we ask through Christ our Lord. Amen.*

◆━━◆━━◆

ST. BLANE, Bishop
August 10

BLANE lived in the sixth century. He was born on the island of Bute, Scotland, and pursued studies in Ireland. He remained there for seven years as a disciple of Sts. Comgall and Canice and became a monk.

Eventually Blane returned to Scotland and was ordained by his uncle, St. Cathan. He then engaged with considerable success in missionary work as he sought to spread the Faith.

As a reward for his efforts, Blane was made a bishop. Sometime later, he undertook a pilgrimage to Rome and returned home by foot.

After a lifetime of evangelization, Blane died around the year 590 on the Scottish isle where he was born. Because of his holiness of life and the miracles attributed to him, he was quickly accepted as a Saint.

REFLECTION Over many centuries countless individuals like St. Blane have given their lives to teach all nations. Like him we are called to follow the ancient and hallowed tradition of spreading God's Word. We can do this in many ways. For example, we can practice holiness of life, hidden works of charity, and steadfast devotion to the Church.

PRAYER *Almighty God, Father of our Lord Jesus Christ, as we celebrate the memory of St. Blane, may we imitate his vigor and zeal for spreading Your Word. This we ask through Christ our Lord. Amen.*

ST. ALEXANDER OF COMANA, Bishop
and Martyr
August 11

ALEXANDER lived in Pontus, Africa, during the third century and was surnamed "the

Charcoal-burner" because of his profession, which he carried out meticulously. That profession, however, concealed a man of deep wisdom and holiness.

One day, St. Gregory the Wonderworker, Bishop of Neocaesarea, was searching for a bishop for the See of Comana in that region. His efforts were fruitless, however, until someone submitted Alexander's name out of derision.

The desperate bishop called Alexander to him and was astounded by the latter's intelligence and grace. As a result, the "charcoal-burner" was appointed Bishop of Comana. Alexander ruled his See wisely and well and willingly accepted a martyr's death by burning during the persecution of Decius about the year 275.

REFLECTION The life of Alexander the Charcoal-burner reminds us that God's call can come in many ways even through a seeming act of scorn. We must take pains to examine every circumstance of our lives— no matter whence it comes—in the light of eternity.

PRAYER   *Almighty God, You give us grace in many ways. Through the example and intercession of Your servant St. Alexander the Charcoal-burner, teach us to recognize Your will in every event and carry it out faithfully. This we ask through Christ our Lord. Amen.*

STS. PORCARIUS AND COMPANIONS,
Martyrs
August 12

PORCARIUS was abbot of a monastery at Lérins, located off the coast of Provence in France. The monastery was greatly renowned, having been founded by St. Honoratus.

When Porcarius was abbot, more than five hundred monks lived at Lérins. He was warned in a vision that the abbey would be attacked. Thereupon he sent many of the younger monks to safety aboard a ship.

Porcarius and those monks who remained behind were slaughtered by marauding Saracens, except for four who were taken as slaves to Spain or North Africa. The year of this martyrdom was around 732.

REFLECTION   As leader of his monastery, St. Porcarius could have claimed a place in the escape vessel for himself. His unselfish concern that the young must live so that the tradition of the monastery could be carried on stands today as an admirable model for civil and religious leaders.

PRAYER   *God, in Your wisdom You ask us to follow Your Son Jesus on the royal road of the Cross. Through the example and intercession of Sts. Porcarius and Companions, may we unite our sufferings with His to further the work of Your Church. This we ask through Christ our Lord. Amen.*

ST. BENILDUS, Religious

PETER Romançon was born at Thuret, France, on June 13, 1805. He was taught by the Brothers of the Christian Schools founded by St. John Baptist de la Salle for the free education of boys.

At the age of fifteen Peter joined that congregation and took the name Benildus. After receiving the habit, he taught at several of its schools. In 1841, he was appointed director of a community at Saugues and instructed to found a school there. He remained at Saugues for the rest of his life.

The school at Saugues was highly acclaimed, and Benildus was known for his sanctity, effective teaching, and spirit of generosity toward his pupils, confreres, and townspeople. He died on August 13, 1862, and was canonized in 1967 by Pope Paul VI.

REFLECTION   St. Benildus vividly reminds us of our Lord's desire to receive the little children. We are called to emulate Christ's care and concern for young people, one of the most precious possessions of the Church.

PRAYER   *O God, through Your humble servant St. Benildus we have come to know and understand the necessity of guidance and good example for young people. May we always teach by lives of love, compassion, and understanding. This we ask through Christ our Lord. Amen.*

ST. ARNULF, Bishop
August 14

ARNULF was born in Flanders around 1040. He grew up in France during a time when soldiers were in high regard. After a successful military career, he felt God's call and exchanged army life for that of a monk.

Arnulf joined the monastery of St. Medard in Soissons and lived as a hermit. Owing to his administrative and spiritual gifts, he was eventually chosen as the abbot.

In 1081, Arnulf was made Bishop of Soissons. He was deprived of his See by a usurper and resigned his episcopacy. The saintly man then founded a monastery at Aldenburg, Flanders, where he died in 1087.

REFLECTION St. Arnulf served both God and country during his short stay on earth. His life should inspire us to do the same. It should particularly bring to mind the virtue of patriotism—a love and respect for one's country.

PRAYER *Lord, You gave each of us both a religious and a secular heritage. Through the example and intercession of St. Arnulf, help us to love our country by being model citizens and to love You by being good Christians. This we ask through Christ our Lord. Amen.*

ST. TARCISIUS, Martyr of
the Holy Eucharist

E ARLY editions of the *Roman Martyrology*
stated: "At Rome on the Appian Way today
marks the passion of St. Tarcisius the acolyte.
When he was carrying the Sacrament of the
Body of Christ he was stopped by pagans who
demanded to know what it was that he carried.
Tarcisius refused to tell them, deeming it a
shameful thing to cast pearls before swine.
Therefore, he was attacked by them with clubs
and stones for a prolonged length of time until
he finally gave up his spirit.

"When the assailants turned over his body,
they could not find any trace of Christ's Sacrament either in his hands or among his clothes."
This happened about the year 257.

This story of the Martyr of the Holy Eucharist
is taken from the fourth-century poem of Pope
St. Damasus, in which he compared Tarcisius to
St. Stephen the Protomartyr. Hence, it suggests
that Tarcisius may also have been a deacon. According to a sixth-century translator, Tarcisius
was taking the Sacrament as a young acolyte to
certain Christian prisoners who were the victims
of the persecution of Valerian (253-260).

REFLECTION   St. Tarcisius gave his life to prevent the
profanation of the Blessed Sacrament that he was car-

rying. He is the model of true devotion to the Body and Blood of Christ. We should pray to him to inspire in us a love and devotion to this august Sacrament of the altar.

PRAYER   *O Lord, You inspired Your servant St. Tarcisius to defend the Sacrament of Your Body and Blood with his very life. Through his intercession, help us to have great devotion to the Blessed Sacrament and cherish it all our lives. You live and reign forever with the Father and the Holy Spirit. Amen.*

ST. ROCH (ROCCO), Layman

August 16—*Invoked against Pestilence*

IT is believed that St. Roch was born in Montpellier, France, in 1350, the son of the governor. At the age of twenty he went to Rome and while there devoted himself to the care of plague victims, effecting many miraculous cures.

Roch himself fell victim to the plague, but eventually he recovered. When he returned to France, he was thrown in jail as a spy. He died in prison about the year 1379, at the age of thirty, and only then was it discovered that this prisoner had been a former governor's son.

After his death, many miracles were reported through Roch's intercession. He is still invoked in times of pestilence and plague.

REFLECTION   In reaching out, like St. Roch, to those who are sick or rejected, we open our arms to the living Christ Who dwells in all people. Christ responds by bringing us to eternal salvation.

PRAYER *O God, in Your great goodness You sent Your Son among us to show us the way, the truth, and the life. Through the example and intercession of Your servant St. Roch, may we always continue to follow Jesus in our sick and needy brothers and sisters. This we ask through Christ our Lord. Amen.*

ST. CLARE OF MONTEFALCO, Virgin

August 17

CLARE was born at Montefalco, Italy, around 1268. As a young woman she joined a convent of Franciscan tertiaries. This group established Holy Cross Convent at Montefalco in 1290, adopting the Rule of St. Augustine.

Clare's sister Joan was the abbess of this community, but at her death Clare succeeded her. She led an austere life, being particularly devoted to the Passion of Christ and His Cross.

When Clare died in 1308, an image of the Cross was found imprinted on her heart, and her body remained incorrupt. She was canonized in 1881 by Pope Leo XIII.

REFLECTION The life of St. Clare reminds us that we are all called to a life of prayer and dedication. Still, we must not expect or anticipate special favors. We are to be satisfied with the simple relationship we establish with God.

PRAYER *Loving Father, You call us to the heights of prayer and love. Yet we are constantly aware of our humanity. Through the example and intercession*

*of Your servant St. Clare of Montefalco, help us to re-
main faithful to You in good times and in bad. This we
ask through Christ our Lord. Amen.*

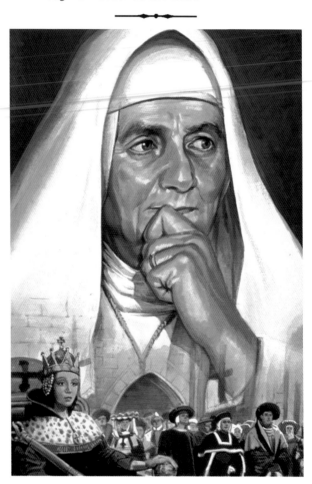

ST. BEATRICE DA SILVA MENESES,
Religious
The Same Day—August 17

BEATRICE Da Silva Meneses was born in Ceuta, Portugal, in 1424. She was the daughter of the Count of Viana, and the sister of St. Amedeus of Portugal. In Portugal, Beatrice is known as Brites.

Raised in the household of Princess Isabel, Beatrice went to Spain with her when Isabel married John II of Castile. Eventually, she tired of court life and entered the Cistercian convent at Toledo.

In 1484, Beatrice founded the Congregation of the Immaculate Conception of the Blessed Virgin Mary. The group's first house was the castle of Galliana, a gift from Queen Isabel. Beatrice died at Toledo on September 1, 1490, and was canonized by Pope Paul VI in 1976.

REFLECTION   In His wisdom God calls each individual to a particular vocation. The life of St. Beatrice reminds us of how important it is for us to be always open to God's designs in our regard and to pray that His will be done.

PRAYER   *O God, come to our help as we walk the narrow path to salvation and send us Your Spirit to teach us how You want us to live. Through the example and intercession of Your servant St. Beatrice, indicate to us Your will, so that we may work out our salvation and that of others. This we ask through Christ our Lord. Amen.*

ST. MACARIUS THE WONDERWORKER,
Priest
August 18

MACARIUS was born in Constantinople around the beginning of the ninth century and became a monk in a monastery at Pelekete. He was soon elected abbot and gained widespread fame as a wonderworker.

The holy man was ordained a priest and opposed Emperor Leo's ban on images (Iconoclasm). As a result, he was thrown into prison and subjected to torture.

Macarius gained his release under Emperor Michael the Stammerer but incurred exile by continuing to uphold the right of God's people to make use of images. He died on the island of Aphusia in Bithynia in 850.

REFLECTION   St. Macarius fought to retain the right of Catholics of his day to make use of religious images. His action should remind us of the great part that religious images and symbols play in our life and lead us to make better use of them.

PRAYER   *God of heaven, You raised up your servant St. Macarius to defend Your people's right to have religious images. Through his intercession, help us to use sacred images to safeguard our union with You. This we ask through Christ our Lord. Amen.*

ST. BERTULF, Abbot
August 19

ST. Bertulf, of Frankish origin, was converted to the Faith by his relative St. Arnulf of Metz. He became a monk of the Abbey of Luxeuil in 620 and learned the principles of the religious life and the discipline of St. Columban from the latter's successor St. Eustace.

A few years later, the Saint went to the Abbey of Bobbio in Italy and in 627 was chosen its abbot because of his holiness, learning, and apostolic zeal. He maintained the austere Rule of St. Columban (who had also headed Bobbio) and successfully battled the Arian heresy, which was widespread in the region.

St. Bertulf is also remembered for obtaining from Pope Honorius I the exemption of his abbey from episcopal jurisdiction—the first such case recorded in history. He died in 639, much esteemed for his holiness and miracles.

REFLECTION   Once Bertulf was converted to Christ, he followed Him in the religious life. He went on to become a great model for that life and attracted others to it. We should pray God to send many like-minded laborers into his vineyard day after day.

PRAYER   *Heavenly Father, You bestowed graces on Your Abbot St. Bertulf that enabled him to live up to his commitment. By his prayers, grant that we too may remain faithful to the end and come to share the joy of Your devoted servants. This we ask through Christ our Lord. Amen.*

ST. MARY DE MATTHIAS, Virgin

August 20

MARY de Matthias was born at Vallecorsa, Italy, in 1805. In 1834, Bishop Lais appointed her head of a school at Acuto, but she wanted to establish a religious community after the model of St. Caspar del Bufalo.

In 1835, Mary founded the Sisters Adorers of the Sacred Heart, whose twofold objective was adoration of the Most Blessed Sacrament and the education of children. She gained many followers through her piety and eloquence.

Despite frequent opposition from local clergy, the Congregation spread rapidly. Mary died at the age of sixty-one in 1866. She was beatified by Pope Pius XII in 1950 (by which time her sisters were conducting more than four hundred schools) and canonized by Pope John Paul II in 2003.

REFLECTION   In cooperating with the grace of God in her life, St. Mary de Matthias was blessed with many followers. She died worn out by her labors, but thousands continue to benefit from her zeal even today.

PRAYER   *O God, through the Congregation founded by Your servant St. Mary de Matthias, many young people come into contact with Your love and Divine presence. Through her intercession, may we always care for the salvation of the young and teach them the joy of Your Sacramental presence in their lives. This we ask through Christ our Lord. Amen.*

ST. SAMUEL, Judge and Prophet
The Same Day—August 20

SAMUEL was the son of Elkanah and Hannah who was born in answer to his mother's prayers (1 Samuel 1:11). He was dedicated to God at Shiloh, where he ministered to Eli and received a message from God for Eli (1 Samuel 3).

When the boy grew up, he became one of Israel's Judges (1 Samuel 7:15) as well as a Prophet (1 Samuel 9:9). In obedience to the Lord, he became instrumental in establishing a monarchical form of government (1 Samuel 9), anointing Saul, whom the Lord later rejected because of his infidelity, and David from whose line the Messiah would eventually come forth.

Samuel guided Israel all his life and when he died all the people came together and mourned for this holy man of God.

REFLECTION   St. Samuel was ever eager to carry out what the Lord asked of him, for he knew that God is ever active in human history to work out His purposes, weaving His will through our free acts. He wants our action and our devotion to go together. Yet even when we fail to do His will, God deals with us through His mercy, not according to our sins.

PRAYER   *O God, in Your wisdom You raised up Your Judge and Prophet Samuel to inaugurate the monarchy in Your people and to anoint David from whom the Messiah was to come. By his prayers, help us to realize that, as sharers in the role of Christ the Priest, the Prophet, and the King, we have an active*

*part to play in the life and activity of the Church. This
we ask through Christ our Lord. Amen.*

ST. LUXORIUS, Martyr

August 21

ALL that is known for certain about St. Luxorius is that he died for the Faith during the
persecution of Diocletian in the fourth century
(about 303). The Saint's unreliable Acts recount
that he was a Roman soldier at Sardinia who
was converted to Christ by reading the Psalms,
then the Prophets, and finally the Gospels.

When the persecution broke out, Luxorius
was arrested and brought before the prefect Delphinus together with two young boys Ciscellus
and Camerinus who were still clothed in the
white garments of salvation. Luxorius was
ordered to deny Christ but steadfastly refused to
do so. Instead, he sang Psalms to glorify God,
forget his own sufferings, and encourage his two
small companions.

Delphinus saw that these three would not be
moved from their belief, so he had all three put
to death by the sword. Their martyrdom took
place at Forum Trajanum.

REFLECTION St. Luxorius was led to the Faith by
praying the Psalms, reading the Prophets, and studying the Gospels. And at the point of martyrdom he re-
lied on praying the Psalms to remain steadfast. We

should strive to spend some time with the Sacred Scriptures every day.

PRAYER   *God of the Bible, You enabled St. Luxorius to be converted and accept martyrdom with courage by meditating on Sacred Scripture. Through his prayers, help us to read the Bible every day and so remain faithful to You in all we do. This we ask through Christ our Lord. Amen.*

ST. PHILIP BENIZI, Priest

August 22

PHILIP Benizi was born of a noble family at Florence, Italy, on August 15, 1233. He studied medicine at Paris and Padua and received his doctorates in Medicine and Philosophy at age nineteen.

After a year's medical practice, however, Philip joined the Servites at Monte Senario, near Florence, in 1254, and he was ordained at Siena in 1258. Later, he became superior of several houses and, in 1267 over his protests, was elected prior general. He became well known for codifying his Order's rules and for the miracles attributed to him. On one occasion, his name was proposed as a papal candidate, but he went into hiding until someone else was elected.

Philip was renowned as a preacher and for his peacemaking efforts between the Guelphs and the Ghibellines as well as for his success in gain-

ing converts to Christianity. He helped establish the Servite third order in 1284 and sent the first Servite missionaries to the Far East. In 1285, he was obliged to resign as general because of poor health and retired to an impoverished community at Todie. He died on August 22, 1285, and was canonized in 1671 by Pope Clement X.

REFLECTION   Despite his intellectual gifts and noble background, St. Philip, although a successful professional, devoted his life's energies to the welfare and benefit of others. What we do for others we do for God, no matter what our talents happen to be.

PRAYER   *O God, Your servant St. Philip Benizi shows us the way to You through helping others. Through his intercession, help us to utilize the gifts and talents You have given us for the benefit of our needy brothers and sisters. This we ask through Christ our Lord. Amen.*

STS. CLAUDIUS, ASTERIUS, AND NEON, Martyrs

August 23

CLAUDIUS, Asterius, and Neon were three well-to-do brothers who were Christians in Aegea, Cilicia, at the time when the persecution of Diocletian broke out. Their stepmother wanted to inherit their estate, so she accused them to the Magistrate.

Haled before the Magistrate, the brothers remained steadfast and could not be moved in their desire not to sacrifice to the gods. As a result, they were crucified or (according to another account) decapitated.

Originally, two women with a small child were also among the martyrs celebrated on this day: Domnina and Theonilla, but the *Revised Roman Martyrology* does not couple them with these three brothers. Domnina was beaten to death, and Theonilla was cruelly tortured and then slain by having burning coals placed on her stomach.

REFLECTION   Sts. Claudius and his brothers were denounced out of their stepmother's greed and attained the crown of martyrdom. They remained strong in their Faith and professed it in spite of all kinds of torture and verbal abuse. They show forth the truth of St. Paul's words that for a Christian "life means Christ and dying is gain" (Philippians 1:21). This is an axiom that might very well be ours.

PRAYER   *Heavenly Father, through cruel pain and suffering many like Sts. Claudius, Asterius, and Neon have come directly to You. Through their prayers, may we accept the trials and tribulations of this life in hopes of gaining an eternity of happiness with You. This we ask through Christ our Lord. Amen.*

ST. OUEN (or OWEN) Bishop
August 24

OUEN (also known as Audoenus and Owen) was born at Sancy, France, in 610. He was the son of St. Authaire. Following his education at St.

Médard Abbey, he served in King Clotair II's court as well as that of Dagobert I and Clovis II.

In 636, although still a layman, Ouen built a monastery at Rebais. He was very active in fostering religion and inveighed against simony. Eventually he was ordained, and in 641 he became Archbishop of Rouen.

Known for his personal austerities, Ouen founded several monasteries, favored many charities, and sent missionaries to pagan areas. He died near Paris on August 24 in the year 684.

REFLECTION   St. Ouen teaches that it is important for all people, priests, religious, and laity, to be aware of their individual responsibility to spread the Gospel. This is best done by each according to his or her talents.

PRAYER   *Lord God, may we always walk in the way of truth as we have come to know it through Jesus and His disciples. Through the example and intercession of Your Bishop St. Ouen, help us to carry forward their work. This we ask through Christ our Lord. Amen.*

ST. GENESIUS, Martyr

August 25—Patron of Actors and Musicians

BORN at the end of the third century, St. Genesius was a catechumen and a notary at Arles in Gaul, who refused to obey a decree of Emperors Diocletian and Maximian condemning

Christianity in a Roman persecution. Denouncing the decree, he fled in search of receiving Baptism. It was denied him because of his youth, but he achieved a Baptism of Blood when he was caught and beheaded on the banks of the Rhone River about the year 303.

After a church had been dedicated to the Saint in Rome, a legend arose that identified Genesius as a Roman comedian who, during a derisive theatrical representation of Baptism before the emperor, received the gift of faith in Christ.

St. Genesius was presented to the emperor and declared himself to be a Christian. Enraged, Diocletian turned him over to Plautian, prefect of the praetorium. Plautian submitted Genesius to torture in an effort to make him sacrifice to the gods. When the Saint persisted in his Faith, he was beheaded. He is the Patron of Actors and Musicians.

REFLECTION St. Genesius placed God's rights above those of his emperor. And he willingly gave up his life to restore God's rights to Him. We should remember that when these two rights clash, those of God must be preserved.

PRAYER   *O Lord, You enabled St. Genesius to remain faithful to You till the end. Through his prayers, grant us the grace to remain faithful to Your commands all our lives. This we ask through Christ our Lord. Amen.*

ST. TERESA OF JESUS IBARS, Virgin

August 26

TERESA of Jesus Ibars was born in 1843 in the town of Aytona in Catalonia, Spain. Her life on her parents' farm was a difficult one, but her dream of becoming a teacher was finally realized when she was accepted for a position at Lérida.

At the same time, Teresa was a deeply spiritual individual inclined toward the religious life. When her efforts in this respect were unsuccessful, her spiritual director suggested that she develop her own religious community. As a result, she gathered a group around her and founded the Little Sisters of the Poor, at Barbastra, on January 27, 1872.

Owing to her great faith, hard work, and courage in the face of difficult circumstances, Teresa was able to establish fifty-eight houses of her institute during her lifetime. She died in 1897, was beatified in 1958, and was canonized by Pope Paul VI in 1974.

REFLECTION St. Teresa was not discouraged by her rejection from religious life. Following the advice of her spiritual director, she established a worldwide organization that serves the elderly and sick poor and affords her sisters the opportunity to give themselves to God through the poor and needy.

PRAYER   *Lord our God, we give You thanks and praise for the great good Your servant St. Teresa of Jesus Ibars provides through her beloved institute.*

Through her prayers, may we imitate her desire to serve You in the poor and continue to support her followers. This we ask through Christ our Lord. Amen.

———◆———

ST. MELCHIZEDEK, King and Priest

The Same Day—August 26

MELCHIZEDEK (whose name means "King of Righteousness") lived in the time of Abraham. He was the king of Salem and priest of God who offered bread and wine as an unbloody sacrifice in thanksgiving for Abraham's victory over the Four Eastern Kings. He blessed Abraham and accepted a tenth of the booty (Genesis 14:18-20).

Psalm 110:4 explains the significance of Melchizedek. He is recognized as a type of the priesthood of the future Messiah.

The full significance of the non-Levitical priesthood of Christ (Who belonged to the tribe of Judah, not Levi) is developed in the Letter to the Hebrews (7:1-28), which shows that Melchizedek is the type of Christ: both are kings as well as priests; both offer bread and wine to God; and both have their priesthood directly from God.

Thus, an antiphon in the new Rite of Ordination of a Priest reads: "Christ the Lord, a priest for ever, according to the order of Melchizedek, offered bread and wine." Melchizedek's sacrifice is also a type of the Eucharist, and in Eucharistic

Prayer I the Church prays that God will accept the offerings at Mass as He accepted the sacrificial gifts of Melchizedek.

REFLECTION   St. Melchizedek prefigured the Priesthood of Christ and the Sacrifice of the Mass. We should be ever grateful for the gift of the Eucharist, which brings Christ to us during our time on earth and anticipates our participation in the eternal worship in heaven.

PRAYER   *O God, in Your wisdom You raised up St. Melchizedek Your servant as a king and priest who prefigured the true King and Priest Jesus Christ, Your Son. By Melchizedek's prayers, send us true priests who will offer Mass "in the person of Christ" Who is Priest and King. This we ask through Christ our Lord. Amen.*

———◆◆———

ST. POEMEN (or PASTOR), Abbot

August 27

POEMEN lived in the fourth/fifth century and is sometimes called by the Latin form of his name: Pastor. Together with a few of his brothers, he embraced the eremitical life in the Egyptian desert of Skete in the abandoned ruins of a temple at Terenuth.

Under Poemen's rule, during the night the hermits slept for four hours, worked for four hours, and chanted the Divine Office for four hours. By day they worked until noon, read until three, and did chores for the rest of the time.

Poemen became one of the most famous of the Desert Fathers, noted for his sayings, such as:

"Silence is not a virtue when charity calls for speech" and "A living faith consists in thinking little of self and showing consideration for others." He died in the fourth/fifth century.

REFLECTION   Although St. Poemen retreated to the desert to serve God, he continued to do good to those who remained in the world. His example should lead us who live in the world to be considerate of others, who are our brothers and sisters in Christ.

PRAYER   *Almighty God, You called St. Poemen to serve You in the eremitical life. Through his example and intercession, help us to serve You in the world and in our neighbor. This we ask through Christ our Lord. Amen.*

———◆———

ST. MOSES THE BLACK, Anchorite
and Martyr
August 28

MOSES was an Ethiopian born into slavery around the year 330. At first, he worked in an Egyptian official's house, but because of his stealing, his vicious nature, and his evil tendencies, he was dismissed from service. He then became the leader of a band of brigands who terrorized the countryside.

Later, the whole tenor of Moses' life changed, perhaps when he fled from the authorities and took refuge among hermits at the monastery of Petra in the Skete desert in Lower Egypt. Eventually he became a monk at that monastery.

Known for his severe discipline, Moses lived as a hermit, although he was later ordained a priest by Archbishop Theophilus of Alexandria. About 400, at the age of seventy-five, he along with six other monks was murdered by marauding Berbers when—in imitation of his Divine Master—he refused to defend himself.

REFLECTION   The lesson of St. Moses the Black's life is quite clear. No matter how sinful a life we might have led, mercy and forgiveness are always available to us if we turn back to God. We have His word on it.

PRAYER   *O God, we rejoice in Your forgiving love. Through the intercession of Your Martyr St. Moses the Black, grant that we may always have the grace to turn to You in time of difficulty and temptation, assured as we are of Your constancy in our regard. This we ask through Christ our Lord. Amen.*

ST. SABINA, Martyr

W E know St. Sabina only through legend, and there is some question as to its trustworthiness. Even the century in which she lived is unknown.

Supposedly Sabina was converted to Christianity by her Syrian servant Serapia. During the persecution of Emperor Hadrian, Serapia suffered martyrdom for her Christian Faith. It is believed that St. Sabina was murdered for the Faith about a month later.

The renowned basilica on the Aventine in Rome is dedicated to and named after her. Some sources hold that Sabina herself had it constructed in 422-432.

REFLECTION In an age when our Faith is ridiculed as being outmoded, we take heart in the lives of so many Martyrs, like St. Sabina, who gave their lives under terrible conditions to defend and sustain their Faith. This confers on us a strong desire to persevere in God's love.

PRAYER *O God, our Creator and Redeemer, Maker of all good things, You call us to that perfection of faith which inspires us to put all our trust in You. Through the intercession of Your Martyr St. Sabina, grant us the courage to do Your will day after day. This we ask through Christ our Lord. Amen.*

ST. PAMMACHIUS, Layman

August 30

PAMMACHIUS was a Roman senator, a man of learning and holiness, married to one of the daughters of St. Paula. In 395, his wife Paulina died, and he decided to devote the rest of his life to study and charitable works.

Pammachius began to care for the physical ills of sick pilgrims who came to Rome. He also arranged for their spiritual care by erecting a church in his house.

At the same time, Pammachius corresponded with St. Jerome concerning the Christian Faith and the people's orthodoxy. He also tried in vain to moderate the caustic language used by St. Jerome against some writers. Pammachius died in 410.

REFLECTION St. Pammachius was a happy blend of the Roman culture and the Christian Faith. He exemplifies the best of both worlds. His life is a reminder that we should utilize the culture of our time and people in our Christian experience.

PRAYER *Almighty God, You make use of all classes of people to further Your work. Through the intercession of Your servant St. Pammachius, teach us that true nobility consists in leading Christian lives. This we ask through Christ our Lord. Amen.*

ST. RAYMOND NONNATUS, Priest

August 31—Patron of Midwives

RAYMOND Nonnatus was born at Portella, Spain, in 1204, delivered by cesarean section after his mother died. Thus, he was called Nonnatus (*non-natus*, or not born). As a youth, Raymond joined the Mercedarians, an order formed to effect the release of Christian captives from the Moors.

While in Algeria ransoming slaves, Raymond was captured and enslaved for several years. He was sentenced to be impaled but was spared because of the large ransom he would bring. Nevertheless, he was forced to run the gauntlet and suffer other tortures before being rescued by St. Peter Nolasco.

In 1239, after returning to Barcelona, Raymond was made a cardinal by Pope Gregory IX at the age of thirty-five. The following year, on his way to Rome, he died at Cardona. He was canonized in 1657 by Pope Alexander VII and is the Patron of Midwives.

REFLECTION The life of St. Raymond Nonnatus teaches us to show concern for and practice good works toward others. However, in doing so, we are rarely required to suffer imprisonment, torture, and the threat of death. Since this is so, why are we so often reluctant to become involved in charitable works?

PRAYER *O God, You honor Your people with the example of Your Priest St. Raymond Nonnatus. May we, like him, be willing to give ourselves completely to others for Your honor and glory. This we ask through Christ our Lord. Amen.*

———◆———

ST. VERENA, Virgin

September 1

ST. Verena lived in the fourth century and is honored throughout Switzerland. Her tomb, which is near Zurich, contains an illustration of the Saint holding a comb and a bowl, which symbolize her charitable works among the poor in the region.

The Saint's Acts, which are not very reliable, portray her as coming from Egypt in search of the relics of St. Victor, who had been martyred in the Theban Legion. She settled at Soluthurn in Switzerland.

Despite the fact that information about her life is lacking, St. Verena's cult is on solid ground since she is listed in the venerable *Hieronymian Martyrology*, which is the forerunner of the *Roman Martyrology.*

REFLECTION St. Verena found joy in praising and loving God and doing good works for the poor and needy. She thus carried out the first and second commandments stressed by our Lord: "You shall love the Lord your God with all your heart, all your soul, and all your mind" and "You shall love your neighbor as yourself" (Matthew 22:37, 39). By doing the same, we too will be known as Christians.

PRAYER   *Heavenly Father, You called St. Verena Your servant to a life of wholehearted service to You and the needy. By her prayers, help us to see and serve You in everyone we meet. This we ask through Christ our Lord. Amen.*

———◆———

ST. JOSHUA, Servant of the Lord
The Same Day—September 1

JOSHUA was the successor to Moses (Joshua 1:1ff), and a Servant of the Lord. He commanded the Israelites in the battle with the Amalekites (Exodus 7:9ff), accompanied Moses to the sacred mountain (Exodus 24:13; 32:17), and was the custodian of the Tent of Meeting (Exodus 33:11).

Joshua was also one of the spies who scouted the land of Canaan (Numbers 13:8, 16; 14:6) and was promised entrance into the Promised Land (Numbers 14:30, 38). When Moses laid his hands on Joshua, he was filled with the spirit of wisdom and was ready to lead the people.

The Saint led the Israelites across the Jordan and into the land (Joshua 3:14-17). He conquered Jericho (Joshua 6) and then the rest of the land and divided it among the twelve tribes (Joshua 7ff; 14ff). Then after convening the tribes at Shechem for a farewell address (Joshua 24), he went on to his eternal reward.

REFLECTION   Although the victories of Joshua depended on the action of God, they also called for the active collaboration of his people. The same is true in our day. We must pray and ponder in order to make the right choices so as to be in tune with God's will.

PRAYER   *O God, in Your wisdom You called Your servant St. Joshua to bring Your people into the Promised Land. By his prayers, help us so to live that we may one day deserve to enter the eternal Promised Land of heaven. This we ask through Christ our Lord. Amen.*

———◆·◆·◆———

BL. SOLOMON LE CLERQ, Religious

September 2

NICHOLAS Le Clerq was born on November 14, 1745. Son of a Boulogne wine merchant, Nicholas was seemingly destined for a career in his father's business. But this was not to be so.

After a rather ordinary life as a young man in the French wine district, Nicholas decided to follow a vocation to the teaching brotherhood.

Nicholas entered the Novitiate of the Brothers of the Christian Schools at St. Yon, on March 25, 1767, and took the name Brother Solomon. He was sent to several of the Brothers' schools throughout France and experienced the tensions that were dividing France in his time.

Nonetheless, Brother Solomon remained a man of deep piety, something quite evident even in his earliest years. His many letters to his brothers and sisters show an individual of deep prayer and piety.

Following several years as a teacher, Brother Solomon was selected as director of novices for his community. Later, he was to serve in the Congregation's motherhouse as procurator, and finally as secretary to the superior general.

In all these positions Brother Solomon remained an exemplary religious and an individual of deep prayer and genuine piety. He was open to God's grace and cooperated with it unstintingly.

It was a time of deep fervor among the Christian Brothers, so that Brother Solomon was not necessarily outstanding in his piety and holiness. It was the circumstances of the French Revolution that finally led to the great grace of martyrdom for Brother Solomon. Throughout it all, Brother Solomon demonstrated unflinching courage.

In the summer of 1792, following a brief incarceration, Brother Solomon, along with a number of other priests, brothers, and religious, was slaughtered in the garden of the Carmelite Convent in Paris. He and his companions were beatified 130 years later by Pope Pius XI in 1922.

REFLECTION Brother Solomon's words shortly before his death demonstrate the tenacity of his faith. "As for us, we hold to what we believed ten and twenty years ago; to what our forefathers believed one hundred years ago, and one thousand years ago, and to that which the whole Catholic world has always believed."

PRAYER   *Loving God, You crowned with triumph Your Martyr Bl. Solomon. You crowned with glory his constancy in teaching and firmness in confessing the Faith. Through his intercession, grant that in the confession of the same Faith we too may be found fervent until death. This we ask through Christ our Lord. Amen.*

———◆—◆———

ST. REMACLUS, Bishop
September 3

REMACLUS was born in Aquitaine, France, in the seventh century. He completed his theological studies under St. Sulpicius of Bourges, and after ordination he was appointed the first abbot of Solignac by St. Eligius. Later he headed the monastery at Cugnon, in the duchy of Luxemburg.

Eventually, Remaclus became affiliated with the court of King Sigebert III. In 648, he convinced the king to found the double abbey of Stavelot and Malmedy for the purpose of evangelization, and he became abbot there.

Known for his personal holiness and austere self-denial, Remaclus became a missionary bishop for the last twenty-five years of his life. He died on September 3, around 671-679.

REFLECTION As people of all ages resume their schooling, we are reminded of the long tradition that monastic communities had of preserving and conveying knowledge, especially during the Middle Ages. Today when we are challenged by the sacrifices needed to foster Christian education, we can admire the many holy persons, like St. Remaclus, who over the centuries have dedicated their lives, frequently under very difficult circumstances, to preserving the great body of knowledge fostered by the Church of Christ.

PRAYER   *Lord our God, open our minds and hearts to the lessons in the lives of the Saints. Through the example and intercession of Your Bishop St. Remaclus, grant that we may imitate their zeal in spreading Your wisdom. This we ask through Christ our Lord. Amen.*

———◆◆◆———

ST. IDA OF HERZFELD, Widow

September 4

IDA of Herzfeld was the great-granddaughter of Charlemagne and thus was raised in his court. She was married to a lord named Egbert, but in a short time she was widowed.

Thereafter, Ida spent most of her time aiding the poor, while practicing self-denial and austerities. She also built a chapel in Westphalia where she devoted herself to prayer.

When her son became a monk at Corvey, Ida moved from Westphalia to Herzfeld. She built a convent there and continued to perform good works up till the time of her death, which took place in 825.

REFLECTION St. Ida teaches us that we have to learn to accept things with faith no matter how difficult they appear to be. At the same time, our spirit of charity must continue to be the earmark of our lives.

PRAYER   *God our Father, in Your goodness and wisdom You give us strength as we move through this life of travail. Through the intercession of Your servant St. Ida, may we always continue to share what we have with others despite any personal adversity we might endure. This we ask through Christ our Lord. Amen.*

———◆◆———

ST. MOSES, Prophet and Lawgiver

The Same Day—September 4

MOSES most likely lived in the thirteenth century before Christ. He is one of the greatest figures of the Old Testament, a Prophet and the founder of Israel as well as leader, lawgiver, and proponent of monotheism. He was saved from death at birth (Exodus 2:1ff) and brought up by Pharaoh's daughter (Exodus 2:5ff).

When Moses grew up, he ended up slaying an Egyptian in protecting one of his countrymen (Exodus 2:11-12). So he fled to Midian, where he stayed with Jethro and married his daughter Zipporah (Exodus 2:15-21).

While Moses was tending his father-in-law Jethro's flock, the Lord appeared to him in the form of a burning bush (Exodus 3:2). God then revealed His plan for Moses to lead His people out of Egypt (Exodus 3—4). Moses, however, considered himself not equal to such a task, so God gave him an assistant, his brother Aaron (Exodus 4:16).

The Saint persuaded his people to leave Egypt and enabled them to pass through the Red Sea (Exodus 14:5ff). He then guided them for forty years in the wilderness (Exodus 16:35). While there, Moses was summoned to the top of Mount Sinai, where God gave him the Law (Exodus 20:1ff), which was to be the charter of the Covenant between God and the Israelites. Eventually, Moses brought them to the entrance of the Promised Land and was allowed by God to see the land from Mount Nebo before he died.

Moses is credited as the author in some way of the Pentateuch, the First Five Books of the Bible. And it was Moses who told the people that the Lord would send another Prophet like him. i.e., the Messiah (Deuteronomy 18:15-19).

In the New Testament, Moses is presented as a personification of the Law, i.e., of the Old Covenant, and at the same time as a figure of Christ come to establish a New Covenant (John 1:17; 1 Corinthians 10:1-12).

REFLECTION Moses is the ideal Prophet, the model for all later Prophets through whom God revealed Himself and His will to humankind. Yet the Law he delivered to Israel was not God's final word. Moses is the type of the greatest Prophet, Jesus, Who came to reveal the fullness of God's love and grace (John 1:17, 45).

PRAYER   *O God, in Your wisdom You raised up St. Moses Your Prophet to deliver Your chosen people and to prefigure Jesus the Messiah. By his prayers, help us to acknowledge Your Son, our Lord, as the Redeemer of the world and to follow Him wholeheartedly every day. This we ask through Christ our Lord. Amen.*

———◆———

BL. TERESA OF CALCUTTA, Virgin

September 5

NAMED Agnes (i.e., Gonxha) Bojaxhui, Teresa was born an Albanian in Skopje, Yugoslavia (now the Republic of Macedonia) in 1910. In 1928, she joined the Sisters of Loretto, an Irish order of missionary nuns, who worked in Calcutta, India. In 1931, she concluded her novitiate and made her vows, becoming *Sister Teresa* in honor of the Little Flower of Lisieux who emphasized joy in menial tasks.

In 1937, she became *Mother Teresa* through further vows. In 1946, she received permission to found a new Congregation, which she did in 1948 as the Missionary Sisters of Charity. The members took a fourth vow to provide wholehearted free service to the poorest of the poor.

Mother Teresa's Congregation grew rapidly all over the world, taking care of the neediest cases. She was obliged to found a Congregation of men in 1948: the Missionary Brothers of Charity.

In 1979, Mother Teresa was awarded the Nobel Peace Prize. She was honored by governments, universities, and organizations throughout the world because she came to the aid of those who felt unwanted, unloved, and uncared-for throughout society.

On September 5, 1997, Mother Teresa's heart failed and she went to the Lord for Whom she had worked all her life, "doing a beautiful thing for God." She was beatified by Pope John Paul II in 2003.

REFLECTION Describing her motives for her work, Mother Teresa spoke of Christ's love and His commands to respect each human life. She also said: "Because we cannot see God, we cannot express our love to Him in person. But our neighbor we can see, and we can do for him or her what we would love to do for Jesus if He were visible. . . . Joy is a net of love by which we can capture souls. God loves the person who gives with joy."

PRAYER *God our Father, You called Your servant Mother Teresa to found a new Congregation that would minister to the poorest of the poor. By her prayers, help us to come to the aid of the poorest by prayer and works. This we ask through Christ our Lord. Amen.*

———◆———

ST. BEGA (or BEE), Virgin
September 6

LEGENDARY accounts indicate that St. Bega (also known as Bee) was the daughter of an Irish king in the seventh century. Arrangements had been made for her to marry the son of the

King of Norway. However, she had vowed virginity, and she fled on her marriage day.

Miraculously transported to Cumberland, for some time she lived as a hermitess. However, St. Oswald advised her to enter the religious life. She consented and received the veil from St. Aidan.

Soon thereafter, Bega founded St. Bee's monastery. She became abbess and was noted for her generosity to the poor and the oppressed. She died in the aura of sanctity.

REFLECTION The life of St. Bega reminds us that no matter what lifestyle we feel called to, care for the poor and the oppressed must be one of our most important concerns. It is an affirmation of our willingness to do God's will.

PRAYER   *O God, through Your servant St. Bega many of Your poor and oppressed were well served. Through her intercession, may we always be open to imitating her generous spirit. This we ask through Christ our Lord. Amen.*

———◆◆———

ST. ZECHARIAH, Priest and Prophet

The Same Day—September 6

ST. Zechariah is one of the Minor Prophets. He was the son of Berechiah and grandson of Iddo (Zechariah 1:1, 7). His initial prophecy is dated to 520 B.C., the same year in which Haggai received the prophetic call.

The Saint's prophecies promote the work of rebuilding the Temple (as do those of Haggai) and encourage their leaders, Joshua and Zerubbabel. They also portray the Messiah and the triumphant Messianic Age.

Zechariah portrays the Messiah as a Good Shepherd rejected by the people (11:1-7), Who would enter Jerusalem in great honor and riding on a donkey (9:9f), be sold for thirty pieces of silver (11:12f), have His side pierced (12:10), shed His Blood for the sins of all human beings (13:17), and come to the world a second time (14:4).

REFLECTION Through his words, St. Zechariah showed that God is in total control of life and history. Just as Jesus, the Messiah, did what God willed for Him (and had the Prophets prophesy about Him), so should we do whatever God wills for us. In this lies our earthly as well as our eternal happiness.

PRAYER *O God, in Your wisdom You raised up St. Zechariah Your Prophet to prophesy about the Messiah, Your Son. By his prayers, let us never cease praising and thanking You for Your goodness in sending Jesus to save us. This we ask through Christ our Lord. Amen.*

———— ◆ ————

ST. CLOUD (or Chlodoard), Priest

September 7

ST. Cloud (also known as Chlodoard) was the grandson of King Clovis and St. Clotilda of the Franks in the sixth century. When Clovis died, his kingdom fell to his four sons. Internecine warfare broke out among the brothers resulting in Cloud's father being killed. This meant the kingship fell to Cloud and his two brothers aged seven and ten who were being raised by St. Clotaire.

Unfortunately, the two brothers were assassinated, but Cloud escaped by being sent to Provence. He gave up any idea of claiming the throne and became a priest, a recluse, and the founding abbot of a hermitage at Nogent on the Seine, which is now called St. Cloud after him.

The Saint labored incessantly to teach the Faith to the people of that region. Then worn out by the time he was thirty-eight, he passed on to his heavenly reward in 560.

REFLECTION St. Cloud saw at first hand the dangers of seeking worldly honors as his father and his brothers were murdered to prevent them from ruling Gaul. We should always be aware of the evils that come with the thirst for earthly power and riches. True happiness comes only from serving God and doing His will.

PRAYER   *God of love, You called Your Priest St. Cloud to renounce earthly power and to serve You. By his prayers, keep us free from the evils of worldly ways so that we may attain eternal happiness with You in heaven. This we ask through Christ our Lord. Amen.*

BL. THOMAS TSUGI, Martyr

The Same Day—September 7

THOMAS Tsugi was born of a noble Japanese family about 1571. He was educated by the Jesuits at Arima, and in 1587, he entered the Jesuit community.

Known for his eloquent preaching, Thomas was exiled to Macao because of his religious convictions. Later, he returned to Japan in disguise, but he was eventually arrested and imprisoned for about a year.

On a hill outside Nagasaki, Thomas was burned at the stake, refusing to the very end to allow his influential family to buy his freedom. As the flames enveloped his body, Thomas was heard to proclaim: "Praise the Lord of All Nations." He was beatified on July 7, 1867, by Pope Pius IX.

REFLECTION Bl. Thomas's zeal for the spread of the Faith was such that he did not fear death for his convictions. The entreaties of his family to give in were to no avail. What a model for us in time of temptation!

PRAYER *Almighty God, grant that this remembrance of Your Martyr Bl. Thomas Tsugi may bring us joy. May we who depend on his prayers glory in his entry into heaven. This we ask through Christ our Lord. Amen.*

ST. SERGIUS I, Pope

September 8

SERGIUS was born and raised at Palermo, Sicily, in the seventh century, the son of a wealthy Syrian merchant. He was educated at Rome and was ordained there. On December 15, 687, he was elected Pope.

In 693, Sergius became involved in a direct confrontation with the Byzantine Emperor Justinian II, refusing to sign the decrees of the Council of Trullanum, composed of Eastern bishops. Such decrees would have made Constantinople equal to Rome in authority. The controversy ended when Justinian was deposed in 695.

Sergius fostered missionary efforts in Germany and Friesland, and he encouraged liturgical music, decreeing that the *Agnus Dei* ("Lamb of God") be sung at Mass. He died in Rome on September 8, 701.

REFLECTION At times, individuals are called upon to stand up to political leaders, as St. Sergius felt obligated to do. In such cases, care must be exercised at all times to clearly distinguish between matters civil and matters ecclesiastical.

PRAYER   *O God, in our daily lives we are constantly required to stand firm in Your service. Through the example and intercession of Your Pope St. Sergius I, grant us the courage to persevere in the face of opposition, especially in matters of faith and justice. This we ask through Christ our Lord. Amen.*

BL. SERAPHINA SFORZA,
Widow and Religious
The Same Day—September 8

SUEVA Sforza was born at Urbino, Italy, around the year 1432. The daughter of a count, she was orphaned as a child and raised in the Roman villa of her uncle, Prince Colonna.

At the age of sixteen, Sueva married Alexander Sforza, and for a while they were very happy. Later, Alexander had an affair with another woman, and after failing in an attempt to poison Sueva, he cast her out of his house in 1457.

Sueva then joined the Poor Clares at Pesar and took the name Seraphina. For twenty years she lived an extremely devout life in the convent and was elected abbess in 1475. She died in 1478, and her public honor was approved by Pope Benedict XIV in 1754.

REFLECTION In life one can experience many disappointments and failures. Like Bl. Seraphina, we are called to turn these occasions to good by becoming closer to God in our lives.

PRAYER *O God, in our weakness we call upon You for help when faced with trial and temptation. Through the example and intercession of Your servant Bl. Seraphina, help us to come closer to You in difficult times. This we ask through Christ our Lord. Amen.*

ST. KIERAN, Priest and Abbot

September 9

SURNAMED "The Younger" to distinguish him from St. Kieran of Saighir, the Saint honored on this date was born in Connacht and trained in the monastic life by St. Fintan of Clonard, when he was one of the "Twelve Apostles of Ireland."

St. Kieran then spent seven years at Inishmore on Aram with St. Enda, after which he went to a monastery in the center of Ireland called Isel.

Finally, the Saint traveled to the banks of the Shannan River in Offaly, where he dwelt and became the abbot of the famous Clonmacnois Monastery, which went on to become the center of Irish learning for centuries. He died at a young age around 556.

REFLECTION   St. Kieran started a monastery that became a beacon of light and understanding for Catholics throughout the centuries. We should strive to grow in knowledge of the Faith day by day so that we may be aided by its many wonderful teachings.

PRAYER   *Lord of Wisdom, You called Your Priest and Abbot St. Kieran to found a monastery that would bring the Faith to people. By his prayers, enable us to know our Faith better and follow its teachings to the letter. This we ask through Christ our Lord. Amen.*

ST. PULCHERIA, Virgin

September 10

PULCHERIA was born to Byzantine Emperor Arcadius and Empress Eudoxia on January 19, 399. When her father died, and her younger brother Theodosius was named emperor, Pulcheria, though only fifteen years old, was made regent and placed in charge of his education.

Pulcheria took a vow of chastity, raised her brother, and changed the court's atmosphere to one of virtue and piety. When her brother married in 421, his wife convinced him to banish Pulcheria, and from exile Pulcheria supported Pope St. Leo the Great against her brother in the Monophysite controversy.

After the death of Theodosius, Pulcheria was named empress. She sponsored the Council of Chalcedon in 451, which condemned Monophysitism, and she was a major force in overcoming the Nestorian and Eutychian heresies. Pulcheria built many churches, hospitals, and hospices and a university at Constantinople. She died at Constantinople in 453.

REFLECTION The life of St. Pulcheria is a good indicator that to a greater or lesser degree we are all endowed with gifts. It is our task to exercise them for the welfare of the community and the advancement of God's Word.

PRAYER *O God, You desire that we always follow You in faith and trust. Through the example and intercession of Your servant St. Pulcheria, help us to use our gifts for the good of all and the advancement of Your Word. This we ask through Christ our Lord. Amen.*

ST. JOHN GABRIEL PERBOYRE, Martyr

September 11

JOHN Gabriel Perboyre was born at Puech, France, in 1802. At the age of fifteen he joined the Vincentians and was ordained in 1826. He then served as a seminary professor of Theology, as rector of a minor seminary, and as assistant director of the Paris novitiate.

In 1835, his request to be sent to China as a missionary was granted. He was sent to the mission in Hunan where he rescued many abandoned children.

John was at Hupeh when persecution broke out. Betrayed by a catechumen, he was imprisoned and tortured so as to give his companions' names, which he refused to do. On September 11, 1840, John was strangled to death. He was beatified in 1889 by Pope Leo XIII and canonized in 1996 by Pope John Paul II.

REFLECTION The life of St. John Gabriel Perboyre reminds us that the Martyrs worked without fear in many lands to bring the comfort and solace of the Gospel to the outcasts. Their good example is a worthy model for us.

PRAYER   *O God, You willed that St. John Perboyre should be a shining example to your Church by his labors and his sharing in Your Son's Cross. Through his intercession, help us to follow his footsteps and share in Christ's sufferings as we joyfully proclaim Your salvation to all people. This we ask through Christ our Lord. Amen.*

———◆◆———

ST. GUY OF ANDERLECHT, Layman

September 12

GUY of Anderlecht was born near the end of the tenth century, close to Brussels. His parents were very poor and unable to provide for his education but they gave him a strong religious upbringing.

Guy practiced great austerity and self-denial, and he proved to be a good friend of the poor. For a while he served as a church sacristan, but when his resources were depleted, he made a pilgrimage to Rome and Jerusalem, walking the entire distance.

After seven years Guy returned to Belgium, seriously ill as a result of his arduous journeys. He died at the hospital in Anderlecht around the year 1012. Before long, miracles were reported at his grave, and as a result a shrine was built to house his remains.

REFLECTION   The seemingly simple, unimportant life of St. Guy can be a source of hope for individuals who feel that their lives have little impact on society. His simple, virtuous life drew the attention of many after his death, and the miracles at his tomb seem to say much for the worth of a life of simplicity and poverty.

PRAYER *Loving Father, You bless the poor in a very special way. For their joy and emulation You raised up Your servant St. Guy as a model for those who are destined to be relegated to the humble tasks of this life. Through his intercession, may we come to understand the truth of letting go of the goods of this world in favor of the poor. This we ask through Christ our Lord. Amen.*

ST. AMATUS, Abbot

September 13

AMATUS was born in Grenoble, France, around the year 567. He entered the abbey of St. Maurice of Agaune in Switzerland at a very early age, and he remained there for thirty years as a schoolboy, as a Benedictine monk, and as a hermit.

In 614, St. Eustace passed through Agaune while returning from Rome. While there he met Amatus and convinced him to return with him to the monastery of Luxeuil and become a monk there.

Amatus was the major factor in the conversion of a Merovingian nobleman named Romaric. Romaric gave all his wealth to the poor, became a monk, and in 620 founded the abbey of Habendum under Benedictine rule. St. Amatus was the first abbot there. He died around the year 629.

REFLECTION To spend one's entire life in the service of God, as St. Amatus did, is an ideal that can be met even in modern times. In order to meet it, we do not have to enter the religious state or any particular state of life. All that is necessary is a conscious awareness of God's presence in everything we do.

PRAYER *O God, You call us all to a life of prayer and contemplation. Through the example and intercession of Your Abbot St. Amatus, help us as we move through the duties of our state in life to be constantly aware of Your guiding presence. This we ask through Christ our Lord. Amen.*

———◆———

ST. NOTBURGA, Virgin

September 14—*Patroness of Servants*

NOTBURGA was born at Rattenberg in Tyrolean Austria, in the thirteenth century. The daughter of a peasant, at the age of eighteen she became a kitchen maid in the house of Count Henry of Rattenberg.

Since Notburga got into the habit of giving leftover food to the poor, she was dismissed from her position by the count's wife, and she became a servant girl on a farm. After his wife died, Count Henry remarried, and Notburga was rehired.

Notburga spent the remainder of her life as the count's housekeeper. Many miracles were attributed to her before her death in 1313, and Pope Pius IX approved local devotion to her in

1862. In the Tyrol today, St. Notburga is honored as Patroness of Servants.

REFLECTION   The life of St. Notburga is a vivid reminder that God frequently channels His most favored graces to the poor, lowly, and simple. No matter what our station in life, He sanctifies us according to our own desires.

PRAYER   *O God, in Your wisdom You raised up for us Your servant St. Notburga as a model of charity and grace. Through her intercession, help us to humbly accept the station in life that gives You the most honor and glory. This we ask through Christ our Lord. Amen.*

ST. ALBERT OF JERUSALEM, Bishop

The Same Day—September 14

ALBERT was born to a well-known family in Parma, Italy, in 1149. After studies, he became a canon at Holy Cross Abbey in Mortara. In 1184, he was named Bishop of Bobbio and then Bishop of Vercelli.

Having mediated a conflict between Frederick Barbarossa and Pope Clement III, Albert was appointed Pope Innocent III's legate to northern Italy. In 1205, he became Patriarch of Jerusalem.

Albert is most remembered for the Rule he wrote for St. Brocard and his hermits, which later became the rule of the Carmelites, of whom he is regarded as a co-founder. In 1214, he was stabbed to death by an individual he had been forced to remove as administrator of a hospital.

REFLECTION Although St. Albert of Jerusalem was an individual of many talents, his energies were for the most part directed toward things spiritual. All of us are called to do the same no matter what our station in life may be.

PRAYER   *O God, through the intercession of Your Bishop St. Albert of Jerusalem, may we remain true to our goal of friendship with You no matter how many distractions arise during our days. This we ask through Christ our Lord. Amen.*

ST. CATHERINE OF GENOA, Widow

September 15

CATHERINE of Genoa was born in 1447 of a noble family in that renowned city of Italy. At the age of sixteen she married Julian Adorno. His lifestyle reduced the couple to destitution.

Julian then reformed and became a Franciscan tertiary, and he and Catherine agreed to live in continence. They devoted themselves to prayer and to work in a hospital of which eventually Catherine became the director.

In 1493, owing to sickness from the plague, Catherine was forced to resign her position. The following year Julian died. Catherine persevered in her life of sanctity and wrote two famous works on mysticism: *Dialogue between the Soul*

and the Body and *Treatise on Purgatory.* She died in 1510, and was canonized in 1737 by Pope Clement XII.

REFLECTION Sometimes, as in the case of St. Catherine of Genoa, a drastic change in lifestyle is called for. In such cases, God's grace is readily available to us for conversion of mind and heart.

PRAYER *O God, You call us back from the brink of death to live, as Your Son Jesus did, in the light of Your truth. Through the example and intercession of Your servant St. Catherine of Genoa, keep us ever faithful to You. This we ask through Christ our Lord. Amen.*

———◆———

ST. EDITH OF WILTON, Virgin

September 16

EDITH was the daughter of King Edgar of England and Queen Wulfrida. Born at Kemsing, England, in 962, she was placed at the Wilton Abbey at a very young age, and she never left there for the rest of her life.

Edith was educated at the royal court. She learned letters, script and illumination as well as sewing and embroidery.

Edith's mother became a nun at Wilton, and was later made abbess. At the age of fifteen, Edith became a nun. Her father offered her the abbacies of three houses, but she declined, preferring to remain where she was.

Later when her half-brother Edward the Martyr was murdered, Edith refused to leave the convent and become queen. She died about the year 984 at the age of twenty-two with a great reputation for sanctity.

The young noblewoman was renowned for her personal service of the poor. She also had a knack for communicating with wild animals.

REFLECTION The life of St. Edith reminds us that, at times, we may be tempted to become completely immersed in worldly affairs. However, we must maintain a balance between the necessities of the duties of our state in life and our faithfulness to spiritual progress.

PRAYER   *Loving God, You call us to a life of inconceivable joy in Your Kingdom. Through the example and intercession of Your servant St. Edith, may we share that joy in this world through intimate prayer with You. This we ask through Christ our Lord. Amen.*

ST. JOHN MASSIAS, Religious

The Same Day—September 16

JOHN Massias was born at Ribera del Fresno in Estramadura, Spain, on March 2, 1585. Although his family was of the nobility, at the time of John's birth they were very poor.

Orphaned as a youth, John labored as a shepherd and later found work on a cattle ranch in Peru. After a few years, he went to Lima and became a lay brother in the Dominican Order, serving as the doorkeeper for the remainder of his life.

As time passed, John developed a reputation for miracles. Many of the poor and sick of Lima and its environs flocked to him, and he ministered to them as best he could. He died on September 16, 1645, and was canonized in 1975 by Pope Paul VI. In some places he is known as St. John Macias.

REFLECTION St. John Massias turned his poverty into the riches of holiness and contemplation. Given the Word of God, he shared his spiritual riches of holiness with the impoverished, performing the humblest of tasks in the monastery. His life disproves the concept that happiness is derived only from material possessions.

PRAYER *Loving Father, You blessed the goodness and poverty of Your servant St. John Massias. Through his intercession, may we share both our physical and our spiritual riches with those who are most in need. This we ask through Christ our Lord. Amen.*

━━━◆━◆━━━

ST. HILDEGARD OF BINGEN, Virgin

September 17

HILDEGARD was born at Böckelheim, Germany, in 1098. Afflicted with fragile health as a child, she was placed in the care of her aunt, Bl. Jutta, who lived as a recluse.

Jutta eventually formed a community of nuns, and Hildegard joined the group, becoming prioress of the house when Jutta died in 1136. Hildegard moved the community to Rupertsburg, near Bingen on the Rhine, and she established still another convent at Eibengen around 1165, overcoming great opposition on many occasions.

Hildegard was known for visions and prophecies, which at her spiritual director's request she recorded. They were set down in a work called *Scivias* (i.e., *sciens vias Domini:* the one who knows the ways of the Lord) and approved by the Archbishop of Mainz and Pope Eugenius III at the recommendation of St. Bernard of Clairvaux.

Living in a turbulent age, Hildegard put her talents to work in the quest for obtaining true justice and peace. She corresponded with four Popes, two emperors, King Henry II of England, and famous clergy. Her pronouncements attracted the fancy of the populace—drawing down upon her both acclaim and disparagement.

Hildegard wrote on many subjects. Her works include commentaries on the Gospels, the Athanasian Creed, and the Rule of St. Benedict as well as Lives of the Saints and a medical work on the well-being of the body. She is regarded as one of the greatest figures of the twelfth century—the first of the great German mystics as well as a poet, a physician, and a prophetess. She has been compared to Dante and to William Blake.

This remarkable woman of God died on September 17, 1179. Miracles were reported at her death, and she was proclaimed a Saint by the multitudes. She was never formally canonized, but her name was inserted in the *Roman Martyrology* in the fifteenth century.

REFLECTION The life of St. Hildegard of Bingen shows that even those who are dedicated to God and involved in monasticism are subject to opposition when they pursue justice. Yet the Gospel calls all to strive for the ideal of justice in all actions and to protect those whose rights have been unjustly blocked.

PRAYER *Almighty God, You endowed Your servant St. Hildegard with wondrous gifts of mind and heart to enable her to work for justice and peace. Through her intercession, help us to spread Your justice and peace by our daily lives patterned after the image of Your Son. This we ask through Christ our Lord. Amen.*

ST. COLUMBA OF CORDOVA,
Virgin and Martyr
The Same Day—September 17

COLUMBA was born at Cordova, Spain, in the eighth century. Her brother was an abbot, and Columba's sister and brother-in-law founded a double monastery at Tabanos.

Columba's widowed mother wanted her to marry, but Columba was determined to dedicate her life to God. Eventually, she entered the monastery at Tabanos.

In 853, during the Moorish persecutions of the Christians, the nuns fled Tabanos and hid at Cordova. However Columba openly proclaimed her Faith to a Moorish magistrate, and as a result she was beheaded.

REFLECTION We must, like St. Columba of Cordova, always be ready to profess our Faith. Despite the call of evil in the world we must remain true to God's Word and His way.

PRAYER   *O God, in our hour of need we turn to You. Through the example and intercession of Your Virgin and Martyr St. Columba of Cordova, help us never to falter in our faith as we await with joy Your Son's Second Coming. This we ask through Christ our Lord. Amen.*

ST. RICHARDIS, Empress and Religious

September 18

RICHARDIS was the daughter of the Count of Alsace. At the age of twenty-two, she married Charles the Fat. Nineteen years later, in 881, she and Charles were crowned Empress and Emperor of the Holy Roman Empire by Pope John VIII in Rome.

Some years later Charles accused Richardis of infidelity, suspecting her of being involved with the Bishop of Vercelli. Richardis denied the charge, and at her insistence she underwent trial by fire, which she passed.

Richardis then left Charles and became a nun at Hohenburg. Later, she founded the abbey of Andlau and stayed there until her death around the year 895.

REFLECTION   False and unjust accusations cannot always be resolved in a practical way like trial by fire. If we are unjustly accused, we must remain self-confidently silent and allow the truth to become evident.

PRAYER   *O God, You are the light of the world, and all truth rests in You. Through the example and intercession of Your servant St. Richardis, teach us to courageously bear the cross of slander and injustice in our regard. This we ask through Christ our Lord. Amen.*

ST. EMILY DE RODAT, Virgin

September 19

EMILY de Rodat was born in Rodez, France, in 1787. Raised by her grandmother, she attended school at Maison Saint-Cyr. At the age of eighteen, she began to teach in that same school. Later, she joined three different orders of sisters but found none of the three to her liking.

In 1815, Emily and three companions began teaching poor children in a room at Maison Saint-Cyr. This proved to be the beginning of the Congregation of the Holy Family of Villefranche. She started a free school in 1816 and eventually established thirty-eight foundations.

The work of the group was expanded to include nursing the sick poor, visiting prisoners, and caring for orphans, the aged, and wayward women. Emily also established many cloistered convents. She died on September 19, 1852, and was canonized by Pope Pius XII in 1950.

REFLECTION   St. Emily de Rodat bears witness that the dedication of one's life and talents to the welfare of others can be a fulfilling lifestyle. Like Jesus, one thus forgets one's own needs completely in order to serve the wants of others.

PRAYER   *O God, through the love and charity of St. Emily de Rodat, Your Church continues to be well served. May her example and intercession lead others to offer their lives in Your service. This we ask through Christ our Lord. Amen.*

BL. FRANCIS DE POSADAS, Priest

September 20

FRANCIS de Posadas was born at Cordova, Spain, in 1644. Early in life he decided that he wanted to be a priest, and in 1663, at the age of nineteen, he entered the Dominican novitiate.

Following his ordination, Francis developed a widespread reputation for the effectiveness of his preaching. As a result, he was sent through western Spain to give missions. At the same time, people were drawn to him as a confessor because of his holiness, spirit of prayer, and spiritual gifts, which may have included the gift of levitation.

In addition to his great missionary work over forty years, Francis also wrote several books, including a biography of St. Dominic. He died on September 20, 1713, at the Cordova novitiate, and was beatified in 1818 by Pope Pius VII.

REFLECTION   The life of Bl. Francis de Posadas reminds us that those who are called to serve God as priests or religious often have to overcome periods of great trial and desolation and to nurture patience and trust in God. We should pray for an increase in vocations to the priesthood and religious life and that our seminarians and religious candidates will have the courage and generosity to persevere in their call.

PRAYER   *God our Father, in Your love for Your people You raised up Bl. Francis de Posadas as Your holy priest. Through his intercession, may we share his great zeal for souls and his patience in helping people to return to the fullness of Your peace. This we ask through Christ our Lord. Amen.*

———◆———

ST. EUSTACE (or EUSTACHIUS), Martyr

The Same Day, September 20—Patron of Hunters and Invoked for Intestinal Diseases

ST. Eustace, also known as Eustachius, is one of the most famous martyrs of the Church, venerated by Catholics throughout the centuries, and one of the Fourteen Holy Helpers.† However, we do not know anything more about him that is certain.

The unreliable Acts of the Saint state that he was an officer in the Roman army under Emperor Trajan and he had a wife and two sons. He became converted to the Faith by having a vision of a stag with a crucifix between its antlers while he was hunting. So he changed his name from Placidas to Eustace and was recalled to the army.

† See p. 223.

The Saint soon lost all his wealth and was separated from his family. Then, after winning a great victory, he was reunited with his loved ones. During the victory celebration, he refused to sacrifice to pagan gods. He and his family were roasted to death around the year 461. He is invoked for intestinal diseases and is the Patron of Hunters.

REFLECTION   Although little is known about St. Eustace, he was one of the most popular Saints during the Middle Ages as one of the Fourteen Holy Helpers. He shows us one of the characteristics that Vatican II attributed to the Saints: "For our own greater good and that of the whole Church, we seek from the Saints . . . aid by their intercession."

PRAYER   *Heavenly Lord, You strengthened St. Eustace Your servant so that he was able to obtain the crown of martyrdom. By his prayers, help us to die to self so that we may live for You. This we ask through Christ our Lord. Amen.*

———◆———

ST. MAURA OF TROYES, Virgin

September 21

MAURA was born at Troyes, France, in 827. Her prayers as a young girl brought about her father's conversion after a worldly life.

Maura continued to live with her mother after her father's death and was instrumental in the spiritual growth of her brother Eutropius who became Bishop of Troyes. She devoted most of her time to prayer and works of charity, fasting on bread and water two days a week.

It is believed that Maura was the beneficiary of miracles, but she went to great lengths to conceal them, preferring a life of humble service and obscurity. She died about the year 850 at the age of twenty-three.

REFLECTION   The life of St. Maura of Troyes is a vivid reminder of the necessity of prayer in our lives. Where so much frustration exists in the world, prayer can easily remedy the pangs of distraught souls.

PRAYER   *O God, You ask us to come to You and pray, and You entertain us with the delights of Your presence. Through the example and intercession of Your servant St. Maura of Troyes, may we constantly respond to Your invitation to pray. This we ask through Christ our Lord. Amen.*

ST. JONAH, Prophet

The Same Day—September 21

ST. Jonah lived in the eighth century B.C. and was the protagonist and probable author of the Biblical Book of Jonah and one of the Minor Prophets.

He prophesied in the days of Jeroboam II (786-746 B.C.) and was the first Prophet sent by God to a Gentile nation. He was called to go to Nineveh, the capital of Assyria, and preach repentance.

Jonah refused to do his task and attempted to escape it by boarding a ship for far-off Tarshish. In punishment, he was thrown overboard and swallowed by a great fish (probably a whale). After three days and nights he was washed ashore. Then, properly chastened, he completed his mission, which ended with the people repenting and being spared by God.

In New Testament times, the "sign of Jonah" was regarded as a prophecy of Christ's Resurrection, and it was used by Him to assure the Scribes and Pharisees that through His Death both Gentiles and Jews would be converted and saved (Matthew 12:40; 16:4; Luke 11:30).

REFLECTION Jonah shows that God is the God of all peoples and He is loving and merciful. His love extends to Ninevites and all pagans, and even to the creatures of the field that He has made. The vocation of the People of God is to reveal to all nations the triune God Who loves them.

PRAYER *O God, in Your wisdom You called St. Jonah to be a Prophet to Your people and led him to understand that no one is deprived of Your grace and mercy. By his prayers, help us to believe more firmly in the Resurrection of Your Son, which is prefigured by the sign of Jonah. This we ask through Christ our Lord. Amen.*

STS. MAURICE AND COMPANIONS,
Martyrs
September 22

MAURICE was an officer of the Theban legion in the army of Emperor Maximian Herculius. The members of this legion were Christians recruited from Upper Egypt.

Around the year 302, the legion was encamped in Switzerland on a march to suppress a rebellion in Gaul. When Maximian ordered the entire army to sacrifice to the gods to ensure a victory, Maurice and his fellow legionnaires, numbering more than six thousand men, refused to do so.

Maximian thereupon ordered the entire Theban legion to be executed. Maurice and two officers encouraged the soldiers before they too were massacred.

REFLECTION   When we are tempted by the gods of greed, slander, deceit, and sensuality, we should readily recall the graced courage of the Martyrs of the Theban legion who resisted the worship of any gods except the one true God.

PRAYER   *O God, through the heroic deeds of Your Martyrs Sts. Maurice and Companions, we are constantly reminded of our duty to persevere in good to the end. Through their intercession, may we not be found wanting. This we ask through Christ our Lord. Amen.*

BL. HELEN OF BOLOGNA, Widow

September 23

HELEN Duglioli was born in Bologna, Italy, in 1472. At the age of seventeen, she married a man named Benedict dall'Oglio. They were married for thirty years, and during that time they were known to have lived a very Christian life.

Shortly after Benedict died, Helen likewise passed away in 1520. After her death, the memory of the holiness of her life was spontaneously celebrated, and a public cult rapidly developed.

Helen's public cult was confirmed in 1828 during the pontificate of Leo XII. Undoubtedly the testimony of the Archbishop of Bologna, who later became Pope Benedict XIV (1740-1758), helped Helen's cause for beatification.

REFLECTION The lives of Bl. Helen and Benedict cannot help but inspire and motivate married couples to holiness of life. The grace of the Sacrament of Matrimony fully accepted and lived can very easily lead a couple to sanctify the pedestrian tasks of married life.

PRAYER *God of love and compassion, You bless marriage in a special way, and You call married couples to sanctity. Through the example and intercession of Your servant Bl. Helen of Bologna, grant to all married couples an awareness and understanding of Your grace-filled presence with them. This we ask through Christ our Lord. Amen.*

STS. ELIZABETH AND ZECHARIAH,
Parents of John the Baptist
The Same Day—September 23

ELIZABETH and Zechariah, the parents of John the Baptist, lived in the first century. Zechariah was a priest of the Old Law, and Elizabeth belonged to the house of Aaron. For a long time, they had not been blessed with children.

One day, while Zechariah was serving in the Temple, he was told by an angel in a vision that he would have a child by Elizabeth, despite their age. At the same time, Zechariah was told what name to give the child who was to have a very special mission. Shortly afterward Elizabeth conceived.

When Mary, Elizabeth's cousin, visited her, John the Baptist in Elizabeth's womb was filled with the Holy Spirit. Following John's birth, Zechariah proclaimed the famous *Benedictus*, which begins with the words "Blessed be the Lord, the God of Israel, Who has visited and redeemed His people."

After the birth of John we know little about Zechariah and Elizabeth. However, some Church Fathers believe that Zechariah was killed in the Temple by Herod's followers when he would not reveal the whereabouts of his son John.

REFLECTION When we look at the lives of St. Elizabeth and St. Zechariah, it seems perfectly clear that God had a special role or mission for them. It reminds all who have been exposed to God's Word and gifted with faith of the necessity of developing a sense of responsibility for our lives. Our faith and knowledge of God are not to be hidden; they must be lived openly in a positive and enlightening manner.

PRAYER   *O God, You chose St. Elizabeth and St. Zechariah to play a central role in our Redemption. Their openness to Your Will is a model for us. May we follow You faithfully as St. Elizabeth and St. Zechariah did. This we ask through Christ our Lord. Amen.*

———◆•◆———

ST. GERARD SAGREDO, Bishop and Martyr

September 24—Apostle of Hungary

GERARD Sagredo was born early in the eleventh century in Venice. As a very young lad, he joined the Benedictine monastery of San Giorgio Maggiore in Venice, but later he left the monastery and went on pilgrimage to Jerusalem.

While traveling through Hungary, Gerard was appointed by the king, St. Stephen, to tutor his son. Gerard then began to gain a reputation as a fine preacher, and eventually Stephen appointed him as the first Bishop of Csanad. The people of the area were open to Gerard, and he was successful in bringing them to the Faith. Gerard's habit of contemplation undoubtedly aided his pastoral endeavors.

When King Stephen died in 1038, there was a general uprising against Christianity in Hungary. When Gerard was in the town of Buda, he was ap-

prehended by some idolatrous soldiers, run through with a lance, and tossed into the Danube River. His martyrdom took place on September 24, 1046. He is known as the Apostle of Hungary and venerated as the Protomartyr of Venice.

REFLECTION   St. Gerard Sagredo's life tells us that in our journey on the road to salvation we must constantly remind ourselves of the necessity of trusting solely in God. Our human companions, even those with whom we work closely, can quickly turn on us. God alone remains our faithful supporter.

PRAYER   *God our Father, you call us to eternal union with You. Through the example and intercession of Your Bishop and Martyr St. Gerard Sagredo, may we make progress day by day on our way to You in Heaven. This we ask through Christ our Lord. Amen.*

━━━━◆━◆━━━━

ST. FIRMIN, Bishop and Martyr
September 25

S T. Firmin was most likely a missionary bishop who lived at Amiens in the fourth century. A later Bishop of Amiens, St. Firmin the Confessor, built the church now called St. Acheul.

The martyrologies and liturgical books of the tenth/eleventh centuries mention one or the other Firmin of Amiens but on different days. Firmin the Martyr is the titular Saint of two ancient English churches.

The Saint's unreliable Acts say he was born at Pamplona, Spanish Navarre, received Baptism from St. Honoratus, and was consecrated Bishop by the same Prelate.

St. Firmin then went to Gaul as a missionary and built his church at Amiens. He was tortured and beheaded for his Faith during Diocletian's persecution in the fourth century.

REFLECTION   Although the lives and times of the early bishops like St. Firmin are shrouded in mystery, we know that it was they who carried the Faith forward and built churches in which the people could worship God. Without them there would be no Church or Catholic teaching today. We should pray to the Lord every day to send laborers into His vineyard—to take care of His people's spiritual needs.

PRAYER   *Almighty God, You called Your Bishop and Martyr St. Firmin to give his life for his flock. By his prayers, remember the needs of Your Church and send forth workers to aid Your people. This we ask through Christ our Lord. Amen.*

———◆◆———

ST. THERESA COUDERC, Virgin

September 26

THERESA was born at Masle, France, on February 1, 1805. Early in life she joined a community of teachers founded at Aps by Father Terme. In 1824, Father Terme established a community of sisters called the Daughters of St. Regis, and Theresa was appointed superior.

After Father Terme's death in 1834, the Jesuits took charge and asked Theresa and her companions to give retreats for the laity. This led to the establishment of the Congregation of Our Lady of the Retreat in the Cenacle.

Theresa resigned as superior in 1838 because of fiscal difficulties. She went to Lyons to found a house, and except for a short time as superior at Paris, she remained a humble sister until her death on September 26, 1885. She was canonized in 1970 by Pope Paul VI.

REFLECTION The life of St. Theresa Couderc is a graphic reminder that the Lord bids us to come aside and rest awhile. When we do this, events in our lives fall into perspective. The Lord opens Himself to us in a special way in time of retreat.

PRAYER *O God, in You we have our hope, joy, and contentment. Through the intercession of Your servant St. Theresa Couderc, may we always be faithful to You and share our lives with You in Your presence. This we ask through Christ our Lord. Amen.*

———◆◆◆———

ST. GIDEON, God's Judge and Faithful Warrior
The Same Day—September 26

DURING the early days of the chosen people's stay in the Promised Land, they were ruled by Judges, who helped them ward off attacks of their neighbors. During one such attack, God called Gideon, a man from the tribe of Manasseh, to be Judge over Israel. As Judge, he was to lead the Israelites into battle in the Name of their king, the Lord (Judges 6:11f).

Gideon's first reaction to his call was one of disbelief. There were stronger men in Israel whom God could have chosen. Yet God assured Gideon that he was to be an instrument of God.

Therefore, the Saint broke down the local altar to Baal (Judges 6:25ff) and called out the Israelites to face the foe (Judges 6:33ff). He asked for a sign of Divine support (Judges 6:36ff) and with only three hundred men routed the Midianites (Judges 7—8).

The elders of Israel were grateful to Gideon for his powerful deeds, and they begged him to be their king. However, Gideon refused, for he knew that Israel had only one king, the Lord, and He was the true author of his fabulous victory. Gideon's rule is said to have lasted forty years.

REFLECTION When the Lord called, Gideon reacted. He did not question his call—he just pitched in and did what the Lord asked of him. This should teach us that as long as God is with us whatever He asks us to do is possible. We should be ready to respond to His call.

PRAYER   *O God, in Your wisdom You called St. Gideon to come to the aid of Your people who were under attack. By his prayers, help us always to discern Your will for us and to carry it out with Your assistance. This we ask through Christ our Lord. Amen.*

ST. ELZEAR, Layman

September 27

Elzear was born of a noble family in Provence, France, in 1285. He was educated at St. Victor's Monastery in Marseilles, and at the age of sixteen, he married Bl. Delphina, who also was sixteen.

As the heir to his father's estate, Elzear became Count of Ariano in Naples. He was greatly beloved by the people, and his marriage was an outstanding one, characterized by virtue and charity. In 1317, he and Delphina joined the Court of King Robert of Naples, and Elzear became tutor to the king's son Charles.

Elzear went on diplomatic missions for King Robert and was appointed by him to other positions of honor. While on a trip to arrange a marriage for Charles, Elzear became ill, and he died at Paris in 1323. He was canonized in 1369 during the pontificate of his nephew Urban V.

REFLECTION The life of St. Elzear reminds us that marriages lived according to God's law can be of great importance to the married couple and the society in which they live. Love, joy, peace, and salvation attend marriages marked with piety.

PRAYER *O God, You have raised up Your servant St. Elzear as an example of Christian marriage. May his prayers help Your Church today in her struggle to preserve the family. This we ask through Christ our Lord. Amen.*

ST. EUSTOCHIUM, Virgin

September 28

EUSTOCHIUM was born around 370. She was the daughter of St. Paula, and, like her mother, she chose St. Jerome as her spiritual director when he visited Rome in 382. Soon thereafter, she took a vow of perpetual virginity.

Later, Eustochium went with Paula and Jerome to the Holy Land. They settled at Bethlehem, where she and Paula helped Jerome with the translation of the Bible when his sight failed.

When Paula died in 404, Eustochium became directress of three communities of women who had been under Paula's direction. Almost everything we know of her comes from the writings of St. Jerome. She died at Bethlehem around 419.

REFLECTION Through her friendship with St. Jerome, St. Eustochium came to love and protect God's Word. We are called by God to do the same. In a very simple way, our guardianship can be one of living exactly according to the way of God's Word.

PRAYER   *Lord, keep us in Your care. Through the intercession of St. Eustochium, may we love and protect Your Word and never stray from it. This we ask through Christ our Lord. Amen.*

BL. CHARLES OF BLOIS, Layman

September 29

BORN in 1320, Charles was of noble heritage. His father was Count Guy de Chantillons of Blois, and his mother Margaret was the sister of King Philip VI of France. In 1337, Charles married Joan of Brittany. As a result, he became involved in a number of conflicts with John of Montfort over Charles's claim to Brittany's dukedom.

Naturally, Charles's claim was based on his marriage to Joan. However, de Montfort was backed by King Edward III of England, who defeated the French troops at Crecy in 1346. Charles was captured at the Battle of La Roche-Derrien and was held in the Tower of London for nine years until he was ransomed and released in 1355.

Undeterred by his time in jail, Charles continued his quest for the dukedom, fighting many battles over another nine years. But at the Battle of Auray Charles was killed on September 29, 1364.

Despite his long and rancorous struggle, Charles always showed compassion for his enemies and had a reputation for a deeply religious spirit. Moreover, he founded several religious houses. Although he was the object of veneration in France for many years, Charles's public veneration was approved only in 1904 during the pontificate of St. Pius X.

REFLECTION   One does not usually associate a military career with holiness of life. Bl. Charles's life demonstrates that one can be involved in the works of the world and still maintain a religious focus in one's life. It is of special note that the popularity of Bl. Charles in France was due to his spirituality rather than his military activities.

PRAYER   *O God, come to our aid as we struggle to make our way along the path to eternal salvation. Through the intercession of Bl. Charles of Blois, help us to turn away from worldly desires and to live for You alone. This we ask through Christ our Lord. Amen.*

———◆———

ST. HONORIUS OF CANTERBURY, Bishop
September 30

HONORIUS was born in Rome. As a young man, he joined the Benedictines and was sent to England by Pope Gregory the Great at the request of St. Augustine, to work toward the conversion of that country.

In 627, Honorius was named Archbishop of Canterbury, and he remained in that position for the remainder of his life. The Pope gave Honorius the right to consecrate bishops.

Honorius appointed St. Paulinus as Bishop of Rochester. When Paulinus died in 644, Honorius then appointed St. Ithmar as his successor. Ithmar was the first English-born bishop. Honorius died on September 30, 653.

REFLECTION   St. Honorius of Canterbury was obedient to God's call. When obedience makes its demands upon us, we know that we surely do God's will as long as what we are asked to do is not against His law.

PRAYER   *O God, You blessed the people of England with the pastoral care of Your Bishop St. Honorius. Through his intercession, may we foster the Spirit of Christ among all those with whom we live and work. This we ask through Christ our Lord. Amen.*

———◆━◆———

ST. ROMANOS THE MELODIST, Deacon
October 1

ROMANOS is known as the "Melodist" because almost nothing but hymns have remained of his life—hymns in Byzantine Greek. His holiness on earth took place through melody, so to speak. But if the poetic material left by Romanos is imposing, the details of his life are very scarce.

A Syrian by birth, Romanos served for a short time as deacon at the Church of the Resurrection in Berytus and then made his way to Constantinople where he was incardinated into the clergy as a deacon. After ministering to the people through music, he died around 556.

Romanos has been called the greatest of hymnwriters not only in the East but also in the whole Church. He is credited with writing one thousand hymns composed for the Liturgy—some very lengthy. Unfortunately, only eighty of them are extant, each consisting of twenty-four strophes.

The hymns that remain are unsurpassed in early hymnody for inspiration, diction, and poetic quality and are based on accent rather than on the ancient meter (i.e., the quantities of the syllables). However, in the course of time and as a result of many factors, their place in the liturgical books was taken by inferior compositions.

REFLECTION   St. Romanos the Melodist reminds us of the importance of music in our lives and especially in the Liturgy. When we participate at the Eucharist, we should strive to recall that it is a celebration and join wholeheartedly in the music and song that have become an integral part of it. As St. Augustine put it, "Those who sing pray twice!"

PRAYER   *Almighty God, You have given us the gift of music to accompany us on our way to You. Through the example and intercession of St. Romanos the Melodist, teach us always to make melody to You both in our hearts and in our liturgical celebrations. This we ask through Christ our Lord. Amen.*

ST. LEODEGARIUS (or **Leger**), Bishop and Martyr, **AND GERINIUS,** Martyr
October 2—(St. Leodegarius) Invoked against Diseases of the Eyes

L EODEGARIUS was born around the year 616. Raised in the court of King Clotaire II, he was eventually ordained, and around 651 he became abbot of Maxentius Abbey, where he installed the Benedictine Rule.

In 663, Leodegarius was named Bishop of Autun, where he introduced many reforms. However, he incurred the enmity of several rulers and was banished to Luxeuil. Eventually, he was restored to his See of Autun.

When Autun was later attacked, Leodegarius surrendered the town in order to save it. The mayor of the palace, who was named Ebroin, then had him blinded, his lips cut off, and his tongue pulled out. Later that same enemy accused Leodegarius and his brother Gerinius of murder. So Gerinius was stoned to death and Leodegarius was cast into prison.

After two years, in 678, the Saint was summoned by Ebroin to a court at Marly, deposed, and executed, all the while protesting his innocence to the end. Although his death seems to have been for political reasons, he was regarded as a martyr and given a cult. He is invoked against Diseases of the Eyes.

REFLECTION We sometimes like to put aside the reality of evil in the world. The lives of Sts. Leodegarius and Gerinius are vivid reminders that personal hatred is one of the most devastating of the human passions. We must fight against this great evil in our lives.

PRAYER *O God, in Your wisdom You call upon Your people to love one another. Through the intercession of Sts. Leodegarius and Gerinius, may charity prevail in all our thoughts, words, and deeds. This we ask through Christ our Lord. Amen.*

ST. HESYCHIUS, Monk

October 3

HESYCHIUS lived in the fourth century and became a monk at the monastery of Majuma and a disciple of its founder, St. Hilarion of Palestine. When the latter left for Egypt in search of more solitude, Hesychius went with him.

In time, still in search of solitude, Hilarion fled to Sicily in secret without informing his devoted disciple. Hesychius was not daunted by this turn of events. He began a search for St. Hilarion that lasted three years and took him through the deserts and ports of Egypt to Greece—without success.

It seems every time the people heard about Hilarion's spiritual gifts, they flocked to him, intruding on his solitude; thereupon, the Saint withdrew to another location.

Finally, Hesychius was able to catch up with his master in Sicily, and together they practiced the solitary life in Dalmatia and then in Cyprus at Paphos. Two years later, Hesychius journeyed to Gaza at Hilarion's request to see how the brothers were doing there. On his return, he found Hilarion on the verge of withdrawing once again. He convinced the aged hermit to remain on a deserted spot twelve miles away, where Hilarion died in 371.

Hesychius took the body secretly back to Palestine and returned to the monastery of Majuma. It was here that he himself died around the year 380.

REFLECTION The life of St. Hesychius is one long example of communion with God and dedication to a friend. In his search for solitude, Hesychius never lost sight of the fact that his friend Hilarion needed him. We should cultivate dedication to God, to our state, and to those dear to us.

PRAYER   *God of goodness, You gave us the gift of friendship. Through the intercession of Your servant St. Hesychius, may we always be totally dedicated to You and to our true friends. This we ask through Christ our Lord. Amen.*

ST. PETRONIUS, Bishop

October 4

IT is believed that St. Petronius was the son of a prefect of the praetorium in Gaul. It is further believed that he was himself a Roman official.

At one point in his life, Petronius became a cleric. He then made a trip to Palestine, becoming very interested in Eastern architecture.

When Petronius returned from Palestine, he became Bishop of Bologna around the year 432. He is remembered for rebuilding many of the churches destroyed by the Goths. Moreover, he oversaw the construction of several other churches along the lines of those in Jerusalem. He died around 450.

REFLECTION Enemies of the Word of God constantly attempt to destroy goodness, virtue, love, and generosity in our society. St. Petronius reminds us that as Christians we are called to be the bulwark of virtue against the destructive forces of evil.

PRAYER   *Loving God, You call us to stand up to the followers of Your enemies. Through the example and intercession of Your Bishop St. Petronius, may we have the grace to live lives of Christian courage and virtue. This we ask through Christ our Lord. Amen.*

ST. FAUSTINA KOWALSKA, Virgin
October 5—*Apostle of the Divine Mercy*

BORN on August 25, 1905, in Glogowiec, into a devout Catholic family, St. Faustina had only three years of formal education and began working as a domestic at the age of sixteen. In 1925, she joined the Sisters of Our Lady of Mercy and filled the posts of cook, gardener, and doorkeeper in various convents of the Congregation.

On February 22, 1931, the Saint had a vision of Jesus with one hand raised in blessing and the other hand at His breast. Jesus told her to have an image made about what she saw and have the following words printed on it: "Jesus, I trust in You." He also asked her to promote the Second Sunday of Easter as a celebration of the Divine Mercy. This request was fulfilled on April 30, 2000, when Pope John Paul II officially proclaimed the Second Sunday of Easter as Divine Mercy Sunday.

St, Faustina, by order of her confessor, recorded her visions, revelations, hidden Stigmata, gifts of reading souls, and prophecies in a diary. Through Faustina's work, devotion to the Divine Mercy grew by leaps and bounds. She died on October 5, 1938, and was canonized in 2000 by Pope John Paul II.

REFLECTION St. Faustina was chosen by God to bring to the world a devotion to the Divine Mercy. And in her short life she did just that. May we follow her in giving thanks to God for the great mystery of His mercy.

PRAYER *Lord Jesus, You appeared to St. Faustina Your Virgin and asked her to propagate the image of the Divine Mercy. By her intercession, may we have frequent recourse to this devotion and at the hour of our death receive Your mercy. For You live and reign forever and ever. Amen.*

BL. ISIDORE OF ST. JOSEPH, Religious

October 6

ISIDORE de Loor was born in Flanders, Belgium, on April 13, 1881. He was the eldest of three children in a devout Catholic family that was engaged in farming.

At the age of twenty-six, leaving his beloved field work, Isidore entered the Passionist Congregation and took the name Isidore of St. Joseph. He was professed as a lay brother on September 13, 1908. Besides his humble community service, Isidore was known for his intense prayer life and penance as well as for his charity, simplicity, recollection, and dedication.

After much suffering, Isidore died of cancer and pleurisy on October 6, 1916, at the age of thirty-five. He was beatified by Pope John Paul II on September 30, 1984.

REFLECTION Even though Jesus turned the world upside down, simplicity was one of the most pronounced characteristics in His life. Like Bl. Isidore of St. Joseph, we would do well to model this simple approach to spirituality.

PRAYER *O God, in Bl. Isidore of St. Joseph's spirit of humility and work You have given us an example of a life hidden in the shadow of the Cross. Through his intercession, help us to imitate his life in service to our brothers and sisters. This we ask through Christ our Lord. Amen.*

ST. MARK, Pope
October 7

ST. Mark, a Roman by birth, was installed as Bishop of Rome on January 12, 336, and occupied the See for less than nine months, dying on October 7 of that same year. Very little is known about his life. He was the first Pope after Constantine's grant of freedom to Christianity.

During Mark's short reign, St. Athanasius was exiled from Alexandria to Trier, Marcellus of Ancyra and other leaders of orthodoxy were deposed, and Arius was on his deathbed. However, there is no evidence that St. Mark was in any way involved in the Arian controversy.

The Saint founded the Church of St. Mark, originally named after him but later placed under the patronage of St. Mark the Evangelist. He also founded the basilica in the cemetery of St. Balbina on the Via Ardeatina. There is also some evidence that during his reign there were begun the very important lists of anniversaries of the deaths of Roman Bishops and Martyrs.

REFLECTION It is believed that St. Mark granted or approved the right of the Bishop of Ostia to consecrate the Bishop of Rome. It is also believed that a poem by Pope St. Damasus (366-384) is about St. Mark, stressing his disinterestedness and spirit of prayer. We should make it our concern to pray for the Pope every day because of the enormous task that is his in this world.

PRAYER   *Almighty God, You called St. Mark to be Pope at a time when the office of Roman Pontiff was in its early stages. By his intercession, grant Your grace to the present Holy Father that he may guide the Church through the dangerous times in which we live. This we ask through Christ our Lord. Amen.*

ST. REPARATA, Virgin and Martyr
October 8

REPARATA lived at Caesarea in Palestine during the fourth century. Nothing is known about her parents or other early background.

When Reparata was only twelve years old, she was discovered to be a Christian. A persecution was under way at the time, and she was arrested in Caesarea.

Reparata was tortured, but she refused to worship pagan gods. She was then thrown into a furnace but escaped unharmed. Since she continued to refuse to worship those pagan gods, she was then beheaded.

REFLECTION Despite the terrors of torture and fire, St. Reparata remained staunch in her faith. As the world mounts its attack on the virtues of faith, hope, and charity, Christians are called to imitate Reparata's unwavering faith.

PRAYER *O God, You call us to be a people of faith as we await Your coming. Through the example and intercession of Your Virgin and Martyr St. Reparata, may we always remain true to the Faith without fear. This we ask through Christ our Lord. Amen.*

ST. PUBLIA, Widow and Religious
October 9

PUBLIA lived in Antioch, Syria, during the fourth century. After the death of her husband, she gathered a number of women around her to form a community.

In 362, when Julian the Apostate was journeying through Antioch on his way to fight the Persians, he stopped to listen to the community chanting Psalms. However, he took offense at the words of some of the Psalms that he felt were directed as a reproach to him, if not an outright condemnation.

Julian summoned Publia before him and allowed his men to slap her. He then left, planning to kill the community upon his return from Persia. However, he died in battle there, and Publia and her sisters were spared to die in peace.

REFLECTION The life of St. Publia reminds us that sometimes the Word of God upsets people. When we live the Word of God, this too can cause people to oppose us, even to the point of violence. The courage of our convictions must prevail.

PRAYER   *O God, we are constantly exposed to the wrath of the Evil One. Through the example and intercession of Your servant St. Publia, may we always abide in Your presence so as to frustrate his designs. This we ask through Christ our Lord. Amen.*

ST. ABRAHAM, Patriarch

The Same Day, October 9—Father of All Believers

ABRAHAM lived in Ur of the Chaldees at the beginning of the second millennium before Christ. One day, God called him to leave his native country and journey to an unknown distant land, which became the Promised Land (Genesis 12:1ff). After a sojourn in Egypt (Genesis 12:10), he settled in Canaan with his wife Sarah and his nephew Lot.

God made a Covenant with Abraham and promised the land to him and his descendants (Genesis 17:4). A sign of this was the rite of circumcision. Despite the fact that Sarah was long past childbearing age and that Abraham was also very old, God enabled them to have a child, who was named Isaac (Genesis 21:2-3).

God also promised to make Abraham the father of many nations and to be the God of His people, the Lord (Genesis 17:4-8). Abraham believed the Lord, and it was credited to him as an act of righteousness (Genesis 15:6). In his dedication to the will of God, Abraham was even prepared to sacrificed his only son as a burnt offering; seeing Abraham's obedience God spared Isaac at the last moment (Genesis 24).

After a long life founded on faith, Abraham went to his reward. He was called the "Friend of God" (Isaiah 41:8), and is among the heroes of faith (Hebrews 11:8, 17).

REFLECTION   Abraham lived a long and eventful life in the service of the Lord, and he survived because he believed fully in God's Word. We should strive to emulate his faith, to be people of faith in our God.

PRAYER   *O God, in Your wisdom You called Abraham out of his native land so that he could become the father of many nations. By his intercession, keep us close to You every day of our lives and enable us to trust You in every circumstance. This we ask through Christ our Lord. Amen.*

———◆◆———

STS. DANIEL AND COMPANIONS, Martyrs

October 10

INSPIRED by the martyrdom of Berard and his companions in 1220, contemporary Franciscans vied with one another to suffer a similar fate. In 1227, Daniel, the provincial superior of Calabria, Italy, with six companions (Samuel, Angelus, Donulus, Leo, Hugoline, and Nicholas) received permission to preach the Gospel in Morocco.

Arriving in Ceuta, the holy men learned from Christian merchants that a recent decree punished Christian evangelizers with death. Ignoring this decree, Daniel and his companions began to preach the Gospel openly in the public places of the city.

Consequently, the preachers were arrested and imprisoned in chains for eight days. Neither threats nor bribes could persuade them to renounce Christian teaching and they were all be-headed. Their bodies were exposed to ridicule, but their remains were gathered together and buried at Ceuta by Godfearing people. In 1516, Pope Leo X permitted their feast to be observed liturgically by the Franciscans.

REFLECTION   Sts. Daniel and his Companions shed their blood for the Lord. They loved Christ during their lifetime and imitated Him in their death. Therefore, they merited the crown of victory. May we too love the Lord during life and imitate Him in dying to the world.

PRAYER   *Almighty and eternal God, You gave Sts. Daniel and his Companions the grace to suffer for Christ. By their prayers, support our weaknesses with Divine strength so that we may not waver in professing our faith in You, even as they did not hesitate to die for You. This we ask through Christ our Lord. Amen.*

ST. MARY SOLEDAD, Religious

October 11

E MANUELA Torres-Acosta was born on December 2, 1826, at Madrid, Spain. From her earliest days, she felt called to the service of God as a vowed religious. Accordingly, she applied to enter the Dominican Order, but she was rejected because of poor health.

In 1848, Emanuela was asked to head a new community of women religious whose purpose was to minister to the sick poor. Taking the

name Mary Soledad, she oversaw the beginnings of the fledgling community, which experienced significant internal discord and split into two groups in 1855.

Half of the sisters remained with Mary Soledad, and under the direction of a new moderator, Father Gabino Sanchez, a new community was formed. It was named Handmaids of Mary Serving the Sick. It received diocesan approbation in 1861, and Mary Soledad was recognized as the superioress, a position she went on to hold for the next thirty-five years.

The Handmaids of Mary received tremendous public acclaim for their heroic work during the Madrid cholera epidemic of 1865, and the community expanded throughout Europe and the Americas. After founding forty-six houses, Mary Soledad died on October 11, 1887. She was raised to Sainthood by Pope Paul VI in 1970.

REFLECTION   St. Mary Soledad dedicated her entire adult life to the care of the sick poor. She thus manifested the Church's option for the poor. Her life should lead us to imitate her efforts to the extent that we are able.

PRAYER   *Lord God, Your Son showed us throughout His life on earth His deep care for the poor. Through the example and intercession of Your servant St. Mary Soledad, may we cultivate a loving concern for the poor both in prayer and in works. This we ask through Christ our Lord. Amen.*

STS. CYPRIAN AND FELIX
AND COMPANIONS, Martyrs

October 12

BOTH Cyprian and Felix were bishops in North Africa in the fifth century. Cyprian was somewhat younger than Felix, who was very old and partially paralyzed.

Around 484, both bishops, along with thousands of members of the faithful, were driven into the Libyan desert during the Vandal persecution by King Hunneric. Hunneric was an Arian, and his hatred for Christians was so intense that he refused to allow the aged Felix to be exempt from torture although the bishop was close to death.

After being subjected to the cruelest of tortures, Cyprian and Felix and their 4,966 followers, including women and children, received the glorious crown of martyrdom.

REFLECTION The destruction of the North African Martyrs reflects the enormity of evil in the world at all times through history. Like the Martyrs, we are sustained by courageous adherence to our Faith.

PRAYER *O God, through the intercession of Sts. Cyprian and Felix and their Companions may we stand strong in our faith and bring the consoling message of Your Word to those who are most in need. This we ask through Christ our Lord. Amen.*

BL. MAGDALEN PANATTIERI, Virgin

MAGDALEN was born in 1443 in the tiny town of Trino in Piedmont, Italy, where she remained for her entire life. Although she continued to live at home, she became a Dominican tertiary at the age of twenty.

Living a very austere life, Magdalen spent most of her time in prayer and care for the poor and young children. She also gave inspiring spiritual talks to women and children and later to priests and religious as well.

Magdalen died at Trino on October 13, 1503. Public devotion to her was approved during the pontificate of Pope Leo XIII.

REFLECTION   The life of Bl. Magdalen Panattieri is a graphic reminder that holiness of life does not require special gifts or talents. Life lived according to the Commandments in union with God is sufficient to bring others to seek His presence in their lives.

PRAYER   *O God, You gift us with Your presence through the inspirational lives of many Saints. Through the intercession of Your servant Bl. Magdalen Panattieri, grant us the wisdom to follow their good example. This we ask through Christ our Lord. Amen.*

ST. ANGADRISMA, Virgin

October 14

ANGADRISMA was born in the seventh century and educated at Thérouanne by St. Omer, and by a cousin, St. Lambert. As a young woman, she wanted to enter the convent, but she was promised in marriage by her father to St. Ansbert of Chaussy.

Angadrisma prayed to be spared this situation, and shortly thereafter she contracted leprosy. Ansbert then married someone else, and the leprosy disappeared when Angadrisma received the veil from St. Ouen.

Angadrisma eventually was selected as abbess of Aroër, a Benedictine monastery near Beauvais. She was known for her holiness, and miracles were attributed to her. She died around the year 695.

REFLECTION In all our needs we should turn to God in prayer. Still, as the life of St. Angadrisma shows, it is most important that we be fully open to God's will in our regard no matter whether our prayers seem to be heard or not.

PRAYER *Loving Father, You bid us turn to You in time of trial. Through the intercession of Your servant St. Angadrisma, may our happiness rest on Your will rather than ours. This we ask through Christ our Lord. Amen.*

ST. THECLA OF KITZENGEN, Virgin

October 15

THECLA of Kitzengen was a community member of Wimborne Abbey in England during the eighth century. Eventually, she was sent to Germany under the leadership of St. Lioba.

The purpose of Thecla's assignment to Germany was to help St. Boniface in his missionary activities. At first, she resided at Bischofsheim Abbey, and later Boniface made her abbess of Oschenfurt. Then she became abbess of Kitzengen.

At Kitzengen, Thecla was known as Heilga. This name means Saint, and Thecla had a reputation among both her sisters and the women of the area as an individual of humility, gentleness, and charity. She died around the year 790.

REFLECTION In His public life, the gentleness of Jesus was clearly evident. St. Thecla of Kitzengen shows that cultivation of this trait in one's life can allow for much goodwill and acceptance of the principles enunciated by Jesus.

PRAYER   *O God, we cry out to You in pain, aware as we are of our lack of gentleness. Through the intercession of Your servant St. Thecla of Kitzengen, grant us the grace to be true lambs of Your flock. This we ask through Christ our Lord. Amen.*

ST. BERTRAND, Bishop
October 16

BERTRAND was born in the eleventh century. He was the son of a military officer, and the expectations were that he would enter military service. However, he joined the canons of Toulouse and eventually became an archdeacon.

Around 1075, Bertrand was named Bishop of Comminges, France. He remained in that position for forty-eight years, inaugurating extensive reforms and placing the cathedral canons under the Rule of St. Augustine.

Bertrand's holiness and zeal were not always appreciated by his people. Once, while preaching at the Val d'Azun, he encountered a great deal of hostility and had all he could do to calm his audience.

In atonement for their boorish behavior toward their prelate, the people of that district promised to provide Comminges with free butter every year during the week after Pentecost. This custom continued until the time of the French Revolution.

In 1100, Bertrand was one of the fathers of the Synod of Poitiers who excommunicated King Philip I and were in turn stoned by the enraged populace. He was also present at the consecration of the cemetery of St. Mary at Auch when embittered monks of St. Orens attempted to burn the church down.

Several miracles were attributed to Bertrand during his lifetime. He died around 1123 and was canonized before 1309 (probably by Pope Alexander III).

REFLECTION   Many facets of life demand great sacrifice and discipline—for example, athletics, scholarly activities, writing, art, music. St. Bertrand shows that the same is true for a life of virtue. Yet this goal, once achieved, will last forever.

PRAYER   *O God, in Your wisdom You allow us to choose in life what we want to do. Through the intercession of Your Bishop St. Bertrand, may we share the wisdom of the Saints in always choosing to do good and avoid sin. This we ask through Christ our Lord. Amen.*

ST. JOHN OF EGYPT, Hermit

October 17

JOHN of Egypt was born at Lycopolis in Lower Egypt around 304. At the age of twenty-five he left the world and retired to a mountain near Lycopolis, under the spiritual direction of an aged recluse who trained John in obedience and self-surrender.

Following his director's death, John spent about five years visiting monasteries. Then he finally settled on top of a hill near Lycopolis, where he walled himself in with only a small window to receive life's necessities. He devoted himself solely to prayer and meditation for five days a week, but he provided spiritual guidance to male visitors who sought his counsel on weekends. His disciples eventually built a hospice for his numerous visitors.

John was known for cures, prophecies, miracles, and the knowledge of secret sins of those who visited. Finally, sensing that the end was approaching, he asked that no one come near for three days. On his knees at prayer, he died on the third day, in 394, at the age of ninety.

REFLECTION St. John of Egypt's life-style was not unusual for hermits who lived in the fourth century. Completely divested of any material possessions, he devoted himself entirely to prayer, yet many were drawn to him and benefited from his spirituality. As we commemorate the Passion and Death of Jesus Who died stripped of everything, St. John's good example encourages us to strip ourselves of all sin and attachments.

PRAYER   *Loving Father, Your servant St. John of Egypt spent his life entirely in Your service. May we seek out Your love and presence in all that we do as we bring our penitential season to an end. This we ask through Christ our Lord. Amen.*

———◆—◆———

ST. HOSEA, Prophet

The Same Day—October 17

ST. Hosea is one of the Twelve Minor Prophets. His ministry to the Northern Kingdom (which seceded from Judah after the death of Solomon) followed closely upon that of Amos, i.e., after 746 B.C. While the latter had spoken as a southerner to the prosperous Israel enjoying an era of peace, Hosea spoke as a native to his own people who were suffering from war with Assyria and in virtual anarchy.

The Prophet's personal life is an incarnation of God's redeeming love. He spoke out against the influence of pagan practices and is known as the cantor of God's redeeming love, which is opposed and frustrated by the people's infidelity.

Hosea recalls God's blessings on His people, urges repentance, and promises salvation. His revelation foreshadows that of Jesus, the revealer of the God of love.

REFLECTION Hosea shows that the God of Christians is the God of love. He loves us with a faithful and everlasting love and He desires our faithful love in return—indeed, He desires love over sacrifice and knowledge of God over burnt offerings (6:6). God's love knows no bounds and can forgive all faults—provided we repent for our infidelity and return to Him.

PRAYER *O God, in Your wisdom You called St. Hosea Your Prophet to preach about Your great love to the people. By his intercession, help us to repent of our sins and be ever faithful to You, Who truly are the God of love. This we ask through Christ our Lord. Amen.*

ST. PETER OF ALCÁNTARA, Priest

October 18—Patron of Brazil

PETER was born at Alcántara, a small town in Estremadura, Spain, in 1499. Like that of most of the Saints, his childhood was virtuous. After studying Philosophy at home and Canon Law at Salamanca, he resolved to enter religion. At sixteen years of age he received the habit of the Franciscans in the solitary convent of Manjarez.

From the beginning of his religious life his characteristic virtue, mortification, manifested itself. About three years after his profession, though he was but twenty years old, he became superior of a small convent at Badajoz, and at the expiration of his term he was promoted to the priesthood, in 1524, and soon after was employed in preaching. His greatest delight was solitude, and he obtained permission of his superiors to take up his abode in the convent of St. Onuphrius, situated in a most remote locality.

In 1538, he became provincial of the province of St. Gabriel in Estremadura, and upon the expiration of his term, in 1541, he went to Lisbon to join Father Martin, who was laying the foundation of an austere reformation of the Order. In 1555, he began a reformation of his own, which was characterized by its extraordinary rigor, and which bears the name Strictest Observance. The following year he was appointed commissary of his Order in Spain, and in 1561 he was chosen provincial of his reformed Order.

Two years previously, while making the visitation of some of his monasteries at Avila, he met St. Teresa, who was then suffering much in endeavoring to reform her own Order. He rendered her great assistance by his encouragement and advice. St. Peter was then approaching the end of his career, for he died soon after in his convent of Arenas, in 1562.

Peter was canonized by Pope Clement IX in 1669 and was declared Patron of Brazil by Pope Pius IX in 1862.

REFLECTION   The life of St. Peter of Alcántara is a providential reminder that one of the essential elements of any spirituality is a spirit of penance and austerity. Such austerity aims to root out those characteristics that are opposed to the essentials of a virtuous life.

PRAYER   *O God, Your servant St. Peter of Alcántara has shown us how to suppress our personal desires so that Your presence to us might grow more and more. Through his intercession, may we always strive to be faithful to his good example. This we ask through Christ our Lord. Amen.*

ST. AQUILINUS, Bishop of Evreux
October 19

ST. Aquilinus was born about 620 in Bayeux, France, and was part of the courts and wars of Clovis II. On coming back from a battle against the Visigoths in 660, he was married at Chartres. Then the couple moved to Evreux and for the next ten years worked for the poor in the service of God.

On the death of St. Aeternus, Aquilinus was chosen to be his successor as Bishop of Evreux. The holy man, who lived with his wife in continence, preferred to be a hermit but agreed to accept the role of Bishop. However, he built a cell close to his cathedral and spent much time there in prayer and penance for his people.

The Saint lost his sight during the last few years of his life but received the gift of miracles and always retained his pastoral concern. He died around 695 in the aura of sanctity.

REFLECTION St. Aquilinus is one of many Frankish Saints of Merovingian times who were part of the political and military sphere before entering the clerical sphere and becoming prelates. He was imbued with love of God and neighbor, especially the poor, which he took with him in whatever sphere he was working. This should remind us that love of God and neighbor can be practiced in every state of life.

PRAYER   *Heavenly Father, You called Your Bishop St. Aquilinus to serve You and the poor in three different states of life. By his prayers, help us to do Your will and accept whatever state of life You call us to follow. This we ask through Christ our Lord. Amen.*

ST. JOEL, Prophet

The Same Day—October 19

JOEL is one of the Minor Prophets. He was from the Southern Kingdom and lived probably after the Babylonian Exile at the time of the Persian domination of Israel, possibly between 350 and 200 B.C.

The Saint was concerned with an invasion of locusts who threatened to eat the land dry. He calls the people to a great liturgical assembly of sincere repentance. He also holds out the promise of Divine restoration, renewed prosperity, and protection from enemies so long as the people repent (Joel 2:12-14).

Joel also refers to the eschatological "Day of the Lord" (or the last days) and the outpouring of the Spirit that took place on Pentecost as well as the judgment of God on the universe. His famous promise is quoted by St. Peter on Pentecost Day: "Your young men shall see visions, and your old men shall dream dreams" (Joel 3:1).

REFLECTION   St. Joel is the Prophet of repentance. He says God stands ready to forgive our sins if only we repent. He also orders all things, in His infinite wisdom, for the good of those who are devoted to Him, those who know how to maintain harmony with creatures and with God. We must be wise enough to see natural events and phenomena as signs of the Lord's liberating presence in our midst.

PRAYER   *O God, in Your wisdom You called St. Joel Your Prophet to preach penance to Your people.*

By his prayers, teach us to do penance all our lives and to discern Your authentic signs as Your presence among us. This we ask through Christ our Lord. Amen.

———◆•◆———

ST. BERTILLA BOSCARDIN, Virgin

October 20

BERTILLA was born into a peasant family on October 6, 1888, at Brendola, Italy. She worked for a time as a servant, and then she joined the Sisters of St. Dorothy of Vicenza.

At first Bertilla was given menial assignments in the convent. Later, she was trained to be a nurse at the Treviso hospital, which was operated by her Order.

Despite a debilitating illness, Bertilla devoted herself to the care of the sick, eventually being placed in charge of the children's ward. She died of cancer at Treviso on October 20, 1922. Many healing miracles were reported at her tomb, and she was canonized in 1961 by Pope John XXIII.

REFLECTION Sometimes we are asked to accept the burden of serious illness in life. St. Bertilla Boscardin used the opportunity to direct her failing energies toward the welfare of others. This was heroic virtue well worth imitating.

PRAYER *O God, Your Son Jesus and His Saints have shown us how to forget ourselves and reach out to others. Through the example and intercession of Your servant St. Bertilla Boscardin, may we have the*

courage to carry forward their great tradition. This we
ask through Christ our Lord. Amen.

---◆─◆◆─◆---

ST. HILARION, Abbot

October 21

BORN near Gaza in Palestine of pagan parents in 291, Hilarion went to study in Alexandria and became a Christian while still a teenager. Drawn to solitude, he spent a few months with St. Antony in the desert of Egypt, then returned to Gaza in 306.

Hilarion lived the solitary life of an anchorite for some twenty years and brought about many conversions. Disciples flocked to him, and in 329, he was led to establish the first monastery in Palestine—at Majuma, the port of Gaza. However, his reported miracles and unmistakable holiness of life attracted crowds of pilgrims to him, and he withdrew to Egypt in 360.

The persecution under the Roman Emperor Julian the Apostate plus his natural desire for greater solitude caused him to flee to Libya and then to Sicily. It was there that his dedicated disciple St. Hesychius found the aged Saint after a three-year search for him.

There too, the Saint's magnetism turned his hermitage into a place of pilgrimage. Accordingly, Hilarion together with Hesychius once again withdrew—to Dalmatia, to Paphos in Cyprus, and finally to a more deserted spot nearby. There the Saint's own pilgrimage on earth ended in 371, and his body was secretly returned to the monastery of Majuma in Gaza by St. Hesychius.

REFLECTION   The life of St. Hilarion reminds us that in our search for God it is not our state of life that is important but our dedication to that state. It was not the solitude itself that enabled St. Hilarion to find God, but his lifelong carrying out of God's will for him. We should be totally dedicated to finding God in our state of life.

PRAYER   *God of goodness, You hold out Your grace to all who genuinely seek You. Through the example and intercession of Your Abbot St. Hilarion, may we never cease to seek You in our state of life by doing Your will day after day. This we ask through Christ our Lord. Amen.*

STS. NUNILO AND ALODIA,
Virgins and Martyrs
October 22

STS. Nunilo and Alodia were the daughters of a Muslim father and Christian mother. They lived at Huesca, Spain, and were raised as Christians.

When their father died, their mother married another Muslim. Despite his objections, Nunilo and Alodia were determined to live lives of chastity, refusing many marriage proposals.

Nunilo and Alodia were arrested during the persecution of the Moor, Abdur Rahman II, when they refused to disavow Christianity. They held firm despite the fact that they were sent to live with prostitutes. Their refusal finally earned them martyrdom through beheading in 851.

REFLECTION The love of chastity exhibited by Sts. Nunilo and Alodia reminds us that both within and outside marriage chastity is a virtue that contributes to the well-being of both the individual and society. This discipline of dedicated chastity often builds up interpersonal relationships through respect and a sense of self-worth.

PRAYER *O God, the lives of Your holy Martyrs inspire us to bring a strong sense of discipline into our lives. Through the intercession of Sts. Nunilo and Alodia, we ask the grace to exercise Your gift of sexuality within the bounds of Your will. This we ask through Christ our Lord. Amen.*

———◆———

BL. ARNOLD RECHE, Religious
October 23

NICHOLAS-JULES Reche was born of an impoverished family on September 2, 1838, in the French province of Lorraine. There was a deeply religious atmosphere in the family home. By the time Nicholas was twenty-one, he was a deeply religious individual, well versed in doctrine, spirituality, virtue, and prayer. He was terrified of sin.

Eventually, Nicholas moved away to work on his own. He went to Charlesville and was attracted to the social life of the industrial town. Marie Brulefer, his aunt, chided him for this and suggested he attend Sunday school conducted by the Brothers of the Christian Schools. He mended his ways, and became an individual of intense prayer and mortification.

At the age of twenty-eight, he entered the Brothers of Christian Schools, becoming a model religious and teacher. As director of novices for the congregation he developed a reputation for sanctity. However, he did not lead a reclusive life, and during the Franco-Prussian War, he was awarded the bronze cross for his work with the wounded. At the same time, Brother Arnold's spirituality led him to a deep sense of self-denial and much mortification.

After a sudden illness of only a few hours, Brother Arnold died on October 23, 1890, at the age of fifty-two. He was beatified by Pope John Paul II in 1987.

REFLECTION   Dedication to prayer and humility enabled Bl. Arnold to lead many others to repentance and an idea of self-worth. Let us imitate his gentle and humble manner when dealing with young people.

PRAYER   *O God, You give us models in Your Saints. Through the intercession of Your servant Bl. Arnold Reche, may we come to imitate his virtues and share his heavenly reward. This we ask through Christ our Lord. Amen.*

ST. MARTIN OF VERTOU,
Deacon and Abbot
October 24

MARTIN of Vertou was born at Nantes, France, in the sixth century. Later he was ordained a deacon by St. Felix. Unfortunately, as a preacher he was not very successful.

Martin then decided to follow the life of a hermit, and he took up residence in the Dumen forest in Britanny. So many followers were attracted to him that Martin eventually established Vertou Abbey, of which he was the first abbot.

During his lifetime at Vertou, many notable miracles were attributed to Martin. He died around the end of the sixth century at the convent in Durieu which he had also founded.

REFLECTION Although every person has many gifts, we are all different and it is important that we decide how best to serve God. The life of St. Martin shows us that although in the process we might experience failure, we should continue to search for the way we can best serve God and neighbor.

PRAYER *O God, You want us to search for Your will in our regard. Through the example and intercession of Your Abbot St. Martin of Vertou, may we always be open to that will and accept the service we are meant to accomplish for Your Kingdom. This we ask through Christ our Lord. Amen.*

STS. CRISPIN AND CRISPINIAN, Martyrs

October 25—Patrons of Shoemakers,
Cobblers, and Leatherworkers

STS. Crispin and Crispinian lived in the third century and were shoemakers by trade. In the Middle Ages, these two Saints were well known throughout northern Europe. Today they are known in England mainly from the speech Shakespeare attributes to King Henry V on the eve of Agincourt (*Henry V*, act IV, scene 3).

The Acts of these two Martyrs are unreliable. They state that the brothers were from a noble Roman family and left their city to preach the Gospel in Gaul. They settled at Soissons and began practicing the trade of shoemakers to avoid drawing attention to their missionary work.

The Saints accepted payment only when it was offered, and the poor always received free service. Their example impressed the pagans and led to the conversion of many. When Emperor Maximian came to Gaul, the brothers were accused of preaching the Faith and were handed over to an enemy of Christians, Rictius Varus. Remaining steadfast in their Faith, they survived inhuman tortures and were finally beheaded around the year 285.

REFLECTION   There is an English tradition that Sts. Crispin and Crispinian lived for a time in Faversham, Kent, during a persecution. Regardless of where the two brothers went, it is fair to assume that they asked no payment of the poor to fix their shoes or to preach

Christ to them. They show us that no matter what we might do for a living, we can always preach Christ to others at least by our example.

PRAYER   *Heavenly Father, You called Sts. Crispin and Crispinian to ply the trade of shoemakers and at the same time preach the Faith until martyrdom. By their prayers, help us to proclaim the Faith at our workplaces by our good example. This we ask through Christ our Lord. Amen.*

BL. DAMIAN DEI FULCHERI, Priest

October 26

DAMIAN dei Fulcheri was born at Petri, near Genoa, Italy, at the beginning of the fifteenth century. As an infant he was kidnaped by a lunatic, and was discovered after a long search aided by a miraculous light that indicated his whereabouts.

As a young man, Damian entered the Dominican Order at Savona. In a short time, he became famous for his preaching in every area of Italy, and many miracles were attributed to him.

Damian died in 1484, at Reggio d'Emilia. Pope Pius IX approved public veneration of him in 1848.

REFLECTION   There are many ways of effectively spreading God's Word. Most of us are not called to be great preachers like Bl. Damian. However, lives of charity, peace, forgiveness, and gentleness can be very effective in spreading God's Kingdom.

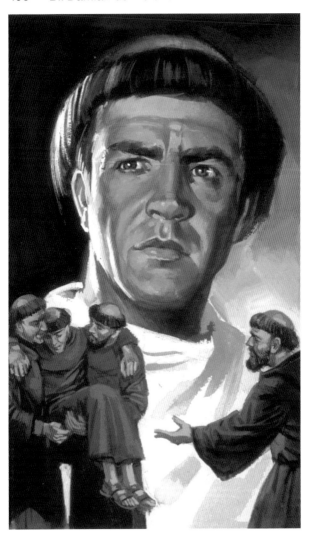

PRAYER　*Loving God, You gave Your servant Bl.
Damian the gift of effective preaching. Through his intercession, may our lives be such as to call others to
holiness of life. This we ask through Christ our Lord.
Amen.*

———◆—◆———

ST. NAMATIUS, Bishop
October 27

WE do not know much about St. Namatius,
and what we do know comes from St. Gregory of Tours. Namatius was the Bishop of Cler-
mont, France, in the fifth century—and he was
married. At that time, bishops were accustomed
to be selected from among the most worthy an-
cients of the Christian communities.

And there was no case of a bishop selected
whose wife was lacking in a certain degree of
wisdom and moral elevation. After the bishop's
election, husband and wife interrupted their life
in common and dedicated themselves completely
to the religious life and to works of charity.

All this was true of St. Namatius and his wife.
In addition, each had a great love for sacred art.
St. Gregory, the historian of Christian France,
describes the great church built by St. Namatius
where, he says, "the faithful inhaled an effluvium
of most sweet fragrance."

St. Gregory also describes another church—this
one built by Namatius's wife. He says too that she

had her church adorned with pictures, "reading the stories in a book that she carried always with her and indicating to the painters what they were to portray on the walls." This was the birth of the so-called Bible of the Poor—sacred images figuratively transcribed from the revealed texts.

REFLECTION   St. Namatius built a beautiful cathedral in which his flock loved to worship the Lord. His wife is credited with building a beautiful church in which the faithful not only were inspired to pray but also learned their Faith better through the Bible stories drawn on the walls. We should strive to pray well in church and also learn our Faith better.

PRAYER   *Heavenly Father, You called Your Bishop St. Namatius and his wife to the religious life after they had been married and enabled them to build churches for his flock. By his prayers, may we learn our Faith and how to participate in the Eucharistic Sacrifice. This we ask through Christ our Lord. Amen.*

ST. FARO, Bishop

October 28

FARO was raised in the court of King Theodebert II of Austrasia during the seventh century. The brother of St. Chainoaldus and St. Burgundofara, he married and moved to the court of Clotaire II.

When he was thirty-five, Faro and his wife agreed to separate. He became a monk at Meaux and was later ordained.

Around 626, Faro was made Bishop of Meaux. In that role, he became known for his generosity to the needy, for his fostering of monasticism, and for the many converts he brought into the Church. He died around the year 670.

REFLECTION   Living God's Word with joy and satisfaction can be a source of great attraction for those who do not have the Faith. St. Faro had the gift of bringing people into the Christian fold in this way. We should strive to emulate him.

PRAYER   *O God, You open the road to salvation through the ministry and mission of Your Son Jesus. Through the example and intercession of Your Bishop St. Faro, may we always follow Him, especially in reaching out to the poor and needy. This we ask through Christ our Lord. Amen.*

———◆━◆———

ST. COLMAN OF KILMACDUAGH, Bishop
October 29

THE name Colman is possessed by quite a few Irish Saints. St. Colman of Kilmacduagh was the son of an Irish chieftain born at Corker in Kiltartan at the end of the sixth century. He became a monk at Aranmore.

Later, Colman lived as a solitary at Burren among the mountains in County Clare. He is said to have hidden there because he had been made a bishop against his wishes. Only one disciple was with him, and they are reputed to have lived solely on wild vegetables and water for many years.

The Saint then founded a great monastery on land given him by King Guaire of Connaught and named after him "Kilmacduagh" (i.e., "the cell of the son of Dui"). He is venerated as its first bishop, but in his old age he returned to the Burren mountains. Colman died around the year 632 with a reputation for holiness, and his cult was approved in 1903.

REFLECTION St. Colman, like other monastic Saints, is reputed to have had a special affinity with animals: a cock used to wake him for the night office; a mouse prevented him from falling asleep during it; and a fly kept his place in the liturgical book. We should always remember to be good to other creatures who inhabit this planet with us.

PRAYER *Heavenly Father, You called St. Colman Your Bishop to live in harmony with everyone living on earth including nonhuman living things. By his prayers, help us to refrain from hurting other inhabitants of the earth. This we ask through Christ our Lord. Amen.*

———◆———

BL. BENVENUTA BOJANI, Virgin

October 30

BENVENUTA Bojani was born at Cividale, Italy, in 1254. As a young girl she became a Dominican tertiary, spending her entire life at home.

Benvenuta lived a life of extremely severe penance and austerity. For over five years she

was confined with a serious illness, but she seems to have been miraculously cured. Moreover, she was known to have experienced both heavenly visions and confrontations with the Evil One.

After a life characterized by cheerfulness and confidence in God, Benvenuta died on October 30, 1292. Pope Clement XIV approved public honor for her in 1763.

REFLECTION We are not privileged to experience visions or open assaults by Satan, as Bl. Benvenuta was. Nonetheless, we can become closer to God through prayer, fasting, and good works. Overcoming sensual pleasures and living totally in God's presence is the work of a lifetime.

PRAYER   *Loving God, as we prepare for Your coming to take us to Your Kingdom, our senses are assaulted with every kind of distraction and sensual allurement. Through the intercession of Your servant Bl. Benvenuta, help us always to practice the mortification and prayer necessary to remain faithful to You. This we ask through Christ our Lord. Amen.*

———◆———

ST. FOILLAN, Abbot and Martyr
October 31

FOILLAN was born in Ireland in the seventh century. He had two brothers, St. Fursey and St. Ultan. All three brothers went to England around 630 where they established a monastery near Yarmouth and did missionary work.

Eventually the brothers moved on to Gaul. Welcomed by King Clovis II, Foillan established a monastery at Fosses and became abbot. The monastery lands were a gift of Bl. Itta, located near the convent of Nivelles that Itta had founded and where her daughter St. Gertrude was abbess.

Foillan proved to be a successful pastor. However, in 655, a band of outlaws attacked and slew him and three friends in a local forest on October 31. Since he was traveling on Church business, he is venerated as a Martyr.

REFLECTION   The life of St. Foillan is a graphic reminder that the dangers to life and limb in this world lurk everywhere. At the same time, we continue to be subjected to the temptations of the Evil One. Thus, we are called to a deeper spirituality marked with prayer and fasting so that we may preserve ourselves pure in mind and spirit.

PRAYER   *God of love and mercy, You promised to be with us as we make our way to You. Through the intercession of Your Abbot St. Foillan, help us to live virtuously and thus bring light into a world of selfishness and sin. This we ask through Christ our Lord. Amen.*

———◆◆———

BL. PETER PAUL NOVARRA
AND COMPANIONS, Martyrs of Japan

November 1

PETER Paul Novarra was born in Calabria, Italy, in 1560. He joined the Jesuits at Naples in 1578 and, after his ordination in Goa, India, was sent to Japan as a missionary in keeping with his explicit desire.

Peter made the Japanese language and customs a part of his life in order to show the people that these were no hindrance to conversion. In 1614, he went underground because of an edict expelling foreign missionaries. In the course of bringing the Mass and Sacraments to his Japanese faithful, he assumed many disguises—beggar, wood seller, farmer, and tradesman among them.

Peter wrote *An Apology of the Christian Faith against the Calumnies of the Pagans* and translated a book on our Lady—both in Japanese. During his last years, he was working in Shimbara in western Kyushu with two catechists as associates—eighteen-year-old Peter Onizzuca Sandaju and thirty-nine-year-old Denis Fugiscima.

In December 1621, all three men together with their house servant Clement Kuijemon were arrested by priest hunters and cast into prison. For a time, it seemed as though they would be set free, but on October 27, 1622, their deaths were ordered by the Shogun.

On November 1, 1622, the two catechists pronounced their Jesuit vows at a Mass celebrated by Father Peter. Then all went resolutely to their death while chanting the Litany of Our Lady. They were beatified by Pope Pius IX in 1867.

REFLECTION The intrepid faith of these Martyrs of Japan and their indomitable love for Christ present a shining example for us. In our pluralistic world, we should strive by every means at our command to bring Christ and His Good News to those who do not know Him.

PRAYER   *Lord of all, You desire that all people come to the truth. Through the example and intercession of Bl. Peter Paul Novarra and his Companions, may we advance the coming of Your Kingdom through our daily prayers and bear constant witness to Christ by our everyday lives. This we ask through Christ our Lord. Amen.*

ST. VICTORINUS OF PETTAU,
Bishop and Martyr
November 2

ST. Victorinus was born in Greece in the second century. He is remembered for having written a number of commentaries on several books of the Old and New Testament. St. Jerome comments at some length on his scholarly works on Scripture, calling them "sublime."

Victorinus also had a reputation as a fine preacher, and eventually he became the Bishop of Pettau in Upper Pannonia. As bishop, he opposed certain heresies of his day, but apparently he was convinced of the truth of Millenarianism, which held that Christ would reign on earth as a temporal leader for one thousand years.

Victorinus is believed to have suffered martyrdom during the persecution under Diocletian. The year of his death was probably 304.

REFLECTION   The life of St. Victorinus of Pettau is a vivid reminder that Martyrs have come from all classes, from Popes to peasants, from bishops to scholars. However, in the mind of God there is no distinction. Whoever dies for the Faith is admitted to the presence of God. To die to oneself without losing one's life can likewise lead to the everlasting dwelling of God's presence.

PRAYER   *O God, through the intercession of Your holy Martyr St. Victorinus of Pettau, grant us the courage to live out our daily lives in the face of many obstacles and temptations. May we abandon ourselves entirely to You. This we ask through Christ our Lord. Amen.*

ST. WINIFRED, Virgin and Martyr

The Same Day—November 2

ST. Winifred was born of a wealthy family in Wales. She was the niece of St. Beuno who had a great religious influence on her in her formative years.

According to legend, Winifred was beheaded by a chieftain named Caradog when she refused to submit to his advances. St. Beuno is said to have restored her head, and later Winifred became a nun. At one time she served as abbess at the convent of Gwytherin in Denbighshire.

Fifteen years after her miraculous restoration to life, Winifred died, around 650. Where her head had fallen, a spring developed, and the area

became a great pilgrimage center, with many cures reported there.

The cult of St. Winifred became widespread during the Middle Ages. Six ancient churches in the area are dedicated to her.

REFLECTION When one wants to lead a life of virtue and holiness, as St. Winifred desired to do, one must expect challenge and even sometimes anger and hatred from others. Here patience and trust in God are called for.

PRAYER   *O God, in times of trouble You have given us the gift of faith to sustain us. Through the intercession of Your servant St. Winifred, may we be true to this gift in good times and bad. This we ask through Christ our Lord. Amen.*

———————•———————

BL. MARGARET OF LORRAINE, Religious

The Same Day—November 2

MARGARET of Lorraine was born of a noble family in Lorraine, France, in 1463. At the age of twenty-five, she married Duke René of Alençon. Four years later, he died, leaving Margaret with three children.

Margaret took care of the family estate and was generous in her charities while leading an austere life. Once her children were grown, she entered a convent at Mortagne, where she labored with the sick and the poor.

Sometime later, in concert with other nuns, Margaret founded a Poor Clare house at Argentan, Britanny. Refusing the position of abbess in the new convent, Margaret died there in 1521. Pope Benedict XV approved public devotion to her in 1921.

REFLECTION The life of Bl. Margaret of Lorraine is a good reminder that no matter what our state in life, we are to seek out ways and means of extending ourselves on behalf of the sick and poor. This is a dictate of the Gospel that should not be lightly dismissed.

PRAYER *O God, through the example and intercession of Bl. Margaret of Lorraine, may we always strive to serve You in Your poor and abandoned brothers and sisters. You entrust us with this great privilege so that we may become more like Your Son Jesus Who lives and reigns with You and the Holy Spirit, one God for ever and ever. Amen.*

ST. JOANNICIUS, Monk and Hermit

November 3

JOANNICIUS was born in Bithynia around 754. A swineherd as a youth, he lived a wild life. Later, he entered the military and retired at the age of forty.

Influenced by a holy monk, Joannicius became a hermit on Mount Olympus. Later he joined a monastery at Eraste. A former Iconoclast (one who opposes the veneration of images), he now preached vigorously against Iconoclasm but defended priests ordained by Iconoclast bishops.

Joannicius was noted for both prophecy and miracles, and he was one of the most renowned ascetics of his time. He died in 846, at the age of ninety-two, leaving us the celebrated aphorism by which he lived: "God is my hope, Christ is my refuge, and the Holy Spirit is my protector."

REFLECTION   We must not be discouraged with the vagaries and conduct of young people. Much love, patience, and good example over a period of time frequently will win them back to Christ, as the life of St. Joannicius well shows.

PRAYER   *Loving God, we regret the sins and misdeeds of our youth. Through the intercession of Your servant St. Joannicius, let us always be open to Your will and grateful for the grace of conversion that You generously confer on us. This we ask through Christ our Lord. Amen.*

BL. HELEN ENSELMINI, Virgin

November 4

BL. Helen belonged to the noble Enselmini family of Arcella, near Padua, Italy. In 1220, she received the habit of the Poor Clares from the hands of St. Francis himself. Six years later, she was afflicted with a painful illness that stayed with her for the rest of her short life.

Helen bore her suffering with Christian patience and received some remarkable heavenly consolations. She is said to have been shown in a vision the glory of the Elect in heaven, especially of St. Francis and his followers, and to have had a vision of purgatory and seen the souls set free by the prayers and good works of the faithful on earth. She is also said to have lived for several months solely on the nourishment provided by the Sacred Host.

Helen was fortunate to receive St. Anthony of Padua as her spiritual director toward the end of her life. She died in 1242, having in the end also been afflicted with blindness and the loss of speech. Her cult was approved in 1695 during the reign of Pope Innocent XII.

REFLECTION   Bl. Helen suffered greatly during the short thirty-four years of her life. But she united her sufferings with those of her Lord Jesus Christ. Her life reminds us to bear our sufferings and problems patiently and without complaining even while striving to be free of them.

PRAYER   *Heavenly Father, You called Bl. Helen Your Virgin to show the faithful how to deal with suffering. By her prayers, teach us to unite our sufferings in this world with Your Son's sufferings for our salvation and that of the whole world. This we ask through Christ our Lord. Amen.*

BL. GUIDO MARIA CONFORTI,
Bishop and Founder
November 5

BORN in Italy on March 30, 1865, Guido felt called to the religious life. He worked as a diocesan priest until December 3, 1895, when he founded a seminary for missionaries. Then in 1898, he founded the Congregation of St. Xavier for Foreign Missions.

On June 11, 1902, Guido took his vows as a Xaverian priest and became more active in providing for missionary work. In 1907, he was made Archbishop of Parma and oversaw both his flock at home and his missionaries hundreds of miles away.

The Congregation achieved enormous growth, spreading to Asia, Africa, Brazil, the Philippines, Taiwan, Mexico, Spain, and the United States. The missionaries conducted parishes, hospitals, orphanages, schools, and colleges. Guido died in 1931 and was beatified in 1996 by Pope John Paul II.

REFLECTION Bl. Guido, said Pope John Paul II, caused a new current of Divine life to flow into the souls of believers, increasing in them the fire of great missionary zeal. May we learn to pray and work always that the true Faith be spread to everyone on earth both near and far.

PRAYER *Lord of all, You called Bl. Guido Your Bishop to found a new missionary congregation in*

Your Church. Through his intercession, help us to work and pray for the spread of the Catholic Faith to all on earth. This we ask through Christ our Lord. Amen.

ST. WINNOC, Abbot
November 6—*Patron of Millers*

WINNOC lived at the end of the seventh century and was probably of British origin, though he was raised in Brittany. With three companions he joined the newly founded monastery of St. Peter at Sithiu (St. Omer) under the Rule of St. Bertin.

In time, the Saint was sent with his three companions to found a monastery among the Morini at Wormhout not far from Dunbarton and to be its abbot. He built a church and hospital there and evangelized the whole neighborhood. After the three companions died, a legend arose that God took pity on the aged St. Winnoc and caused a mill stone to turn by itself. This explains how Winnoc became the Patron of Millers.

The Saint provided a great example of devotion as well as of a zealous workman with his hands. He died about the year 716, and his memory is perpetuated by the Cornish village of St. Winnoc.

REFLECTION Many miracles are attributed to St. Winnoc, who always served both his monastic brothers and his pagan neighbors. He ground corn for the poor—even in his old age. He took seriously that ancient Catholic axiom: "To labor and to pray!" And we should too.

PRAYER   *Dear Lord, St. Winnoc Your Abbot has left us a wonderful example of the loving shepherd who takes care of his sheep. By his intercession, grant that we may follow his example combining prayer and work all our days. This we ask through Christ our Lord. Amen.*

———◆·◆———

ST. ENGELBERT, Bishop and Martyr

November 7

ENGELBERT may be termed the prototype medieval prince-prelate. Born around 1185, he was the son of the powerful Count of Berg. Because of his family's influence, he received several ecclesiastical benefices even as a boy, and as an adult (in 1215) he was made Archbishop of Cologne.

However, Engelbert turned into a dedicated prelate. He instituted discipline into the clergy, fostered monastic life, and instilled a spirit of learning among his people. He also became tutor to the emperor's son and chief minister of the empire.

In the course of time, Engelbert incurred the hatred of his cousin, Frederick of Isemberg. Frederick had abused his position as administrator of the goods of the nuns of Essen by stealing from them, and the archbishop had removed him from it. In retaliation, Frederick plotted his cousin's death.

On November 7, 1225, while Engelbert was taking a short trip, he was waylaid by a band led by Frederick and stabbed to death. He was pronounced a Martyr by the papal legate of the time and was eventually inserted into the *Roman Martyrology*, although never formally canonized.

REFLECTION   The life of St. Engelbert is a strong reminder that God calls us in many ways. Although he may have become archbishop through the power of his family, Engelbert grew into the post and turned into an outstanding churchman. He also fought for justice on behalf of God's people.

PRAYER   *Almighty God, in Your relations with human beings, You have continually indicated to us that You love justice. Through the example and intercession of Your servant St. Engelbert, may we ourselves be truly just and strive to bring about more justice in the world. This we ask through Christ our Lord. Amen.*

ST. WILLEHAD, Bishop

November 8

WILLEHAD was born in Northumbria, England, in the eighth century. Educated at York, after his ordination he went to Friesland in 776 to evangelize the pagans, and barely escaped with his life when those pagans tried to put him to death.

Willehad then went to Utrecht, but when he and his friends destroyed pagan temples, he was again in danger of losing his life. In 780, Charlemagne sent him as a missionary to the Saxons, but when the Saxons revolted against the Franks, Willehad fled to Friesland.

After a two-year hiatus at Esternach, where he gathered more missionaries, Willehad went back among the defeated Saxons. In 787, he was ordained Bishop of the Saxons, with his See centered at Bremen. There he built a cathedral and many other churches. He died at Bremen on November 8, 789.

REFLECTION Sometimes when we attempt to bring the truth to the attention of others we encounter serious opposition. With faith let us put our trust in God and continue to work for His honor and glory as St. Willehad did.

PRAYER *God our Father, as we work in Your vineyard we ask that You sustain us. Through the intercession of Your Bishop St. Willehad, may we always be endowed with courage and an abiding faith in Your constant care. This we ask through Christ our Lord. Amen.*

———◆•◆———

BL. ELIZABETH OF THE TRINITY, Virgin

November 9

ELIZABETH Catez was a French Carmelite mystic. Born in 1880 at Camp d'Avor, Bourges, France, she lost her father at the age of seven. At fourteen, she took a vow of virginity, and at twenty-one she entered the Carmelites at Dijon.

Elizabeth placed great emphasis on the indwelling of the Blessed Trinity and strove to be ever aware of the presence of God. In 1903, she was afflicted with a rare sickness of the adrenal glands called Addison's disease and offered herself to be conformed to the death of Christ. She died on November 9, 1906, with the words: "I'm going to the light, to love, to life."

Bl. Elizabeth is regarded as one of the great mystical writers of modern times, and Pope John Paul II beatified her in 1984.

REFLECTION   Bl. Elizabeth exhibited an openness to the Word of God. With it she nourished her prayer and reflection so that she found therein her reasons for living and consecrating herself to the praise of the glory of this Word. We should try to follow her along this same path.

PRAYER   *Triune God, You enriched Bl. Elizabeth Your servant with the grace to become Your herald in the world. By her prayers, grant us the grace to dwell daily upon the indwelling of the Trinity within us. This we ask through Christ our Lord. Amen.*

ST. ANDREW AVELLINO, Priest

November 10

ANDREW Avellino was born at Castronuovo, in Naples, Italy, in 1521. After earning Doctorates in both Civil and Canon Law, he was ordained and was assigned to work in the ecclesiastical courts.

In 1556, Andrew took up pastoral work. Later, he joined the Theatines in Naples. At one time, he was named superior there, and he worked hard to improve the quality of the community.

In 1570, Andrew founded houses in Milan and Piacenza where his reform policies were successful. In 1582, he went back to Naples and lived out his life there, ministering to the people with great compassion and effecting many conversions. He died in Naples on November 10, 1608.

REFLECTION Despite his expertise in Canon Law, St. Andrew Avellino dedicated himself to reform and evangelization. No matter what our station in life, we cannot excuse ourselves from the privilege of spreading the Faith.

PRAYER   *O God, in Your plan of salvation for all people You ask us to share the task of spreading Your Word. Through the intercession of Your Priest St. Andrew Avellino, may we always live so as to reflect Your Gospel values. This we ask through Christ our Lord. Amen.*

ST. BARTHOLOMEW OF ROSSANO, Abbot
November 11

BARTHOLOMEW was born at Rossano in Calabria, Italy. He eventually became a follower of St. Nitus, who around the beginning of the eleventh century had founded a Greek abbey at Grottaferrata, near Rome.

Bartholomew joined the monastery, later became abbot, and completed the buildings started by Nitus, meanwhile strengthening the community's spiritual foundations. He turned Grottaferrata into a center of education and the copying of manuscripts.

Bartholomew was responsible for convincing Pope Benedict IX to resign after a turbulent and scandal-ridden papacy and to become a monk at Grottoferrata. Benedict died at Grottaferrata, preceded by Bartholomew who passed away in 1065.

REFLECTION The actions of St. Bartholomew toward Pope Benedict IX remind us that a very healthy aspect of Christianity is the conviction to do penance for one's sins. Prayer, fasting, and almsgiving tend to remind us of the reality of the frailty of life in this world.

PRAYER   *O God, we acknowledge our sinfulness in the presence of Your great love for us. Through the intercession of St. Bartholomew of Rossano, may we always strive to do penance and become closer to You. This we ask through Christ our Lord. Amen.*

————◆●◆————

ST. NILUS THE ELDER, Abbot

November 12

NILUS was born in Byzantium in the fourth century and became an official of some importance at Constantinople. Two children were born to him after his marriage. However, some time later, he and his wife agreed to separate and devote their lives to God. Nilus became a monk on Mount Sinai, joined by his son Theodulus.

A few years later, Theodulus was abducted by Arabs during a raid. Nilus went in search of him and found him at Eleusa, where he had been ransomed by the local bishop. Nilus and Theodulus then returned to Sinai after the bishop had ordained them.

Nilus became renowned as the author of theological and ascetical works. He also served as Bishop of Ancyra and was a close friend of St. John Chrysostom. He died around the year 430.

REFLECTION The call to perfection is made to all without exception. Today it may be unusual to find perfection by following two vocations, namely, married and religious life, as St. Nilus the Elder was able to do. Nonetheless, no matter what our vocation is, the invitation to perfection and holiness of life remains universal.

PRAYER *Loving God, You invite us to share the infinity of Your wisdom, the power of Your Holy Spirit, and the forgiving love of Your Son Jesus. Through the intercession of Your servant St. Nilus the Elder, may we generously turn to You in all things with praise and thanksgiving. This we ask through Christ our Lord. Amen.*

ST. NICHOLAS I, Pope

November 13

ST. Nicholas was a Roman by birth and a member of the clergy of Rome. He has been surnamed "the Great" because of the tremendous effect he had on the Church of his day. He was elected Pope in 858, and in that office exhibited much energy and courage until his death on November 13, 867.

Nicholas excommunicated among others John the Archbishop of Ravenna (for recalcitrance), King Lothair II of Louvain (for breaking the marriage bond), and Photius, Patriarch of Constantinople (for intrusiveness). He also brought Archbishop Hincmar of Rheims to acknowledge the papal appellate jurisdiction.

The Saint was hailed as the champion of the people. He confirmed St. Ansgar as papal legate in Scandinavia and brought about the conversion of Bulgaria.

REFLECTION St. Nicholas was the very model of what a Pope should be. He was strict and temperate, humble and chaste, handsome of face and graceful in body. His speech was at the same time learned and modest, while he was illustrious by his great deeds. Devoted to penance and the Holy Mysteries, he was the friend of widows and orphans, and the champion of all the people.

PRAYER *Heavenly Father, Your Son Jesus established the Church and chose St. Peter and his successors to rule and guide her throughout the ages. Through*

*the intercession of Your servant St. Nicholas I, help us
to love the Church and follow her teachings all our lives.
This we ask through Christ our Lord. Amen.*

ST. LAWRENCE O'TOOLE, Bishop

November 14

BORN at Castledermot in County Kildare, Ireland, in 1128, St. Lawrence was taken
hostage in a raid when he was ten years old. He
was released two years later to the Bishop of
Glendalough, and became a monk there.

Lawrence was named Abbot of Glendalough
in 1153, at the age of twenty-five. Eight years
later, he was appointed Archbishop of Dublin. In
that position, he inaugurated many reforms, including acceptance of the imposition of the English form of the Liturgy on Ireland in 1172.

Living in an age of political upheaval and wars,
Lawrence steadfastly tried to help the peace. On
one occasion, he was attacked while visiting the
shrine of St. Thomas Becket in England.

In 1179, Lawrence attended the General Lateran Council in Rome and was appointed papal
legate to Ireland. However, he died on the way
back to Ireland on November 14, 1180. He was
canonized by Pope Honorius III in 1225.

REFLECTION   Despite difficult times and open hostility, our goal, like that of St. Lawrence O'Toole, must be to bring as much peace as we can to ourselves and to those for whom we are responsible. This can be life-threatening at times, for Gospel demands are not always pleasing to the worldly-minded.

PRAYER   *O God, Your Son Jesus left us with the command to live in peace and love with one another. Through the intercession of Your Bishop St. Lawrence O'Toole, grant us the grace we need to overcome hatred and distrust in our communities. This we ask through Christ our Lord. Amen.*

———◆—◆———

ST. LEOPOLD OF AUSTRIA, Layman

November 15

LEOPOLD was born at Melk, Austria, in 1073. He was educated by Bishop Altman of Passau, and at the age of twenty-three he succeeded his father as military governor of Austria.

In 1106, Leopold married Emperor Henry IV's daughter, who bore him eighteen children, eleven of whom survived childhood. Known for his piety and charity, in 1106 he also founded three monasteries.

In 1125, Leopold refused to become emperor upon the death of his brother-in-law Henry V. He died in 1136 at one of the monasteries he had founded. He was canonized by Pope Innocent VIII in 1486.

REFLECTION   When one carries out the duties of one's state of life with fairness, justice, and virtue, as did St. Leopold, many people are won over not only to a peaceful political scene but also to a life of faith and virtue.

PRAYER　*O God, in Your goodness You raised up for us St. Leopold who as a public figure fulfilled his office with responsibility and virtue. Through his intercession, may we always strive to make a similar contribution to our society. This we ask through Christ our Lord. Amen.*

ST. AGNES OF ASSISI, Virgin

November 16

AGNES, born in Assisi in 1197, was the younger sister of St. Clare. At the age of fifteen, she joined the Benedictines of Sant' Angelo di Panzo, wishing to follow a life of poverty and penance.

Despite her relatives' efforts to get her out of the convent, Agnes accepted the habit from St. Francis of Assisi and was sent to San Damiano, where Clare lived. This marked the foundation of the Poor Clares.

Agnes became abbess of the Poor Clares convent at Monticelli near Florence in 1219, and later she founded convents at Mantua, Venice, and Padua. She died in 1253, three months after Clare's death.

REFLECTION　In developing one's spirituality, two widely recognized characteristics of the interior life are poverty and penance. As we detach ourselves

from the cares of this life, as St. Agnes of Assisi did, we become more absorbed in the life of God.

PRAYER   *O God, through the intercession of Your servant St. Agnes of Assisi, grant us the wisdom to accept the necessity of detaching ourselves from this world's goods. This we ask through Christ our Lord. Amen.*

ST. HILDA, Virgin

November 17

HILDA was born in Northumbria, England, in 614, but it was not until she was thirteen years old that she was baptized by St. Paulinus.

Until the age of thirty-three, Hilda lived a life of a noblewoman, but then she decided to enter Chelles Monastery in France. At the request of St. Aidan, Hilda returned to Northumbria and became abbess of a double monastery at Hartlepool. She held the same position later at Whitby.

Hilda had a wide reputation for her spiritual counsel, and her monastery was known for its scholarly and spiritual life. Five of her monks became bishops, and she ranks as one of the great Englishwomen of history.

Although Hilda favored the Celtic Liturgy, following the Synod of Whitby she accepted the Roman Liturgy when King Oswy ordered its use in Northumbria. Hilda died on November 17, 680.

REFLECTION   Although St. Hilda was exposed to the comforts and pleasures of the nobility, at a later age she chose to follow Jesus more closely in prayer, poverty, obedience, and self-denial. In this she won many over to God's Word.

PRAYER   *O God, through the intercession of St. Hilda, who set aside her personal wishes for the Divine Liturgy, may we faithfully adhere to the norms and traditions espoused by Your Son's Vicar the Pope. This we ask through Christ our Lord. Amen.*

ST. ODO OF CLUNY, Abbot
November 18

ODO was born in Le Mans, France, around 879. He spent his early life with Count Fulk II of Anjou and Duke William of Aquitaine. At the age of nineteen, Odo received the Order of Tonsure, while, at the same time, he took the canonry of St. Martin of Tours.

For some time, Odo studied music and theology in Paris. Eventually, he joined the monastery at Baume, under Abbot Berno's direction. Later, he was made headmaster of the Baume Monastery School, and when Berno became Abbot of Cluny in 924, Odo was elected Abbot of Baume.

In 927, Odo became Abbot of Cluny. And in consideration of his reputation as a reformer, Pope John XI asked him in 931 to reform all the monasteries of northern France and Italy.

In 936, Pope Leo VII asked Odo to Rome to negotiate peace between Heberic of Rome and Hugh of Provence. Over a six-year span, Odo had to go to Rome twice to renegotiate between the two. However, Odo's work in monastic reform was outstanding. In many instances, he persuaded secular leaders to give up their unlawful control of monasteries so that good order and recollection might be had. On November 18, 942, Odo died at Tours while on his way to Rome.

REFLECTION   Monastic reform might seem something completely foreign to our experience. St. Odo's career as a reformer ably demonstrates the need for personal reform and holiness of life.

PRAYER   *Heavenly Father, through the intercession of St. Odo, inspire good and holy men and women to serve You and the Church according to the great monastic traditions. This we ask through Christ our Lord. Amen.*

ST. BARLAAM, Martyr
November 19

BARLAAM was an illiterate peasant who lived in Antioch in the third century. During the persecution of Diocletian, when he professed his faith in Jesus Christ, he was jailed for a long time before being brought to trial about 303.

At his trial, Barlaam was mocked by the judge. After that he was scourged, put on the rack, and subjected to other instruments of torture, but he continued to hold firm.

Finally, Barlaam was brought before an altar and one of his hands was held over hot coals and had incense sprinkled on it. The judge thought that the burning incense would force Barlaam to shake his hand as if he were offering sacrifice. However, Barlaam did not move and his hand was consumed. Immediately thereafter he was martyred.

REFLECTION   The judge's mockery of St. Barlaam demonstrates that no matter what station in life we occupy there is no partiality with God. We are all good, equal, and destined for salvation in His eyes.

PRAYER   *O God, through cruel pain and suffering many have come directly to You. Through the example and intercession of Your Martyr St. Barlaam, may we accept the trials and tribulations in this life in hope of an eternity with You. This we ask through Christ our Lord. Amen.*

ST. OBADIAH, Prophet

The Same Day—November 19

NOTHING is really known about Obadiah, one of the Minor Prophets and the author of the shortest book in the Old Testament (twenty-one verses). His oracle against Edom, a long-standing enemy of God's people, indicates a date of composition around the fifth century B.C.

His message is divided into two parts: (1) Edom has been judged by the Lord and will incur destruction for its social injustice (1-9) because it has taken part in the fall of Israel (10-14); (2) indeed, the Day of the Lord will come for all nations, and Israel will be restored (15-21).

The principal message of Obadiah appears to be that it is not only dangerous for peoples to fight against God but also just as dangerous for them to fight against His people.

REFLECTION   St. Obadiah tells us that social injustice is just as abhorrent to God as personal sin. Yet God is always faithful to His promises, even when His people are unfaithful to Him and unworthy of them. Those who repent as Israel did will be blessed. Those who remain in indifference and rebellion as Edom did will incur the same fate—separation from God.

PRAYER   *O God of justice, You raised up Your Prophet St. Obadiah to preach against social injustice. By his prayers, help us to seek true justice for every situation in this world, including social justice. This we ask through Christ our Lord. Amen.*

ST. EDMUND THE MARTYR
November 20

ST. Edmund came of Saxon stock and was brought up as a Christian. He was elected King of the East Angles in 855 when only fourteen and of Suffolk the next year. He ruled his people wisely and protected them until 870.

At that time, a great invasion of England by the Danes under Ingmar (which had begun in 866) reached his domain.

Edmund courageously led his army to hurl back the invaders, but he was soon defeated and taken prisoner. Though greatly pressured, the King refused to deny the Christian Faith or to rule as Ingmar's puppet. The Saint was scourged, pierced with an arrow, and finally beheaded. He died with the Name of Jesus on his lips.

REFLECTION   St. Edmund ruled his people from an early age. He ruled wisely and well, acknowledging Christ as the only real King. When he was still a relatively young man, he was cut down by pagan invaders and gave his life as a martyr for the real King of the world. May we always realize that our only King or Ruler is Christ and act accordingly.

PRAYER   *Lord Jesus, as the King of kings, You chose to make St. Edmund King of the East Angles and bestowed upon him many graces, including that of martyrdom. By his intercession, help us to offer our life to You and at our death have on our lips Your Name. For You live and reign forever. Amen.*

ST. GELASIUS I, Pope

November 21

GELASIUS was born in Rome, in the fifth century, the son of an African named Valerius. Later, ordained a priest, he was elected Pope on March 1, 492.

Gelasius had a reputation for learning, justice, holiness, and charity. However, he was burdened with difficulties caused by a conflict with Euphemius, the Patriarch of Constantinople, over the Acacian heresy. He also protested the encroachments by Constantinople on Alexandria and Antioch.

Gelasius was influential in setting aside Roman pagan festivals. Moreover, in opposition to the Manichaeans, he ordered reception of the Eucharist under both species.

Gelasius is known to have composed liturgical Prefaces and Orations for Sacramentaries, which may be part of the *Leonine Sacramentary*. However, he had nothing to do with the *Gelasian Sacramentary* or the *Gelasian Decree* (listing the Canonical books of the Bible)—which have been erroneously attributed to him. He died at Rome on November 21, 496.

REFLECTION   The life of St. Gelasius bears witness that the human element in the Church can be the cause of a number of difficulties. Nevertheless, we are assured that God will sustain the Church till the end time. Through personal holiness, we contribute to the Church's vitality.

PRAYER   *O God, in Your goodness You promised to be with Your people until Jesus comes a second time. Through the intercession of Your servant St. Gelasius, grant us the wisdom to grow in grace and holiness as we await His coming. This we ask through Christ our Lord. Amen.*

STS. PHILEMON AND APPHIA, Martyrs

PHILEMON, a Christian, lived at Colossae in Phrygia in the first century. It is believed that he was converted by St. Paul, and was the object of St. Paul's writing known as the Letter to Philemon.

In this rather personal letter, Paul tells Philemon that he is sending back Onesimus, Philemon's runaway slave. However, he asks Philemon to receive Onesimus as a brother, not as a slave.

Tradition holds that Philemon freed Onesimus. Later Philemon and his wife Apphia were stoned to death at Colossae for their avowal of their Christianity.

REFLECTION What is clearly a precept of God's Word is the universality of our brotherhood and sisterhood. The Gospel demands that we constantly work toward complete freedom from prejudice or discrimination of any kind, as Sts. Philemon and Apphia did.

PRAYER   *O God, You counsel us to seek out those who are the most poor and rejected in our societies. Through the intercession of Your servants Sts. Philemon and Apphia, may we minister to them with love, care, and compassion. This we ask through Christ our Lord. Amen.*

ST. TRUDO, Priest

TRUDO was born to Frankish parents in the province of Brabant in the seventh century. He studied as a youth at the Metz cathedral school and eventually was ordained by St. Clodulf.

Following ordination, Trudo returned to his hometown of Hasbaye. There he built a church and monastery on his paternal estate.

Around the year 660, Trudo founded a convent near Bruges. He also was renowned for his zealous preaching to the pagans of Hasbaye. He died around 690.

REFLECTION Not only did St. Trudo share his life for the spiritual welfare of his people, but he also gave completely of his worldly possessions. Even today, this same generous spirit of detachment is called for by those who wish to serve God's people.

PRAYER *O God, through the intercession of St. Trudo, call up from among Your people individuals of detachment and generosity, so that they may effectively serve Your people and bring them to Your Word. This we ask through Christ our Lord. Amen.*

———◆———

ST. COLMAN OF CLOYNE, Bishop

COLMAN was born in Munster, Ireland, in 530. As a youth he showed himself to be a poet of great skill, and eventually he became the royal bard at Cashel.

When Colman reached the age of fifty, he was baptized by St. Brendan. Shortly thereafter, he was ordained. Moreover, he is said to have been St. Columba's teacher.

Colman became the first Bishop of Cloyne in eastern Cork, of which he is the Patron today. He died between 604 and 608.

REFLECTION   The life of St. Colman reminds us that age is no barrier to growth in the love of God and in the initiation of work in His service. There is much to be done in the Christian community, which adjusts itself to the abilities and talents of its members.

PRAYER   *Loving God, You call many into Your special service. Through the intercession of Your Bishop St. Colman, bless in a special way Your brothers, sisters, and priests so that their lives may truly reflect Your Gospel. This we ask through Christ our Lord. Amen.*

———◆◆◆———

ST. MERCURIUS, Martyr

November 25

ALL we really know about St. Mercurius is that he was martyred for the Faith. His various Acts are pious fiction and may be summed up as follows.

The Saint was the son of a Scythian officer of the Roman army. He himself also became a soldier and, with a sword given him by an uncle, led the army to a great victory against the barbarians who attacked Rome at the time of Emperor Decius (248-251).

When Mercurius professed his Christianity before Decius, the Emperor sent him to Caesarea in Cappadocia where he was subjected to torture and then beheaded when he did not deny his Faith. Since that time, he has been one of the warrior-Saints so popular in the Eastern Church. He is reported to have appeared with St. George and St. Demetrius at Antioch to the soldiers of the First Crusade.

REFLECTION St. Mercurius is known as "the Father of swords" on account of the weapon he wielded and his military might. His battle, however, is always against evil and in favor of the Church. We should remember that our whole life is one long struggle against evil and frequently call on St. Mercurius for help.

PRAYER *Lord, You made Your Martyr St. Mercurius a member of the heavenly hosts in defense of Christians who are threatened by evil. By his prayers, help us to be safeguarded against the snares of the devil. This we ask through Christ our Lord. Amen.*

ST. LEONARD OF PORT MAURICE, Priest

November 26—*Patron of Parish Missions*

PAUL Jerome Casanova was born at Porto Maurizio on the Italian Riviera in 1676. Disowned by his uncle for refusing to become a physician, in 1697 he joined the Franciscans of the Strict Observance, taking the name Leonard.

Ordained in 1703 in Rome, Leonard went to Florence in 1709, and from there he preached throughout Tuscany with great success. For six years he gave missions around Rome, ardently promoting the Stations of the Cross.

In 1744, Pope Benedict XIV sent Leonard to Corsica to preach and establish peace, but owing to the political situation, the Saint was unsuccessful. Returning to Rome after an exhausting missionary tour, Leonard died there in 1751. Patron of Parish Missions, he was canonized in 1867 by Pope Pius IX.

REFLECTION Today many young people in the Church are burdened with the attractions of high-paying professional careers. St. Leonard's life demonstrates how rich and effective one can be in living and preaching Christ Crucified.

PRAYER   *O God, in Your mercy and goodness inspire many young people to opt for the service of their brothers and sisters in the Church. Through the intercession of St. Leonard, show them the delights of intimate union with You in working for the spiritual welfare of others. This we ask through Christ our Lord. Amen.*

ST. VIRGIL, Bishop

November 27—*Patron of the Slovenes*

VIRGIL, an Irish monk, was born in the eighth century. In 743, he traveled to the Holy Land, and then through France to Bavaria. While there he was appointed Abbot of St. Peter's at Salzburg, Austria.

Shortly afterward Virgil was appointed administrator of the See of Salzburg by Duke Odilo. Around 765, he was made Bishop of Salzburg. Twice denounced to Rome by St. Boniface of Mainz, he was cleared of charges each time.

Virgil rebuilt the Cathedral of Salzburg, and in addition he sent many missionary priests to Carinthia. After a pastoral visit to his missions in 784, he died at Salzburg shortly after his return. Canonized in 1233 by Pope Gregory IX, he is known as the Patron of the Slovenes.

REFLECTION   The life of St. Virgil is a graphic reminder that misunderstandings can be painful not only for the individuals involved but also for others for whom they are responsible. Disagreements should be cleared up as soon as possible.

PRAYER   *Lord our God, fill us with the zeal of Your servant St. Virgil. May we continue to work for the Kingdom even in the face of misunderstanding and criticism. This we ask through Christ our Lord. Amen.*

ST. STEPHEN THE YOUNGER,
Monk and Martyr
November 28

STEPHEN, surnamed "the Younger," was born at Constantinople in 714. At the age of fifteen, he entered the monastery of Mount St.

Auxentius, not far from Chalcedon, where he was in charge of obtaining the monastery's daily provisions.

Upon the death of his father, Stephen journeyed home to receive his inheritance. He immediately sold it and distributed the proceeds among the poor. Then, he returned to Mount St. Auxentius after locating a home for his mother and sister in a nearby monastery.

At the age of thirty, Stephen became Abbot of Mount St. Auxentius and ruled it with wisdom and compassion. Nonetheless, twelve years later, he resigned his post and retreated to an out-of-the-way cell in the desire for more solitude.

At that time, the emperor Constantine Copronymus was following in his father Leo's misguided footsteps, obsessed with stamping out the use of sacred images in the Church. Because of St. Stephen's fame, the emperor was determined to persuade the holy man to join the Iconoclast side. But St. Stephen steadfastly refused to go against the teaching of the Church.

As a result, the Saint was subjected to pressures of all kinds, including exile, over the course of two years. Among other things, Stephen was falsely accused of wrongdoing with a holy widow, but he was proven innocent.

Throughout all this time, Stephen put his trust firmly in God and his Catholic Faith, reiterating the good that sacred images do for all the members of the Church. He even fearlessly defended the teaching on images before the emperor himself. This act of courage, however, only increased the wrath of the emperor toward the man of God.

At length, the saintly man was clubbed to death in 764.

REFLECTION   St. Stephen the Younger energetically defended the Church's use of sacred images against a tyrannical emperor. He was well aware that sacred images do much good and are necessary to the spiritual life of Christians. We should show our gratitude for this gift of God to us by using images to good effect in our lives.

PRAYER   *Almighty God, You have enabled us to make use of sacred images of Jesus, Mary, and the Saints to keep us close to You. Through the intercession of Your servant St. Stephen the Younger, help us to utilize sacred images in our everyday lives. This we ask through Christ our Lord. Amen.*

BL. DIONYSIUS AND REDEMPTUS,
Martyrs
November 29

PIERRE Berthelot was born at Honfleur, France, in 1600. For a time he served as a cartographer and naval commander in the service of the French and Portuguese crown.

In 1635, Pierre joined the Discalced Carmelites at Goa. As a priest, he was known as Dionysius of the Nativity.

At Goa, Dionysius met Thomas Rodriguez da Cunha. Thomas had been born in Portugal in 1598 and had become a professed Carmelite Brother in 1615, taking the name Redemptus of the Cross.

In 1638, Dionysius was asked to serve as pilot for a Portuguese diplomatic mission to Sumatra, and Redemptus accompanied him. Both of them suffered martyrdom in 1638 when they refused to deny their Faith. They were beatified by Pope Leo XIII in 1900.

REFLECTION The martyrdom of Bl. Dionysius and Bl. Redemptus reminds us that we may suffer contradiction because of our dedication to the ways of the Lord. It is then that we should rejoice and be glad to be privileged to suffer with and for Christ.

PRAYER *O God, we celebrate the memory of Bl. Dionysius and Bl. Redemptus who died for their faithful witness to Christ. Give us strength to follow their example by remaining loyal and faithful to you to the end. This we ask through Christ our Lord. Amen.*

ST. CUTHBERT MAYNE, Priest and Martyr

November 30

BORN at Youlston, Devonshire, England, in 1544, St. Cuthbert was raised as a Protestant by his uncle, a schismatic priest, and persuaded by him to become an ordained minister. While studying at Oxford in 1870, he was converted to the Faith through the efforts of St. Edmund Campion.

The Saint studied for the priesthood at Douai and was ordained in 1575. In 1576, he was sent back to England as the fifteenth missionary priest sent from Douai. While acting as the estate steward for Francis Tregian at Goldon, Cornwall, he was arrested inside of a year. He was convicted for the "crime" of being a priest celebrating Mass and was hanged, drawn, and quartered on November 25, 1576.

St. Cuthbert was the first priest Englishman trained at Douai to be martyred. He was beatified by Pope Leo XIII in 1886 and canonized by Pope Paul VI in 1970.

REFLECTION St. Cuthbert was arrested and martyred for trying to attend to the spiritual welfare of English Catholics at a time when persecution reigned. We should thank God that we are free to practice our religion and to worship God in perfect freedom. And we should be sure to put this freedom into practice.

PRAYER *God our Father, You called St. Cuthbert to become a priest and minister to the members of the Church in England, and he did this so well that he attained the crown of martyrdom. By his prayers, grant us the grace to worship You in peace and freedom all the days of our lives and to offer prayers for those who are not free to do so. This we ask through Christ our Lord. Amen.*

ST. ELIGIUS (or Eloi), Bishop

December 1—Patron of Metalworkers

ELIGIUS (also known as Eloi) was born around 590, near Limoges in France. He became an extremely skillful metalsmith and was appointed master of the mint under King Clotaire II of Paris. Eligius developed a close friendship with the king and his reputation as an outstanding metalsmith became widespread.

With his fame came fortune. Eligius was very generous to the poor, ransomed many slaves, and built several churches and a monastery at Solignac. He also erected a major convent in Paris with property he received from Clotaire's son King Dagobert I.

In 629, Eligius was appointed Dagobert's first counselor. Later, on a mission for Dagobert, he persuaded the Breton King Judicael to accept the authority of Dagobert.

Eligius later fulfilled his desire to serve God as a priest, after being ordained in 640. Then he was made Bishop of Noyon and Tournai. His apostolic zeal led him to preach in Flanders, especially Antwerp, Ghent, and Courtai where he made many converts.

Eligius died on December 1, around 660, at Noyon. He is the Patron of Metalworkers.

REFLECTION The use of one's talents and wealth for the welfare of humanity is a very true reflection of the image of God. In the case of St. Eligius, he was so well liked that he attracted many to Christ. His example should encourage us to be generous in spirit and kind and happy in demeanor.

PRAYER   *Loving Father, through the example and intercession of Your Bishop St. Eligius, may we share with others our faith, talents, possessions, and knowledge in a joyful and convincing manner. This we ask through Christ our Lord. Amen.*

ST. NAHUM, Prophet

The Same Day—December 1

ST. Nahum was one of the Minor Prophets of the Old Testament and came from Elkosh in Judah. Nothing else about him is known apart from his Book, which was written between 664 and 612 B.C. and is regarded as a literary masterpiece.

The contents of the Book (three chapters) is believed by scholars to be a "battle curse" (voiced shortly before an attack) that announces the coming punishment of the enemy Nineveh because of its unprecedented pride, idolatry, and oppression, especially against Israel. (At the time, Israel has already been destroyed, Judah has been humbled, and King Manasseh has been made a prisoner in Assyria; 2 Chronicles 33). It thus becomes a word of comfort for the Prophet's people.

Yet Nahum also indicates that God was willing to save the doomed city if its people repented. For He is always seeking the lost, is slow to anger (1:3), good (1:7), and a refuge for those who trust in Him (1:7). Indeed, God sends Good News to those who will listen (1:15). All this is told with matchless poetic style and great literary power.

REFLECTION The Prophet tells us that God rules over all the earth, even over those who do not acknowledge Him as God. This one God holds us all accountable for our actions, whether we know it or not. Those who repent for their wrongdoing and rely on God will be saved, for He is their refuge in time of trial. He cares for all who trust in Him. Hence, we should always trust in the Lord.

PRAYER *O God, in Your wisdom You called St. Nahum the Prophet to announce the punishment coming to those who do evil. By his prayers, help us to repent for our sins and receive Your merciful forgiveness. This we ask through Christ our Lord. Amen.*

ST. CHROMATIUS OF AQUILEIA,
Bishop
December 2

CHROMATIUS was born in Aquileia, near Venice, in the fourth century. Raised by his widowed mother, brother, and several sisters, eventually he was ordained a priest.

In 381, Chromatius attended the Synod of Aquileia, which was famous for its denunciation of Arianism. In 388, he was elected Bishop of Aquileia, and his friend St. Jerome dedicated several books to him. Chromatius also befriended Rufinus and eventually baptized him.

In pursuit of his scholarly interests, Chromatius paid Rufinus to translate Eusebius's *Ecclesiastical History*, and he also financed Jerome's translation of the Bible. He wrote several Scriptural commentaries of his own, and at one time tried in vain to reconcile Rufinus and Jerome.

Chromatius was also a friend of St. John Chrysostom. When the latter was suffering persecution at the hands of Emperor Arcadius, Chromatius issued a vigorous protest, which like the protests of many others went unheeded. Worn out by his labors, Chromatius died on December 2 around the year 407.

REFLECTION In his support of scholarly works associated with Sacred Scripture, St. Chromatius reminds us of the great significance that Scripture studies should have in our lives. Called as followers of Jesus, we can more easily live a Christian life if we steep ourselves in Scripture.

PRAYER *Almighty God, in Your mercy You have made available to us Your inspired Word. Through the example and intercession of Your Bishop St. Chromatius, may we carefully listen to and live Your Word as it has been given to us. This we ask through Christ our Lord. Amen.*

ST. HABAKKUK, Prophet

The Same Day—December 2

ST. Habakkuk is one of the Minor Prophets of the Old Testament, but we know nothing about his personal life and background. His prophecy was written toward the end of the seventh century B.C. (605-597), at a time when Israel was under heavy attack from the Chaldeans and in desperate straits.

In the first two chapters, the Prophet carries out a dialogue with the Lord and even dares to question His ways. Habakkuk speaks in the language of complaint and protest. He is concerned with such profound themes as the sovereignty of God and His justice in His rule over human history.

After listening to the Lord's reply, the Prophet concludes that after bad times there will always be good times for those who are faithful to the Lord. The third and last chapter is a magnificent religious lyric filled with reminiscences of Israel's past and expressions of authentic faith in the Lord.

REFLECTION Habakkuk calls for faith and complete confidence in God's power to rule earthly affairs and in His providence to protect His faithful. The righteous will live by their faithfulness (2:4), by their unwavering attachment to God. This was later reiterated and refined by St. Paul (Romans 1:17). We should dwell on it often.

PRAYER *O God, in Your wisdom You raised up St. Habakkuk Your Prophet to be the herald of faith in*

You. By his prayers, help us to live by faith in You every day of our lives. This we ask through Christ our Lord. Amen.

———◆◆◆———

ST. CASSIAN, Martyr

December 3—Patron of Stenographers

ST. Cassian was a court stenographer at the trial of St. Marcellus the Centurion before Deputy Prefect Aurelius Agricolas at Tangiers, under Emperor Diocletian. When Marcellus was unjustly sentenced to death for refusing to deny his Faith, Cassian became indignant and denounced the injustice being done. He flung down his writing instrument and declared himself to be a Christian.

As a result, Cassian was arrested and imprisoned. A few weeks later, he too was put to death. He was brought to the place where Marcellus had been tried and gave the same replies and statements that Marcellus had given, thus meriting to obtain the victory of martyrdom.

The date of his death was December 3, about the year 300.

REFLECTION St. Cassian loved justice and could not stand to see injustice carried out before his very eyes. So he instinctively fought against this injustice. His action caused him to lose his life in this world but to gain it in the next. We should make it our practice to combat injustice in every way.

PRAYER   *God of justice, You inspired St. Cassian to battle injustice and gain eternal life. Through his intercession, help us to work for justice in the next. This we ask through Christ our Lord. Amen.*

———◆•◆———

ST. ZEPHANIAH, Prophet
The Same Day—December 3

ST. Zephaniah is one of the Minor Prophets of the Old Testament, and the last before Judah's Seventy Years' Captivity. His ministry took place during the first decade of King Josiah's reign (640-609 B.C.).

The Prophet sets forth the judgment against Judah and Israel (1—2), the woes against other peoples (3:8), and the Messianic promise for Israel (i.e., a Remnant will remain—3:9-13), and eventually all nations.

Zephaniah is especially important for his delineation of the *Poor of the Lord.* Instead of a social group within the chosen people, he broadens the idea to include all the *oppressed* who see God as their only defense and all the *indigent* who know God as the only One Who can fill their needs.

REFLECTION   St. Zephaniah's word to us is that like the People of the Lord we should be always cognizant of our insufficiency and put our trust in God. We should repent for our sins, adore the Almighty Lord, and abandon ourselves to His Will—for He seeks nothing else but our good.

PRAYER   *O God, in Your wisdom You raised up St.
Zephaniah Your Prophet to preach about the Day of
the Lord and to utter the promise of a Remnant. By
his prayers, help us to rely upon You alone as true
People of the Lord. This we ask through Christ our
Lord. Amen.*

———◆————

ST. BARBARA, Virgin and Martyr

December 4—Patroness of Architects and Builders

BARBARA lived in the fourth century, but
much of what is said about her seems to be
legend. She is believed to have been the daughter of a pagan named Dioscorus during the reign
of Emperor Maximian.

Barbara resisted her father's wish that she
marry. Then on one occasion, during her father's
absence, Barbara had three windows inserted
into a bathhouse her father was constructing.
Her purpose was thereby to honor the Trinity.

Dioscorus was enraged by Barbara's action.
Therefore he took her to a mountain place and
killed her. Reportedly Dioscorus was destroyed
by fire from heaven immediately afterward as he
descended from the mountain. She is the Patroness of Architects and Builders and one of the
Fourteen Holy Helpers.†

REFLECTION   The life of St. Barbara is a vivid reminder that there can be much anger in our world and

---

† See p. 223.

in our lives. Being in touch with God's presence in a very special way can do much toward relieving ourselves of our tendency to allow anger to control us.

PRAYER   *O God, Your Son Jesus patiently instructed His followers in Your Word. Through the intercession of Your servant St. Barbara, may we always imitate the patience of the God-made-man and be satisfied with Your gifts. This we ask through Christ our Lord. Amen.*

———◆•◆———

ST. CRISPINA, Martyr

December 5

CRISPINA, born in the third century, was a citizen of Thagara, Africa. A person of means, she was the mother of several children.

During the persecution of Diocletian, Crispina was arrested because of her Christianity. Then she was brought to trial in Thebeste, before the proconsul Anulinus.

Crispina was ordered to sacrifice to the gods. She refused and offered a splendid defense of her Christian Faith. She was then sentenced by the proconsul to die by the sword. She exclaimed: "Praise to God Who has looked down and delivered me out of your hands!"

Crispina was beheaded in 304. St. Augustine often mentioned this holy Martyr in his preaching.

REFLECTION In defense of the Faith, Crispina was willing to forego the company of her most cherished possessions, her children. The love for and nurture of children, if accepted generously, can itself merit eternal salvation.

PRAYER   *Loving Father, Your holy Martyrs teach us the true meaning of life. Through the intercession of Your Martyr St. Crispina, help us to appreciate and defend the gift of life. This we ask through Christ our Lord. Amen.*

———◆•◆———

BL. PETER PASCHASIUS,
Bishop and Martyr
December 6

PETER Paschasius was born in Valencia, Spain, around the year 1227. He studied for the priesthood in Paris where he was ordained in 1249. On his return to his native country, Peter joined the Mercedarian Order and dedicated himself to the redemption of captives. He had great devotion to Mary as Our Lady of Mercy and was a strong advocate of her Immaculate Conception.

In 1296, the holy man was made Bishop of Jaen, Spain. During a pastoral visit to his diocese, he was captured by the Moors and kept in prison for three years.

While in prison, Peter wrote various works in defense of the Catholic Faith. On December 6, 1300, after many sufferings, Bishop Peter was beheaded by the Moors.

REFLECTION   Peter Paschasius was great in mind and heart and strove to be perfect in virtue. He took part in monastic life and pursued Jesus' image. As Bishop, he fed his sheep with Christ's Word and Living Bread. For this he was imprisoned and met a martyr's death. Let us strive to imitate him.

PRAYER   *O God, in Bl. Peter Paschasius, outstanding champion of Mary's Immaculate Conception, You gave to the Christian captives a heroic teacher and defender of the Faith. By his prayers, let us be truly rooted in Your Word, conduct ourselves as true children of Mary, and continually express our faith in works of mercy. This we ask through Christ our Lord. Amen.*

ST. JOSEPHA ROSSELLO, Virgin

December 7

BENEDETTA Rossello was born at Liguria, Italy, in 1811, and at the age of sixteen she became a Franciscan tertiary. For nine years, she cared for an invalid, and when he died, Benedetta, along with Paula Barla, and her two cousins Angela and Domenica Pescio, established a community at Savona in 1837.

The new community was called the Daughters of Our Lady of Pity, and its members engaged in the education of poor girls, the founding of hospitals, and other charitable works. Benedetta took the religious name Josepha and was mistress of novices. She was later elected superior in 1840, and she remained in that post till her death.

In 1846, the group received diocesan approval, and the number of its foundations increased rapidly. During Josepha's lifetime, the congregation numbered sixty-eight houses. During the last years of her life, Josepha was quite ill and her prayer life was terribly arid. Nonetheless, she persevered till the end. She died on December 7, 1880, and she was canonized by Pope Pius XII in 1949.

REFLECTION   Jesus, Whose birth we anticipate, preached the Good News of care and concern for others. When we put Jesus' words into action, we can readily see what can be accomplished, as was the case with St. Josepha and her sisters.

PRAYER   *O God, may we always be faithful to Your invitation to be caring for others. Through the intercession of Your servant St. Josepha, be with us as we reach out to those who are most in need of our care and love. This we ask through Christ our Lord. Amen.*

————◆·◆————

ST. EUTYCHIAN, Pope

December 8

ST. Eutychian was Pope from January 4, 275, to December 7, 283. Other than this fact and that he was a Tuscan, son of a certain Marinus, no other reliable information exists about his activity or personality.

The Saint is listed as a martyr in the second edition of the *Roman Martyrology* and as someone who personally buried 342 martyrs. Scholars maintain that this can hardly be the case since he reigned within the period of peace that occurred between the persecutions of Emperors Valerian (253-260) and Diocletian (284-305). Records of his reign may have perished during the havoc caused by the later persecution of Diocletian.

St. Eutychian was buried in the cemetery of Callistus (the last Pope to be interred there) where fragments of his Greek epitaph have been found. He is credited with establishing the custom of blessing fresh fruits at Mass, but scholars believe this is an anachronism The usage is attested much later in the *Gelasian* and *Gregorian* Sacramentaries.

The Roman calendar of 354 included Eutychian in its list of episcopal burials, but not in that of martyrs.

REFLECTION St. Eutychian led the Church when there was no official toleration of Christianity in Rome. However, there was no persecution, and the Church was able to develop and grow while awaiting the advent of Constantine the Great and his edict of toleration in 313. Sometimes, it is our task just to be patient and wait for God's time to come—as St. Eutychian did.

PRAYER *Provident God, You called St. Eutychian to rule Your Church during a trying but not yet dangerous time. By his prayers, help us to stay close to You in every type of situation, waiting for Your time to come. This we ask through Christ our Lord. Amen.*

ST. GORGONIA, Laywoman

December 9

GORGONIA, who lived in the fourth century, came from a very virtuous family. She was the daughter of St. Gregory Nazianzen the Elder and St. Nonna, and the sister of St. Gregory Nazianzen and St. Caesarius.

Married and the mother of three children, Gorgonia had a reputation for holiness. She was devoted to her children, and lived a life of self-denial in order to be generous toward the poor.

Although she suffered ill health, and prayed to be relieved of her pain, Gorgonia accepted God's will. Baptized later in life with her husband, children, and grandchildren, she died shortly thereafter, around the year 370.

REFLECTION   The life of St. Gorgonia is a vivid reminder that holiness of life is open to all Christians. No matter what our vocation or life status, all of us are called to prayerful union with God, especially through an abiding awareness of His presence in our lives.

PRAYER   *O God, You promised to be with us until the end of time. Through the intercession of Your servant St. Gorgonia, grant us the grace to be united with You through an awareness of Your presence. This we ask through Christ our Lord. Amen.*

ST. EULALIA OF MÉRIDA, Virgin and Martyr

December 10

EULALIA of Mérida was born in Spain in the last decade of the third century. It is almost universally accepted that she suffered martyrdom for the Faith. What little else is known of her to date is based mostly on legend.

It is believed that Eulalia, as a twelve-year-old girl, tried to remonstrate with Judge Dacian of Mérida for forcing Christians to worship false gods in accord with the edict of Diocletian. Even though Dacian was at first amused and tried to flatter her, Eulalia would not deny Christ.

Finally, Dacian ordered that her body be torn by iron hooks. Fire was applied to her wounds to increase her sufferings, and in the process her hair caught fire. She was asphyxiated by the smoke and flames, gaining the crown of martyrdom in 304.

REFLECTION In a very subtle way, the world beckons to us to worship the false gods of greed, lust, and anger. Like the young girl St. Eulalia, we are called to stand fast and cast aside the urgings of worldlings.

PRAYER *O God, Creator of Heaven and earth, You generously share with Your people the fruits of Your creation. Through the intercession of Your servant St. Eulalia of Mérida, may we in turn share our gifts with others generously. This we ask through Christ our Lord. Amen.*

ST. DANIEL THE STYLITE, Priest

December 11

DANIEL was born in Maratha, Syria, in 409 and became a monk in nearby Samosata on the Upper Euphrates. He learned of St. Simeon Stylites the Elder living on a pillar at Antioch and got to see him twice.

At the age of forty-two, Daniel decided that he too wanted to become a stylite (from the Greek word *stylos* meaning pillar) and live on a pillar at a spot near Constantinople. Therefore, Emperor Leo I built a series of pillars with a platform on top for him, and Daniel was ordained there by St. Gennadius.

The Saint quickly became an attraction for the people. He celebrated the Eucharist on his pillar, preached sermons, dispensed spiritual advice, and cured the sick who were brought up to him. He also gave prudent counsel to emperors Leo and Zeno and the Patriarch of Constantinople.

All the while, Daniel lived his particular type of pillar spirituality. He came down from his perch only once in thirty-three years—to turn Emperor Baliscus away from backing the heresy of Monophysitism. Daniel died in 493 and became the best-known Stylite after St. Simeon Stylites the Elder.

REFLECTION The life of St. Daniel the Stylite is an apt reminder that there are many ways to live the spiritual life. All of us have our own way to be close to

God every day. Our task is to find that way and follow it to the very end.

PRAYER   *Loving Lord, You are the Creator of all things and of all styles of life on earth. Through the example and intercession of Your servant St. Daniel the Stylite, may we practice the type of spirituality suitable for each of us and remain in loving union with You daily. This we ask through Christ our Lord. Amen.*

ST. SPIRIDION, Bishop

December 12

SPIRIDION lived in the fourth century. As a native of Cyprus, he was a shepherd. Early in life he married, and he was known as an individual of self-sacrifice and generosity.

Later, Spiridion was appointed Bishop of Tremithus near Salamis. During a persecution under Emperor Galerius Maximian, he had an eye put out and a leg hamstrung. He was then sent to the mines for the remainder of the persecution.

An individual of holiness and simplicity, Spiridion had a great knowledge of Scripture and is believed to have been the source of several miracles. He died around 348.

REFLECTION   Although clerical celibacy was not observed in the fourth century, St. Spiridion's life gives witness to the necessity of bringing virtue and holiness into family life.

❖━━◆━◆━━❖

ST. ODILIA, Virgin and Abbess

December 13

ODILIA was born in France in the seventh century. Since she was born blind, her father wanted to have her put to death, but because of her mother's pleas it was agreed to give Odilia away anonymously to a peasant.

At the age of twelve, Odilia was placed in a convent at Baume. She was baptized by Bishop St. Erhard of Regensberg, and her eyes were opened when touched by chrism during the baptismal liturgy. When her father was told of the miracle, he was so angered at his son for arranging for Odilia's return that he struck and killed him.

Later, the father repented and accepted Odilia. However, she fled when he wanted her to marry. Finally, he agreed to let her turn his castle into a convent. She became abbess and then founded another convent at Niedermünster, where she died.

REFLECTION   In the life of St. Odilia, we can readily see the devastating effects of anger on family life. The energies of anger channeled into love would be more

Godlike and worthy of the example offered by Jesus Christ.

PRAYER　*O God, through the intercession of St. Odilia, may we work so as to have our family life free of the cancer of anger. This we ask through Christ our Lord. Amen.*

———◆◆———

ST. VENANTIUS FORTUNATUS,
Bishop and Poet
December 14

VENANTIUS Honorius Clementianus Fortunatus was born near Treviso, Italy, about 535. He was educated at Ravenna and then left for Germany and later Poitiers where he lived from 567 to 587.

After his ordination, Venantius became an adviser to st. Radegund, the wife of King Clotaire I. About 600 he was made Bishop of Poitiers, but died shortly afterward.

The Saint was a voluminous writer and notable poet. He composed the lives of the Saints in his region and several outstanding hymns, among which are two standards that form part of the Liturgy.

The first great hymn is *Pange Lingua Gloriosi* ("Sing My Tongue the Glorious Battle"), which extols the triumph of our Savior's Cross and is used on Good Friday during the Adoration of the Cross and in the Latin Liturgy of the Hours on feasts of the Cross. This hymn is filled with sentiments of respect and love, penetrating tenderness and veneration for the Cross and the Crucified One.

The second outstanding hymn is *Vexilla Regis Prodeunt* ("The Royal Banners Forward Go"), which is sung at Evening Prayer from Passion Sunday to Holy Thursday and on the feast of the Exaltation of the Cross. The hymn is essentially about the triumph of Christ through suffering. The Cross becomes a throne for the Redeemer-King and the glory of the redeemed.

REFLECTION St. Venantius in his two greatest hymns has given us sentiments that fit in perfectly with our worship, e.g., "Fulfilled is all that David told / In true prophetic song of old; / 'Amid the nations, God,' said he, / 'Has reigned and triumphed from the tree.'" We should strive to meditate on these two beautiful hymns from time to time.

PRAYER   *Heavenly Father, You called St. Venantius to serve You as Bishop and as Poet. By his prayers, help us to love the Liturgy and always participate in it fully, consciously, and actively. This we ask through Christ our Lord. Amen.*

ST. MARY DI ROSA, Virgin

December 15

PAULA Frances Mary di Rosa was born on November 6, 1813, at Brescia, Italy. Educated by the Visitandine nuns, she left school at the age of seventeen to manage her widowed father's household.

Mary was not interested in marriage since she was attracted to the convent. She took care of the spiritual needs of young girls working in her father's mills, and she volunteered to work in the Brescia hospital during the 1836 cholera epidemic. Later, she founded a home for girls and a school for deaf mutes.

In 1840, her spiritual director made her superior of a group of religious who cared for the sick. She took the religious name Mary Crucifixa because of her devotion to the Crucified Christ. Called the Handmaids of Charity of Brescia, her group was approved by the Bishop of Brescia in 1843, and papal approval was granted in 1850. Mary died at Brescia in 1855 and was canonized by Pope Pius XII in 1954.

REFLECTION We cannot always copy the things some Saints did in their lives. However, one of the things St. Mary di Rosa did is easy to imitate. She put life and its concerns in proper perspective, especially comparing time with eternity.

PRAYER   *God our loving Father, the life of St. Mary di Rosa reflects Your generosity for Your people. Through her intercession, may we respond generously to those who seek our care and attention. This we ask through Christ our Lord. Amen.*

BL. MARY FONTANELLA, Virgin

December 16

MARY Fontanella was born at Baldinero, Italy, in 1661. She was one of eleven children, and at the age of twelve she joined the Cistercians at Saluzza. However, when her father died, she left the convent.

Four years later, despite family opposition, Mary joined the Carmel of St. Christina in Turin. Initially, she was subjected to numerous diabolical attacks. Eventually these ceased, and she was gifted with mystical experiences.

Mary became mistress of novices in 1691 and prioress in 1694. Later, she founded a Carmel at Moncaglieri. She died on December 16, 1717, and was beatified in 1865 by Pope Pius IX. She is also known as Mary of the Angels.

REFLECTION As we prepare to celebrate the birth of Jesus, we are reminded by the life of Bl. Mary Fontanella that the true meaning of the Incarnation is anathema to the worldly. Our abstinence from sin and sensuality this Advent will challenge the world.

PRAYER *O God, as we move closer to the celebration of Christmas, may the example and intercession of Bl. Mary Fontanella so direct our lives as to proclaim the stark poverty and detachment of the stable at Bethlehem. This we ask through Christ our Lord. Amen.*

ST. HAGGAI, Prophet

The Same Day—December 16

ST. Haggai is one of the Minor Prophets of the
Old Testament. He received the Lord's word
in the second year of Darius (520 B.C.), and post-
exilic prophecy is said to begin with him.

The Jews who returned from the Exile in
Babylonia had encountered formidable obstacles
in their efforts to reestablish Jewish life in
Judah. The Samaritans had succeeded in block-
ing the rebuilding of the Temple; but after Darius
acceded to the throne permission was given to
resume the work.

At this critical moment, when defeatism and a
certain lethargy had overtaken his repatriated
compatriots, Haggai came forward with his ex-
hortations to them to complete the great task. In
the space of four short months Haggai with five
brief messages managed to turn defeat and dis-
couragement into victory. He was aided in the
last month of his ministry by another Minor
Prophet, Zechariah (Zechariah 1:1-6).

REFLECTION St. Haggai reminds us that we are to
work unceasingly. Once it was to build God's Temple
but today it is to build His Church, a spiritual sacrifice,
which is constructed by our acts of love. To build a
Temple for God nowadays is above all to bring Him to
all people. Thus, Haggai invokes the Messianic Hope,
for in the conversion of the Gentiles that he announces is comprised the coming of the Messiah.

PRAYER   *O God, in Your wisdom You called St. Haggai Your Prophet to help reestablish Jewish life in Judah, and he succeeded. By his prayers, help us to establish the Catholic Faith in every part of the world. This we ask through Christ our Lord. Amen.*

ST. BEGGA, Widow

December 17

BEGGA, who lived in the seventh century, was the daughter of Bl. Pepin of Landen and St. Itta, and the sister of St. Gertrude of Nivelles. Little is known of her early life.

Eventually Begga married Ansegisilus, son of St. Arnulf of Metz. They had a son named Pepin of Herstal, who is remembered as the founder of the Carolingian dynasty in France.

Begga's husband died in 691. In his memory, she built at Andenne seven chapels commemorating the seven churches of Rome, and she also established a convent there, where she became abbess and where she died in 693.

REFLECTION   As we await the commemoration of Jesus' birth, St. Begga reminds us that we are all called to holiness of life. Love, prayer, and forgiveness go far in blessing married and family life according to God's Word.

PRAYER   *O God, Your servant St. Begga, raised by virtuous parents, openly accepted their direction and lived her life in Your service as both a parent and a nun. Grant us the grace to imitate her wisdom and goodness. This we ask through Christ our Lord. Amen.*

———◆———

ST. FLANNAN, Bishop

December 18

FLANNAN was born in Thomond, Ireland, in the seventh century, the son of an Irish chieftain named Turdough. He received his early education from a monk, some of which was more vocational than intellectual.

Despite opposition from family and friends, Flannan became a monk. He then made a pilgrimage to Rome, where Pope John IV consecrated him a bishop.

Upon his return to Ireland, Flannan served as the first Bishop of Killaloe. As a result of his preaching skill, his father became a monk.

REFLECTION   In our determination to fully serve the Lord in others, we sometimes become the victims of ridicule. Like St. Flannan, and like Joseph and Mary at Bethlehem, we lovingly accept these rejections.

PRAYER   *O God, strengthen our faith so that our lives may more eloquently bespeak Your holy Word. May our lives, like St. Flannan's preaching, bring conversion of mind and heart to others. This we ask through Christ our Lord. Amen.*

———◆———

ST. MALACHI, Prophet

The Same Day—December 18

S T. Malachi is the last of the twelve Minor Prophets of the Old Testament. He was an anonymous Prophet who wrote around 455 B.C. using a proper name made out of the Hebrew expression "My messenger" (Malachi), which occurs in 1:1 and 3:1 of his book.

The Prophet reminds the people of God's enduring love and then reprimands them for insincere worship even though the Temple has been rebuilt. He warns them that God's judgment is approaching, and on that day everything will be put into order again.

There will even be a perfect sacrifice offered from morning till night, alluding to the Mass (1:10-12). But first Elijah will have to return to open the New Age. The New Testament applies this description to John the Baptist, the forerunner of Christ (see Matthew 17:12 and Mark 9:13).

REFLECTION   St. Malachi is the Prophet of the true worship, i.e., the Sacrifice of the Mass, which in real truth goes on from morning till night all over the world. He is also the Prophet of God's true judgment, which will be rendered on the Day of the Lord when Jesus returns at the Second Coming. The righteous will achieve full redemption and enter the definitive Kingdom of God. We should strive to know, love, and live the Mass.

PRAYER   *O God, in Your wisdom You called St. Malachi Your Prophet to persuade Your people to offer true worship to You through the Mass. By his prayers, help us to know, love, and live the Mass all our lives. This we ask through Christ our Lord. Amen.*

———◆◆———

ST. ANASTASIUS I, Pope
December 19

ANASTASIUS was born in Rome in the fourth century. Little is known of his youth. According to Jerome, he lived a most virtuous life.

Elected Pope on November 27, 399, Anastasius was almost immediately embroiled in a conflict that resulted from the spread of errors attributed to Origen. Eventually he convened a synod at which certain of Origen's writings were condemned.

Anastasius also implored the bishops of Africa to guard the Church against Donatism. Known as a very holy man and one who was detached from material possessions, he died at Rome on December 19, 404.

REFLECTION   The life of St. Anastasius I reminds us that in our efforts to preserve God's Word we must be willing to undergo the work of prayer, study, vigilance, and humility. Opposition fades in the face of these activities.

PRAYER   *O God, in Your goodness and wisdom You raise up leaders for Your Church who are rooted in Your Word and Your Will. Through the intercession of Your servant St. Anastasius I, may we be loyal to our Faith in following their directions. This we ask through Christ our Lord. Amen.*

———◆—●—◆———

ST. DOMINIC OF SILOS, Abbot

December 20

DOMINIC of Silos was born at Cañas, Spain, in the year 1000. As a boy he was a shepherd. Later he joined the Benedictines at San Millán de Cogolla Monastery, and subsequently he was elected prior there.

Eventually Dominic was driven from the monastery by Garcia III of Navarre when he refused to surrender some monastery lands. He fled to San Sebastian Monastery at Silos where he became abbot. His tenure was one of reform, and his monastery became a great spiritual center, noted for its book design and art.

Many healing miracles were attributed to Dominic, and he expended much effort in ransoming slaves from the Moors. He died on December 20, 1073.

REFLECTION　What can the life of a tenth-century monk teach us? Personal holiness and the willingness to reach out to others even in the most difficult circumstances are characteristics of St. Dominic's life that speak volumes for all ages.

PRAYER　*O God, in Your wisdom You raised up St. Dominic of Silos for the welfare of Your people. May we, like him, dedicate our lives to prayer and good works. This we ask through Christ our Lord. Amen.*

ST. THEMISTOCLES, Martyr

December 21

S T. Themistocles bears the same name as one of the most noble persons in ancient history, the Athenian statesman and military genius Themistocles who lived from about 524 to 460 B.C.

Our Saint is much different from the Greek hero. His person is a lot more modest and his life much more silent. He had no city and country to save, no army to defeat, and no populace to praise or condemn him. However, his action, dictated by a supernatural faith, was no less daring nor humanly speaking less difficult.

Themistocles was a shepherd in Myra, Lycia, where he died and is venerated. He presented himself spontaneously to the imperial tribunal there in order to save another Christian, named Dioscoros, and to undergo torture in his place. In place of his companion in faith, Themistocles was accused and reviled; in his place, he was stretched out on a trestle, dragged on the ground, and beaten with clubs, and finally beheaded. He thus received the crown that had not been prepared for him but one that he well earned. His death took place in the third century, probably during the reign of Decius.

REFLECTION   St. Themistocles gave up his life in keeping with the words of Christ, "There's no greater love than to give one's life for a friend" (John 15:13). He thus followed Christ's example and gained the martyr's crown. We should strive to pray daily for those who are in danger because of their faith.

PRAYER   *Heavenly Father, You enabled Your Martyr St. Themistocles to give up his life for his companion in the Faith. By his intercession, grant us courage to follow his example if ever we are in a similar situation. This we ask through Christ our Lord. Amen.*

ST. MICAH, Prophet

The Same Day—December 21

ST. Micah was one of the Minor Prophets of the Old Testament. He carried out his ministry in the Southern Kingdom of Judah during the reign of Jotham, Ahaz, and Hezekiah in the late eighth century B.C. He was thus a contemporary of Isaiah and Amos.

Micah cried out against social injustice and foretold the fall of the Northern Kingdom because of the people's infidelity to God. He stressed God's judgment but also His loving mercy and is known as the "Prophet of the Divine Compassion" (see 7:18-19).

Micah also gives the fullest description of the coming of the Messiah (5:2-15). The Messiah will come from Bethlehem and be a human being. He will have preexisted and will bring together a Remnant of believers. He will inaugurate a Kingdom of peace and care for the needy. In Messianic times there will be universal peace. Swords will be beaten into plowshares and spears into pruning hooks. It will be an age of peace, prosperity, and plenty (4:1-5).

REFLECTION Micah reminds the people that the cause of war and individual unhappiness in the world is sin (both social and personal). God abhors idolatry, injustice, rebellion, and empty ritualism, but He delights in pardoning sinners who are determined to do justice, love kindness, and walk humbly before Him (6:8). God has promised to take away sin and war at the coming of His Messiah. If we follow Jesus, we will achieve peace and joy in the Lord.

PRAYER *O God, in Your wisdom You called St. Micah Your Prophet to proclaim the coming of the Messiah from Bethlehem. By his prayers, help us to accept Jesus as the Messiah and to receive the peace and joy of His Kingdom. This we ask through Christ our Lord. Amen.*

STS. CHAEREMON, ISCHYRION, AND COMPANIONS, Martyrs

December 22

WE know about these Martyrs only from a letter that St. Dionysius of Alexandria wrote to Fabian of Antioch. He mentioned the Egyptian Christians who suffered under the persecution of Decius (248-251). Many of them, he says, were forced to flee into the desert and perished from hunger, thirst, or exposure to the elements, wild beasts, and human ferocity.

Dionysius mentions Chaeremon, an aged Bishop of Nilopolis. With a single companion, the bishop had taken refuge in the mountains of Arabia, but neither he nor his companion was ever heard from afterward.

Another name mentioned by Dionysius is Ischyrion, who was the procurator for a magistrate in a city of Egypt, which is usually identified as Alexandria. Ischyrion was commanded by the magistrate to sacrifice to the gods. He refused and remained steadfast in spite of being reviled and threatened. In the end, his master ordered him to be mutilated and impaled. These two Saints are honored today together with all the other Martyrs who died in that persecution.

REFLECTION Sts. Chaeremon and Ischyrion gave their lives to remain faithful to their Lord and their Faith. They stand for the many other Christians who passed away during that time. They teach us to remember always that we have no lasting home on earth and should remain ready to depart for our eternal home in Heaven regardless of what sufferings that may entail.

PRAYER *Heavenly Father, You called Sts. Chaeremon and Ischyrion and others to give their lives for their Faith. By their prayers, help us to remain steadfast in the Faith all our days. This we ask through Christ our Lord. Amen.*

ST. SERVULUS, Layman

December 23

SERVULUS was born in Rome in the sixth century. Afflicted with palsy when he was an infant, he was never able to stand, sit upright, or feed himself.

Servulus's family used to carry him to the Church of St. Clement in Rome so that he could beg alms. Whatever he collected that was not needed for his existence he would share with other needy people. He would also purchase books of Scripture that he would ask others to read to him.

Servulus died around 590 after a lifetime spent in thanksgiving to God for His goodness despite the terrible existence he was forced to endure. He was buried in the Church of St. Clement.

REFLECTION Many go through life blessed with good health and talents and some even with great fortune or prosperous circumstances. The challenge of St. Servulus's life is how under such afflictions he continued to praise God and encouraged others to praise the Heavenly Father.

PRAYER   *All-powerful Father, we anticipate with joy the commemoration of Your Son's birth. Through the example and intercession of Your servant St. Servulus, may our celebration be marked with greater generosity to the poor and outcast. This we ask through Christ our Lord. Amen.*

ST. IRMINA, Abbess

December 24

S T. Irmina was a daughter of Dagobert II, son of Sigebert III and King of Austrasia, and lived at the end of the seventh century or the beginning of the eighth. When her intended bridegroom was killed on her wedding day by another man who wanted to marry her, Irmina became a nun of the Benedictine Order. Her father established the convent of Oehren for her near Trier, and she became its Abbess.

St. Irmina was a great supporter of the missionary efforts of St. Willibrord, and in 698, she gifted him with a manor that went on to be the famous monastery of Echternach. This gift was by way of thanking St. Willibrord for miraculously bringing an epidemic to an end that had been raising havoc in her convent.

Irmina died around the year 710 at the monastery of Weissenburg, which her father had also founded.

REFLECTION There is little doubt that St. Irmina continued to aid the missionary efforts of the Saint from Echternach with both spiritual means (i.e., the prayers of her community) and material means. Her life is an apt reminder for us to support the missionary effort of the Church through prayer and any other kind of assistance.

PRAYER *Heavenly Father, You called St. Irmina Your Abbess to work for the spread of the Church through prayer and material assistance. Through her intercession, help us to support the missionary labors of the Church with both our prayers and our material assistance. This we ask through Christ our Lord. Amen.*

ALL THE HOLY ANCESTORS OF JESUS CHRIST
The Same Day—December 24

THIS day the Church honors all the holy ancestors of Jesus Christ, the Son of David, the son of Abraham, the son of Adam, that is, all the fathers who were pleasing to God and were found righteous and died in the Faith. None of them obtained what they had been promised, but they saw and saluted it from afar. From them was born Christ according to the flesh Who is above all things, God blessed forever.

REFLECTION These ancestors or forebears of Christ are as it were our cloud of witnesses, which the author of the Letter to the Hebrews extols (11:1ff). Let us then set aside every encumbrance of sin that clings to us and persevere in running the race that lies ahead, keeping our eyes fixed on Jesus, Who inspires and perfects our faith.

PRAYER   *Heavenly Father, You raised up the Holy Ancestors of Jesus to prepare the way for His coming with the promised Redemption. By their prayers, help us to follow Jesus all our lives and come to share their joy forever in Heaven. This we ask through Christ our Lord. Amen.*

ST. ALBERT OF KRAKOW,
Religious and Founder
December 25

BORN in Igoalomia, Poland, in 1845, Adam Chmielowski gained fame as an artist but felt called to follow Christ by serving his fellow human beings. He became a member of the Franciscan Third Order, taking the name Albert. Brother Albert labored for the good of the most destitute in Krakow.

In 1887, the Saint founded the Brothers of the Third Order of St. Francis Servants of the Poor, known as the Albertines, and in 1891 he added a similar Congregation for women. The members of his two Congregations established shelters and soup kitchens as well as charitable undertakings for the poor. They soon became known as the "Gray Brothers" and "Gray Sisters."

After a lifetime of aiding the poor, Albert died —still at work—on Christmas Day, 1916. He was canonized by Pope John Paul II in 1993.

REFLECTION   St. Albert is the champion of the poorest of the poor. He strove to follow Christ in taking care of the "least of His brethren" and became a brother to them. In the end, he had those wonderful words of Christ directed to him: "Whatever you did to the least of My brethren, you did unto Me. Enter into the joy of your Master" (Matthew 25:40, 23). We should never forget the least of Christ's brethren.

PRAYER   *Heavenly Father, You called St. Albert Your servant to serve the least of Christ's brethren.*

By his prayers, help us to do whatever we can for the poor and never forget to pray for them. This we ask through Christ our Lord. Amen.

———◆—◆———

ST. VINCENTIA MARIA LOPEZ Y VICUÑA,
Virgin
December 26

VINCENTIA was born at Cascante, Spain, in 1847. While being educated in Madrid, she lived with her aunt who had founded a home for domestic servants.

That form of charity impressed Vincentia. Accordingly, she took a vow of chastity and, in concert with her aunt, organized a group of ladies who were interested in ministering to working girls. Between 1871 and 1876, she developed a written rule for her group, and in 1878, with three others, she took the vows of religion.

Out of this grew the institute of the Daughters of Mary Immaculate for Domestic Service. The congregation, having spread throughout Spain, other sections of Europe, and Latin America, was given papal approbation in 1888. On December 26, 1896, Vincentia died at Madrid, and she was canonized in 1975 by Pope Paul VI.

REFLECTION The dedication of one's life to the service of others reflects the depths of devotion and care that Joseph and Mary exemplified at Bethlehem. St.

Vincentia reminds us that reaching out to others allows us to do God's will.

PRAYER   *God our loving Father, You raised up St. Vincentia to work for the welfare of working women. May their lives of virtue and goodness fostered by Vincentia's faithful daughters reflect Your honor and glory. This we ask through Christ our Lord. Amen.*

———◆–◆–◆———

ST. FABIOLA, Widow
December 27

FABIOLA was born in the fourth century to the noble Fabia family of Rome, Italy. Early in life, she was a follower of St. Jerome, but she fell away from the Church.

Fabiola divorced her first husband because of his ribald lifestyle, and she remarried. When her second husband died, she once again accepted her Christian obligations and returned to the Church and her support of St. Jerome.

Fabiola was noted for her charitable works, including the establishment of the first Christian public hospital in the West, where she waited on the patients. Later, she opened a hospice for poor and sick pilgrims at Porto. She died in the year 400.

REFLECTION As the angels herald the newborn King, we echo their joy and prophecy when we return to the full observance of the Commandments and participate in the Sacraments. Like St. Fabiola, may we always share in Christmas joy with the poor.

PRAYER   *O God, Your servant St. Fabiola responded with an open heart to Your generous call to conversion. Through her intercession, may we always be open to Your call to conversion of heart. This we ask through Christ our Lord. Amen.*

———•———

ST. ANTONY OF LÉRINS, Hermit

December 28

A NTONY was born around 468 at Valeria in Lower Pannonia. When he was eight years old, his father died and he was first entrusted to the care of St. Severinus. After the death of Severinus, an uncle, Bishop Constantius of Lorsch in Bavaria, took charge of his upbringing.

While in Bavaria, Antony became a monk. He returned to Italy in 488 and joined the cleric Marius and his companions as a hermit at Lake Como. However, he gained so many disciples that he was forced to flee.

Antony then went to Lérins in Gaul and became a monk there. However, he lived only two years at Lérins before his death in 520, renowned for his miracles and spirituality.

REFLECTION   The life of St. Antony of Lérins recalls to us that as Joseph and Mary watched over Jesus at Bethlehem, all was well, quiet, and peaceful. It is this sense of divine tranquility that ceaselessly calls us to contemplate the newborn Messiah.

PRAYER   *O God, we look to You for peace, solace, and quiet as we turn from our work-filled days.*

Through the intercession of St. Antony of Lérins, remove from our minds and hearts anything that would distract us from Your Spirit dwelling within us. This we ask through Christ our Lord. Amen.

———•—•———

ST. MARCELLUS AKIMETES, Abbot
December 29

MARCELLUS was born at Agamea, Syria, in the fifth century. As a youth, he inherited a large fortune, but after studies at Antioch and Ephesus he became a monk at Eirenaion Monastery in Constantinople. Later he was elected abbot, and the institution grew and prospered.

In 488, Marcellus attended a synod called by St. Flavian and was effective in his efforts against Eutyches. Later he attended the Council of Chalcedon. In 465, when Constantinople was threatened with destruction by fire, his prayers were credited with saving the city.

Around 485, after forty-five years as abbot, Marcellus died on December 29. His surname, which means "non-resters," refers to the unique situation at Eirenaion Monastery where there were three groups of choirs and the Divine Office was chanted twenty-four hours a day.

REFLECTION The life of St. Marcellus Akimetes is a graphic reminder that through a simple offering—our prayers, works, and sufferings, twenty-four hours each day—our entire lives can become a constant prayer.

PRAYER   *O God, be with us as we go through this vale of tears. Through the intercession of St. Marcellus Akimetes, may we always remember Your Son's birth and the positive consequences it has had on humankind. This we ask through Christ our Lord. Amen.*

———◆•◆———

ST. DAVID, King and Prophet
The Same Day—December 29

DAVID was the son of Jesse of Bethlehem who found grace before God and while King Saul was still alive was himself anointed King by the Prophet Samuel. He reigned from about 1010 to 970 B.C.

David became the court musician and gained fame as the slayer of the Philistine giant, Goliath, who was terrifying the Israelites.

Upon Saul's death, David became King of all Israel, both north and south. He chose Jerusalem as his capital and brought the Art of the Covenant there. In the course of his rule, he achieved the definitive victory over the Philistines and increased the boundaries of Israel. He later committed adultery with Bathsheba but repented and received God's forgiveness and promise of salvation. His last words were a prophecy of the future Davidic Messiah and his own salvation, springing from the cross (2 Samuel 23:5).

REFLECTION   David among other things had a hand in fashioning the worship of the Temple. He also wrote many of the psalms that make up the Book of Psalms, which "keep repeating and fostering the hope of the promised Redeemer. They show forth in splendid light the prophesied glory of Jesus Christ: first, His supreme and eternal power, then His lowly coming to this earthly exile, His kingly dignity and priestly power, and finally His beneficent labors, and the shedding of His Blood for our redemption" (Pope Pius XII, *Mediator Dei,* no. 148).

PRAYER *O God, in Your wisdom You raised up St. David Your King and Prophet to rule Israel and prophesy in the Psalms about the Messiah Who was to spring forth from his house. By his prayers, help us to pray the Psalms frequently and gain the spiritual fruits found therein. This we ask through Christ our Lord. Amen.*

ST. EGWIN, Bishop
December 30

EGWIN was born in the seventh century. He was of the nobility and a direct descendant of the Mercian kings. At an early age, he joined a religious order, and in 692, he was named Bishop of Worcester, England.

As bishop, Egwin was charged with being too severe with his clergy, and he made a penitential pilgrimage to Rome. After returning from Rome, he founded the Benedictine Monastery of Evesham.

Evesham was to become one of the greatest Benedictine institutions in England during the

Middle Ages. Egwin died on December 30, 717, and was buried at Evesham.

REFLECTION St. Egwin's feast at the end of another calendar year bids us look at our lives. As followers of Christ, our primary concern is to evaluate our relationship with God and examine the things that are necessary for us to be more in touch with Him.

PRAYER *All-powerful Father, we turn to You with praise and thanksgiving for having brought us to this point in our lives. As we move into the future, may the intercession of St. Egwin lead You to watch over and protect us with Your love and compassion. This we ask through Christ our Lord. Amen.*

ST. COLUMBA OF SENS, Virgin and Martyr

December 31

COLUMBA of Sens was born in the third century. It is believed that she was a native of Spain and belonged to the Spanish nobility.

At the age of sixteen, Columba went to Gaul to avoid being forced to worship pagan gods. Eventually, she was baptized and settled at Sens.

During the persecution of Aurelian, Columba was ordered to be put to death. Legend has it that when her jailers tried to rape her she was defended by one of the bears from the amphitheater. Then she was beheaded in the fourth century, and she was buried by a man whose sight had been restored through her intercession.

REFLECTION The life of St. Columba of Sens cries out to us to go to any lengths to both gain and defend the Christian Faith. As we move into a new year, let our resolve be to strengthen our faith, hope, and charity.

PRAYER   *Lord God, as we come to the end of another year we praise and thank You for many blessings. Aware of our failures, we look forward in faith and hope to serving You and Your people more effectively. Through the intercession of St. Columba of Sens, help us in this quest. This we ask through Christ our Lord. Amen.*